Most men and women lead lives at the worst so painful, at the best so monotonous, poor and limited that the urge to escape, the longing to transcend themselves if only for a few moments, is and has always been one of the principal appetites of the soul.[323]

ALDOUS HUXLEY

Andrew Neher is Professor of Psychology at Cabrillo College, where, for several years, he has taught a course in transcendental experience. He has also done research on the physiology of altered states of awareness; this research has been published in journals in psychology, physiology, and anthropology. In addition, Andrew Neher has a private counseling practice.

Transpersonal Books
JAMES FADIMAN, *General Editor*

Transpersonal Books
explore the psychology of consciousness,
and possibilities for transcendence.

BOOKS IN THE SERIES

The
Psychology
of
Transcendence

ANDREW NEHER

PRENTICE-HALL, INC.,  Englewood Cliffs, N.J. 07632

Library of Congress Cataloging in Publication Data

NEHER, ANDREW.
  The psychology of transcendence.

  (A Spectrum Book)
  Bibliography: p.
  Includes index.
    1. Psychical research.   2. Occult sciences.
  3. Mysticism—Psychology.   I. Title.
  BF1031.N43   133.8'01'9   80-19797
  ISBN 0-13-736652-3
  ISBN 0-13-736645-0 (pbk.)

*To all those who have paid—with their happiness, sanity,
or lives— the price of psychological ignorance.
May their experience encourage in others
the self-awareness that prevents such tragedy.*

Line drawings by Robyn Hall
Editorial/production supervision and interior design: Betty Neville
Cover design by Vincent Ceci
Manufacturing buyer: Cathie Lenard

10   9   8   7   6   5   4   3   2   1

Printed in the United States of America

Prentice-Hall International, Inc., *London*
Prentice-Hall of Australia Pty. Limited, *Sydney*
Prentice-Hall of Canada, Ltd., *Toronto*
Prentice-Hall of India Private Limited, *New Delhi*
Prentice-Hall of Japan, Inc., *Tokyo*
Prentice-Hall of Southeast Asia Pte. Ltd., *Singapore*
Whitehall Books Limited, Wellington, *New Zealand*

Contents

Figures

Exercises

Forewords

Dr. Robert Morris, School of Social Sciences
University of California, Irvine

Human experience is incredibly diverse; the multiplicity of factors that contribute to each moment of awareness are considerably beyond our present capacities to analyze and understand. Given the resultant uncertainties, we are free to speculate endlessly about the "true meaning" of any experience that has complex characteristics. Our society currently allows extensive experiential experimentation. We have the technology to induce in ourselves and others an extraordinary diversity of experiences, including "psychic" and "transcendent" ones, which occasionally seem to maintain even the intensity of some of the world's noted religious experiences.

In coming to grips with transcendent experiences, we tend rather quickly to reject attempts to apply the scientific method, preferring more subjective methods to evaluate subjective experiences. Andy Neher's book helps to remind us that excluding science so quickly is a mistake, that in fact we know a great deal about the bases of many aspects of such experiences. Although science is not presently in a position to claim thorough understanding of transcendent experience, it nevertheless has made some good beginnings. Additionally, the methods of science have frequently enabled us to build considerable evidence against certain esoteric interpretations of anomalous experience.

I personally look forward to the publication of this book because I intend to use it as a required text in my parapsychology classes. I generally use at least one "pro" and one "con" book in such classes, to guarantee that students get a balanced perspective. In the past, my "con" books have given me trouble—they tend to be written by arrogant individuals who display an all-too-obvious counterbias and manage to insult and turn off many open-minded students. Three of them have gone out of print, much to my students' relief. The present work should have a kinder fate, however, as the author writes with a consistent basic respect for the experiences and the personal validity they may come to have for the individual. The information is presented fairly and straightforwardly.

I do not regard this book as a "debunking" of parapsychology. A true debunking attempt would be another book at least this size, involving intensive analysis of a very dense and frequently confusing experimental literature. It does present some very useful, very legitimate alternative explanations for what have been construed as "psychic" events, and I am sure it will be a welcome addition to the literature for all serious educators in the area of parapsychology, transpersonal psychology, and related topics.

Dr. Ray Hyman, Department of Psychology
University of Oregon, Eugene

Transcendental experiences lead to convictions that one has come in contact with The Truth. The contents of this truth, however, vary widely depending upon the setting and the individual having the experience. In most cases the sorts of truths that become "known" to these experiencers have no demonstrable validity in terms of modern science. One answer that experiencers often give is that science is limited in what it can know. There are other ways of knowing, and these other ways can tap into higher truths of the sort that are inaccessible to modern science.

Such an answer, however comforting to those who want to hang onto their received truths, will not do. For one thing it naively assumes that "scientific knowing" is basically different from some other sorts of "knowing." The characterization of scientific thinking is too complicated to take up here. But Andy Neher, the author of *The Psychology of Transcendence*, provides illustrations of how transcendental experiences have contributed to scientific knowledge. The sources of scientific knowledge are just as varied and rich as those employed by mystics, occultists, artists, and others. As far as we can tell, there is, in fact, no difference. What characterizes science is not its sources of ideas, hypotheses, theories, and the like, but its commitment to put each of these ideas to as many stringent tests as possible.

Another reason why the claim of other ways of "knowing"

makes little sense is that it fails to face up to the fact that the "knowing" that flows out of transcendental experiences results in claims that conflict with one another. Obviously all these "truths," no matter how strongly held and clearly seen, cannot be correct. In the past month, for example, I have met three different groups whose transcendental experiences have convinced them beyond any doubt that the world will soon end. One group has placed the date in 1981 and has assured me that every occupant of the earth will be evacuated in spaceships by that time. Another group has told me that the earth will be subject to severe earthquakes in 1982, which will destroy civilization as we now know it. The third group has already begun making plans to be secluded in caves by 1984 when, as they assure me, the earth will be struck by a gigantic planetoid. The resulting fire and radiation will destroy most of the population, and those dedicated individuals who emerge from the caves will reconstruct civilization according to secret lore.

The third reason for being dubious about transcendental experience as a sufficient way to knowledge is amply documented in this book. We typically do not realize how the contents of transcendental experience are a product of our own subconscious operating on buried memories and sensitive to immediate group demands. Because both the experience and its contents are strange to us, we project them outward onto the external world. We attribute the experience and "knowledge" to outside, often paranormal, forces.

Every experience is a product of both external or environmental inputs and our own bodily and psychological states. The immediate environment and our own memories and expectations contribute to the experience. We usually do not realize the extent to which the experience is actually a construction based upon our own contributions. In most ordinary interactions with the environment, this failure to keep separate our own contributions from those of the environment is of little consequence. Indeed, it might be an advantage because it enables us to focus on what is going on around us rather than on how we know what it is that is going on.

But under unusual circumstances, especially those conducive to transcendental experiences, the failure to distinguish between what the environment is and what we are contributing to the experience can result in a variety of false commitments, many of which are superbly discussed by Andy Neher.

The fault, as Neher argues, is not in transcendental experiences as such. He avoids the trap of putting down such experiences just because they have mistakenly resulted in false beliefs. The fault lies in the failure of a cultural and educational system to teach us about how our bodies and minds operate. Psychology already knows much that can help us to account for many of the "strange" features of transcendental experiences. By learning how our bodies operate during such experiences, we can avoid the pitfalls of false commitments and exploit positive features of the experiences.

The problem of transcendental experience presents many challenges to psychology and to a writer. One challenge is to cope with the myriad of paranormal, occult, and other claims made for systems that involve such experiences. Andy Neher would deserve plaudits if only because his book meets this challenge in as comprehensive a manner as I have seen. I know of no other single source that covers such a wide range of fringe and borderline beliefs with such knowledge and critical evaluation. But Neher goes beyond a critical evaluation of the evidence and arguments. He also brings to bear the best and most contemporary psychological and physiological mechanisms to help account for why these varied beliefs have been so persuasive to their adherents.

But Andy Neher's most important accomplishment is, in the words of an old popular song, to accentuate the positive and eliminate the negative. He has avoided the debunker's defect of throwing out the baby with the bath water. And he has not fallen into the believer's trap of making mysteries out of every interesting anecdote. His message is positive. You can learn to cultivate and profit from transcendental experiences. Such profits can best be achieved if you learn how to separate the sense from the nonsense made in behalf of such claims. Being sure that you are right, unfortunately, has little to do with actually being right. And a healthy use of transcendental experiences goes along with a healthy skepticism of feelings of certainty. Experiences do not have to be paranormal to be valuable. The quest for truth, human dignity, and romance does not have to suffer because so-called claims of paranormality have no basis in fact.

Andy Neher has given us good reason to doubt the validity of prophets, but I cannot refrain from making a prediction—that you will find reading this book an educational and rewarding experience.

Preface
and Acknowledgments

I have long been fascinated by experiences that are commonly called *psychic*, *occult*, or *mystical*. Growing up, I had some of these experiences myself and was convinced of their potential value, in spite of the fact that they were considered not quite respectable by many people. However, when I sought an understanding of my experiences, I was in for a disappointment. Readily available, but of little help, were writings by "true believers," who labeled such experiences *paranormal* or *supernatural* and usually considered them basically mysterious or unfathomable. Less common were writings by "debunkers," such as D. H. Rawcliffe,[539] who did seem to have a grasp of some of the dynamics involved; however, their negative attitude did little to encourage my interest and enthusiasm.

These and other interests eventually launched me into a study of psychology. Here I did gain some of the understanding I was after, but much of it was hard won; most psychologists seemed to share the general feeling that mysticism and occultism were freakish or frivolous concerns and not worth serious study. Fortunately, it wasn't long until this attitude was challenged by expanded research efforts on topics such as the physiology of consciousness and altered states of awareness, which promised to shed a great deal of light on experiences that had previously seemed inexplicable. I myself became involved in this research effort.

A few years later, I began teaching college courses in psychology. I could not help noticing, in talking with and counseling students, that psychic, occult, and mystical experiences were often very important to them, sometimes reaching the level of a passion or a life's work. Not surprisingly, however, I found that their understanding of their experience was usually minimal and often naive. Furthermore, some were clearly suffering from their inability to grasp what was happening to them.

Believing that research efforts and popular interest in extraordinary states of consciousness and experience had both reached fairly high levels, I decided to offer a course in what I had by that time begun to call *transcendental psychology*—that is, the study of experiences that go beyond our usual levels of functioning and, for that reason, often seem inexplicable. I soon found, however, that curriculum materials had not kept pace with recent research developments and that, if I wanted satisfactory readings for my course, I would have to develop my own. In this effort, I had a number of objectives.

1. I wanted to lay a foundation of solid understanding of psychological principles and research.

2. I wanted to show how transcendental experiences— visions, automatisms, etc.—far from being merely freakish or peculiar, had inspired many great geniuses as well as lesser ones. In other words, I wanted to point out the potential usefulness of such experience.

3. I wanted to incorporate some exercises I had found useful in helping people develop their potential for transcendental experience.

4. I wanted to deal with the issue of paranormal influences by presenting and evaluating the relevant research evidence.

5. In general, I wanted to shed the light of understanding on experiences that were often cloaked in mystery.

This curriculum is now several semesters old and has benefitted greatly from helpful critiques by numerous students. I have found student interest in this material not only to be high, but also to be an excellent vehicle for introducing students to a wide range of important psychological principles and research.

The curriculum I have just described forms the basis of this book. Although it was written for a college course, my idea from the start was that there was a great need for a book on extraordinary experience that would serve the needs of the general reader.

Consequently, I have kept the writing as nontechnical as possible and have attempted to explain psychological principles in terms that the nonpsychologist can understand. Also, wherever possible, I have incorporated examples so that readers can relate the concepts being discussed to their own lives.

At this point, a comment about the term *transcendental* might be helpful. According to the *Oxford English Dictionary*, transcendental means "surpassing . . . going beyond the ordinary limits . . . extraordinary." Thus the term is a good one for labeling experiences that significantly exceed our usual levels of functioning and, therefore, often seem mysterious. However, many readers are probably more familiar with another term, *transpersonal*, which is used in a similar, although not identical fashion. Transpersonal refers to a wide range of experiences that "go beyond the personal," including many seemingly inexplicable experiences, but *also* many experiences—self-actualization, synergy, and so on—that, although they may be unusual, are not considered particularly mysterious. Thus, *transcendental* and *transpersonal* are complementary and not synonymous terms.

I am grateful to many people for their help at various stages in writing this book. The administration at Cabrillo College, by granting a sabbatical, provided the time and mental space necessary to initiate the project. Many others at the college lent their assistance. Students in my "transcendental experience" course read and critiqued early drafts of the manuscript and also conducted many small-scale research studies, which are summarized at appropriate points in the book. Sally Douglas and David Hucklesby, of the college computer center, calculated and verified some of the statistical tests presented in the book. Marnell Hillman, in the college library, located and obtained, through Interlibrary Loan, many hard-to-find books and journals; unknown and unsung Interlibrary Loan staff in libraries across the country aided this effort.

As my search for materials progressed, my sister, Topsy Smalley, helped track down obscure sources during a summer visit to the Library of Congress. Many other staff in university and public libraries up and down the West Coast lent their assistance when I visited in search of materials. Parapsychology researchers kindly shared their experiences in long discussions in their laboratories and at professional meetings. And many friends graciously put me up when I visited labs or libraries in their area.

As the book took form, numerous colleagues and friends shared with me their thoughts on various topics; Hilding Carlson, Steve Evanson, Jim Fadiman, Neil Fashbaugh, Jim Funaro, Ray Hyman, Harry McCune, Bob Morris, Neal Smalley, and Marcello Truzzi were particularly helpful in this regard. Of those who read various drafts of the manuscript, Dan Harper and Mel Tuohey spent many hours advising on writing style and Karin Harrington did a thorough and valuable critique from the perspective of an advanced psychology student. Several typists worked hard on the book. Chimey Anderson, Sue Daugherty, and Lauri McInerny, in particular, were a great help in getting the manuscript typed in decent form.

Robyn Hall, the cartoonist for the book, deserves special thanks. An artist of many talents, her delightful caricatures and sense of the comic add a refreshing dimension to the book.

My family helped in many ways. Linda, my wife, shared her expertise at many stages of conception and writing. She and my children, Anya and Kevin, also put up with my frequent absences into the study and away from home. My parents not only read and offered suggestions on the manuscript but also get credit for certain helpful influences during my formative years—my father for setting the example of a questioning attitude, my mother for setting the example of a receptive attitude.

Finally, I want to thank the many people who took the time to relate to me their psychic, occult, and mystical experiences. Although our understanding of the experience often differed, we generally share the conviction that such experiences are significant and worthy of serious attention and study.

Excerpts from Phil Santora's "Life and Death in Africa," *New York News*, May 28, 1972 are reprinted by permission of the publisher. Copyright 1972 New York News Inc.

The excerpt from *The Sufis* by Idries Shah—copyright © 1964 by Idries Shah—is reprinted by permission of Doubleday & Company, Inc., and W. H. Allen & Co. Ltd.

The excerpt from Hans Selye, *The Stress of Life*—copyright © 1956 by Hans Selye— is used with permission of McGraw-Hill Book Company.

The excerpt from *The I Ching or Book of Changes* is from the Richard Wilhelm translation rendered into English by Cary F. Boynes, Bollingen Series XIX. Copyright 1950, copyright © 1967 by Princeton University Press. Copyright © renewed 1977 by Princeton University Press. Reprinted by permission of Princeton University Press and Routledge & Kegan Paul Ltd.

The excerpt from Charles Rycroft, *Wilhelm Reich* is reprinted by permission of Viking Penguin Inc.

Excerpts from *Lost Continent: The Atlantis Theme,* 1975, by L. Sprague de Camp are used by permission of Dover Publications, Inc.

The excerpts from *Chariots of the Gods* by Erich von Daniken are used by permission of G. P. Putnam's Sons, Souvenir Press Ltd., and Econ-Verlag G.M.B.H.

The excerpt from "The Nature of Scientific Evidence: A Summary," by Philip Morrison is from *UFO's: A Scientific Debate* by Carl Sagan and Thornton Page. Copyright © 1972 by Cornell University. Used by permission of the publisher, Cornell University Press.

The excerpts from *The World of Flying Saucers* by Donald H. Menzel and Lyle C. Boyd—copyright © 1963 by Donald H. Menzel and Lyle C. Boyd—are used by permission of Doubleday & Company, Inc.

Excerpts from *The UFO Enigma* by Donald Menzel and Ernest Taves—copyright © 1977 by Florence Menzel, Executrix of the Estate of Donald H. Menzel and Ernest H. Taves—are used by permission of Doubleday & Company, Inc.

Excerpts from *The Bermuda Triangle* by Charles Berlitz—copyright © 1974 by Charles Berlitz—are reprinted by permission of Doubleday & Company, Inc.

The excerpt by Henri-Frederic Amiel, from Franklin P. Adams, *F.P.A.'s Book of Quotations,* is used by permission of Harper & Row Publishers, Inc.

The excerpt from *The Dark Night of the Soul* by Georgia Harkness is used by permission of Abingdon Press.

Figure 3 is used by permission of Jean-Claude Lejeune.

Figure 7 is from page 73 of *Visual Illusions: Their Causes, Characteristics, and Applications* by Matthew Luckiesh. It is used by permission of Dover Publications, Inc.

Figure 10 is used by permission of United Press International.

Figure 11 is used by permission of Ken Heyman.

Figure 14 is used by courtesy of Edmund Scientific Co.

Figure 15 is from *Clever Hans* edited by Robert Rosenthal. Preface and Introduction by Robert Rosenthal Copyright © 1965 by Holt, Rinehart and Winston, Inc.; text Copyright 1911 by Henry Holt and Company. It is reprinted by permission of Holt, Rinehart and Winston.

Figure 16 is *Automatic Drawing* by André Masson. Done in 1924, it is ink,$9\frac{1}{2} \times 8''$. Private collection, New York. © by ADAGP, Paris, 1980. Courtesy Harry N. Abrams, Inc., New York.

George Tooker's, *The Waiting Room* is used by permission of National Collection of Fine Arts, Smithsonian Institution; gift of S. C. Johnson and Son, Inc.

Figure 18 is used by permission of Alinari.

Figure 20 is photo no. 245-MS-2624L in the National Archives.

Figure 22 is used by permission of Milbourne Christopher.

Figure 27 is used by permission of Rare Book Division, The New York Public Library, Astor, Lenox and Tilden Foundations.

The excerpt from *The UFO Experience* by J. Allen Hynek, 1972, is reprinted with the permission of Contemporary Books, Inc., Chicago and Abelard-Schuman Ltd.

The epigraph on page i from *Doors of Perception*, by Aldous Huxley is reprinted by permission of Mrs. Laura Huxley, Harper & Row, Publishers, Inc., and Chatto & Windus Ltd. Copyright 1954 by Aldous Huxley.

Figure 21 is used by permission of D. Scott Rogo.

Figure 23 is used by permission of Steven Neher.

Figure 24 is used by permission of Sandy Solmon.

Figure 26 is used by permission of Charles Pender.

Figure 28 is used by permission of Peter Farquhar.

1

Introduction

*Our normal waking consciousness . . . is but one special type of consciousness, whilst all about it, parted from it by the filmiest of screens, there lie potential forms of consciousness entirely different. We may go through life without suspecting their existence; but apply the requisite stimulus, and at a touch they are there in all their completeness, definite types of mentality which probably somewhere have their field of application and adaptation. No account of the universe in its totality can be final which leaves these other forms of consciousness quite disregarded.[336] ***

WILLIAM JAMES

We have all heard of experiences so strange and unusual that we are hard put to explain them. Consider the following example:

Colin Turnbull is an anthropologist, noted for his fieldwork over a period of many years in several different cultures. It seems unlikely that he would be affected by "superstitions" such as hexes or black magic. Yet when the people of a village in the Congo, angry at Turnbull, used witchcraft against him, it almost cost him his life. As Turnbull explains:

> The witchcraft business started off simply enough and at first I was secretly amused. Not for long. They do things to upset you. Unexpected things. If you walk through the village and greet someone by name, he will just walk past as though you didn't exist . . .
>
> No matter what I did, it was wrong. If I approached a group, they would stop talking except for a word or two they wanted me to hear.

*See Reference section, which begins on page 297.

1

The words usually indicated that Sabani, the local ritual doctor, had made witchcraft against me and that my fate was sealed.

Then I began to feel sick. Food wouldn't stay down and I began to vomit. Here I was, an Oxford graduate, sitting in the midst of a little African village succumbing to psychological warfare. There might have been humor in it but I couldn't see it . . .

. . . I was becoming very weak—and I recognized the danger. I couldn't leave my house because I could scarcely move.[586]

Convinced of the seriousness of his condition, Turnbull finally turned to the only medicine that seemed appropriate.

. . . one of the pygmies said the only way I could save myself was to make magic back. Things were serious and I was so desperate that I didn't think of the absurdity of a veteran anthropologist making magic against a native witch doctor.

I felt foolish but I made a fire and I put some of my personal belongings into it—which is considered very powerful medicine. To make sure that the entire village knew what was going on, I had one of the local boys get me the wood and stand by while I made some Turnbull magic. . . .

For whatever reason . . . the next day I was feeling a little better. Within three days I was back to normal.[586]

Turnbull's illness and recovery are examples of transcendental experience—that is, experience that goes beyond our accustomed levels of functioning. Here, seemingly, "magic" was able to produce illness and then cure it. What is going on here? Can we hope to understand such experiences that seem, at first glance, so mysterious? And what about other experiences that also go beyond our ordinary expectations and understanding? For example:

Have you ever felt "tuned in" to someone you feel close to—as if you could read that person's mind?

Have you, perhaps when tired or under stress, had visions in which you perceived a "separate reality" unlike the reality of ordinary consciousness?

Have you ever had a dream that turned out to be an accurate portrayal of an event of which you had no conscious knowledge?

Have you ever experienced a flash of inspiration or insight that seemed, in its suddenness, to come "out of the blue"—in other words, from outside of yourself?

Have you ever had the feeling—when dancing, performing music, or playing a sport exceptionally well—that your actions are flowing "automatically," as if directed by an entity other than your own consciousness?

Have you at times experienced heights of ecstasy during which you felt "at one" with the universe?

In large part, as we will see, such transcendental experiences appear mysterious because they arise from processes outside of our ordinary conscious awareness. As you read further in this book and become more familiar with the subtle psychological processes that are involved, you will find that a wide variety of extraordinary experiences no longer seem as foreign or strange to you. As a dividend of your enhanced self-awareness, you should also find it easier to tap into and benefit from your latent transcendental capacities. Hopefully, in this process, you will find that you have gained an expanded vision of human potential.

The Perspective of this Book

Neither shall they say, Lo here! or, lo there! for, behold, the kingdom of God is within you.

LUKE 17:21

Transcendental psychology is concerned with a whole spectrum of experiences that entail heightened functioning. Transcendental psychology encompasses, for example:

1. Heightened sensitivity that appears to go beyond the capacity of the senses.
2. Visionary states in which elaborate and seemingly real images are experienced.
3. Mental elicitation of physiological processes to facilitate healing and to maintain a state of health.
4. Altered states of consciousness in which consciously forgotten experiences are remembered in elaborate detail.
5. Flashes of creative insight, which seem to come "out of nowhere."
6. States of consciousness in which intricate tasks are performed without conscious awareness and beyond ordinary capabilities.
7. Mystical and ecstatic states that involve overwhelming feelings of joy and contentment and that can add meaning and significance to life.

Transcendental experiences are not, by definition, necessarily paranormal in nature. However, because such experiences are so exceptional and seemingly mysterious, many people believe that they *are* paranormal. We will discuss the meaning of paranormal at greater length later. For now, it is sufficient to say that someone who believes in the paranormal believes in the existence of processes that lie outside the range of known natural processes. For example, many people believe that witchcraft, such as resulted in Colin Turnbull's illness and also his recovery, involves some paranormal mechanism. Thus the question arises: To what extent, if any, are paranormal processes involved in transcendental experience?

Later, we will consider the evidence for paranormal factors in transcendental experiences of various kinds. At this point, it is sufficient to say that this evidence is far from conclusive. For this reason, we will devote most of our attention to understanding the psychological mechanisms that are involved in transcendental experience rather than to speculation about paranormal factors for which the evidence is less convincing. At the same time, since so many people believe in paranormal phenomena, we will also examine some of the motivations for such beliefs.

Nevertheless, because terms that imply paranormal experiences are so common and widespread, I will use such terms—for example, *psychic, out-of-body experiences, visions*—without meaning to indicate that the experiences to which they refer are necessarily paranormal in nature.

The Risks vs. the Benefits of Faith

To believe with certainty we must begin to doubt.[689]

ST. STANISLAUS

The belief of some people in paranormal phenomena approaches the level of faith. It is important to realize that belief based solely on faith can have unfortunate consequences.[175, 217, 313, 561] Recently, for example, Lawrence and Alice Parker of Barstow, California, took their eleven-year-old diabetic son, Wesley, to a faith healer. Believing that faith was infallible, the Parkers withheld Wesley's medication after the healing ceremony. Their son died soon afterward. At last report, his parents were confident that their faith would restore him to life.[195]

Many less tragic cases are also on record. For example, a number of years ago, an "earthray" panic struck the Netherlands, and dowsers were hired by many people, including the royal family and government officials, to search out the dangerous rays by "dowsing" public and private buildings. Antiearthray devices were then installed to protect the occupants. The panic died out only after an investigation by the Royal Academy of Science revealed earthrays to be a hoax.[658]

Although these cases certainly demonstrate the risks of blind faith, we also must recognize that faith is sometimes beneficial, as Colin Turnbull discovered when he put his faith in a counterhex and began to recover from his illness. Must we, then, accept the risks of faith as the price of its benefits? No, for, generally speaking, knowledge can take the place of faith and provide its benefits without its risks. For example, as you read further in this book and learn about various psychological healing processes, you should be able to activate more easily your own latent capacities for healing without needing to put faith in a dubious practice or belief.

Neither Believer Nor Debunker

To doubt everything or to believe everything are two equally convenient solutions; both dispense with the necessity of reflection.[434]

JULES HENRI POINCARÉ

As we have seen, many people who undergo extraordinary and seemingly mysterious experiences are *believers,* who assume these experiences are paranormal in nature. At the other extreme are *debunkers,* who assume such experiences are based on "imagination" or "wishful thinking" and therefore are not worthy of serious consideration.

Both believers and debunkers have retarded the development of a psychology of transcendental experience. A good example is provided by the history of hypnosis. A forerunner of what is now called hypnosis was a treatment known as animal magnetism, which Franz Anton Mesmer popularized in the late eighteenth century. By passing his hands over his patients, supposedly to affect the "magnetic fluids" of the body, Mesmer treated a wide range of illnesses successfully.[95] Unfortunately, believers in animal magnetism did little to foster an understanding of hypnosis, since the "magnetic fluids" they believed were producing the effects they observed have never been shown to exist. On the other hand, debunkers of animal magnetism showed little interest in the phenomenon beyond discrediting Mesmer. Eventually, Hippolyte Bernheim, James Braid, and others devoted serious efforts to understanding the processes and applications of hypnosis.[463] As a consequence, hypnosis is now employed in many contexts, and, at the same time, paranormal explanations of its effects are now less common.

In this book, we will steer a middle course between the believers and the debunkers. We will adopt the believers' interest without adopting their blind faith, and we will adopt the debunkers' questioning attitude without adopting their cynicism.

Just as our understanding of hypnosis has increased over the years, so has our understanding of many other transcendental experiences. The foundations of much of our current knowledge concerning transcendental experience can be traced to the latter half of the nineteenth century. During this period, while the Fox sisters and others were popularizing spiritualism and occultism in general[329], psychology got its start as a science. Also, at this time, the newly established societies for psychical research in England and the United States, which included dedicated researchers such as William James[336] and Frederic Myers[474, 475] among their members, studied many of the subtle subconscious mechanisms involved in transcendental experience.

In recent years there has been a resurgence of interest in transcendental experiences, and psychologists such as Donald Hebb, [293] Joseph Kamiya, [356] Nathaniel Kleitman, [371] James Olds, [487] and Roger Sperry, [641] using highly sophisticated instruments and techniques, have rekindled research interest in altered states of awareness, the physiology of consciousness, and other fields relevant to transcendental experience. At the same time, there has arisen a "human potential" movement, which stresses the importance of self-awareness and self-development. In part, transcendental psychology reflects the mutual influence of these two movements; the renewed research interest in transcendental experience has been inspired by and has, in turn, encouraged the expanding popular interest in developing one's latent potentials.

An Integrated Approach

Nasrudin, ferrying a pedant across a piece of rough water, said something ungrammatical to him.
"Have you never studied grammar?" asked the scholar.
"No."
"Then half of your life has been wasted."
A few minutes later Nasrudin turned to the passenger.
"Have you ever learned to swim?"
"No. Why?"
"Then all your life is wasted—we are sinking."[608]
SUFI TALE

Although it is true that our understanding of transcendental experiences has increased significantly in recent times, understanding is not the same as experiencing, and experience is the essence of transcendence. Although, as we have seen, people who interpret their transcendental experience as paranormal sometimes pay dearly for their belief, they *do* experience transcendental states. On the other hand, people who debunk transcendental experience may do so partly because such experience is foreign to them. Ideally, understanding and experience reinforce each other. An example will help to clarify this point.

George Estabrooks, a psychologist and also a hypnotist, was once recuperating in a hospital. To pass the time, he hypnotized himself so he could enjoy of a vision of ". . . a pet polar bear which [Estabrooks] was able to call up merely by counting to five. This animal would parade around the hospital ward in most convincing fashion, over and under the beds, kiss the nurses and bite the doctors. It was very curious to note how obedient he was to 'mental' commands, even jumping out of a three story window on demand."[191] Estabrooks also "conjured up" symphonies for his enjoyment.

An amusing example, perhaps, but sufficient to illustrate the point that Estabrooks' understanding of the process involved in creating visions, together with considerable prior preparation and experience, enabled him to employ this capacity in a useful and enjoyable fashion.

In contrast, believers who attribute visions to mysterious "energies" or "spirits" may be incapacitated by visionary experience, not only because it seems alien to them, but also because they feel helpless to control it. On the other hand, debunkers probably could not benefit from transcendental experience because they would not allow themselves such experience in the first place. Throughout the book, you will see that many creative geniuses have been able to reap the benefits of transcendental experiences that are latent in all of us. Generally speaking, these remarkable people who have benefited so greatly from transcendental experience are found neither in the camp of those who mystify such experience nor in the camp of those who debunk it. Maybe we can learn from their example.

As you read, I will invite you to participate in exercises, which will be set off from the text in italics. The exercises will acquaint you firsthand with many transcendental experiences and help you draw upon your hidden potentials in a constructive way. There is a Sufi saying: "He who tastes knows."[290] However, should you feel uncomfortable about any of the exercises, it is possible to omit them and still understand the concepts being discussed.

The book is organized so that the basic psychological processes involved in transcendental experience are presented first, in Chapters 2, 3, and 4. In Chapters 5, 6, and 7, we discuss some psychic, occult, and mystical experiences of current interest and learn how a knowledge of the psychological processes discussed in the first chapters helps us to understand these experiences.

Now you are invited to read and to experience.

2

Physiological Effects in Transcendental Experience

Know thy body.[606]

HANS SELYE

To return to the example at the beginning of Chapter 1, there is little question that Colin Turnbull underwent physiological changes as his illness progressed and that the reversal of this condition resulted in his recovery. Likewise, physiological processes are involved in many transcendental experiences. In this chapter, we will discuss these processes, along with the psychological mechanisms that relate to them. The effects of conditioning—that is, basic learning processes—will be discussed in the next chapter, since the physiology of learning is not well understood.[679]

The mechanisms described in this chapter are, to a large extent, hereditary. In transcendental experience, hereditary processes play an important role. It is highly likely, for example, that genetic as well as experiential factors are involved in cases of exceptional capacities, such as the following:

1. Eidetic imagery—the capacity to create a vivid mental image of re-membered or reconstructed experience.[254]

2. Hyperamnesia—the capacity for perfect recall of extensive, detailed material after the passage of many years.[412]

3. Synesthesia—the capacity to experience sensations of several kinds as a result of stimulation of one sense only.[421]

4. Psychosomatic ideomotor response—the capacity to alter bodily processes, voluntarily and significantly, through thought alone.[412]

5. Computational wizardry—the mental capacity to perform long, complex arithmetic computations extremely rapidly and accu-rately.[238]

Don't worry if these feats seem beyond your capacity. Most of us would develop abilities such as these only with great effort, if at all. In contrast, almost all of us possess the capacity for most of the experiences we will discuss in the remainder of this chapter.

Let us now examine some of the physiological processes that will help us to understand the psychic, occult, and mystical experiences that we consider in depth later in the book.

Peculiarities of Our Senses

Clearly, there is enough going on within the eye to provide the basis for a full-length Hollywood spectacular.[559]

ALAN RICHARDSON

Can you remember a time when you saw patterns or colors that did not seem to be related to objects in your visual field at the moment? If so, your experience may have resulted from certain peculiarities of your visual sense that can create spectacular images in the absence of any external stimulus.

The word *peculiarity* aptly characterizes the phenomena discussed in this section; these are features of our senses that indeed seem peculiar at first glance. They are important to transcendental psychology for two reasons.

First, learning about sensory processes opens up a new world of appreciation. The optical peculiarities of our eyes, for example, are well worth observing for the learning experience of watching our physiology at work as well as for the "light show" that they provide. Some works of major artists, for example, have been inspired by such optical displays.[579]

THEATER OF THE EYE

PECULIARITIES OF THE SENSES

Second, many people are sufficiently unaware of their own sensory functioning that, when they become conscious of a peculiar sensory process, they may ascribe the experience to a mysterious or paranormal source. As Alan Richardson says with regard to afterimagery:

> ... most people remain unaware of their ... after-imagery, because they have learned to ignore it. It is a distraction and it has no positive value in most of the practical activities of life. ... It is possible that when imagery *is* experienced by someone who is either unfamiliar with it or defensively protected against it, that a reality [that is, external] status is more likely to be attributed to it.[559]

In extreme cases, there is evidence that optical peculiarities of the eye sometimes serve as a basic pattern around which hallucinations are developed.[309] The lesson for us is that if we learn about our bodies, we will not be surprised by what our bodies can do.

Described below are some sensory peculiarities of which many people are unaware, but which can easily be experienced by almost everyone.

1. Floaters and blood cells[462, 730]—Vitreous humor is the jellylike substance that fills the major portion of the eyeball. Detached cells in the vitreous humor cast shadows on the back of the eyeball (the retina), which contains the receptors for vision. We see these cells as round transparent objects often combined in chains and interesting patterns of various kinds. Ordinarily floaters are indistinct compared to the richness of most visual stimuli.

> *You can become aware of floaters by looking at a well-lit homogeneous background; the daytime sky is a good backdrop for a floater show. Notice that the floaters "float" along as you move your eyes.*
>
> *Under these same conditions, you can become aware of cells in the blood vessels that crisscross the retina. These are perceived as darting pinpoints of brightness that rapidly appear and disappear.*

With practice, these darting blood cells can be seen almost everywhere you look. I once knew a psychic study group who thought, when they saw such displays, that they had successfully trained themselves to perceive the movements of molecules in the air!

2. Phosphenes[492]—These are images that arise from stimulation of the retina by pressure or any stimulus other than light.

One way to see phosphenes is to close your eyes and rub them with your palms or fingers; "scrunching" the muscles around your eyes may also help. Do not, however, apply too much pressure; no pain is necessary in order to enjoy phosphenes.

Phosphene patterns can be truly kaleidoscopic and spectacular; several acquaintances of mine were at one time convinced that the phosphenes they were seeing were really paranormal displays of psychic energy.

One theory concerning phosphene patterns is that they reflect the pattern of organization of the neural networks for vision; if so, phosphenes are a rare opportunity to "see" inside your eye and brain, utilizing the very mechanisms you are "watching."

An artist's portrayal of phosphenes can be seen in Figure 1.

Figure 1. Phosphenes

3. Autokinetic effects[426]—Autokinetic means "self-movement" and refers to the perceived movement of objects that occurs, under certain conditions, when the objects are, in fact, stationary. This effect usually occurs only when an object is seen against a plain (usually dark) background that does not contain other objects that could serve as a frame of reference. In this situation, a stationary object will often appear to move. In part, this perception seems to be due to the continuous movement of the eyes, a process of which most people are unaware. That is, when looking at an object, we do not fix our gaze directly on it, but rather we move our eyes slightly and continuously without being conscious of it. This causes the image of the object to move, and, in the absence of other objects that could serve as a frame of reference, we assume that the object itself is moving.

> *To experience, in an exaggerated manner, how movement of your eyes can be interpreted as movement of external objects, close one eye. Then place your finger on the eyelid at the outside edge of your open eye. Now jiggle your eyeball slightly and notice that the objects in your field of vision seem to move around.*

> *Autokinetic movement can be observed by watching a small source of light in a dark setting (a solitary star or planet, or a small light in a dark room). After a minute or so, you should notice that the light source seems to move around in an apparently random manner.*

In light of the effects of autokinetic movement, we should not be surprised that people in the darkness of a seance or lying in bed at night sometimes think they see objects move in a mysterious fashion.

4. Afterimages[559]—A visual stimulus produces more than the visual sensation usually ascribed to it; it also produces an afterimage due to changes that occur in the retinal cells when they are stimulated. As soon as a visual stimulus ceases to stimulate an area of the retina, an afterimage, with the same outline as the stimulus, will appear in that area. The color, brightness, and duration of the afterimage are determined by the color and brilliance of the stimulus, the length of time the stimulus is observed, and the background against which the afterimage is viewed. Commonly, the

afterimage is the complementary color of the stimulus so that, for example, if the stimulus is red, the afterimage will be green. Typically, the characteristics of the afterimage will change as the image fades.

> *One way to see an afterimage is to look at a bright light (a light bulb, for example) in a dark room for several seconds; then, when you look into the darkness or close your eyes, you should see an afterimage.*

With a little practice, you should be able to notice afterimages almost everywhere you look. For example, you should be able to see the afterimage "aura" that is formed around any person you are watching. This aura is a result of the small movements of your eyes that cause the image to shift on the retina. The afterimage that forms in the areas of the retina that are stimulated in this fashion appears as an aura surrounding the person or object you are watching. Afterimage auras probably account for a large percentage of auras that are often felt to arise from some kind of mysterious psychic energy.

5. Neural habituation[682] and inhibition[214]—One reason for the normal continuous eye movements mentioned previously is that our neural networks are designed to respond most strongly to stimulus change; we soon cease to notice a continuous, unvarying stimulus. Thus, movement of our eyes shifts the image on the retina so that no single group of neurons is stimulated for an extended period.[524]

> *To some extent, however, this movement of the eyes can be controlled,[289] as you can experience with the help of Figure 2. When you look at this figure and fix your gaze on the dot, notice that sections of the circle begin to fade. After a time, these sections reappear and other sections fade. If you shift your gaze from the dot, if only slightly, notice that the faded sections reappear in your perception.*

This decreasing sensitivity of our senses to a constant stimulus is reflected in a general decline, known as habituation, in the response of our neural circuits to repetitive stimulation. For example, as Robert Ornstein notes: "When we drive to work the first time, everything appears quite new and interesting—a red house, a big tree, the road itself—but gradually, as we drive the same route over and over, we 'get used' to everything on the way. We stop 'seeing' the trees, the bridges, the corners, etc."[488]

It is sometimes difficult to distinguish between the effects of habituation and the effects of inhibition. Inhibitory neurons, as their name indicates, inhibit the firing of other neurons. Occasionally, when concentrating intently on one object in your visual field, you may have noticed that large sections of the rest of the visual field have faded away. Slight movement of your eyes does not bring the absent objects back into view, so that habituation can be ruled out, and the effect then can be ascribed to neural inhibition. I occasionally have this experience when I am engrossed in watching a musical performance. Only the performers remain visible while all peripheral vision is blocked out.

If you would like to experience one kind of sensory inhibition, hold a finger up in front of your eyes while you are looking at a distant object. You will, of course, see two images of your finger because your eyes are focused on the object in the distance. As

Figure 2. Disappearing circle—stare at the dot and watch the circle disappear.

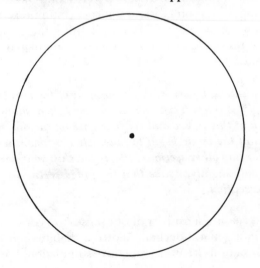

you continue to watch the two images of your finger, notice they sometimes appear to be transparent and sometimes solid; this means that inhibitory neurons are sometimes succeeding in blocking the competing image of the background and sometimes not. With practice you will find that you can make the background fade in and out at will, demonstrating voluntary control over inhibitory processes.

Habituation and inhibition also operate in hearing and serve to "tune in" and "tune out" sounds from our environment. For example, a composer describes the inhibition process, which occurs when she is writing music, as follows: "I am really quite oblivious to my surroundings after I really get going. I think that the phone could ring, and the doorbell could ring [and I wouldn't hear them]. . . . When I start working, I really do shut out the world. Once I stop, I can let it back in again."[143]

Ordinarily, habituation and inhibition are useful since they serve to tune out the features of our environment to which we no longer need to attend and to concentrate our attention on important or new and unusual stimuli. However, as useful as habituation and inhibition are, they also can lead us to misinterpret events. When magicians (or psychics or mediums) make an object "appear" or "disappear," they are often merely manipulating your focus of attention, and thus the mechanisms of habituation and inhibition.

6. Sensory driving[716]—The neurons of the brain are basically rhythmic in their mode of firing. The resultant brain rhythm is particularly sensitive to incoming sensory stimulation that has a similar rhythm. A number of years ago, I demonstrated that a rhythmic auditory stimulus is capable of causing the brain rhythm to increase in amplitude and to change in frequency.[477] This effect is called "driving." Interestingly, an ideal stimulus turned out to be a drum, and the subjective effects seemed similar to those observed in drum ceremonies in various cultures in which participants go into trance and experience visions.[478] Some idea of these effects is given in the following account by an American who participated in a Haitian drum ceremony. "My skull is a drum; each great beat drives that leg, like the point of a stake, into the ground. The singing is at my very ear, inside my head. This sound will drown me! . . . I am caught in this cylinder, this well of sound. There is

nothing anywhere except this. . . . It is too much, too bright, too white for me. . . . The bright darkness floods up through my body, reaches my head, engulfs me."[162]

You will probably find visual driving easier to produce than auditory driving. All that is necessary is to face an extremely bright light (the sun is ideal if you are careful) with your eyes closed. Then spread the fingers of one hand and pass your fingers back and forth a few inches in front of your eyes. This causes a rhythmic stimulation of your eyes that will produce a changing array of patterns and colors. By moving your fingers faster or slower, you can modify the sensation. Driving effects rival phosphenes in their beauty and fascination. However, the illusory colors and patterns seen in sensory driving are generally more organized and consistent than those characteristic of phosphenes. If you have access to a bright strobe light, you can create the same effects by facing the strobe (with your eyes closed) and varying the frequency of flashes between about five and fifteen flashes per second.

Caution is required, however. This form of stimulation of the brain can trigger a seizure in certain epileptics and rhythm-sensitive individuals. A wise policy is to refrain from this experience if you are epileptic, and, epileptic or not, you should stop the procedure if you begin to feel uncomfortable.

To this point, we have seen that certain peculiarities of our senses can create perceptions of colors, patterns, movements, and the appearance and disappearance of objects in the absence of any corresponding external stimulus. Because many people are not aware of their physiological basis, these fascinating effects are sometimes ascribed to mysterious forces, and thus contribute to various psychic and occult beliefs. We have seen that by becoming aware of our sensory peculiarities, we can enjoy and experiment with their sometimes spectacular effects in a way that is denied to those who believe that mysterious or paranormal forces are producing these effects.

The sensory effects discussed thus far are transducer effects; that is, they arise because our senses are imperfect transducers, or converters, of external stimuli to internal sensations. In addition, there are perceptual effects that arise not from sensory processes, but from the effect on the brain of alterations of various bodily processes. In general, perceptual changes (illusions, hallucinations) can be expected whenever basic bodily processes are altered drastically.[84, 410] Some effective alterations are:

1. Drugs—psychedelic drugs, alcohol, opiates, and a variety of anesthetics directly affect brain chemistry and are perhaps the best-known route to unusual perceptual and feeling states.

2. Alterations in breathing—underbreathing (holding the breath or breathing very slowly) and overbreathing or hyperventilation (deep, rapid breaths) are ways of altering the oxygen/carbon dioxide balance in the blood, often producing perceptual alterations.

3. Fasting—lack of certain nutrients can create altered perceptions and mental states.

4. Fever—the altered states of awareness—delusions, delirium—produced by fever are well known to most people.

5. Excitement, exertion, fatigue, and loss of sleep—these conditions produce blood constituent and other changes that can alter perception.

If you are familiar with methods of achieving transcendental states in other cultures, you will immediately recognize the methods described above. Although the perceptions achieved are assigned a multitude of meanings by various peoples, quite similar methods are used for achieving them in a wide variety of cultures.

We see, then, that various physiological conditions can produce altered states of awareness, including illusions and hallucinations. We should neither fear these effects nor, in the absence of other evidence, assume that they arise from paranormal or supernatural influence.

How We Process Information

When people's eyes are open, they see landscapes in the outer world.

When people's eyes are closed, they see landscapes with their mind's eye.[585]

Samuels and Samuels

We have seen that, given the proper physiological conditions, our senses and nervous system can portray a highly distorted picture of the world that, nevertheless, may be very enjoyable and even enlightening. In this section, we will broaden our scope and discuss several general features of our capacity to process information from our senses. Becoming aware of these processes will help us understand some important characteristics of transcendental experience.

1. First, we process input from our senses through various stages. The first stage of sensory processing is, of course, the sense organ itself. We have already discussed enough peculiarities of our senses to realize that we are, even at this stage, a significant step away from the external stimulus.

The second stage is the perceptual stage—that is, our immediate evaluation of the stimulus, which is based not only on the sensory input as it reaches the brain, but also on how we interpret that input according to our needs and prior conditioning.

The third stage includes the processing that the perception undergoes with the passage of time and encompasses memory, thought, fantasy, and so on.

It should be evident that, in general, as the initial stimulus is processed through these stages, the correspondence between the stimulus and our interpretation of the stimulus declines, and the opportunity for subjectivity increases. In other words, unlike a computer, the human brain does not store information "as is." Instead, information stored in memory undergoes processing and modification. The likelihood that memories will be distorted is important to keep in mind when recollections of "miraculous" experiences are cited as evidence for supernatural or paranormal influences in transcendental experience.

2. A second important characteristic of our sensory input and processing mechanism is its limited capacity. In terms of input, we can be aware of very few stimuli at any one time.[449] In terms of processing information, we generally exhibit a "unitary consciousness," meaning that we process information in a one-thing-at-a-time, step-by-step fashion (although, to some extent, subconscious processing of different information can be occurring simultaneously). Two quite different consequences of interest to us follow from our limited capacity to receive and process information.

First, usually without being aware of it, we look out at the world through a very narrow "window." Often we cannot possibly take in enough information to comprehend fully many situations.

This is particularly true if we are distracted, have restricted our attention to a few elements in the environment, or are confronted with a great number of unfamiliar stimuli. When we are mystified by a magician, it is partly because magicians are masters at exploiting these limitations in order to direct our attention away from crucial aspects of the trick. Many psychics and mediums use similar techniques.[313]

A second consequence of our limited capacity to receive and process information is that, if we focus our attention on one thing, we cannot worry about other concerns at the same time. This release from obsessive worry can be an ecstatic experience and is an important component of such approaches to transcendental states as meditation, dance, and ritual.

You can experience these limitations of consciousness in various ways. First of all, take time to notice what you are aware of at this moment. Now direct your attention to various aspects of your environment—sights, sounds, smells. Which of these stimuli were you unaware of previously? Now become aware of your body. Can you sense your skin—the pressures, the itches? Can you sense your muscles—which are tense and which are relaxed? Can you sense your internal organs—your stomach, your bladder? Which of these stimuli were you unaware of previously? Now attempt to attend to all these stimuli at the same time. Can you do it, or do you shift your attention from one stimulus to another?

Now let's try thinking of more than one thing at once. Here is a multiplication problem: 14 × 41. Solve this problem in your head and, at the same time, try to think of something else.

Don't be discouraged if you are unsuccessful at such tasks; to a large extent, these limits on our consciousness are quite absolute. It is useful, however, to be aware of these limits and of their implications.

3. A third important characteristic of our information processing mechanisms concerns how we deal with extremes of data input. At one extreme, bombardment by rich and varied stimuli can surpass our capacity to deal with stimulus input. We sometimes respond to this condition of "sensory overload" by going into an

altered state of consciousness.[269] Such a response is often experienced at rock concerts, light shows, and religious revivals. The following description of a religious revival, for example, gives the flavor of the involvement of sensory overload—among other influences—in the production of altered states of awareness.

> Men, women, and children begin dancing with jerks. Women begin speaking in tongues. A youth dances for a long time by himself, eyes closed, bent sideways. A girl about twenty years old stands in the aisle beside me, her eyes closed, teeth chattering, and talking to herself in a high voice. A woman gets up with a shriek and rushes out. People stand and give impromptu sermons and testimonials. The evangelists sing and beat on little drums with cymbals. One little girl about eight years old watches the scene with open-mouthed wonder. The children begin imitating. Now the climax is reached. The whole crowd flows down in front to meet with the evangelists, singing, praying, crying, hands raised, embracing, receiving holy touches. Women fall unconscious, stretched out on the floor, trembling and twitching.[368]

At the other extreme of sensory input is a condition known as sensory deprivation. To understand it, we must realize that we need a certain level of stimulus input to function normally. This need is closely related to our capacity for learning and thinking and to such drives as curiosity, play, manipulation, exploration, and competency.[221] That is, we ordinarily seek contact with, and information from, our environment. When we are deprived of this contact, we experience certain altered states of consciousness, often including hallucinations and delusions of various kinds.[757] It is as if the mind creates its own reality when external reality is excluded. Although this process occurs every night when we dream, its occurrence during ordinary waking consciousness is less common. In the laboratory, of course, relatively complete sensory isolation can be achieved. However, religious ascetics in isolated quarters, solitary wanderers or explorers, and others in similar situations sometimes undergo sufficiently reduced levels of stimulation to experience sensory deprivation effects.[92] Joshua Slocum, for example, the first man to sail alone around the world, once awakened to see the figure of a sailor at the helm. Later, on several occasions, the vision of the sailor returned to keep Slocum company.[627]

At this point, you may want to experience sensory deprivation. One method is to lie down in a semilit room with half of a ping-pong ball over each eye. With the ping-pong ball halves, you can open your eyes and still see only a homogeneous field (called a "ganzfeld"); do not close your eyes or lie in a completely dark room because you are then likely to fall asleep. To exclude sounds you can use earplugs, or you can tune a radio to a spot between stations where the hissing "white" noise will mask other noises. Pick a time and place so that you will not be disturbed. Then lie as quietly as possible; it may take an hour or more to experience deprivation effects.

So we see that our information gathering, processing, and storage mechanisms contribute in their own ways to transcendental experience. Because these mechanisms are imperfect, they can distort our internal images of the world to the point where our perceptions at times seem strange and inexplicable. Through understanding these processes, however, we can enjoy and benefit from their sometimes extraordinary effects without being frightened or mystified by them.

The Example of Meditation

It is the mind that maketh good or ill,
That maketh wretch or happy, rich or poor.[689]

EDMUND SPENSER

The scene pictured in Figure 3, of a meditator in deep meditation, is becoming a common one in our society as people seek to achieve the transcendence that meditation can provide. Meditation is a particularly good example of transcendental experience for our consideration because it illustrates how our conception of an experience changes as our understanding increases. In the past, the transcendental effects of meditation were often thought of as paranormal or supernatural. However, now that our knowledge of the processes involved in meditation is more advanced, its effects are commonly thought of as normal and natural, although still extraordinary.

Figure 3. Meditator

Now let us see if we can understand meditation in the light of the sensory and sensory-processing features we have considered to this point.

1. Habituation and inhibition—Most systems of meditation involve monotonous stimulation, fostered by a constant posture

and a repetitive thought (word or mantra, visual image, concentration on breathing, etc.). You will recall that when a stimulus is unvarying for a period of time, our nervous system habituates so that we cease to be aware of the stimulus. You will also remember that there are inhibitory neurons, which, when active, inhibit sensory impulses, thus effectively excluding stimuli from awareness. There is now ample research to demonstrate that meditation can indeed produce habituation and inhibition and that practiced meditators can remain unresponsive, physiologically and psychologically, even to very loud noises that ordinarily would produce an involuntary startle response.[12] This sensory isolation also can create altered states of awareness—hallucinations, etc.—similar to those of sensory deprivation. Aside from meditation, practices such as stereotyped dancing, chanting, and rituals also sometimes appear to involve sufficient repetitive stimulation, and thus habituation, to produce sensory withdrawal and hallucinations.

Of the various effects produced by habituation, one deserves special mention. Perception of body location and movement depends upon sensations from receptors, called proprioceptors, in the inner ear and in the muscles, tendons, and joints of the body. During meditation, when the body is quiet and habituation and inhibition are operating, these receptors sometimes cease to supply a sense of body location. Then the mind can perceive the body as changing in various ways—expanding, levitating—or the psyche as detached and independent of the body.[257] You may have experienced this feeling just before dropping off to sleep. Such "out-of-body" experiences undoubtedly have contributed to the widespread belief that it is really possible to levitate or travel out of your body.[393, 749]

2. Dishabituation—The approach to meditation we have discussed to this point is sometimes called "concentrative" because the meditator concentrates on a mental image that, as we have seen, has the effect of blocking out external stimuli. Another effect of this withdrawal from environmental stimuli occurs after meditation when the habituated sensory neurons are subjected, once again, to stronger and more varied stimulation as the meditator gets up and attends to other affairs; the previously habituated neurons now respond strongly to surrounding stimuli. Physiological studies demonstrate that practiced concentrative meditators do, in fact,

show increased response to environmental stimuli and increased resistance to habituation for a period following meditation.[264] This process is known, appropriately, as dishabituation.

Robert Ornstein describes the process leading to dishabituation in concentrative meditation as follows:

> The practice of meditation, then, can be considered as an attempt to turn off conceptual activity temporarily, to shut off all input processing for a period of time, to get away for a while from the external environment.
>
> A result of this "turning-off" of our input selection systems is that, when we introduce the same sensory input later, we see it differently, "anew."[488]

However, it should be noted that some systems of meditation, notably some forms of Zen-Buddhist meditation, train their meditators to maintain heightened awareness instead of blocking out external stimuli as concentrative meditators seek to do. As Fred Griffith says, ". . . Zen meditators seek to remain aware of each here and now moment without getting carried away into discursive thoughts."[264] Consequently, Zen meditation is sometimes called "open meditation." Physiological studies confirm that practiced Zen meditators do show a high resistance to habituation during meditation.[295]

Nyanaponika Thera describes dishabituation in open meditation this way:

> . . . the normal visual perception . . . will rarely present the visual object pure and simple, but the object will appear in the light of added subjective judgments, as: beautiful or ugly, pleasant or unpleasant, useful, useless, or harmful. . . .
>
> It is the task of Bare Attention to eliminate all those alien additions from the object proper that is then in the field of perception. . . .
>
> . . . therefore it will happen with progressive frequency that things will have something new and worth while to reveal.[677]

The psychological effects of open meditation that Thera describes have been studied by Arther Deikman, who asked subjects to sit and look at a vase for a series of sessions of approximately 15 minutes each spread out over several weeks.[158] Deikman's subjects reported a variety of unusual experiences, including perceiving the vase with increased clarity and vividness.

"Perceiving anew" can be an ecstatic experience, akin to children's naive wonder as they encounter the world. The ecstasy that can accompany the new experiences which sometimes result from meditation probably derives in part from the fact that these experiences meet our powerful need for stimulus change and for discovering new aspects of our environment.[221] This "seeing with fresh eyes" is also closely related to creative processes insofar as creativity consists of perceiving the world in new ways. Indeed, Transcendental Meditation, in particular, places considerable stress on this aspect of meditation.[416]

Of course, dishabituation can result from almost any change, almost any new, different, or unexpected stimulus. Perhaps you can recall when a vacation, a new lover, a move to a new home, or even a change in the weather served to "wake up" your senses and produce a feeling of "aliveness." Even illness, shock, pain, and risky situations evidently are sometimes valued because of their dishabituation effects.[370]

3. Nonconceptual attention—During meditation, concentrative meditators focus on mental imagery, while open meditators attend to varied sensory input. The effect, in both cases, is to exclude rational, conceptual thought as well as worries and disturbing fantasies in general. This is in accordance with the principle of unitary consciousness: you cannot attend to two things at once. Such redirection of attention is not easy. Beginning meditators are often surprised to discover that the chatterbox of the mind is quite incessant and resistant to conscious control. However, meditators do learn to exclude distracting thoughts. Many studies have shown that the quieting of the mind thus achieved is accompanied by relaxation more profound than would be expected from merely sitting quietly.[59, 713] This absorption in meditation and exclusion of other concerns is often accompanied by feelings of euphoria. As Gopi Krishna states:

> . . . meditation or sustained concentration is a natural process. . . . It is the moments of intense absorption that provide . . . the happiest, most beautiful, and most harmonious intervals in [our] lives. . . .
>
> When we listen enraptured to music, when we see a masterpiece of painting or sculpture. . . . It is then that we forget ourselves and our

surroundings in the intensity of our feelings. The same thing happens in the play of love. We forget ourselves and remain in a state of intense absorption during all the period while the contact lasts, forgetting even the flow of time.[380]

Similar effects can be achieved, of course, in a wide range of endeavors—sports, hobbies, martial arts, and so on—that require total attention and concentration.

So we see that meditation involves a number of physiological processes that can produce a variety of impressive psychological effects. Although some of these effects—for example, out-of-body experiences and visionary states—are spectacular, they are also, to a large extent, understandable.

Now that we have considered some of the processes involved in meditation, perhaps you would like to practice some concentrative meditation. Choose a quiet spot where you will not be disturbed for twenty minutes or so. Sit on the floor in a posture that is relatively easily maintained; a cross-legged position is commonly used. If you must sit on a chair, be sure it is not so comfortable that you are likely to go to sleep; for the same reason, do not lie down. Whether you meditate on the mental image of a sound, a visual object, etc., is up to you. Although some schools of meditation claim that only a narrow range of potential images is suitable for meditation,[416] there is little evidence to support this notion.[106] However, whatever image you choose should be simple, unvarying, and not psychologically disturbing. A simple one-syllable sound that is pleasant to you, or a simple geometric figure, will suffice. Beginning meditators will probably find it best to close their eyes. At first, your mind will probably often wander from the image you have chosen; when this happens, merely redirect your attention to your focus of meditation. As you gain more experience, you will be able to maintain your focus of attention for longer periods. If you find it extremely difficult to clear your mind of its myriad other concerns, at least you will have become aware of the relative lack of control that you have over your own mental processes and possibly the importance of learning such control. Meditate for twenty minutes or so; the exact period of time is not crucial. Many meditators meditate in this fashion twice a day, in the morning and at night.

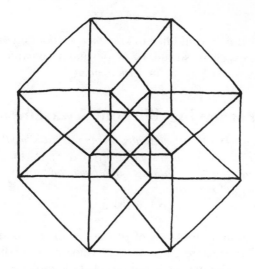

Figure 4. Sufi meditation image

If you would like to practice open meditation, it may be easier first to experience a form of meditation that partakes of both concentrative and open meditation. First, choose a quiet spot and an appropriate position as described above for contemplative meditation. Then choose a stimulus object on which to meditate—a vase, a painting, a piece of paper—almost anything will serve. You may want to meditate on a design such as the one in Figure 4, which is similar to those used by certain Sufis for their meditation. Then, as you look at your chosen object, let it impress itself upon you without, as far as possible, selection, thought, or evaluation on your part. Keep your attention directed to it and let its richness fill your consciousness. When you feel successful at this form of meditation, you may want to try open meditation. Here you will be "open" to the sights, sounds, and other stimuli of your total environment rather than to one particular stimulus; again, refrain as much as possible from thinking or evaluating. This is not easy, but it can be rewarding.

Many of the effects of meditation, of course, will not be experienced until you have meditated for a period of time. There is a Zen saying: "Devotion frees."[545]

Finally, if you would like to know more about meditation, you will find an excellent summary of pertinent research in Patricia Carrington's book, *Freedom in Meditation.*[106]

Perceiving Without Awareness

Things are being "automatically" arranged just below the level of consciousness; "subconsciously perceived" factors are being sorted out, fall "automatically" into place, and are integrated into the final impression.[63]

ERIC BERNE

In addition to the kinds of processing of stimuli that we considered in the previous section, there remains to be discussed the processing of minimal, or subtle, levels of stimulation. That individuals are sensitive to stimuli outside of the range of ordinary conscious perception is of particular interest to transcendental psychology.

Most of us have met people who are particularly sensitive or intuitive—that is, who often "know" what another person is feeling or thinking even though it is not obvious to anyone involved how they know such things. In this section we will discuss how people, through subliminal perception and hyperesthesia, can "pick up" information from others without being aware of how they do it.

Subliminal perception refers to perception without conscious awareness. Stimuli of two basic kinds can be perceived subliminally: (1) stimuli that are just beneath the minimal intensity, or threshold, that is required for conscious awareness, and (2) stimuli that are just outside of the current focus of conscious attention.[168] We all perceive subliminally. Perhaps you can recall humming a tune that you realized after a time was playing softly on a distant radio, although at first you were not aware that your humming was initiated by hearing the tune. More importantly, there is considerable evidence that much of the nonverbal communication that takes place between individuals occurs on a subliminal level.[437] Also, intuition as well as *déjà vu* experiences (the feeling that the present situation is duplicating an experience from the past) are probably often the result of the sudden conscious awareness of information acquired subliminally.[63, 631]

Hyperesthesia refers to heightened sensitivity to stimuli. People who exhibit hyperesthesia are able to sense subtle stimuli to which most of us are oblivious. This sensitivity is probably not due to more acute receptors in the eye, ear, or other senses. Rather, hyperesthesia may be the result of any of several conditions that we have already discussed: (1) dishabituation, (2) cessation of inhibition, and (3) focused attention.[622] In addition, hyperesthesia is undoubtedly greatly facilitated by practice.

Let us see, then, what kinds of experiences appear to result from hyperesthesia and subliminal perception. Bear in mind that these processes are often associated; that is, people who are acutely sensitive to subtle stimuli are often unaware of the nature of their own sensitivity.

1. Blind persons often seem to have a mysterious capacity to avoid obstacles. Experiments have shown that this "sixth sense" consists of an acquired ability to hear faint echoes that bounce off objects in the environment.[664]

2. The mechanic who can detect and identify subtle engine noises, the physician who is sensitive to slight changes in skin color or condition of the fingernails, the wine expert who can identify the vintage and place of origin of fine wines by taste and smell—these and many other practitioners are aware of cues to which most of us are oblivious.

3. Fortune tellers, mind readers, and astute therapists, who often seem mysteriously perceptive, are experienced at deriving useful information from subtle facial expressions, body movements, and tones of voice.

Sometimes the feats of individuals with hyperesthesia are so spectacular that many people credit them with paranormal abilities. Mind readers, for example, are sometimes thought capable of *really* reading minds.[144] However, most mind readers do not claim to possess paranormal powers. For this reason, we will discuss their feats here rather than in the later chapter on psychic phenomena.

Mind readers typically are individuals who have learned to pay attention to extremely subtle cues "leaked" involuntarily by the person whose mind they are attempting to read.[120] Often, mind readers must be in some kind of physical contact with the person whose "mind" is being read, in which case they are guided by small involuntary muscle tensions.[170] The psychologist Clark Hull relates

HYPERESTHESIA

how he was thus able, while blindfolded, to locate a ring which had been hidden previously by "Miss X."

Miss X meets me at the door. I direct her to grasp my right wrist firmly with her thumb on the lower side and the tips of her four fingers on the back. I tell her to think constantly and intently of where the object lies hidden. . . . I begin to move slowly away from the door. . . . I make gentle movements in various directions, but find that the subject's hand makes a slight resistance in all directions except towards the right. I therefore begin moving slowly towards the right, watching intently for signs of resistance or leading. . . . At length I detect a faint pulling of my hand forward and somewhat to the left. I follow the lead slowly and tentatively. By moving carefully I can feel that slight pulling nearly all of the time now. It leads me around the corners of the table. At length I feel my hand touching the shoulder of a man's coat. I start to move my hand upward, thinking the object may be lying on top of the man's head, but encounter marked resistance from my subject's hand, which presses downward. I completely relax my arm and the subject quite definitely moves my hand down the front of the man's coat and pauses at a pocket. I reach into the pocket, feel the ring, and pull it out. Here the audience applauds and I know I have been successful. I remove the blindfold and ask Miss X if she intentionally led me to the ring. She vigorously denies leading me either intentionally or otherwise.[319]

32

However, some mind readers do not need to be in contact with the person whose mind they are reading. In this case, they pay attention to visual and sometimes other kinds of cues.[120] One mind reader describes how he trained himself to be aware of such cues.

> . . . I asked a subject to fix his mind upon certain concepts, such as "up" or "down," "right" or "left," "yes" or "no," and others, in any order he pleased. . . . Standing opposite the subject, I tried to guess at the mental content of the person's mind. . . . With twelve subjects (a total of 350 tests) I made an average of 73% correct responses and in the more favorable cases I attained even 90 to 100% correct responses. Very slight involuntary movements of the head and eyes . . . were the signs which I used as cues. . . . [For example,] "zero" was expressed by a movement of the head describing an oval in the air. Indeed, it was even possible to discover whether the subject had conceived of a printed or written zero, for the characteristics of both were revealed in the head-movements.[509]

Some feats of mind readers are truly amazing; for example:

1. Eugene de Rubini could enter a room and pick out a person or an object, chosen by common agreement by the occupants of the room, by observing their involuntary reactions.[708]

2. Fred Marion could identify which of a number of small cans contained an object; he did this by noting the involuntary reactions of observers who knew which can the object was in.[636]

3. Washington Irving Bishop could drive blindfolded through city streets, guided by the involuntary muscle reactions of a passenger who placed his hand on Bishop. In addition, Bishop could drive to a location anywhere in the city where his passenger had hidden an object and, still through reading his guide's muscle reactions, would locate the object in its hiding place. Bishop could also write down or draw what a subject was thinking, again by being aware of the subject's subconscious muscle responses to what he was writing or drawing.[561]

If the development of hyperesthesia always took years of training and its usefulness were confined to stage demonstrations, it might be of marginal interest to us. But cases of hyperesthesia in otherwise unremarkable individuals have been noted and studied, indicating that it may be more common than usually realized.[166] The case of Ilga K. is particularly interesting. Ilga was a somewhat retarded girl who seemed, nevertheless, to possess remarkable academic skills. These skills were revealed, however, only when an observer was present. For example: ". . . the teacher discovered that Ilga could 'read' any and every text, even one in a language foreign to her, as soon as he stood beside her with the text before him. She did not need to look into the book. The mother made similar observations. In her presence the child uttered results of calculations which were far beyond her calculating ability."[55] It is little wonder that Ilga was thought by many observers to possess psychic abilities and that many scientific observers were baffled by her feats.

Eventually, investigators found that Ilga's remarkable abilities vanished when they put her out of hearing range of those observing her work. In other words, Ilga evidently was able to pick up subtle auditory cues "leaked" by her observers as they watched Ilga work, sometimes from a distance of several meters. Specifically, she was picking up the faint sounds given off by the activation of her observers' vocal chords, which corresponded to their thoughts about what she was working on. As one investigator puts it, Ilga ". . . is capable of 'hearing' something which I with my normal . . . auditory sense could *not* hear even with the highest degree of amplification"[55]

There is little question that we all have the capacity to be exquisitely sensitive to other people and the world around us. Although some people seem to acquire this kind of sensitivity in the normal course of events—perhaps because of the demands of their jobs or family lives—others need special practice to reach the same degree of awareness.

> *If you feel you are relatively insensitive to other people and would like to develop your sensitivity, begin by observing several people from a distance—for example, in a restaurant, in a park, or at a party. Pay attention to their clothing and hair styles, facial expressions, body positions and movements, hand gestures, and tone of voice (if this can be heard). See if you can guess something about their upbringing, what kind of life they lead, and how they are feeling at the moment. As you do this, be aware of what sorts of cues lead you to your conclusions. If people are interacting, see if you can also guess, to some extent, the content of their interaction and how they feel about one another.*

Sometimes it is helpful—and fun—to "people watch" with another person, in which case you can discuss and compare your impressions. Consulting a book on nonverbal communication, such as Albert Mehrabian's **Silent Messages**,[437] *can also help you in this process. Of course, ordinarily you will have no way of knowing if your guesses are correct, but you will at least become aware of some possibilities that you can check out with further experience.*

You will, of course, want to try paying attention to these same nonverbal cues as expressed by people with whom you interact. This is more difficult since, in our personal interactions, we usually concentrate on the verbal message rather than on non-verbal expression. Nevertheless, with practice you can become aware of much nonverbal behavior on the part of people with whom you are interacting, the meaning of which you can then check out with them if you like. However, because nonverbal expression is often not admitted to consciousness, this checking process will seldom be simple or easy. This difficulty will become evident if you ask your friends or acquaintances what kinds of nonverbal messages they feel you have conveyed to them and in what manner. Although at first you may have a difficult time confirming or denying their impressions, with practice you should find that you are increasingly aware of how you express yourself to others, which should help you become sensitive to how they express themselves to you.

Obviously, developing sensitivity to subtle cues is very much an art that is not accomplished overnight. Nevertheless, it is possible to develop such sensitivities and, as you do so, your awareness and understanding of yourself and others should increase accordingly. Eventually, your newly acquired sensitivities will function "automatically," without your conscious direction or awareness.

Creative Imagery

Insofar as the experience of hallucination is synthesizing and unifying it is a unique experience of the same type as the moment of illumination in an act of discovery.[45]
STEPHEN BAUER

There are many definitions of creativity, but most involve the concepts "new and useful."[646] That is, creativity involves a way of seeing, thinking, or dealing with the world that is not only new, but also better than previous ways.

In several respects, the human nervous system is designed to be creative. To understand this, we need to understand some basic physiology.

The human brain is made up of an "old brain" portion, so called because these regions of the brain have persisted over millions of years of evolution and are found in many lower animals, and a "new brain" portion, which evolved relatively recently and reaches its highest development in humans. This evolutionary distinction between old and new brain is reflected in their functioning. The old brain is responsible largely for ordinarily subconscious and involuntary functions, such as emotional arousal and body maintenance and repair processes. In contrast, the new brain is responsible largely for the conscious, voluntary functions of sensation, thinking, learning, and body movements. The new brain, or cerebrum, is in turn dominated by two major structures called cerebral hemispheres. The left hemisphere, in most people, tends to be analytical and rational in its functioning, while the right hemisphere is more intuitive and holistic and often functions outside of conscious awareness.[164] Creative insights often seem to result from right brain processes.[28, 177]

These distinctions, however, are very rough, and there is more reciprocal interplay and sharing of functions than can be indicated here. For example, most old brain functions are initially subconscious, but, as we shall see later, many can be brought under conscious control through training. Likewise, many initially conscious images, thoughts, and behaviors become subconscious with the passage of time, when they can lie dormant waiting for the proper stimulus to release their creative energies.

Also important to our consideration of creative processes is the fact that the human brain consists of billions of neurons, which can be connected in an almost infinite variety of different patterns or networks. In addition, the neural network that represents any particular perception, feeling, thought, or behavior intersects with many other networks for related perceptions, feelings, thoughts, and behaviors.[176] These vast arrays of intersecting neural networks result in two features of particular importance to our creative ca-

CREATIVE IMAGERY

pacity: 1. our capacity to relate separate items of experience—in other words, our capacity to think and to be creative—and 2. our related capacity to confuse and misinterpret experiences since there is no guarantee that the mental connections we make will, in fact, accurately reflect the workings of the external world.

In addition, these neural networks may be active even though we are not consciously aware of this activity. Particularly when our ordinary conscious awareness is altered in some manner—for example, as in dreaming or reverie—this subconscious neural processing can dominate mental activity, producing the unusual or bizzare thoughts and images familiar to us all, as well as—if we are lucky—an occasional creative flash of insight.[115, 268, 577] As John Eccles puts it, "[Through] weaving the spatio-temporal patterns of its engrams in continually novel and interacting forms, the stage is set for the deliverance of a 'brainchild' that is sired, as we say, by creative imagination."[176]

However, important as subconscious processes are in creative activity, conscious, voluntary processes are definitely involved in certain stages of most creative endeavors, particularly in the lengthy initial formulation and information-gathering stages and in the final stages in which the creative insight is evaluated.

The importance of the processes discussed above can be seen in the following account by the chemist Otto Loewi. He describes how the idea for an experiment, which proved to be a milestone in the understanding of neural mechanisms, came to him after a long dormant period when he did not consciously work on the problem.

> The night before Easter Sunday of that year (1920) I awoke, turned on the light, and jotted down a few notes on a tiny slip of thin paper. Then I fell asleep again. It occurred to me at six o'clock in the morning that I had written down something most important, but I was unable to decipher the scrawl. The next night, at three o'clock the idea returned. It was the design of an experiment to determine whether or not the hypothesis of chemical transmission that I had uttered seventeen years ago was correct. I got up immediately, went to the laboratory, and performed a simple experiment on a frog heart. . . .[407]

That subconscious creative processes can produce solutions that go beyond the bounds of conscious thought processes is clearly shown in the following example:

> Somewhere in the spring. . . . I attacked this problem:—Given an ellipse, to find the locus of the foot of the perpendicular let fall from either focus upon a tangent to this ellipse at any point. I endeavoured to solve this analytically. . . . No thought of attempting a geometrical solution ever entered my head. After battling with these equations for a considerable time—it was over a week and may have been two weeks—I came to the natural conclusion that I was bogged, and that all my efforts, if continued, would only sink me deeper in the bog; the proper thing to do was to call a halt . . . and return to it afresh. . . . After about a week, I woke one morning and found myself in possession of the desired solution under circumstances to me strange and interesting. . . . First:—the solution was entirely geometrical, whereas I had been labouring for it analytically without ever drawing or attempting to draw a single figure. Second:—it presented itself by means of a figure objectively pictured at a considerable distance from me on the opposite wall. . . . On opening my eyes on the morning in question, I saw projected upon [a] blackboard surface a complete figure, containing not only the lines given by the problem, but also a number of auxiliary lines, and just such lines as without further thought solved the problem at once. . . . I sprang from bed and drew the figure on paper; needless to say, perhaps,

that the geometrical solution being thus given, only a few minutes were needed to get the analytical one.[481]

As the preceding example indicates, imagery can be an important element in creative endeavor.[618] (Imagery can involve any perceptual mode: vision, hearing, etc.) Although children, with their imaginary playmates and easy expression of fantasy, seem particularly in touch with the processes of imagery,[56] this capacity is by no means lacking in adults. Many achievements in many different fields can be traced, directly or indirectly, to imagery experiences. As Evelyn Underhill says: "Thus the painter really sees his unpainted picture, the novelist hears the conversation of his characters, the poet receives his cadences ready-made, the musician listens to a veritable music. . . ."[697] For example:

> Robert Louis Stevenson, early in his life, discovered that he could dream complete stories and even go back to them on succeeding nights if the end was unsatisfactory. He once described his dreaming consciousness as filled with "little people" who every evening provided him with "truncheons of tales upon their lighted theater." Perhaps his greatest dream achievement came one night when he pictured a criminal, pursued by the police, who imbibed a potion and changed his appearance. This dream eventually appeared as the classic story of Dr. Jekyll and Mr. Hyde.[378]

Creative imagery can also work in a less direct fashion, as can be seen in the following account by the composer Richard Wagner.

> When I commenced work on *Rheingold* in 1853, I was lying in bed. I felt suddenly as if I were immersed in a flood of flowing water. I imagined myself lying at the bottom of the Rhine. I could certainly feel and hear the moving, surging water sweeping over me. Musically this took the form of the chord of E flat major, commencing with the low contra E flat in the double basses. . . .
>
> I was in a semi-trance condition and when I awoke, I immediately realized that this vision was an inspiration—that my prelude to *Rheingold* had taken shape in my inner consciousness.[2]

Imagery can be conceptualized by a continuum, from the weak imagery of fantasies and daydreams, at one end, to the strong imagery of hallucinations and dreams at the other. There is a wide variation in the degree to which individuals ordinarily experience imagery.[559] If you have relatively weak imagery, the following description may help you understand what strong imagery is like.

> For R, the world of actual perception is readily annihilated, as a whole or in part, and replaced by . . . imagery. Thus, she can abolish the perception of a person who is standing before her open eyes, and in his place see a . . . vision of some absent person. . . . She can also add many kinds of . . . details to the things in the real world, e.g. she can place green leaves upon barren winter trees, or supply a smooth shaven man with a full beard. . . . R seldom mistakes her . . . images for reality, but this does happen occasionally. Thus, when riding in an automobile, she has sometimes warned the driver against objects in the road which, as she soon discovered, were figments of her . . . vision. . . .
>
> R's . . . imagery in the nonvisual sense departments is also strong. . . . If R imagines the roar of the sea, the auditory impression is so intense as to weaken actual sounds . . . in her environment. Sometimes, she declares, these real sounds are completely blotted out. . . . When R imagines that an insect is crawling upon her skin, she reports an image that is as intense and irritating as the feeling of a real insect.
>
> By exerting an effort, she can make a human being appear to rise in the air and float across the room. After such an apparent movement has started, she cannot always control its course completely. Thus, when she is asked to make the body float out the window, she reports that it perches itself on the window-sill and refuses to go further.[527]

Of all imagery experiences, hallucinations such as these probably are the most puzzling. Many people feel that experiencing vivid images while asleep—that is, dreaming—is understandable, but that experiencing vivid images while awake—that is, hallucinating—is not. We have already discussed some conditions that give rise to hallucinations—namely, sensory and bodily alterations of various kinds. However, a variety of other conditions can produce hallucinations,[728] including hypnosis and simple conditioning, discussed in the next chapter. As Samuels and Samuels say, ". . . all people need to experience an image is for the right neuronal pathways to fire. It does not matter whether they fire because of stimulation to the retina or other sense organs, or because of an internal stimulus."[585]

Hallucinations are also common in mental illness, but this is not to say that hallucinations necessarily imply mental illness. Many otherwise normal individuals experience hallucinations.[724] For example, Friedrich Kekulé arrived at the concept of the benzene ring, an important advance in organic chemistry, through a series of visions which he describes as follows:

> I fell into a reverie, and lo! the atoms were gamboling before my eyes. Whenever, hitherto, these diminuitive beings had appeared to me, they had always been in motion; but up to that time I had never been able to discern the nature of their motion. Now, however, I saw how, frequently, two smaller atoms united to form a pair, how a larger one embraced two smaller ones; how still larger ones kept hold of three or even four of the smaller; whilst the whole kept whirling in a giddy dance. I saw how the larger ones formed a chain.[205]

His final vision was of a snake, with its tail in its mouth, in the midst of the flames in a fireplace; this image provided Kekulé with the notion, which turned out to be correct, that the benzene atoms were joined in the shape of a ring. Kekulé had been puzzling for some time over the structure of benzene, and, as Richardson demonstrates, strong imagery often occurs after long periods of concentration.[559]

Artists, as well as scientists, often develop strong imagery. Simone Martini, for example, ". . . saw so vividly the imaginary pictures which he painted that he one day asked a visitor to move away from between him and his hallucination so that he might go on with the picture."[283]

Among composers, Mozart, Schumann, Wagner, and Tschaikovsky evidently had highly developed auditory imagery. For example, "When listening to piano music, [Schumann] could fill it in with the tones of other instruments, hearing it as though played by an orchestra." And ". . . whenever Tschaikovsky wrote a symphonic work, he already heard it in imagination as it would sound in the concert-room at Moscow."[7]

Obviously, the capacity for vivid imagery is an important element in a wide range of creative endeavors.

At this point, you may want to try an imagery experience. First, some simple "mind's eye" exercises. With your eyes closed, imagine a simple geometrical figure of your own choosing: dot, line, circle, whatever you like. Note the relative strength of the image and to what extent you are able to maintain the image without having it change. Now, embellish your figure in whatever way you would enjoy—that is, make it more complex, perhaps lace it with flowers, let your imagination run wild. If you are able to see a relatively strong image with your eyes closed, try opening your eyes and looking at a plain background. Can you still "see" your figure?

An alternative method is to begin by looking at an object for an extended period. Then look at a plain background and see if you can maintain the image of the object when the afterimage has faded. If you have poor visual imagery, such exercises might help you develop yours.

Or you might rather try an auditory, touch, taste, or smell exercise. Again, you may prefer to call the image to mind unassisted or to start with an external stimulus—a piece of music, the smell of a flower—and see if you can create the perceptual impression after the stimulus is removed. For most people, this is not an easy exercise, but, as with most abilities, practice helps.

The other major forms of imagery are dreams and dreamlike states. First of all, strong imagery often appears during the period just before we drop off to sleep. This is known as hypnagogic imagery.[591] Likewise, the period just as we are waking up often is accompanied by what is known as hypnopompic imagery. If you cannot recall experiencing these forms of imagery, the following example may help you become aware of them. This sequence is from a recording of a subject describing the hypnagogic images he is experiencing as he falls asleep.

I'm falling asleep and talking, it's like I copied something that was (inaud. mumbling) . . . Anyway . . . uh . . . uh . . . wonder if I'm supposed to feel like I'm drowsing? It sounds like water smacking against rocks. Why did I say that? That was part of a dream I slipped into as I just closed my eyes, impossible . . . Uhu . . . oh the image I have before my head where did it come from? . . . It's a broad green field . . . It's a bluish building with a thin bottom . . . bluish building . . . thin bottom. Fell asleep. That's right . . . I actually had just fallen asleep. I found my lips moving . . . an image, a dream I was dreaming . . . then I woke up and then my eyes closed again . . . so easy.[65]

Sometimes hypnagogic imagery seems to arise from specific earlier experiences,[277] as can be seen in the following description.

> When I was studying anatomy, I was fairly frequently subject to an hypnagogic hallucination familiar, I believe, to medical students. While in my bed, the eyes closed, I would see, with great definiteness and a perfect sense of objectivity, the anatomical preparation with which I had been occupied during the day: the likeness was exact, the impression of reality and, if I may express myself thus, of intense life which emanated from it, was perhaps more intense than if I had been in the presence of a real object. It seemed to me also that all the details, each artery, vein, muscle insertion, all the various features which during waking life I had so much trouble to remember and to recall visually, were there before my eyes. . . .[396]

It can be seen that, in another context, imagery as strong as in the above examples might be interpreted as a vision of paranormal origin.

An excellent exercise for experiencing hypnagogic imagery is given by Charles Tart:

> *"The problem in studying the hypnagogic state in oneself or others is that the material experienced is generally forgotten rapidly, especially as subsequent sleep intervenes between experience and reporting. A simple method to overcome this in studying hypnagogic phenomena is to lie flat on your back in bed, as in going to sleep, but keep your arm in a vertical position, balanced on the elbow, so that it stays up with a minimum of effort. You can slip fairly far into the hypnagogic state this way, getting material, but as you go further muscle tonus suddenly decreases, your arm falls, and you awaken immediately. Some practice with holding the material in memory right after such awakenings will produce good recall for hypnagogic material."*[670]

If you do not ordinarily remember your hypnagogic imagery, try this exercise. You can assume any position—sitting upright, for example–that will change and thus jar you awake as you start to fall asleep. If hypnagogic imagery does not come easily to you, it may be helpful to concentrate on phosphenes—the patterns you see when you close your eyes–and let hypnagogic images arise from them. Finally, immediately writing down or talking about the imagery you experience will help you recall it later.

Compared to many other cultures, ours does not take dreams seriously, although this situation is changing with the new interest in self-awareness. The Senoi culture of the Malay Peninsula provides an instructive contrast. The Senoi consider dreams significant. Dreams of the previous night typically are discussed during the morning meal and may be told at larger social gatherings as well. The Senoi believe that dreams can provide important insights into the social and psychological functioning of the dreamer. For example, if someone dreams of fighting with a relative, the parties might be encouraged to make an effort to head off possible conflict. Thus, dreams are considered a sort of "early warning system." Dreamers are taught to control the course of their dreams in the belief that this may help them to manage situations in the waking state. Kilton Stewart, who studied the Senoi, considered them particularly peaceful and psychologically healthy, partly as a result of the catharsis, resolution of conflict, self-awareness, and general openness that their work with dreams achieved.[653] The emphasis that the Senoi place on dreams receives support from research that indicates that dreams do, in fact, often reflect significant events in the dreamer's life.[533]

Often dreams are the vehicles for creative insights. Stanley Krippner and William Hughes have collected several examples of creative endeavor in which dreams played an important role. For example: "A number of composers reportedly were inspired by melodies heard during the [dreaming] state. Tartini heard in a dream a sonata from which he drew inspiration for his famous "Devil's Trill." Mozart, Schumann, Saint-Saëns, and d'Indy claimed that some of their music was first heard by them in dreams."[378] In another instance:

> [The] inventor, James Watt, had been working on lead shot for shotguns. The standard process involved cutting or chopping metal and was quite costly. About this time, Watt had a recurring dream. He seemed to be walking through a heavy storm; instead of rain, he was showered with tiny lead pellets. Awakening, he surmised that the dream might indicate that molten lead, falling through air, would harden into small spheres. Obtaining permission to experiment in a church which had a water-filled moat at its base, Watt melted several pounds of lead and flung it from the bell tower. Hastening down the stairs, he scooped from the bottom of the moat the tiny leaden pellets—inaugurating a process that revolutionized the lead shot industry.[378]

Perhaps you have been fortunate enough to have had a similar experience of wrestling with a problem just before resting or going to sleep and having the solution come to you in a dream or fantasy.

The psychology and physiology of dreaming have received a great deal of attention in recent years. It is now known that dreaming generally occurs during a light stage of sleep known as REM (rapid eye movement) sleep; this dream state reappears several times each night.[198] Although everyone dreams, it is possible to awaken without remembering any dreams. If this happens to you, perhaps you would like to make an effort to remember your dreams to see what insights you can gain from them. Try putting a tape recorder or a pencil and pad of paper by your bed so that you can record dream memories immediately upon awakening and before they fade. If this does not work, or if you would like help in exploring the psychological significance of your dreams, you might read one of the excellent books available on dreams, such as Ann Faraday's *The Dream Game*[199] or Patricia Garfield's *Creative Dreaming.*[241]

We have seen that imagery—visions, hypnagogic and hypnopompic states, and dreaming—can produce insights that are very useful. Another characteristic of imagery of interest to transcendental psychology is the ecstatic feelings that often accompany creative imagery. Of course, the experience of suddenly and clearly visualizing, through imagery, the solution to a problem with which one has been wrestling can be a powerful and euphoric experience. However, the euphoric feelings that so often accompany imagery have other roots as well. According to H. L. Hollingworth, the hypnagogic state is often accompanied by ". . . feelings of exuberance, buoyancy, confidence, and eager enthusiasm. . . . 'the mental symptoms consist in convictions of emancipation, relief, and happiness, in grand and sublime ideas which in their expansion seem to break down all barriers of doubt and difficulty. . . .' "[300]

One possible reason for these feelings becomes clear if we remember that we often repress not only bad feelings, but also good feelings during our ordinary waking life. For example, we often hesitate to show joyful, loving, or sexual feelings in social situations where they would be considered out of place. However, in the private world of fantasies and dreams, such stored-up feelings are free to emerge.

How We Create Meaning

The search for order, regularity and meaning is a general characteristic of human thought processes.[334] GUSTAV JAHODA

Another important aspect of creativity relevant to our consideration of transcendental experience has to do with our ability and need to create meaning. This tendency is closely related to other characteristics we have already discussed—our curiosity, our capacity for imagery, and our capacity to conceptualize. Fr xmpl, yu r abl to rd ths sntnc bcs yu r abl t crte mnng n yr mnd. If you attempted to make sense out of the last sentence, you experienced the feeling of reading meaning into an ill-defined stimulus. This ability is our glory as human beings, yet various reserach studies indicate that we often read meaning into situations where it does not, in fact, exist. For example:

1. When subjects are given rewards at random times, they tend to interpret the rewards as meaningfully linked with behaviors they happen to be engaging in at the time of the reward; they therefore increase the frequency of those behaviors.[109] Superstitious behaviors, in which individuals perform seemingly arbitrary acts in the belief that they will produce a desired outcome, may somtimes result from this kind of experience. For example, Gustav Jahoda describes ". . . the case of a person who won a large sum on the football pools, and encountered a black and white cat at the time the news arrived. For years afterwards there persisted a ritual of looking out for the cat when the pool results were due."[334]

2. When subjects are told that a point of light is moving and spelling out words, even though it is stationary, they will often "see" the light move and will identify the words they believe it is spelling (this is the autokinetic effect discussed earlier).[541] Thus the perception of events is modified by the expectations we bring to the experience. You may have noticed this tendency in yourself when, alone in a dark place, crumpled newspapers become rats and shadows become lurking figures. Obviously, in such circumstances, we cannot take sightings of ghosts and spirits at face value.

3. When subjects recall events, they tend to forget or distort certain portions of the experience, with the effect of enhancing its psychological meaning at the expense of accuracy of recall.[10] The unreliability of the memory of witnesses, for example, is a peren-

nial problem in courts of law.[94] This tendency of memories to change over time to produce a "better story" undoubtedly underlies many accounts of mysterious happenings, which fit so well the beliefs of the perceiver. As one investigator of seemingly precognitive visions states, ". . . the human mind not only quickly forgets non-coincidental cases, but . . . in the course of time the ones that are remembered become embroidered with coincidental features that they did not in fact possess."[723]

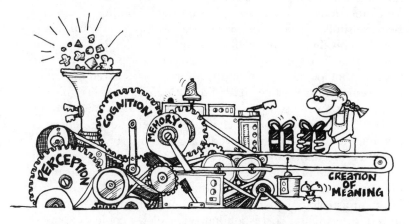

Using astrology as an example, let us consider how this tendency to read meaning into events underlies certain fallacies in reasoning so often characteristic of theories that postulate paranormal influence.

1. Confusion of correlation and cause. There is often a tendency to think that if two events are correlated—that is, if they occur together—there is a direct cause-effect relationship between them.[621] For example, one author wonders, "Why . . . does the number of lemmings born determine the number of eggs the white northern owl will lay?"[88] This author states that the one event determines the other, and this does indeed appear mysterious or even "supernatural." However, when we realize that the number of offspring of lemmings and owls probably vary together because they both depend on other factors, such as fluctuations in the food supply, the relationship seems much less mysterious. Many other relationships that seem mysterious and unexplainable lose their mystery in the light of such analysis. This confusion of correlation

and cause is found in the central tenet of astrology, which states that because my birth "correlates" with the appearance of certain heavenly bodies in particular areas of the sky, I therefore am endowed psychically with the characteristics that are ascribed to those heavenly bodies.

2. Reasoning by analogy. Perceiving meaning in analogies is another form of reasoning of interest to us, since many theories that postulate mysterious psychic and occult influences are analogical theories. Analogical reasoning consists of postulating meaningful connections between two events on the basis of their similarity. Because similarity does not prove relationship, analogical theories are often invalid. Astrology, for example, is analogical when it postulates that heavenly bodies represent certain psychic influences because they possess certain appearances: Mars is red and, therefore, represents a warlike, masculine influence; Venus is white and, therefore, represents a peaceful, feminine influence, and so on.

3. Underestimation of chance and coincidence. There is a tendency to think that, since events are meaningful, they cannot be a matter of chance or coincidence. For example, when given a random series of symbols, subjects tend to perceive meaningful ordering even though there is none.[270] More to the point, a believer in astrology is likely to ascribe meaning to what may be a purely coincidental correspondence between people's experience and their horoscopes.

You can test your own judgment regarding the probabilities of coincidence by answering the questions posed in the following problems.

The "birthday problem": How many people would have to be assembled before there is a 50-50 chance that at least two people in the group would have the same birthday (that is, be born on the same day of the year, but not necessarily the same year)?

The "small world problem": You randomly choose two individuals—hereafter called person A and person B—from the population of all adults living in the United States. You give person A a folder and the name and address of person B with instructions to send the folder to an acquaintance, known on a first name basis, who would have the best chance of either knowing person B or knowing someone in B's acquaintance. The individual who receives the folder from A is given the same instructions for getting the folder to B. The idea is to get the folder from A to B in the smallest number of steps. The question is, assuming that the folder in fact gets from A to B, how many steps are required on the average to link two adults chosen at random in this country?

Now compare your answers with the correct answers below.

Twenty-three people are required on the average for there to be a 50–50 chance that at least two people will have the same birthday.[359]

Five to six such acquaintance links are required on the average to link any two adults chosen at random in the United States.[445]

The guesses of most people are considerably higher than the correct answers, illustrating the tendency to underestimate the role of chance and coincidence in human affairs. Thus, we would expect that some people will be mystified by occurrences that are well within the bounds of chance and coincidence.[348, 375]

Thus we must conclude that our tendency to attribute meaning to events is a mixed blessing. On the one hand, this capacity enables us to learn about the world as we test the meanings that we create. On the other hand, we have seen that we tend to intellectualize our experience and attempt to assign it meaning even in the absence of sufficient understanding. With regard to transcendental experience in particular, with its great intrinsic interest, we should expect that the need to ascribe meaning will be particularly strong. However, given the widespread lack of awareness of many of the underlying processes involved in transcendental experiences, we would also expect that the "meanings" ascribed to such experiences will often stem from personal needs and biases more than from true understanding.[432] This points up the wisdom of Randall Collin's suggestion to ". . . *trust the experiences, not the interpretations.*"[127]

Deprivation and Motivation

Hunger is the best seasoning for meat, and thirst for drink.[689]
CICERO

If you have ever fallen head over heels in love, you know the powerful, even transcendental, impact of feeling your needs for intimacy fulfilled. But "falling in love" presumes a prior state of "not having fallen in love"—in other words, a prior state of deprivation. Can deprivation, then, contribute to transcendental experience? We have already discussed the transcendental experiences that can arise if we are deprived, for example, of sleep, nutrients, or sensory input. We might expect, then, that need deprivation in general would produce transcendental effects, and, as we will see, that is indeed the case.

First, however, we should deal with the feeling, common in our affluent society, that deprivation is necessarily psychologically damaging. This attitude is even expressed in some contemporary psychological theories.[424] Although there is no question that extreme need deprivation is often psychologically damaging,[362] several lines of evidence and theory indicate that some degree of deprivation contributes to psychological well-being.

1. The dishabituation principle we have already discussed, which states that stimuli, including those that satisfy various needs, are appreciated more after a period of deprivation.

2. The Yerkes-Dodson law, which states that efficiency and creativity are enhanced with some degree of deprivation.[751]

3. The cognitive-dissonance theory, which states that, to the extent that deprivation elicits effort, the attained goal will be perceived as valuable.[20]

4. The competence theory, which states that satisfaction results from developing proficiency in overcoming difficult obstacles.[731]

5. The catharsis theory, which states that the release of tension after a period of buildup of frustration and expectation is pleasurable.[228]

It will be helpful at this point to understand some additional physiology. Generally, when the body is deprived of what it needs, it becomes activated to deal with the potential emergency. Internally, the activation of the heart, lungs, and other organs of the body is accomplished by the autonomic nervous system—in specific, the branch known as the sympathetic nervous system. In general, some degree of activation is pleasurable since, in this state, we are motivated, active, and interested in our surroundings.

When the need is finally met, the part of the autonomic nervous system called the parasympathetic nervous system serves to calm the body. This process of restoration of the body to a normal state is known as homeostasis and is also generally pleasurable. In fact, this is reflected in the word *satisfaction,* which can refer both to "satisfaction of a need" and to "feelings of pleasure."

You probably can recall experiences of your own that illustrate this process. In my own life, the birth of my first child was such an experience. I felt intensely involved and alive while Linda was in labor, partly because my needs concerning her and the baby's well-being were not completely met. When Anya was born, I felt an overwhelming rush of relief and joy, and I cried in a tremendous release of feeling. I experienced similar feelings after Kevin, our second child, pulled through a serious illness when he was a few weeks old. Without denying the importance of other factors, it is clear that my "high" on these occasions was due in part to a homeostasis process.

Perhaps the greatest unmet need in our society is the need for close human relationships.[81] It is not surprising, then, that the achievement of intimacy, for lonely people, should be a particularly powerful experience. In my work with people in group situations, I have found that group experiences that bring people closer together often produce feelings of exhilaration. Others also have noted the euphoric feelings that often accompany the achievement of intimacy.[186] Although intimacy is expressed in many ways, there is much evidence to indicate that touching is a basic physiological mechanism that meets this need.[455] Unfortunately, touching has always been something of a taboo in our culture. Given such deprivation, it is little wonder that touching elicits the strong psychological reactions that it does.

Physiologically, touching generally quiets the body through the parasympathetic nervous system. Thus it can alleviate anxiety and elicit feelings of contentment and well-being. Because of its therapeutic impact, touching plays a large role in a wide variety of healing procedures: the massage of conventional hospitals, the "laying on of hands" of faith healing, and the "energy flow" in the touch of psychic healing.

To experience the effects of touch, you may want to exchange a massage with a friend. If you need assistance on techniques, good books are available[602] but technique is not as important as concern and sensitivity. Do not engage in sex during this experience. Although sex entails touch, it often serves for the expres-

sion of a variety of other needs. So keep your touch experience separate, and you can experience the pleasure of touch alone. Do not make your massage too short since it takes time to modify physiological states; allow at least twenty minutes for each massage. You will have to decide whether to keep your clothes on; it greatly inhibits touching, but better a massage with clothes than no massage at all. If you are so inclined, you might try a group massage; the feelings can be that much more intense as your whole body is massaged simultaneously.

Another mechanism sometimes involved in need deprivation is sublimation. Although its physiology is not well understood, psychologically what seems to occur is that energy that would ordinarily be expended in satisfying a certain need will, when that need is no longer directly expressed, be redirected into other areas of concern. These other concerns thus become infused with greater dedication and activity. While writing this book, for example, I have forgone many social activities so that I could devote greater time and energy to writing. The book has become a form of social communication that takes the place of more usual forms of social relationships. Many writers, artists, and scientists undoubtedly sublimate social and other motivations while engaged in their work. One consequence of such sublimation is that feelings of achievement and fulfillment can be considerably heightened, based as they are on extended periods of deprivation and expectation. In the case of religious ascetics, in particular, in both Eastern and Western cultures, it appears that ecstatic mystical experiences, sometimes complete with visions, can result from the long-term sublimation of social and sexual drives in their religious devotions.[396]

We see, then, that need deprivation, far from being a totally negative experience, can facilitate the development of ecstatic states and also the production of creative works, which derive their life force from self-denial.

Healthy Mind, Healthy Body

Every change in the physiological state is accompanied by an appropriate change in the mental-emotional state, conscious or unconscious, and conversely, every change in the mental-

emotional state, conscious or unconscious, is accompanied by an appropriate change in the physiological state.[259]
GREEN, GREEN AND WALTERS

Having briefly discussed how feelings of deprivation can produce a physiological state of activation and stress, we are now in a position to consider more thoroughly the case of Colin Turnbull, the anthropologist mentioned in Chapter 1, who fell ill when he was hexed by African villagers. Turnbull could hardly help feeling stress when he was rejected and vilified by the villagers he had gone to study. How can stress, however, produce physical illness? To answer this question, we need to understand more about the physiology of stress.

During the long span of evolution, our ancestors developed certain ways of responding to threat. When our basic genetic makeup was evolving, most threats could best be met either by physically overcoming the threat or by running away from it. This "fight or flight" reaction was relatively successful in dealing with marauding animals, floods, or attacking tribes. Under conditions of threat, the autonomic nervous system activates the body, preparing it for action. Walter Cannon describes this process: "Respiration deepens, the heart beats more rapidly, the arterial pressure rises, the blood is shifted away from the stomach and intestines to the heart and central nervous system and the muscles, the processes in the alimentary canal cease, sugar is freed from the reserves in the liver, the spleen contracts and discharges its contents of concentrated corpuscles, and adrenin [adrenaline] is secreted from the adrenal medulla."[103]

Although, as we have seen, mild levels of activation are often pleasurable, high levels of stress are usually unpleasant; this is basically adaptive as it motivates us to take immediate action. If we successfully deal with the threat, the energy is expended and the body returns to its normal state. However, most threats we encounter in today's world have to do with relations with others or with our feelings about ourselves. Although such threats usually cannot be dealt with by violence or by fleeing, our bodies nevertheless still prepare us for such action. The consequence is that the physiological activation becomes chronic; that is, it remains because it is not discharged.[503] Chronic stress has a number of detrimental effects.

1. Body organs and cells weaken over time and also become more susceptible to infection.[606]

2. The chronic preparation of the body for violent activity together with the body's attempts to restore balance, can produce a variety of psychosomatic conditions stemming from disturbances in blood sugar balance (diabetes, hypoglycemia), digestive function (ulcers, colitis), respiration (hyperventilation, asthma), connective tissue (arthritis, rheumatism), and cardiovascular function (heart disease, stroke).[71, 398] In addition, many other psychosomatic conditions have been shown to be related to the body's stress response.

3. The psychologically punishing nature of high levels of stress is responsible for a great deal of mental anguish and suffering.

It is not surprising, then, that the stress Colin Turnbull undoubtedly experienced after he was hexed could lead to physical illness. It is also not surprising that his counterhex could psychologically counteract the stress and facilitate recovery. Likewise, sufferers from a wide variety of psychosomatic illnesses are often helped by psychic or occult healing approaches that reduce stress through relaxation, meditation, or the loving touch of a healer's hands.

Summary

Heaven and hell have been located inside the human brain.[674]
JOHN TAYLOR

In this chapter, we have seen that our nervous system is designed, in several respects, to transcend our ordinary modes of functioning.

We have seen that our senses are not simple conveyers of information. On the contrary, our eyes, for example, sometimes provide brilliant phosphene shows of their own.

We have seen that meditation relies on several physiological and psychological mechanisms to achieve such effects as profound relaxation and imagery experiences.

We have seen that sometimes we are sensitive to stimulus cues so subtle that we are not even consciously aware of our own sensitivity.

We have discussed how our brain is designed to create its own images in the form of dreams and fantasies and that this imagery sometimes is strong enough to appear "real."

We have seen how, as in the case of the religious ascetic, we can experience feelings of ecstasy as a result of periods of hardship and deprivation.

And we have seen how the psychosomatic illnesses that result from stress often can be alleviated by psychological approaches that employ such techniques as touch and relaxation.

Finally, we have seen that a knowledge of the physiological processes involved in transcendental experiences not only helps us understand ourselves better, but also can help us develop our potential for these experiences.

3

Conditioning Effects in Transcendental Experience

... the danger that custom will blunt our astonishment.[201]

ERWIN SCHRÖDINGER

Colin Turnbull's illness, which developed when he was hexed and which was discussed earlier, is also a good introduction to this chapter. One reason Turnbull fell ill was undoubtedly because the villagers' actions *suggested* to him that he would. How suggestion can produce illness is one of the questions we consider in this chapter concerning the effects of learning and conditioning. As we shall see, a discussion of these effects will enable us to understand many other out-of-the-ordinary experiences.

It is not surprising that learning is important in transcendental experience. Of all organisms, we, as humans, have the greatest capacity for modifying our experience through learning. The basic forms of learning are known as conditioning, and, although there may be a single physiological process involved, two types of conditioning are recognized: classical and operant. Because we will refer to these forms of conditioning later, it is important to be clear about the differences between them.

Classical conditioning consists of responding to a *new stimulus*, whereas operant conditioning involves learning a *new response*. Classical conditioning is so called because it was the first type of conditioning to be studied systematically. These studies were conducted by Ivan Pavlov, the Russian physiologist who taught dogs to salivate to the sound of a bell by ringing the bell just before food was made available. The dogs did not learn a new response; they already "knew" how to salivate. The learning consisted of *responding to a new stimulus*. This example of classical conditioning is diagrammed in Figure 5.

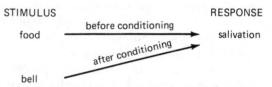

Figure 5.   Classical conditioning—the example of Pavlov's dog.

The traditional example of operant conditioning, on the other hand, is the rat that B. F. Skinner, the American psychologist, taught to press a bar to get a food pellet (known as a reinforcement because it makes bar pressing more likely). This type of conditioning is called *operant* because here the animal operates on the environment, in this case by pressing a bar. In operant learning, the response changes, from relatively nondirected exploration, in this example, to a truly new response—pressing a bar. On the other hand, the stimulus conditions remain the same from the first of the experiment to the last. Operant learning, in other words, consists of *learning a new response*. This example of operant conditioning is diagrammed in Figure 6.

Figure 6.   Operant conditioning—the example of Skinner's rat.

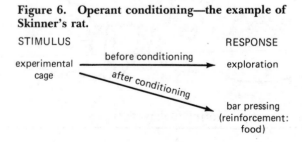

It will help to understand the relevance of classical and operant learning to transcendental psychology if we show how esctatic feelings, for example, can be brought about through both kinds of learning. First of all, we inherit the capacity to respond joyfully to certain stimuli, such as being cuddled and played with as a child. Then, years, later, some stimulus that was associated with those occasions (a melody, an odor, a photograph) evokes their memory in us. Through the mechanism of classical conditioning, this stimulus will reactivate in us the joyful feelings we experienced as a child.[301] In fact, because of the numerous experiences this stimulus may have come to represent, our feeling may be even stronger than it was as a child; as a consequence, adults may be more able than children to experience profound ecstatic feelings. Much nostalgia probably arises from classical associations of this kind.

Operant conditioning, on the other hand, probably accounts, in part, for the differences among adults in the capacity to experience ecstasy. Children who grow up in families that take pleasure in their joyful feelings will likely experience greater and greater joy as they are reinforced in their feelings. In contrast, children raised by families that discourage expressions of joy are, sad to say, likely to grow up to be joyless adults.

We discussed meditation in the last chapter and it is appropriate now that we discuss the conditioning process in meditation. First of all, meditation helps free us from learned fixations such as

CONDITIONED RESPONSE

stereotyped ways of perceiving and obsessional thinking. In addition, the process of meditation conditions us in new ways. For example, one effect of meditation often reported is the learned ability to relax in the face of problems that previously provoked anxiety. Also, it is well known that meditation is a cumulative process and that practiced meditators achieve profound meditative states more easily than novices. This is largely a conditioning effect. With each meditation session, meditators classically condition themselves so that the stimuli present during meditation—the place, the posture, the focus of meditation, and so on—are increasingly effective in producing the meditative state. In addition, this conditioning of mental and physical processes is rewarding—or reinforcing in operant conditioning terms—to meditators; thus they are likely to devote themselves even more to meditation. Finally, most schools of meditation directly or indirectly offer suggestions about what psychological states meditators might experience during meditation, and these suggestions serve as additional conditioning to help produce these states. All in all, the effects of meditation truly would be minimal without the conditioning that occurs during the meditation process.[614]

The Habits in Our Lives

All habits gather by unseen degrees,
As brooks make rivers, rivers run to seas.[689]
JOHN DRYDEN

Do your remember brushing your teeth this morning? If so, do you remember whether you brushed your upper or lower teeth first, or how many times you rinsed your mouth or your toothbrush? Even though most of us perform such behaviors in much the same manner on each of thousands of occasions, we often cannot recall doing them, much less any details of the act.

As this example illustrates, one consequence of learning anything well is that the acquired behavior becomes habitual and stereotyped. Such behaviors are known as sets. Sets tend to be automatic in operation and to resist change. They also can appear mysterious because they often operate outside of immediate awareness. Some examples will help clarify these properties of sets.

HABIT

An example of perceptual set is given in Figure 7. Here the two pairs of eyes appear to be looking in different directions; the left pair is looking to the reader's right and the right pair is looking directly at the reader. Now, with your hand, cover the faces all except for the eyes, and you will see that the two sets of eyes are actually identical; the misperception is the result of conditioned associations that link direction of gaze with facial orientation.

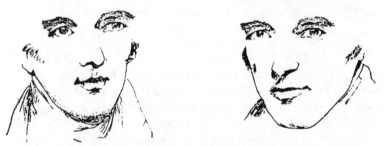

Figure 7. Perceptual set

Many other illusions, both optical and magical, are based on perceptual set.[263]

An example of thinking set is provided by the following problem: Two Indians are standing on a bluff. The little Indian is the son of the big Indian, but the big Indian is not the father of the little

Indian. What is the relationship of the big Indian to the little Indian? In thinking about this problem, most people are affected by past conditioned associations: we expect to see a boy Indian on a bluff with his father. The answer, which contradicts this conditioning, is: The big Indian is the little Indian's mother.

This tendency to think in set ways that may be inadequate to explain new experiences can make these new experiences seem mysterious and inexplicable. For example, magicians and many psychics and mediums mystify their audiences by producing out-of-the-ordinary experiences for which ordinary explanations cannot account.[690]

Here is an example of response set. Hold out your arm and point at a distant object so that the finger you point with is in line between your eyes and the object. Now close your left eye. Is your finger still in line with the object? If it is, you are a "right-eyed" individual for such tasks; that is, you use your right eye, rather than your left, probably without knowing it. If, when you close your left eye, your finger is no longer in line with the object, you are a "left-eyed" individual for this task. We all know whether we are right or left-handed, but eye dominance is much more subtle, and although we habitually use our dominant eye on many such occasions, this awareness escapes most of us.[516]

The concept of set not only helps us understand some apparent mysteries, it also helps us better understand creativity. The word *set* implies rigidity; *creativity* implies new and useful. In large part, then, creativity involves breaking sets; a creative person is one who goes beyond previous conditionings.

Hypnosis

We are all hypnotized.[651]
JOHN STEVENS

Think of a strongly conditioned behavior of yours—brushing your teeth, smoking, lacing your shoes—such as we discussed in the last section, and you will realize that you perform these acts almost as if you were in a trance or were hypnotized. That is, you feel compelled to perform them, yet you often do so without having consciously made a decision about it and without being consciously aware of your actions. This similarity to hypnosis is not accidental; hypnosis is also, to a large extent, a conditioning phenomenon.

There is little question that hypnosis qualifies as an important transcendental experience and, furthermore, that it helps us to understand a wide range of seemingly paranormal experiences. Therefore, it is important to understand some of the processes that seem to be involved in hypnosis. These processes are postulated by various theories, of which the following are representative:[587, 722]

1. "Focused attention" theory. Concentration on the monotonous sound of the hypnotist's voice is similar to the concentration of meditation and might be expected to produce similar effects of relaxation, altered states of consciousness, and oblivion to other stimuli—including ordinarily painful stimuli. Restrictive, repetitive stimuli can even produce a "trancelike" state in some animals.

2. "Role-playing" theory. Through observing other hypnotized subjects or through reading descriptions of such subjects, most of us have learned how to "model" appropriate hypnotic behaviors. In addition, family experiences have usually taught us to play a responsive, submissive role with authority (parental) figures such as the hypnotist.

3. "Ideomotor" theory. As the ideomotor process is undoubtedly involved in producing specific hypnotic behaviors[319], we will need to understand it in some detail.

The word *ideomotor* means, literally, "idea response" and is meant to convey the notion that merely thinking about a behavior will tend to produce that behavior. Classical conditioning explains how this is possible. You will recall that if a stimulus elicits a certain reponse (as, for example, food elicits salivation in a dog) and if we then present a new stimulus (such as a bell) along with the food, eventually the new stimulus will produce salivation. You may have noticed salivation or some other anticipatory response in yourself just before you eat. For example, take a moment, close your eyes, and imagine yourself biting into a juicy, sour lemon. If you salivated, notice that your response is involuntary; you did not consciously "will" yourself to salivate and ordinarily you would not be able to prevent it. Ideomotor responses arise from the fact that words and thoughts are, in part, conditioned stimuli, which can elicit automatic responses in us just as a bell elicits automatic salivation in Pavlov's dog.

> *You can experience how the ideomotor process can create involuntary movement if you rest one of your arms beside you, on your lap, or on the arm of your chair. Now think about your arm lifting up in the air. Think this thought over and over to yourself, using words that represent that movement—for example, "My arm is lifting slowly up in the air, rising more and more." It may take a few minutes, but you probably will feel at least a slight movement in your arm as a result of this exercise, and you may experience your arm lifting in the air, all without conscious effort. If in fact your arm lifts in the air, terminate this exercise by suggesting to yourself, in similar fashion, that your arm is lowering back to its resting place.*

A diagram of this exercise is given in Figure 8; you will notice that it looks exactly like the diagram for Pavlov's dog in Figure 5. In other words, originally a real need situation, such as the need to get a package from a high shelf, was required to produce arm-raising (just as real food was required to elicit salivation in Pavlov's dog). However, after many occasions of associating these situations with a word or thought ("lift your arm"), the word or thought alone is able to produce an involuntary lifting of your arm, just as the bell was able to produce involuntary salivation in Pavlov's dog.

Closely related to the production of "automatic actions" is the creation of "automatic perceptions" through classical conditioning.

Figure 8. Ideomotor response as classical conditioning

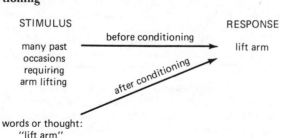

It has long been known that hallucinations can be produced in the manner shown in Figure 9.[188] Here is a basic procedure by which, after many pairings of a light and a tone, the light alone will elicit the (hallucinatory) perception of the tone. In other words, the anticipation of a perception can elicit the perception in the absence of a corresponding external stimulus. All of us have been conditioned to experience at least low level hallucinations of this variety. For example, you may remember looking at a clock and "seeing" the second hand move before you realized that the clock was not running. In other words, your expectation that the second hand would be moving was sufficient to cause you to "see" it move.

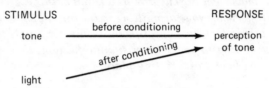

Figure 9.   Conditioned hallucination

In light of this, we should not be surprised if, under conditions of strong suggestion, many people experience hallucinations. Following is an example of this phenomenon.

In the fall of 1903, Professor R. Blondlot, a respected member of the French Academy of Sciences and head of the physics department at the University of Nancy, announced the discovery of still another type of radiation, which he named "N-rays" in honor of his university. In a paper published by the French Academy of Sciences, Blondlot disclosed that N-rays were emitted spontaneously by many different metals, but never by wooden objects. He said that the presence of N-rays could be detected by the human eye in a nearly darkened room. When they were present, N-rays enabled the eye to see objects not otherwise discernible. Within several months, the Academy had published a dozen more papers that confirmed Blondlot's remarkable discovery. One reported that N-rays also improved an observer's sense of hearing and smell. Another disclosed that N-rays were emitted by the human brain, nerves, and muscles as well as by metals. . . .

Soon a variety of French scientists were experimenting with N-rays, including biologists, physiologists, psychologists, chemists, botanists, and even geologists. Still more exciting discoveries were being reported. For example, that N-rays were emitted also by growing plants, by a vibrating tuning fork, and even by a human corpse. All investigators confirmed Blondlot's original findings that *N-rays were never emitted by wooden objects.* . . . Within a year of Blondlot's original paper, *the French Academy had published nearly one hundred papers on the subject.* It came as no surprise when the Academy announced that Blondlot would receive its Lalande prize of 20,000 francs and a gold metal for his discovery of the remarkable N-rays.[369]

However, in 1904 the American physicist Robert Wood visited Blondlot's laboratory and discovered, by secretly changing a series of experimental conditions, that Blondlot continued to see the N-rays under circumstances that Blondlot claimed would prevent their occurrence![603] When Wood published his findings,[748] it was realized that Blondlot and the other French scientists[72] had believed so strongly in N-rays that they hallucinated their existence!

We have seen that classical conditioning can produce seemingly mysterious behaviors, for example, involuntary actions and hallucinations. Likewise, suggestions that elicit hypnotic behaviors are, in effect, classically conditioned stimuli that elicit responses that can appear very strange and incongruous. Of course, the more we practice any kind of conditioned response—for example, the arm-lifting exercise presented earlier—the easier the response becomes as we are further conditioned. Also, in hypnosis, following the initial suggestions of the hypnotist makes it easier to follow later, more involved suggestions.[722] In this manner, truly amazing results can be obtained in good hypnotic subjects,[294] including: 1. vivid hallucinations, 2. enhanced memory, sometimes for events of which subjects have no conscious recall, 3. posthypnotic suggestion in which subjects, at a signal, compulsively and automatically perform a behavior that was suggested to them during hypnosis, and 4. insensitivity to pain, even during major surgery.[382] Figure 10, for example, shows a patient undergoing major surgery, for removal of an appendix, with hypnosis as the sole anesthetic.

Some idea of the effectiveness of hypnosis in relieving suffering is conveyed by the following description of a visit to a clinic where hypnosis was used in the treatment of patients who had suffered severe encephalitis infection.

> . . . I spoke to some of the patients. They were miserable victims of the dread disease, rigid, with abnormal involuntary movements. They had been receiving this [hypnotic] treatment for months, some

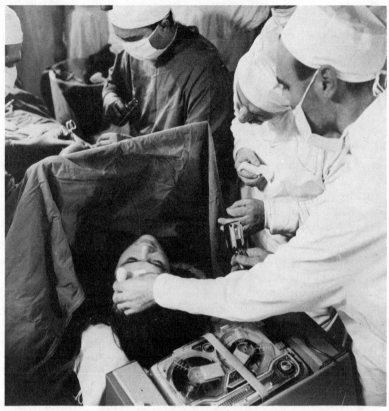

Figure 10. Surgery under hypnosis

of them for a year or more, and all of them, according to their own testimony, were cured! Among them I was especially impressed by one. He was so rigid that he could hardly propel himself with the short, increasingly rapid Parkinsonian gait. His right hand shook violently, his body swayed from side to side incessantly, his head moved continually up and down and from side to side, his mouth was open, and saliva dribbled from it. His speech was of the classical explosive type, scanning and with abrupt pauses. And he, too, was cured! I was as certain of the poor fellow's sincerity as I am that I have not seen many postencephalitic sufferers more pitiable.[573]

Hypnosis certainly is an important transcendental experience, and readers who would like to train themselves in self-hypnosis are advised to obtain one of the publications on the subject; the books by Leslie Le Cron[391] and Laurence Sparks[639] are particularly recommended.

If the effects just described were possible only in a hypnotic trance, they would be useful enough. However, we have seen that many situations produce the equivalent of a hypnotic state. T. X. Barber, in particular, has collected many studies bearing on the equivalence of "real life" experiences to hypnotic induction. For example, he relates an account describing how anesthesia can be achieved in the absence of formal hypnotic induction.

In 1945 these investigators were working under primitive conditions in a prisoner-of-war hospital near Singapore. Since drugs were not available, hypnotic procedures were employed in surgery. Two patients could not be "hypnotized." Since the surgical procedures (incision for exploration of abscess cavity and extraction of incisor) had to be performed without drugs, Sampimon and Woodruff proceeded to operate after giving "the mere suggestion of anesthesia." To their surprise they found that both patients were able to undergo the normally painful procedures without complaints and without noticeable signs of pain. These investigators wrote that "as a result of these cases two other patients were anesthetized by suggestions only, without any attempt to induce true hypnosis, and both had teeth removed painlessly." Other investigators . . . have presented comparable findings with respect to the effectiveness of direct suggestion for pain relief given without the induction of "hypnotic trance."[33]

In the light of this discussion, we should not be surprised that settings in which strong suggestions are present for the relief of pain and discomfort, experiencing visions, and so on should be able to produce these responses in many individuals. Settings such as seances and psychic healing ceremonies provide the elements required for such effects.

Contagious Behavior

Hundreds of people were streaming away from the evening meeting of a certain Sufi, while Nasrudin was making his way toward the house. Suddenly Nasrudin sat down in the middle of the road. One of the people stopped and asked, "What are you doing?"

Nasrudin said:

"Well, I was going to the house of the Sufi. But since everyone else was going away from it, I'm having second thoughts."[612]

SUFI TALE

Think of a time when everyone around you was laughing or crying and you found that you could not keep yourself from feeling these same emotions. Many studies demonstrate that effects of suggestion are magnified in a group of people who mutually reinforce and model one another's behavior.

In one study, for example, Solomon Asch presented lines of various lengths to a group in which all members, except one naive subject, were previously instructed to make incorrect judgments about their relative length. Under these conditions, the naive subject often went along with the group and sometimes actually seemed to misperceive their length.[21]

In another study, Mazafer Sherif presented a stationary light to groups under conditions that would create autokinetic movement—in other words, the illusion of movement. In general, subjects perceived movement more consistently under group conditions than when tested individually.[619]

Spontaneous group processes involving strong mutual suggestion are known as collective behavior, and this seems to account for a number of cases in which large groups of people came to believe in fearful and mysterious forces.

1. In the late 1930s, Orson Welles broadcast a play based on a story by H. G. Wells called *War of the Worlds.* The program was written to sound like news bulletins of an invasion of earth by extraterrestrial beings. The broadcast created in many listeners a state of panic, which seemed to be intensified by the description in the broadcast of general panic and by the mutual reinforcement of one another's fears by people who were listening together.[104]

2. In the 1950s, Seattle experienced a windshield-pitting epidemic in which pits suddenly and mysteriously seemed to appear in automobile windshields around the city. An investigation after the epidemic subsided revealed that apparently groundless initial news reports had prompted many people to examine their windshields carefully (which they had never done before). Many of these people found what were actually old pits and duly reported their "mysteriously caused" pits to the press, thereby eventually creating an epidemic of reports. Many people at the time believed, and many people undoubtedly still believe, that a mysterious force was pitting windshields in Seattle.[435]

3. ". . . in 1969 there was a run on survival kits after astrologers and soothsayers had predicted the imminent end of California in a giant earthquake, in which San Francisco, Santa Barbara, Los Angeles, and San Diego were expected to disappear into the Pacific. Preachers

led hundreds of their congregations out of the state, convinced that California was a den of iniquity about to be visited by divine retribution. A book called *The Last Days of the Late, Great State of California* became a best seller."[368]

To balance the generally negative tone conveyed by the above examples, it should be emphasized that the emotional contagion of groups also can produce heights of ecstasy. Probably you can recall attending a party, a parade, a rally, a concert, a religious ceremony, or an athletic event where good feelings elicited more good feelings until the whole crowd was singing, dancing, laughing, cheering, or crying for joy. Figure 11, for example, shows the excitement of a crowd of teen-aged girls at a rock music concert; the feelings they experience are enhanced by the display of feelings of others around them, although this is by no means the only factor involved.

It is evident that many of our strongest feelings—for example, of terror related to belief in strange forces or, on the other hand, of ecstasy—arise from group processes. Knowing this gives us the choice of being receptive to such experiences when they are enjoyable or of avoiding them when they are incapacitating.

Figure 11. Contagious emotions

How We Learn Health and Sickness

It's as if your body has always been on automatic pilot, and suddenly you find you can take over the controls.[201]

BIOFEEDBACK TRAINEE

We have discussed how suggestion effects are often magnified in groups. It should not be surprising, then, that illness, on the one hand, and cures, on the other, are often a consequence of group suggestion. For example, have you ever been with a group of people, all of whom are feeling tired or depressed, and found yourself "taking on" these symptoms? The cases that follow all illustrate this process carried to an extreme. In each of these incidents, subsequent investigation revealed that the illness probably resulted from emotional contagion; the initial sickness of a few was sufficient to produce similar sickness in others by suggestion. The reaction snow-balled, producing what appeared to be an epidemic.

1. In the 1940s, a "phantom anesthetist" struck a small town in Illinois, causing symptoms of paralysis, nausea, and vomiting in people who

HYSTERICAL ILLNESS

reported that someone attacked them, but that they could never see who it was.[342]

2. In the 1960s, 57 workers at a textile plant in the South came down with symptoms—skin eruptions, stomach pains, nausea—that they attributed to the bite of a mysterious poisonous bug.[361]

3. In the 1970s, more than 30 workers in an office at a midwestern university were struck with symptoms of dizziness, vomiting, and fainting attributed by those affected to the presence of a mysterious gas.[644]

These incidents evidently are examples of group suggestion affecting the health of a large number of individuals. To a significant extent, both sickness and health are the products of suggestion. Placebo therapy, of course, is based on this effect. A placebo is a quasimedical procedure (a sugar pill, a manipulation, etc.), the effectiveness of which is a result of suggestion. It may help to understand placebos and other suggestion effects if we diagram the placebo effect as a classical conditioning phenomenon.

Figure 12 indicates that if a patient's resistance to illness has been activated in the past by an effective procedure (for example, a medical treatment), it will also tend to be activated by stimuli that are associated with that procedure. Thus, a sugar pill, a ritual, certain phrases, almost any stimulus can come to be an effective curative agent.

Figure 12. The placebo effect

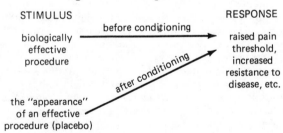

There is little question that placebos can be very effective and that a large portion of patients can gain relief from a wide variety of conditions through the use of a placebo alone.[304] The following, for example, is an:

> . . . illustrative and dramatic case of the placebo effect in a patient with malignant lymphosarcoma [cancer of the lymphatic tissue]. The

PLACEBO

patient was febrile, gasping for air, required oxygen by mask, and every other day required a thoracentesis, which produced one to two liters of milky fluid. Masses, the size of oranges, were present in the neck, axilla and groin, chest, and abdomen. The spleen and liver were greatly enlarged. The patient was . . . bedridden, and his life expectancy was thought to be a matter of days or weeks. Despite this, the patient was not without hope because he had heard of the favorable publicity with which the newspapers had reported a new anticancer drug called Krebiozen. The patient learned that the drug was to be tried at the hospital at which he was confined. His entreaties for the drug were finally granted, although with reluctance and pessimism.

The patient's response was astonishing. After one day of treatment, the tumor masses melted to half their original size. Within ten days all signs of his disease vanished. He breathed normally, and he was discharged. After two months of almost perfect health, conflicting and pessimistic reports about Krebiozen began to appear in the newspapers. The patient lost hope and relapsed to his original state. The physician, however, rekindled the patient's hope by telling him not to believe what he read, that the drug deteriorated with standing, and that a new superrefined, double-strength drug was to arrive the following day. The patient was then given water injections, and his optimistic expectations were restored. Recovery was even more dramatic than before. He became ambulatory and was discharged, and continued symptom-free for over two months. The remission continued until a few days after the press published an American Medical Association announcement that nationwide tests showed Krebiozen to be a worthless drug in the treatment of cancer. Within a few days the patient was readmitted to the hospital and succumbed in less than forty-eight hours.[613]

Closely related to the use of placebos in medical practice is the effectiveness of similar procedures in psychotherapy.[209] In the realm of folk psychotherapies, placebo therapy has a long history, including the approaches of Emile Coué ("Day by day, in every way, I am getting better and better"), Mary Baker Eddy (Christian Science), and Norman Vincent Peale ("the power of positive thinking").[444]

Thus far, we have seen how classical conditioning effects—placebos, group suggestion, and such—can cause and cure illness. However, operant conditioning is often involved as well. For example, illness can develop because people learn it is a great way to get attention and avoid responsibility. In other words, illness can be rewarding.

Operant conditioning is also often involved in cures. For example, the relief from illness that effective placebo therapy provides is a very powerful reward and would be expected to strengthen belief in the particular placebo approach utilized. An elementary diagram of operant conditioning of this nature is given in Figure 13. The diagram indicates that the individual's original response to the belief system is a low level of commitment. If this leads, however, to a cure, the individual's commitment will be greatly strengthened. That the belief system is basically a placebo is usually not understood by the believer. Thus, in part, are "true believers" created. In this way, a wide variety of divergent and even contradictory beliefs come to be effective in producing cures.[409]

Figure 13. Belief through conditioning

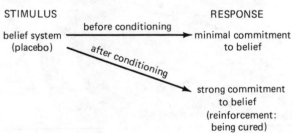

STIMULUS   RESPONSE

belief system ——————*before conditioning*——————▶ minimal commitment
(placebo)   to belief

                    after conditioning

                                                ▶ strong commitment
                                                   to belief
                                                   (reinforcement:
                                                   being cured)

Thus, a complete psychology of illness includes not only illnesses that result from psychological stress, but also "learned" illnesses. In either case, conditions such as ulcers that entail organic impairment are called psychosomatic illnesses,[387] whereas conditions such as a psychological paralysis that do not involve organic damage are known as hysterical or conversion illnesses.[4]

As discussed in the last chapter, the autonomic nervous system regulates the internal organs and basic bodily processes and is intimately involved in most illnesses and emotional states. Therefore, cures based on suggestion generally involve conditioning brain mechanisms that relate most closely to the autonomic nervous system. For example, it appears that suggestions that relieve pain may be effective because they trigger the release of natural opiatelike substances, called enkephalins and endorphins, in these brain centers.[203]

The effectiveness of classical conditioning in modifying autonomic processes has long been known.[387] It has also been recognized that yogis and fakirs train themselves to control autonomic processes,[34] but it was unclear what kind of conditioning was in-

Figure 14. Biofeedback training

volved. Now there is good evidence to indicate that operant, as well as classical, conditioning can produce curative autonomic nervous system reponses.[450] This relatively new approach to health is known as biofeedback training.

Biofeedback training is based on the principle that people can learn to control an autonomic response if they are given "feedback" concerning that response.[89] The subtle nature of most autonomic responses makes it difficult to be aware of their operation. For example, are you aware at this moment of your heart beat, blood pressure, or your general arousal level (indicated by brain rhythms)? Ordinarily, the autonomic nature of autonomic processes is adaptive, since this insures that necessary bodily processes are maintained whether or not we pay attention to them. Under conditions of chronic stress, however, their automatic nature is a liability, as the psychosomatic conditions that often result are not subject to voluntary control. In biofeedback training, a sophisticated instrument measures one of these autonomic processes and feeds back an auditory or visual signal that informs subjects of slight changes in such functions as heart rate, blood pressure, and arousal level. By attending to this feedback, most people can learn to control voluntarily, to some extent, these ordinarily involuntary processes. The chief reinforcement for learning such control is, of course, the relief that it provides from the unpleasant effects of stress. A biofeedback training session can be seen in Figure 14.

Although this book cannot offer you a biofeedback session complete with instruments, it can guide you in an experience that is similar. Before the development of biofeedback, approaches such as progressive relaxation[332] and autogenic training[413] taught patients to control certain physiological processes. Usually these were somatic processes, such as tension of the external muscles, that are part of the stress response, but that are relatively easily controlled voluntarily. Because of the interrelationships between the somatic and autonomic nervous systems, relief of stress in one system ordinarily relieves stress in the other. The following exercise will teach you to be aware of, and to reduce tension in, your somatic muscles, and it should have the effect of reducing your general level of stress.

Before beginning this exercise, be aware of what muscular tensions exist in what areas of your body at the moment. Often we

*are oblivious to these tensions up to the point where pain begins.
To begin the exercise, sit in a comfortable chair or lie on a bed in
a quiet place and relax as completely as possible. Now, by intentionally tensing and then relaxing various groups of muscles in
your body, you will learn to be aware of various degrees of
tension and will learn to relax when you feel this tension. Start
with the muscles of your face and head; tense these muscles for
several seconds, paying attention to the feelings of various degrees of tension. Then relax these muscles as completely as possible for several seconds. Pay attention to the different feeling
produced by relaxation (usually a pleasant feeling compared to
the feeling of tension). Continue the same procedure for the
following groups of muscles in turn: neck, shoulders, upper
arms, forearms, hands, back, abdomen, pelvic region, thighs,
calves, and feet. After you have completed the process for the last
group of muscles, go back over the various muscles and notice if
any are again tense. If they are, relax them. Continued practice
of relaxation will help you to be aware of muscle tension as a
sign of general stress and will help you to reduce such tension
when it occurs.*

In light of the discussion so far, you may agree that conditioning processes indeed underlie many psychic and faith healing
cures. However, you may wonder about some of the more specific
cures that are sometimes reported. Recent research indicates that
conditioning can produce almost unbelievably specific physiological effects.[43] For example, J. V. Basmajian states that ". . . normal
human beings can quickly, in a matter of fifteen or twenty minutes,
isolate only one motor unit [response neuron] from the population
of perhaps a hundred or two hundred which are within an area of
pick up of an electrode pair. They can suppress all of the units, fire
single units, manipulate those units, turn them on and off easily,
suppress the one they started with, pick up another one, train it,
suppress it. . . ."[88]

This remarkable specificity of response may help to explain
conditioning effects such as the following:

1. T. X. Barber presents a number of studies indicating that in some
   subjects, hypnosis, or sometimes mere suggestion, is sufficient to

produce or eliminate cold sores, blisters, warts, and allergic reactions.[34]

2. Oscar Ratnoff, as well as Loretta Early and Joseph Lifschutz, present a variety of case studies indicating that suggestion is a factor in many cases of stigmata (the appearance of wounds in the hands and feet of some Christian devotees, similar to the wounds of Christ on the cross).[174, 535]

3. David Lester presents evidence that, under appropriate cultural conditions, the suggestion of certain fatal illnesses can in fact produce these illnesses and subsequent death in suggestible individuals.[395]

At this point, returning to the example with which we introduced the first chapter, we can better understand why Colin Turnbull fell ill after being hexed. We have seen that the suggestion of illness constitutes a conditioned stimulus that can produce physical illness. In a similar fashion, the suggestion that Turnbull would get well, implicit in his counterhex, probably helped bring about his cure. Likewise, we should expect that suggestions implicit in psychic and occult healing procedures might be very effective in producing cures.

To conclude this section, we return to a point mentioned earlier, namely that, through conditioning, almost any stimulus can come to elicit positive, curative responses. Symbols well illustrate this process since symbols are initially somewhat arbitrary stimuli, which, through conditioning, come to evoke strong responses. The Christian cross is a good example, since the cross was originally an instrument of torture and execution and undoubtedly evoked feelings of fear and horror just as gas chambers and electric chairs do today. However, the symbol of the cross became conditioned to new associations, such as Christ's love, and today the cross is displayed on altars, steeples, and necklaces, and brings comfort to many Christians. The magnitude of this transformation can be felt if you think of your reaction to the idea of a miniature gas chamber or electric chair on a mantel piece or altar. Also, thanks to conditioning, drinking Christ's blood and eating his flesh—symbolically in communion—are comforting rituals instead of the repugnant acts they would be in another context.

A related effect of conditioning is the development of masochistic responses, in which stimuli initially perceived as painful and noxious come to evoke ecstatic and even therapeutic responses.

That conditioning can produce this effect is shown by studies in which animals have been conditioned to seek out stimuli that are initially strongly avoided.[90] This is accomplished by presenting low levels of the noxious stimulus with higher levels of pleasurable stimulation or by rewarding animals when they choose noxious stimulation.

Strange as masochism as a route to transcendental experience may seem, most of us have been conditioned in similar, if less profound, ways. For example, we sometimes prefer medicine to have a horrible taste because we have been conditioned to think that it is then more effective. Or some of us "acquire a taste" for initially disliked substances such as coffee and alcohol because their pleasant effects—the "pick-up" of coffee, the "relaxation" of alcohol—are stronger effects than their originally unpleasant taste. The fact that most of us are "masochists" to some extent may help us understand the cases that follow, both of which involve Christian devotees.

M. Vianney was the curé of Ars, France. ". . . he imposed it on himself that he should never smell a flower, never drink when parched with thirst, never drive away a fly, never show disgust before a repugnant object, never complain of anything that had to do with his personal comfort. . . [Vianney stated,] 'There is in mortification a balm and a savor without which one cannot live when once one has made their acquaintance.' "[336]

Marguerite Marie was the founder of the Sacred Heart Order. "Her love of pain and suffering was insatiable. . . . She said she could cheerfully live till the day of judgment, provided she might always have matter for suffering for God; but that to live a single day without suffering would be intolerable. She said again that she was devoured with two unassuageable fevers, one for the holy communion, the other for suffering, humiliation, and annihilation. 'Nothing but pain,' she continually said in her letters, 'makes my life supportable.' "[336]

We are not talking here about the effects on consciousness of dishabituation, fatigue, exertion, etc., which we discussed in the last chapter and which can account for the reward-value of some degree of pain and deprivation. The levels of feeling in the examples above go far beyond such effects and probably depend on reinforcements such as 1. feeling that guilt is reduced through suffering, 2. pride in forbearance, and 3. implicit or explicit rewards from others in the form of attention of various kinds.

So we see that our state of health, as well as our attitude toward our bodily aches and pains is, to a large extent, a product of learning. The lesson for us is that in various ways we can educate ourselves to achieve an optimal level of health and well-being.

Behaving Without Awareness

It is our less conscious thoughts and our less conscious actions which mainly mould our lives.[42]

SAMUEL BUTLER

The section on hypnosis contained an exercise in which a suggestion can elicit arm movement that occurs without conscious volition. This was called ideomotor response and is related to another class of conditioned behaviors known as automatisms. Whereas ideomotor responses are the result of thoughts that di-

AUTOMATISM

rectly correspond to the actions performed, automatisms are self-sustaining, often complex behaviors that are guided by subconscious associations. Automatisms are thus even more likely than ideomotor responses to be seen as mysterious. Generally, automatisms result when a behavior is so highly conditioned that we no longer need to give conscious attention to it. Also, automatisms can occur when strong suggestions or needs, often unrecognized consciously, dictate our actions. We all have many automatisms. For example, most of us have driven a car somewhere, carrying on a conversation the whole time, and found, when we arrived at our destination, that we could not recall the process of driving there. And many of us doodle while talking on the phone, unaware both of doodling and of the content of the doodles.

Automatisms can be very useful. For example, as in the case of knitting while talking, they allow us to perform habitual behaviors while we devote our conscious awareness to more urgent concerns. This state of consciousness, in which a behavior is performed without conscious awareness, is called dissociation. In highly developed automatisms, as in the case of a nightclub pianist who improvises "automatically," the dissociated behavior is so intricate, and even creative, that it almost seems as if some separate personality makes the fingers move while the pianist carries on a completely unrelated conversation. And, in fact, the more unusual automatisms, such as are involved in water witching, automatic writing, working Ouija boards, and speaking in tongues, are often interpreted as due to the paranormal influence of some external agency or personality.

In the last chapter, we discussed the case of Ilga K., the girl with hyperesthesia who heard subvocalizations and thereby seemed to read minds. Subvocalization has been studied as an automatism for many years[331, 433] and probably accounts for many experiences that have been erroneously interpreted as evidence for telepathy.[539]

> *To experience subvocalization, count from one to ten in your mind. Notice the activation of your vocal chords as you think each number. Now mentally count again and try to keep your vocal chords absolutely still. Difficult, isn't it? As with many other automatisms, most people are unaware of subvocalizing,*

just as people who hear subvocalizations often do so subliminally.

A fascinating example of automatism concerns, of all things, a horse named Clever Hans, which, when he became famous in the early 1900s, seemed to have remarkable intellectual as well as telepathic abilities. The description of Clever Hans that follows is by Oskar Pfungst, the psychologist who published a definitive study of the horse. As you read about Clever Hans, see if you can determine how he accomplished his feats.

> The reader may accompany us to an exhibit which was given daily. . . . The visitor might walk about freely and if he wished, might closely approach the horse and its master. . . . To his left the stately animal, a Russian trotting horse, stood like a docile pupil. . . . He would answer correctly, nearly all of the questions which were put to him in German. If he understood a question, he immediately indicated this by a nod of his head; if he failed to grasp its import, he communicated the fact by a shake of the head. . . . Even though Hans did not appear as willing and reliable in the case of strangers as in the case of his own master, this might easily be explained by the lack of authoritativeness on their part and of affection on the part of Hans. . . .
>
> Our intelligent horse was unable to speak, to be sure. His chief mode of expression was tapping his right forefoot. A good deal was also expressed by means of movements of the head. Thus "yes" was expressed by a nod, "no" by a deliberate movement from side to side; and "upward," "upper," "downward," "right," "left," were indicated by turning the head in these directions. . . . Taking into account his limited means of expression, his master had translated a large number of concepts into numbers; e.g., the letters of the alphabet, the tones of the scale, and the names of the playing cards were indicated by taps. In the case of playing cards one tap meant "ace," two taps "king," three "queen," etc.
>
> Let us turn now to some of his specific accomplishments. He had, apparently, completely mastered the cardinal numbers from 1 to 100 and the ordinals to 10, at least. Upon request he would count objects of all sorts, the persons present, even to distinctions of sex. Then hats, umbrellas, and eyeglasses. . . .
>
> But Hans could not only count, he could also solve problems in arithmetic. . . . The following problems are illustrations of the kind he solved. "How much is $2/5$ plus $1/2$?" Answer: $9/10$ (in the case of all fractions Hans would first tap the numerator, then the denominator;

in this case, therefore, first 9, then 10). . . . "What are the factors of 28?" Thereupon Hans tapped consecutively 2, 4, 7, 14, 28. . . .

Hans, furthermore, was able to read the German readily, whether written or printed. . . . If a series of placards with written words were placed before the horse, he could step up and point with his nose to any of the words required of him. He could even spell some of the words. . . . He could also answer such inquiries as this: "If the eighth day of a month comes on Tuesday, what is the date for the following Friday?" He could tell the time to the minute by a watch. . . .[509]

If you are still baffled at this point, you are not alone. Committees of scientists who observed Hans were likewise mystified. The fact that the horse's trainer need not be present was particularly puzzling, since this eliminated the obvious possibility of subtle but specific cues intentionally given by the trainer. Oskar Pfungst persisted in his observations of the horse and noticed, first of all, that if the questioner did not know the answer, Clever Hans could not correctly answer the question. This seemed to eliminate the possibility that the horse possessed humanlike intelligence and indicated that Hans was picking up some kind of communication from his questioners. Then Pfungst discovered that Clever Hans could not correctly answer a question when he was prevented from seeing his questioner. This seemed to eliminate telepathy as an explanation, but left open the question of what kind of visual cue was conveyed by the questioner. As one committee that studied Clever Hans stated, "In spite of the most attentive observation, nothing in the way of movements or other forms of expression which might have served as a sign, could be discovered."[509]

At this point, Pfungst persisted where others had given up and, through detailed measurements, determined that most questioners did indeed cue Hans with small involuntary movements similar to those that professsional mind readers train themselves to observe. For example, if the problem required Clever Hans to tap his hoof: "As soon as the experimenter had given a problem to the horse, he, involuntarily, bent his head and trunk slightly forward and the horse would then put the right foot forward and begin to tap, without, however, returning it each time to its original position. As soon as the desired number of taps was given, the questioner would make a slight upward jerk of the head. Thereupon the horse would immediately swing his foot in a wide circle, bringing it back to its original position."[509] For other tasks, Hans learned to respond to cues of other kinds. These cues were so subtle and involuntary that ". . . even after he had learned the cueing system very well Pfungst still cued Hans unintentionally, though he was consciously trying to suppress sending the crucial visual message."[509]

The subtle and involuntary nature of the cues probably explains why Clever Hans' trainer, Von Osten, was ignorant of the basis of his horse's success. Von Osten's training method was to reward the horse for correct responses in the belief that he was educating the horse much as any teacher would educate a student; he was unaware of the cues he was furnishing that allowed Clever Hans to perform his remarkable feats. Clever Hans can be seen in Figure 15, together with his trainer, Von Osten, and some of the materials used to test his mental powers.

Both before[509] and after[120] Clever Hans, there have been other animals that have accomplished similar feats, but none has been studied with a thoroughness to match Oskar Pfungst's study of Clever Hans.

Figure 15. A "mind reading" horse

What can we conclude from our discussion of the role of subtle and subconscious auditory cues (as in the case of Ilga K.) and visual cues (as in the case of Clever Hans) in communication? An obvious conclusion is that our sensitivity to other people and to our environment can indeed transcend our normal levels of functioning and our usual conceptions of ourselves. Another conclusion is that, since communication can occur outside of the conscious awareness of all concerned, we should not be surprised that the communication in such cases is often interpreted as paranormal in nature.

In fields of creative endeavor, automatisms have proved very useful. Just as creative imagery illumines the mind's eye, so can automatism inspire the artist's hand. The surrealist school, for example, includes artists who draw, as well as authors who write, "automatically" as a means of expressing subconscious awareness. As Herschel Chipp states: ". . . when all controls by the conscious mind were released, the marvelous and boundless world of images of the subconscious could flow to the surface. The writer had only by various means to shock himself free from the controls and then automatically to record whatever thoughts and images presented themselves. The same method for the painter produced 'automatic drawings.' Surrealism as a movement thus was . . . 'pure psychic automatisms.'"[116]

A noted example of surrealist art employing automatism can be seen in Figure 16.

At this point, you may wish to attempt automatic drawing or writing. The following method for automatic writing is suggested by D. H. Rawcliffe and seems to produce good results with sufficient practice.

> *"Most beginners who wish to develop the art of [automatic writing] simply hold a pencil in one hand over a sheet of paper and purposely allow the attention to wander or else engage in conversation. The expectation of producing [automatic writing] has the effect of mild auto-suggestion, and after a considerable time the pencil will begin to make variegated movements beginning with upward strokes, zigzag lines, or even just a simple line. The next step is the formation of single letters; and then a series of letters, at first devoid of coherence. After further practice these will combine into words and sentences."*[539]

Figure 16. *Automatic drawing,* by André Masson

A similar method, with the suggestion of drawing instead of writing, will serve to produce automatic drawing. If you are successful in either endeavor, you may wish to see what insights into your unconscious you can gain from the result. Automatic writing, in particular, has proved useful in psychotherapy in uncovering unconscious feelings.[465]

Although most of us do not write or draw automatically, many of us have had the experience of playing a sport, performing music, or dancing "automatically," with little conscious direction, and doing much better than when we are in our ordinary state of "self-consciousness." For example, when I play my best tennis, my body movements seem to "flow" without requiring forethought or intellectual analysis. Conscious attention seems to be useful for acquiring skills, but it can interfere with the smooth flow of actions already well established. These experiences of superlative performance understandably are often accompanied by tremendous feelings of exhilaration.

Multiple Personality

The human mind is capable of hiding many things from itself.[736]

RICHARD O'CONNOR

In this last section, we discussed automatisms, in which an individual speaks, writes, or performs other complex behaviors that are not under conscious control. Imagine these behaviors carried to an extreme so that, for all intents and purposes, another personality seems to be in control for extended periods. Psychologists call this condition multiple personality, in which a single individual exhibits, at different times, two or more separate and distinct personalities. Although we have already discussed the classical conditioning basis of many automatisms, such extremes as multiple personality require some additional explanatory concepts.

Multiple personality seems to be the result of severe trauma, usually in childhood, which serves to "punish," and thus repress, the expression of a multitude of needs and personality traits. Thus operant conditioning, in which behavior changes according to rewards and punishments, also helps account for multiple personality. These repressed personalities typically emerge when the needs that they express become extremely strong or when environmental conditions are no longer as repressive. As with automatisms, these ordinarily unexpressed parts of the self can be highly creative in ways that are foreign to the dominant personality; however, the trauma of multiple personality usually overshadows these potential benefits.

It may help make multiple personality more understandable if you can recall an instance in your own experience when you felt "not yourself" and were unable, perhaps, to remember afterward what you had done or said. Perhaps you have walked or talked in your sleep and acted in what appeared to be a coherent manner, but without conscious awareness. Perhaps as a child you created an imaginary playmate to keep you company. Or perhaps you find that you are a radically different "person" at different times in different settings. Multiple personality, then, is a condition different in degree, but not in kind, from experiences that are characteristic of many of us.

The brief descriptions that follow are of three cases of multiple personality. They illustrate many of the fascinating features of this unusual condition.

Morton Prince describes the case of Christine Beauchamp, who exhibited four distinct personalities.[522] One personality was submissive, sickly, and religious; another was assertive, lively, intolerant of religion, and delighted in playing tricks on the first personality. This "devil-angel" split is common in multiple personality cases and probably derives from being severely punished, during childhood, for "devilish behavior." These two personalities communicated by leaving notes where the other personality would find them. In therapy, a third personality emerged who knew of the first two, although they knew nothing of her. All three personalities now vied with one another, each considering itself the rightful owner of the woman's body. Through psychotherapy, Prince was able to integrate the first two personalties into a well-balanced fourth personality, although the third personality objected strenuously, feeling she was being squeezed out of existence.

Corbett Thigpen and Hervey Cleckley describe the case of Chris Sizemore, better known as Eve of "the three faces of Eve."[678] In this case also, two personalities reflected the "devil-angel" split. The "devil-personality," called Eve Black, had the advantage in that she knew of Eve White's existence and used this knowledge for her own ends, while the "angelic" Eve White suffered, in bewilderment, the hangovers and other repercussions of Eve Black's behavior. Unfortunately, other personalities also appeared and, at last report, Chris was still struggling to achieve an integrated personality.[625]

Flora Schrieber describes the case of Sybil, who, before her therapy ended successfully, revealed sixteen different personalities.[600] Sybil suffered greatly as a child at the hands of a sadistic, psychotic mother. Only some of her personalities knew one another, and some of these cooperated with each other. Some of her personalities revealed artistic and other talents unique to those personalities. When her therapist attempted to achieve a synthesis, several of Sybil's personalities objected violently. Eventually these parts of herself were persuaded to give up their independent existence so that a stable, single personality could emerge.

Not surprisingly, the experience of multiple personality, which involves such radical changes of personality, is sometimes interpreted as a sign of being possessed by an external spirit or agency. In a later chapter, we will discuss experiences interpreted as instances of possession, which bear many similarities to cases of multiple personality.

Before leaving this subject, we should discuss one of the mechanisms involved that is of particular interest. This is the phenomenon of cryptomnesia, which refers to the recollection of experiences that are not usually accessible during ordinary waking consciousness.[225, 349] Cryptomnesia seems to be facilitated when the individual is in the same state of consciousness as when the memory was acquired.[208] Thus, in cases of multiple personality, each personality will tend to acquire its own set of memories. In a similar manner, our dreams, the recollection of which is potentially very important for understanding ourselves, are easier to recall when we are in a dreamlike state. I occasionally have been able to recall several dreams from the past that are similar to another dream from which I am just waking. By allowing imagery associations to form during this hypnopompic period, I have remembered a large number of dreams that I had never recalled while in an ordinary waking state of consciousness.

Obviously, cryptomnesia can be very mysterious when it is not recognized as such. For example, mediums who go into trance and recite a large body of information, which, upon emerging from trance, they do not recognize, are likely to be mystified by their experience. Not understanding the psychological processes involved, they may postulate explanations such as having contact with a "spirit personality" or having memories from a prior life.

The World As Our Reflection

Everything unknown and empty is filled with psychological projection; it is as if the [perceiver's] own psychic background were mirrored in the darkness. What he sees in matter or thinks he can see, is chiefly the data of his own unconscious which he is projecting into it.[347]   CARL JUNG

Projection can be defined as the ascription of one's own characteristics to someone or something else. The projection of negative characteristics is a commonly recognized form of projection. For example, paranoids assume people have turned against them either because they think themselves unworthy or because they themselves are basically hostile. Projection of positive characteristics, however, is of particular interest to transcendental psychology, since there is a strong tendency to disown and project many of the transcendental capacities we have been discussing. That is, it is easier for many people to think that a healer, a spirit, the stars, or some mysterious energy has power over them than to recognize that they themselves possess such powers.

A good example from literature of the projection of positive characteristics is the story of the scarecrow, the woodman, and the lion in *The Wizard of Oz*.[46] You will remember that the capacities that each felt he lacked were the very ones that each already possessed: the scarecrow wanted brains, but could always figure the best way to get out of a fix; the woodman wanted a heart, but was always rusting his armor with his tears; and the lion, who greatly desired courage, could always be counted on to stand up to dangers that threatened his friends. Instead of recognizing these capacities within themselves, all three were convinced that only the Wizard's magic could cure them of their deficiencies.

We do not know definitely why some people need to disown and project their own positive, even transcendental capacities, but there are a number of possibilities. For one thing, most of the transcendental experiences we have discussed are subconscious and thus seem to have an independent existence—a vision that one sees seems to originate outside oneself; the pencil that one holds while doing automatic writing seems to be moved by an external force; the communications that one receives subliminally seem to be conveyed in a mysterious way. As Marghanita Laski says: "It is

PROJECTION

characteristic of inspirations . . . that the new idea or purpose feels as if it had arrived independently of the creator's volition and often as if it were communicated by someone or something else."[389]

However, many people have transcendental experiences of this nature and yet only some interpret such experiences as originating outside of themselves. It may help us to understand projection if we see it as a conditioning phenomenon. Thus, people who project their transcendental experiences may have been conditioned: (1) to feel that external events control their lives, rather than vice versa, (2) to distrust their own psychological functioning, or (3) to feel that they are not "good enough" to possess transcendental capacities. For whatever reason, individuals who ascribe their inner experiences to external sources seem to be saying, in essence: "I do not have the capacity to be that sensitive, to know so much, to heal myself, or to produce such ecstasy. Therefore, since I could not have created my experience, it must have arisen from an external source."[574, 594]

Although it is possible to study projection in the laboratory,[604] the richest examples lie in case studies. For example, Carl Jung's autobiography provides a number of cogent examples of the operation of projection. In the early part of his life, Jung experienced several dreams and visions, the origin of which he did not understand and which he therefore ascribed to external sources. For example, here is Jung's description of one image that bothered him considerably: "I saw before me the cathedral, the blue sky. God sits on His golden throne, high above the world—and from under the throne an enormous turd falls upon the sparkling new roof, shatters it, and breaks the walls of the cathedral asunder."[352] Here is Jung's comment regarding this experience. "Who wants to force me to think something I don't know and don't want to know? Where does this terrible will come from? And why should I be the one to be subjected to it? . . . This has happened to me without my doing. Why? . . . At last I asked myself whether it was not the devil's doing. For that it must have been God or the devil who spoke and acted in this way was something I never doubted. I felt absolutely sure that it was not myself who had invented these thoughts and images."[352]

Evidently Jung never did recognize the probable origin of such experiences in his own upbringing as the son of a strict clergyman. Instead, he continued to maintain that images such as these—which he also noted in his patients and in various myths—arose from sources outside of personal experience. Such reasoning eventually formed the basis of Jung's theories of "archetypes," the "collective unconscious," and "synchronicity."[348, 350]

The major problem with projection lies in the disowning of the psychological basis of the projection, not in the projection itself. Psychotics, of course, provide an extreme example of such denial; they assume that their hallucinations and delusions have a "real" existence outside of themselves. This is not to deny that we are products of our environment and that our experience is therefore "caused," in part, by external influences. The problem of projection and denial arises when an immediate experience—for example, an hallucination or automatism—is interpreted as proof of an immediate external stimulus—for example, a ghost or spirit.

On the other hand, projections that are "owned" can be very useful. The artist who can "see" an image on a canvas as if it were really there, the musician who can "hear" a composition as if it were being performed, the writer who can write as if another personality were guiding the pen; all of these are useful projections. It is useful to be able to project meaning into scientific observations to see if a theory "fits," into abstract works of art, and into works of poetry and fiction. In these ways, we also increase our enjoyment of the world and become better acquainted with our own unconscious as it unfolds in our projections. This, of course, is the basis of the Rorschach and other projective tests in psychology.

> *To conclude this chapter, let's try some projection exercises. A good place to begin is with an ill-defined stimulus, such as a cloud formation, textured wall, or abstract painting or sculpture for a visual stimulus, or the sound of machinery, river, or water-fall, or a large conch shell held up to your ear for an auditory stimulus. Take time to let your unconscious impressions emerge. What do you see or hear—figures, voices? See what you can learn from your projections about your unconscious state of mind and trains of associations.*

> *A somewhat different projection exercise starts with a self-generated stimulus. For this exercise, find a quiet place. Then read the paragraph below one sentence at a time, following what it says before going on to the next sentence. Most of you will find it helpful to close your eyes for each segment of the exercise; take plenty of time to get into your feelings at each point.*

> *Imagine that you are a plant, any kind of plant. . . . Now im-merse yourself in the sensations and feelings that arise as you imagine what it is like to be that plant. . . . Become aware of your external appearance—your size and shape, your texture, your color, your odor. . . . Now journey to the inside of your body and become aware of its structure and interconnections; go out to your furthest extremities as well as into your "center". . . . Now become aware of your environment—its sights, sounds, odors; what is going on around you? . . . Now imagine how you came to be where you are. . . . Finally, take some time to imagine how your future will unfold. . . .*

> *By projecting your feelings into a plant, you have perhaps not only enjoyed an out-of-the-ordinary experience, but you also may have become conscious of some feelings about yourself. That is, the kind of plant you choose to be, your feelings about being that plant, and the history and future you project into the plant are likely to indicate feelings you have about yourself. In the flights of imagination during projection, such feelings often emerge*

relatively easily and freely. By becoming aware of our projections as we experience them daily, we can keep in touch with our deepest feelings.

Summary

*What we need is not the will to believe,
but the wish to find out.*[578]
BERTRAND RUSSELL

In this chapter we have discussed the role of conditioning in transcendental experience. We have seen that both classical and operant conditioning are involved in many varieties of transcendental experience. For example, both forms of conditioning probably play a role in the development, at an early age, of the capacity to experience ecstatic feelings, and both forms seem to be involved in the process by which meditators learn to achieve altered mental and body states.

We have seen that hypnosis is, to a large extent, a conditioning process, and that hypnosis, or sometimes merely a placebo or suggestion, can produce remarkable effects, including the creation of visions and the relief of pain.

We have seen how the effects of suggestion can be magnified by group processes and can produce illnesses, on the one hand, or the facilitation of cures in psychic or faith healing ceremonies, on the other.

We have discussed biofeedback, an operant conditioning technique by which people can learn to alleviate anxiety and, consequently, various psychosomatic illnesses. We have noted that yogis and fakirs probably employ conditioning techniques to achieve remarkable control over their bodily processes.

We have seen that the seemingly dissimilar phenomena of symbolism and masochism, both of which are sometimes involved in transcendental experiences, probably are products of conditioning.

We have seen that conditioning also can result in automatic behaviors that are performed without conscious awareness. Although automatisms are characteristic of all of us, forms such as automatic writing or water witching are less common. At the extreme, we have seen that multiple personality and possession behavior are also related to automatisms, although these forms are quite rare.

We have seen that many people project and disown their transcendental experience; that is, they view such experience as arising from outside themselves. Probably this tendency to deny one's own role in transcendental experience is, to a large extent, learned and may relate to a general feeling of inadequacy and insufficiency that many people acquire.

Finally, we have seen that a knowledge of the conditioning processes involved in transcendental experiences enables us to make use of such processes to develop our own capacity for these experiences.

4

The Cultural Context of Transcendental Experience

[Technology] has taught us how to become gods before we have learned to be men.[468]

HERBERT MULLER

In preceding chapters, we discussed a wide variety of transcendental experiences and examined the psychological processes that appear to underlie them. Now we are ready to take up two questions that require a somewhat broader perspective.

What are the appeals of transcendental experience in our particular society?

Why, in today's society, do so many people assume that transcendental experiences are paranormal when, as we have seen, so many of them can be understood in terms of known psychological mechanisms?

Keep in mind that there is probably a reciprocal relationship between transcendental experience and paranormal interpretations. On the one hand, to people who are not in touch with their own psychological processes, transcendental experience is often so mysterious that the only possible explanation seems to be a paranormal one. On the other hand, the idea of a paranormal or supernatural force can contribute to transcendental feelings insofar as it satisfies a longing for a superhuman agency that we can count on for miraculous intervention. However, as previously emphasized, there is no intrinsic relationship between transcendental experience and belief in mysterious paranormal forces. We can enjoy and develop our capacity for transcendental experience and, at the same time, recognize that these experiences are, to a large extent, psychological in nature. The faith that might be directed at an external agent can become faith in ourselves.

Alienation and Identity in Contemporary Society

All the lonely people;
where do they all come from?
All the lonely people;
where do they all belong?[183]
JOHN LENNON AND PAUL McCARTNEY

In our society at present, there seems to be a strong interest in psychic, occult, and mystical experience.[192, 692] However, it is important to recognize that various forms of transcendental experience are almost universally found in cultures around the world. For example, with regard to altered states of consciousness, Erika Bourguignon states:

> . . . of a sample of 488 societies, in all parts of the world, for which we have analyzed the relevant ethnographic literature, 437, or 90%, are reported to have one or more institutionalized, culturally patterned forms of altered states of consciousness. This . . . suggests that we are, indeed, dealing with a matter of major importance, not merely a bit of anthropological esoterica. It is clear that we are dealing with a psychological capacity available to all societies, and that, indeed, the vast majority of societies have used it in their own particular ways. . . .[75]

As is true in most other cultures, Westerners have long been fascinated by transcendental experience and a wide variety of occult beliefs. Why is it that Western civilization, which has almost made a religion of science and rationality, fosters at the same time such an interest in the nonscientific and the nonrational? Perhaps we can gain some insight into this issue from occultists themselves.[494]

A popular writer on occultism, Colin Wilson, describes the roots of his own involvement with the occult as follows:

> I was twenty years old, and I had been married for a year. My wife and our son were living in Earls Court, London, our fourth home in a year, and our half-insane landlady was the fourth—and worst—of a series. I was on the dole, and I found this almost as nervously wearing as the various factory jobs I had worked at since I was married. London seemed not merely alien, but somehow unreal. So I understood . . . that craving for *another world* of deeper meaning, represented by books on the occult. . . . I had only to look at the advertisements in the London tube, or the headlines of the daily paper, to see. . . . Lies, stupidity, weakness, and mediocrity—a civilization without ideals.

> That was why I read . . . books on magic and mysticism that I could find in the local libraries: not only because they were an escape from the world of factories and neurotic landladies, but because they confirmed my intuition of another order of reality. . . .[743]

Wilson's motivations seem oriented around his dissatisfaction with his own life, which he sees as futile, and his disillusionment with the society around him, which he perceives as aimless and meaningless. Evidently, Wilson sees occultism and mysticism as an escape from, and perhaps an answer to, these problems. Such problems are not unique to Colin Wilson; many social scientists feel that they are common in contemporary society.[360, 729] Briefly stated, these problems have to do with the failure to develop a satisfactory identity—which involves feelings that one's life is worthless and meaningless, and with the sense of being alienated from one's fellows—which involves the conviction that one's society is uncaring and unjust. Of course, given the strong social needs of humans, identity and alienation issues are very closely related; a healthy identity grows only in the soil of warm and supportive social relationships.

Not only social scientists, but social observers in many fields—politicians, existential philosophers, novelists, artists—are sensitive to these problems of modern life. The artist George Tooker, for example, has captured some of the essence of self and social estrangement in several of his paintings, one of which—*The Waiting Room*—is shown in Figure 17.

Later, we will discuss how transcendental experience and occultism might ease alienation and identity problems and thus appeal to a great many people. First, however, let us try to understand these problems in greater depth. We will draw on a variety of studies, including historical census data and cross-cultural comparisons.[423, 457, 676] Although there are always competing counterculture influences and short-term fluctuations, most of the social trends discussed below seem relatively well established and, in fact, have reached an extreme in Western cultures never before realized in the history of humankind.

We are a highly mobile people.[451, 496, 700] We wander from place to place and from group to group, seldom finding the "roots" so many of us seem to need.[408, 643] Our culture adds to this instability as it almost overnight changes the face of our countryside as well as the complexion of our social institutions.[302, 685] These forces reach their peak in urban areas where we tend to concentrate our-

Figure 17.   George Tooker, *The Waiting Room*

selves.[699] Here, most people are strangers to us;[446] Here a noisy din,[246] pollution,[83] and crime[110, 702] are ever-present problems, which seem beyond our understanding or capacity to solve.[206, 399]

We grow up in small, socially isolated families in which disruption, from divorce or from geographical separation, is an ever-present threat.[698, 701] As infants, most of us are bottle—not breast—fed, weaned early, and, in general, seldom receive the amount of physical cuddling, rocking, and body contact that is commonplace in so many other societies.[448, 650, 733, 734]

As we gain awareness and attempt to understand the world around us, we may be told that it is "God's handiwork," but, as we grow older, this explanation seems increasingly simplistic. More likely we are told that science has explained the wonders of nature; yet such explanations are not easy to understand, and nature remains largely incomprehensible and a mystery to many of us.

As we grow older, we are bewildered by a wide variety of rival belief systems,[265] each claiming to be superior to all the others. A common religious belief, which serves as a bond between people in most folk societies, has long since been eroded by competing beliefs and scientific advances.

As we grow up, we develop relationships outside our immediate family.[216] However, we soon learn that such relationships often lead to hurt and not fulfillment. When we find compatible friends, which is difficult because of our widely differing backgrounds, they often move away or change life-styles in ways we cannot relate to. If we fall in love, we often find that our love crumbles under the weight of our differing backgrounds and expectations. Eventually, many people insulate themselves from further hurt by withdrawing from potentially deep relationships with their fellow human beings.[665] Thus estranged from one another, we seldom come together for social celebrations and rituals, which in times past have provided a much-needed opportunity for catharsis of feelings, reaffirmation of meaning, and social cohesion.[401]

We are told that what we make of our lives is our choice and our responsibility.[428] This means that if we do not live up to expectations—our own or those of others—we have only ourselves to blame.[575, 576] If we end up in a monotonous job in a large bureaucratic organization,[326] that, after all, is no one's fault but our own. On the other hand, if we are clever enough to find a life's work that meets both our own needs and society's priorities, we can never be sure that we will not soon be replaced by a machine or a computer or that our skills will even be considered relevant at some future date.[617]

In the last years of our lives, we find that, instead of being valued because of our lifetime of experience, we have been outmoded by a rapidly changing culture.[125, 499] Rejected by family and society alike, many of us will spend our last days, not in the warmth and comfort of home, but in an institution.[473] Confronting death, few of us still have our childhood faith in a better life that awaits us in heaven. Rather, we are often terrified of death and seek any palliative to alleviate our fear.

In summary, we can conclude that many of us grow up feeling, to some degree, unloved, isolated, and out-of-step with those around us. In other words, many of us feel alienated from our own society and our fellow human beings. Also, many of us grow up confused and unsure of ourselves, not knowing what to believe or how to cope with our lives or our environment. That is, many of us lack an adequate sense of identity that could provide an inner source of strength.

That these features of contemporary society are, in many ways, psychologically stressful is indicated by studies that compare Western societies to less technologically developed societies on various indices of social and psychological disturbance.[503] Although such studies are difficult to conduct, and many researchers have disputed particular findings, the trend seems to be in the direction of higher rates of mental illness,[57, 514] suicide[386, 649] and crime[26] in the more technologically developed countries such as our own. It is not surprising that so many people seek some way to rise above the cares and worries of their everyday lives.

The Search for Transcendence

A host of . . . cults strive to fill the gap left by the decline of established religion and to reassert the primacy of mystical experience in the face of the dreary progress of secularism.[401]
IOAN LEWIS

The question we now need to consider is, can transcendental

experience, and the occult beliefs that so often accompany such experience, ease the problems of alienation and identity that are so common in our society? If they can, we may be able to understand the appeal of such experience and beliefs.

We have seen that, in a complex and ever-changing society such as ours, many people feel inadequate to understand or to cope with the world around them. Growing up in a science-oriented society, but often lacking in scientific sophistication, these people can be attracted to occult theories, which claim to explain the workings of the world, but which do not require the discipline of true scientific understanding. And if the occult theory postulates a paranormal or superhuman source of power or wisdom, that can be an additional attraction to people who feel lacking in competence and control.[593]

Social complexity and change also can lead to loneliness, as our differences in background make it difficult to find a common ground for relating. Sharing a belief system is one way to overcome these differences. And belief systems that claim to provide access to a superhuman source of knowledge and power are likely to be particularly effective in overcoming differences among adherents as they yield to the higher authority. In addition to the belief itself, a new jargon helps to establish common modes of thought and provide a sense of exclusiveness. And, if the belief and the jargon are occult enough to be offensive to other segments of society, this may be a benefit, since persecution from outside of a group usually strengthens social bonds within the group.

Thus, a belief system and group of believers can constitute a miniature social system within which adherents gain a sense of competence, coherence, and belonging they previously lacked.

Feelings of competence and control are also enhanced in most occult systems by direct participation. In place of reliance on specialists—bureaucrats, scientists, physicians—who are seen as impersonal or inaccessible, occultists feel they are directly affecting the course of events as they themselves conduct the magic ritual or the healing ceremony. Especially when the need is strong—for example, as in the case of a terminal illness—occult practices are an attractive alternative to traditional approaches.[36, 506] As Hans Toch has said: "Miracles provide prospects of change in situations that are objectively hopeless."[684]

To gain access to the paranormal reality they envision, believers sometimes indulge in consciousness-altering activities, which help them feel that they are directly experiencing this "other reality." Some may see visions, while others may feel themselves "possessed" by the higher power. Either experience is commonly seen as a validation of the belief, and "revelations" thus obtained are usually welcomed as a source of guidance.

Experiencing what seems to be another reality can constitute a welcome escape from the tribulations and frustrations of everyday life. In this "other world," needs—for example, for love, for control, for purpose, for excitement—can often be fulfilled, at least in fantasy. In particular, after "seeing a world beyond," some may find that they are no longer burdened by the fear of death. Obviously, the feeling that one's needs have finally been met can be a truly ecstatic experience and can greatly reinforce one's commitment to an occult belief.

Thus, it seems that transcendental experience and occult beliefs can, in fact, meet many needs that are often unmet in contemporary society. Such experience and beliefs can bring people together through mutual sharing of significant experiences and can serve as a much-needed means of affirming meaning, providing a sense of control, and alleviating frustrations. It is no wonder that transcendence and occultism are so appealing to so many in our society.

Of course, the social-psychological conditions we have discussed impinge on each of us in different ways and in different degrees. Therefore, we should expect that particular belief systems and experiences will appeal to different kinds of people and that people will differ greatly in their needs for such belief systems and experience. And, in varying degrees, these needs can be met in other ways. For example, either traditional religious belief[248, 752] or scientific endeavor, opposed as these are in many ways, satisfy many of these same needs. Also there is little doubt that the burgeoning interest in encounter groups and in a wide variety of new psychotherapies constitute efforts to meet needs for social involvement and a sense of identity.[24]

In the light of these considerations, it is not difficult to see why occult beliefs are so resistant to erosion by contrary evidence. Despite claims of scientific validity, occult beliefs gain their life force, not from scientific evidence, but from extremely strong psychological needs. This lack of insight of occultists into the roots of their belief can constitute a problem for them since occult beliefs have been known to retreat in the face of overwhelming proof to the contrary. This is hard on believers as they watch the foundation of their belief crumble around them. During the nineteenth century, for example, phrenology won a large number of converts who believed that the bumps of your skull reveal psychological capacities represented by the parts of your brain underneath the skull.[152] As knowledge accumulated concerning the actual location of psychological capacities in the brain, it became obvious that these bore no relationship to phrenology, which consequently diminished so greatly in popularity that it is remembered today, even by occultists, mainly as a quaint delusion.

If scientific discovery constitutes one threat to occult believers, the fragmented nature of our society constitutes another. Although transcendental experience and occultism are by no means unique to contemporary society, in folk societies they are usually part and parcel of a pervasive and unifying religious perspective. In contrast, in our society seekers are faced with a bewildering assortment of beliefs that become popular only to go out of style. The continued existence of a group of fellow believers, so important to sustaining most believers and most beliefs, can rarely be counted on.

The discussion to this point may seem to portray features of our culture in a somewhat negative light. Therefore, it is important to add that many of these same features contribute to transcendental experience in what might be considered more positive ways; for example:

Our society values social diversity and individual autonomy; this means that a wide range of transcendental experiences and occult beliefs can be promoted and experienced.

Our society values change; this means it also values creative endeavor[687] and, as we have seen in the case of some of our greatest creative geniuses, various transcendental experiences—visions, automatisms, ecstatic feelings—are often involved in the creative process.

Our society values scientific inquiry and, as we will see in the next chapter, scientists involved in searching out the secrets of nature sometimes experience strong mystical feelings; in this sense, in fact, science is truly one of the mysticisms of the West.

Thus, in a variety of distinctive ways, our society fosters transcendental experience and occult beliefs. Such experiences and beliefs are not merely "relics" from earlier cultural periods, but rather they are understandable products of technological society.

Summary

If men define situations as real, they are real in their consequences.[442]

W. I. THOMAS

In this chapter, we have seen that transcendental experience and occult explanations of such experience are almost universally found in a wide variety of cultures. At the same time, we have seen that the particular characteristics of technolgically advanced societies such as our own modify the role of transcendental experience and occultism in distinctive ways. For example, the advance of science and technology has certainly shattered many occult beliefs that were vulnerable to discomfirming evidence. On the other hand, science and technology have also contributed to many social conditions—for example, rapid cultural change and a complex and bewildering society—in the face of which transcendental experience and the miracles of occultism are inviting to many.

We have also seen that, particularly in contemporary society, believers in occult theories run certain risks—for example, of disconfirming evidence and of waning popularity. In the light of these problems, we come back to a point which we have made previously; we need not turn transcendental experience into occultism in order to benefit from it. It is true that, in many ways, our society fosters the tendency to explain transcendental experience in terms of mysterious occult powers. It is also true that many people have neither sufficient knowledge of, nor confidence in, their own minds and bodies to be aware of the role of their own psychology and physiology in transcendental experience. However, it is possible to develop self-awareness, and it is possible to develop faith in ourselves. In this process we can enhance and enjoy our capacities for transcendental experience and, at the same time, avoid the pitfalls that occult belief entails.

5

Mystical Experience

Man is inextricably enmeshed in the universe. It is the beginning of wisdom to understand this fact; it is the beginning of mysticism to enjoy it.[255]

ANDREW GREELEY

In previous chapters we discussed the psychological processes that seem to underlie a variety of extraordinary experiences, often viewed as paranormal, or at least inexplicable. In this and following chapters we will discuss these transcendental experiences at greater length and will consider evidence that bears on the question of the involvement of paranormal processes.

It is fitting that we begin with a discussion of mystical experience. Of all transcendental experiences, mystical experience is unquestionably one of the most powerful and moving. Consider the following example:

> But as I turned and was about to take a seat by the fire, . . . the Holy Spirit descended upon me in a manner that seemed to go through me, body and soul. I could feel the impression, like a wave of electricity, going through and through me. Indeed, it seemed to come in waves and waves of liquid love . . . it seemed to fan me, like immense wings.

> No words can express the wonderful love that was shed abroad in my heart. I wept aloud with joy and love; and I do not know but I should say I literally bellowed out the unutterable gushings of my heart. These waves came over me, and over me, and over me, one after the other. . . .[336]

The powerful nature of this experience is obvious. And, although such experiences often seem unique and indefinable, they commonly share certain features. Notice, in this example, the feeling of overwhelming ecstasy that is perceived as flowing from a universal source of goodness and love, called in this case the "Holy Spirit." These two feelings—of ecstasy and of contact with a universal essence—are so common in such reports that they constitute a good defintion of mystical experience.[68]

The universal essence that is described is often conceived of as supernatural or paranormal. This is not surprising considering the overwhelming nature of the experience and the fact that it is often accompanied by out-of-body sensations, visions, automatisms, and other transcendental feelings. Nevertheless, postulating a superhuman origin for mystical experience is by no means a necessary or universal outcome of such experience.[77]

But is there any evidence that paranormal or superhuman processes are involved in mystical experience? An attempt to answer this question will require the consideration of a range of studies—for example, of visions, of out-of-body states, of possession—which we will take up in the next chapter. For now, we can summarize our later discussion and say that this issue is far from settled and that the belief in a superhuman element in mystical experience is, at the moment, a matter of faith.

Examples of mystical experience come from all historical periods, all varieties of cultures,[68] and are known by a variety of names—for example, samadhi, nirvana, and satori in Hindu and Buddhist traditions; cosmic consciousness, higher consciousness, and peak experience in various Western writings.[23, 93, 425] Here, for instance, is an example of mystical feelings as related by an Eskimo: ". . . I felt a great inexplicable joy, a joy so powerful that I could not restrain it, but had to break into song, a mighty song, with only room for the one word: joy, joy! . . . And then in the midst of such a fit of mysterious and overwhelming delight I became a shaman, not knowing myself how it came about. But I was a shaman. I could see

and hear in a totally different way. I had gained my . . . enlightenment. . . ."[534]

The universal nature of mystical experience underscores the
futility of attempts to derive narrow religious or philosophical
points of view from such experience. Much of the available literature on mystical experience is of this nature and is of little relevance to our present consideration of the psychology of mystical
experience.[292]

Rather, we will draw upon authors—for example, William
James,[336] Marghanita Laski,[389] James Leuba,[396] and Abraham Maslow[425] who concentrate on the nature of the mystical experience
itself. Although I have included accounts by well-known religious
mystics, mostly in the Western tradition, whenever possible I have
included accounts by ordinary people, who, like most readers of
this book, are not devoted mystics, but who nevertheless may have
experienced mystical feelings from time to time.

The Conditions For Mystical Experience

We carry our homes
within us
which enables us to fly.[100]
JOHN CAGE

Before attempting to understand the conditions that appear
to foster mystical experience, let us consider some general features
of such experience.

First, mystical experience is not as rare as many people believe. Depending on how it is defined, studies indicate that anywhere from about 50 to 85 percent of adult Americans say that they
have had such an experience.[76, 77, 255] As discussed in the chapter
on conditioning, one factor that is undoubtedly involved in the
capacity for profound ecstatic experience is whether such experience has met with acceptance by others.

Second, adults seem more able to experience mystical feelings
than children.[389] This may be because learning can enhance the
capacity for profound emotional experience, just as it sometimes

stifles it, and adults have undergone more learning experiences than children.[289]

Third, mystical experiences are often reported to occur unexpectedly. Although, as we shall see, certain conditions seem to precede mystical experience, some people have commented on the rarity of having a mystical experience through "trying,"[389] and a few have commented on the difficulty of resisting a mystical experience when it occurs.[17] The difficulty of "prearranging" a mystical experience may stem from the tension implicit in the effort of trying, which would probably inhibit mystical feelings. The fact that so many of the processes underlying mystical experience are subconscious also might make it difficult to know what is required to "set up" such an experience as well as, perhaps, to avoid one. Nevertheless, a knowledge of the general conditions that seem to underlie mystical experiences may help set the stage for them even if they are difficult to produce "on demand."

What conditions, from accounts of mystical experiences, seem to be important in the creation of such experience? It should be kept in mind that many of these conditions are closely related and that they undoubtedly often work in conjunction with one another. Also, these conditions vary in their proximity to the mystical experience itself; some necessarily operate over a long period of time, whereas others serve as immediate stimuli that seem to "trigger" the mystical experience.[389]

1. One element in many mystical experiences is direct physical effects. In the chapter on physiology, we discussed the altered states of consciousness that can result from such direct physiological alterations as drugs, over- or underbreathing, fasting, fever, excitement, and fatigue. The involvement of some of these factors in mystical experience can be inferred from the following quotations.

William James, for example, states: "The sway of alcohol over mankind is unquestionably due to its power to stimulate the mystical faculties of human nature, usually crushed to earth by the cold facts and dry criticisms of the sober hour. Sobriety diminishes, discriminates, and says no; drunkenness expands, unites, and says yes."[336]

John Wesley, the founder of Methodism, describes the following experience, which may reflect the effects of fever: "The fever came rushing upon me as a lion . . . my body grew weaker every moment. . . . Then it came to my mind, 'Be still, and see the salvation of the Lord; I will not stir hand or foot; but let Him do with me what is good in his own eyes.' At once my heart was at ease; my mouth was filled with laughter, and my tongue with joy; my eyes overflowed with tears, and I began to sing aloud."[389]

William James makes the general point that: ". . . 103° or 104° Fahrenheit might be a much more favorable temperature for truths to germinate and sprout in, than the more ordinary blood heat of 97 or 98 degress."[336]

Omar Michael Burke relates his experience at a dance of dervishes, in which many potential influences, including fatigue and strong rhythms, are present:

> The drum begins to beat, the callers sing a high-pitched flamenco-type air. Slowly the concentric circles begin to revolve in opposite directions. Then the Sheikh calls out, *Ya Haadi!* (O Guide!) and the participants start to repeat this word. They concentrate upon it, saying it at first slowly, then faster and faster. Their movements match the repetitions.
>
> "I noticed that the eyes of some of the dervishes took on a far-away look, and they started to move jerkily, as if they were puppets. The circles moved faster and faster, until I (moving in the outer circle) saw only a whirl of robes and lost count of time. Now and then, with a grunt, or a sharp cry, one of the dervishes would drop out of the circle and would be led away by an assistant, to lie on the ground in what seemed to be an hypnotic state. I began to be affected, and found that although I was not dizzy, my mind was functioning in a very strange and unfamiliar way. The sensation is difficult to describe and is probably a complex one. One feeling was that of a lightening; as if I had no anxieties, no problems. Another was that I was part of this moving circle, and that my individuality was gone, was delightfully merged in something larger. . . . I looked at my watch. Two hours has passed in what seemed like a few minutes.
>
> "I went out into the courtyard to assess my feelings. Something *had* happened. In the first place, the moon seemed immensely bright, and the little glowing lamps seemed surrounded by a whole spectrum of colours."[97]

One element that is probably common to all these experiences is that, in various ways, they alter ordinary consciousness and allow unconscious feelings to emerge. Since we often repress positive emotions—for example, feelings related to sex and love are often repressed because of fear of hurt or rejection—it is not surprising that these unconscious feelings can be highly charged and positive.

In addition, radical changes in consciousness are typically dishabituating as we think, feel, and perceive in new and unusual ways; this can be a highly ecstatic experience as it meets our need for new experience and for discovering new aspects of our world.[221]

2. Another precursor of mystical experience is states of altered attention. Unconscious ecstatic feelings and images can emerge as we change our mode of attention and put aside our usual conscious thoughts and concerns during reverie, fantasy, meditation, drowsiness, or dreaming.

Certainly many people have reported mystical experiences that arise from dreams.[389] Hector Berlioz, the composer, writes: "Last night I dreamt of music, this morning I recalled it all and fell into one of those supernal ecstasies. . . . All the tears of my soul poured forth as I listened to those divinely sonorous *smiles* that radiate from the angels alone. Believe me, dear friend, the being who could write such miracles of transcendent melody would be more than mortal."[7]

Some of my strongest mystical feelings have occurred during dreaming and drowsy states. Once, several days after seeing one of my favorite operas, I heard the opera in my sleep; I awoke feeling deeply moved and crying with joy.

Meditation, in particular, is an approach much favored by the great religious mystics. Evelyn Underhill sees the relationship of meditation to mystical feelings in the following way:

> All that is asked is that we shall look for a little time, in a special and individual manner, at some simple, concrete, and external thing. This object of our contemplation may be almost anything we please: a picture, a statue, a tree, a distant hillside, a growing plant, running water, little living things. . . .
>
> Look, then, at this thing which you have chosen. Wilfully yet tranquilly refuse the messages which countless other aspects of the world are sending; and so concentrate your whole attention on this one act of loving sight that all other objects are excluded from the conscious field. Do not think, but as it were pour out your personality towards it: let your soul be in your eyes. Almost at once, this new method of perception will reveal unsuspected qualities in the external world. First, you will perceive about you a strange and deepening quietness;

a slowing down of our feverish mental time. Next, you will become aware of a heightened significance, an intensified existence in the thing at which you look. As you, with all your consciousness, lean out towards it, an answering current will meet yours. It seems as though the barrier between its life and your own, between subject and object, had melted away. You are merged with it, in an act of true communion.[697]

This heightened awareness and appreciation of surrounding stimuli is, at least in part, an example of dishabituation, characterized by a new awareness of the everyday world.

Renewed awareness and appreciation of everyday events can also result from the deepened understanding of the workings of nature that scientists often experience. For example, Edward Purcell, cowinner of the Nobel Physics Prize for 1952, relates the following experience:

> Professor Bloch has told you how one can detect the precession of the magnetic nuclei in a drop of water. Commonplace as such experiences have become in our laboratories, I have not yet lost the feeling of wonder, and of delight, that this delicate motion should reside in all the ordinary things around us, revealing itself only to him who looks for it. I remember, in the winter of our first experiments, just seven years ago, looking on snow with new eyes. There the snow lay around my doorstep—great heaps of protons quietly precessing in the earth's magnetic field. To see the world for a moment as something rich and strange is the private reward of many a discovery.[526]

That dishabituation and ecstasy can also occur as a consequence of being in a new, unusual, and demanding environment can be seen in the following account of a mountain climbing expedition:

> With the more receptive senses we now appreciated everything around us. Each individual crystal in the granite stood out in bold relief. The varied shapes of the clouds never ceased to attract our attention. For the first time we noticed tiny bugs that were all over the walls, so tiny they were barely noticeable. While belaying, I stared at one for fifteen minutes, watching him move and admiring his brilliant red color.
>
> How could one ever be bored with so many good things to see and feel! This unity with our joyous surroundings, this ultra-penetrating

perception gave us a feeling of contentment that we had not had for years.[119]

3. Another forerunner of many mystical experiences is deprivation and frustration. It is in the great mystical traditions that we find frustration and deprivation carried to an extreme in the quest for mystical enlightenment. In Christian—mainly Catholic—mysticism, and in many Eastern mystical traditions, it is common practice to renounce intimate relations with lovers, parents, children, and sometimes all of humanity.[592] In the East, however, we also find systems—for example, Tantric Hinduism—that advocate sexual activity that omits or postpones orgasm;[592] this can have the immediate effect of sustaining a high level of arousal and anticipation and producing an altered and euphoric state of consciousness. The long-term effects of these practices, in both Western and Eastern traditions, is often some degree of frustration. What are the consequences of such frustration? Earlier we discussed the concept of sublimation; in the case of religious mystics, sexual or love feelings often seem to be redirected and interpreted as a sign of spiritual enlightenment. How this might occur is described by James Leuba:

> ... sexual desire is almost as effectively aroused by representations and ideas as by actual sensations. And, because of the richness of [people's] mental associations, the number of objects perceived, or merely thought of, which can lead to thoughts of sex, is almost unlimited. ... Ideas are not only sufficient in man to awaken amorous desires, but they may adequately replace the physical stimuli and lead to the orgasm itself. That which has happened to nearly everyone in sleep, is a familiar instance in point. ... The subject of the voluptuous excitement may not be aware of the participation of his sex-organs and may, therefore, regard his delight as "spiritual."[396]

In the light of the above, and considering the degree of sexual repression so often characteristic of religious mystics, it is not difficult to see how mystical imagery can be so overwhelming.

That sexual repression is indeed an important ingredient in the experience of many mystics is indicated by the numerous occasions when repression proved inadequate, and erotic impulses— usually explained as being due to possession by the devil—

overwhelmed the mystic.[485] For example: ". . . St. Catherine of Siena, in the interval between her period of joyous illumination and her 'spiritual marriage,' was tormented by visions of fiends, who filled her cell and 'with obscene words and gestures invited her to lust.' "[697]

The erotic nature of some mystical imagery is sometimes quite transparent, as can be seen in the following account by the mystic, St. Teresa:

> I saw an angel close by me, on my left side, in bodily form. . . . I saw in his hand a long spear of gold, and at the iron's point there seemed to be a little fire. He appeared to me to be thrusting it at times into my heart, and to pierce my very entrails; when he drew it out, he seemed to draw them out also and to leave me all on fire with a great love of God. The pain was so great that it made me moan; and yet so surpassing was the sweetness of this excessive pain that I could not wish to be rid of it. The soul is satisfied now with nothing less than God.[697]

St. Teresa's rapture has been portrayed by Bernini in the statue shown in Figure 18.

Sometimes, however, the need for love is expressed in a more general way, as in the following account by Madeleine, a lonely woman who was noted for her mystical experiences and who was also a patient of the French psychiatrist Pierre Janet: "I feel myself under the spell of a pure and sweet hug which ravishes the whole of my being, an inexpressible heat burns me to the marrow of my bones. . . . The flesh, which is dead to the . . . [sense] perceptions is very much alive to the pure and divine enjoyments. I go to sleep sweetly cradled in God's embrace. God presses me so hard to Himself that He causes me suffering in all my body, but these are pains that I cannot but love. . . ."[17]

Madeleine also expressed her longing for children in her fantasies about her relationship with God: "On one occasion she remarks that her nipples are inflamed, 'because He suckles so much.' She is God's mother and wet-nurse, she lets God play, she scolds Him, and so forth."[17]

Instead of satisfying sexual or maternal needs in their spiritual relationship, some mystics seem to regress and become childlike as they envision God as a parent-figure who protects and nurtures them.[523] Of course, God as a father is a common image in

Figure 18. Bernini's *St. Teresa's Ecstasy*

Christianity, but sometimes maternal characteristics are ascribed to God, as Saint Francois de Sales has done: "In this state the soul is like a little child still at the breast whose mother, to caress him while he is still in her arms, makes her milk distill into his mouth without his even moving his lips. So it is here. . . . Our Lord desires that our will should be satisfied with sucking the milk which His Majesty pours into our mouth, and that we should relish the sweetness without even knowing that it cometh from the Lord."[336]

The self-denial of ascetic mystics, however, can go far beyond withdrawal from human intimacy. Many mystics renounce a wide variety of everyday indulgences and pleasures. Such self-denial not only frees these mystics from time-consuming and mind-consuming activities so that they can devote themselves to spiritual concerns, but also can produce a euphoric state as they feel freed from the burden of self-striving and as they see the world in a new light—untainted by personal desire.

A step beyond self-denial lies self-inflicted pain. Here, the list of tortures that some mystics have created for themselves is almost endless.[697] But how could self-torture contribute to mystical experience? There are several possibilities, a number of which were discussed in the chapters on physiology and conditioning.

Self-torture may encourage inhibition of the sense of pain and thus the suppression of ordinary conscious awareness; this could contribute to the development of valued altered states of consciousness.

Certainly pain and discomfort can be dishabituating and might be valued for this reason.

Finally, through conditioning, pain can come to be rewarding as ascetics feel that they are, for example, identifying with the suffering of Christ, atoning for their guilt, or demonstrating the depth of their devotion.

To this point, we have seen that, among the religious mystics, deprivation and frustration seem to facilitate an extremely rich mental life in which various satisfactions are obtained that have been denied to the physical body. Need deprivation for most of us, however, means only that we must postpone gratification for a period of time. Of course, during this period we may dream and fantasize about the time when we will finally feel fulfilled. That the time of fulfillment can then be a truly ecstatic, and even mystical, experience can be seen in the following accounts.

A university professor describes how he felt when he finally found the woman of his dreams:

> Then it was as if the world had changed during the night: everything had become new and fresh, and I specially remember the garden of my hotel, the road under the mountain-side, the lake and the mountains, and above all the sun. It was as if it were the first time I saw real sunshine, everything I had seen before being pale and lifeless as compared to that sunshine. I thought I discovered the real life and beauty of the various colours of the fields and meadows and mountain-slopes as they had never been discovered before. It seems to me now that I never doubted a moment that my new world was

the real one, the old one being somehow defective. . . . It did last, not only that day, but the following days and weeks as well. For days and weeks I lived as in a dream, though I think I did my daily work rather better. . . .[396]

Love for children can produce similar feelings. Childbirth, for example, is an experience of great involvement, concern, and unpredictability, which (usually) is resolved happily; many women cite childbirth as an ecstatic experience.[389] In a similar vein, one woman states that she was joyful and ecstatic upon "[receiving] when my child was ill, a phone message that he was all right."[389]

Love, of course, is not the only kind of fulfillment that can bring ecstasy after a period of frustration. Scientists have described the transcendental feelings they sometimes experience when they finally perceive the solution to a problem over which they have been puzzling. For example, physicist James Lee describes how he felt when he arrived at an insight into a perplexing problem in acoustics:

> I am a physicist, who for his masters degree thesis studied the concert hall problem . . . the problem was shown to be unsolved by the experience of L. L. Beranek, an eminent acoustician, in the original design for Philharmonic Hall, Lincoln Center, New York. I reasoned that the fault was not Beranek's, but rather the state of the theory; this drove me to select the problem for study. . . . About a year after completing the thesis, while designing several theatres, I got hit by the solution. . . . I realized that the problem had been misformulated, that reverberation time is a nearly meaningless criterion, and that the seminal factors are the surface development of the walls and ceiling and the size and shape of the stage. Briefly, the problem is determinate rather than stochastic, as had been assumed since . . . the turn of the century. The emotional state accompanying this discovery was one of tremendous exhilaration, lasting for several months.[392]

Even such experiences as ". . . finding ten chromosomes when I knew they ought to be there. . . ." and ". . . solving mathematical problems. . . ." have been cited as leading to ecstatic feelings.[389]

Artists and musicians, likewise, sometimes experience transcendental feelings when a new idea bursts forth. Peter Tchaikovsky, for example, has written: "It would be vain to try to put into words that immeasurable sense of bliss that comes over me directly a new idea awakens in me. . . ."[7]

Of course, fulfillment after a period of frustration is a feature of many human activities—mountain climbing, sporting events, space exploration—and such activities sometimes trigger mystical feelings.

Sometimes mystical experience follows periods of depression; perhaps the mere lifting of the feeling of depression and deprivation can create an ecstatic feeling of relief. This may be involved in the following example:

> It happened to me about two years ago, on the day when my bed was first pushed out of doors to the open gallery of the hospital. I was recovering from a surgical operation. I had undergone a certain amount of physical pain, and had suffered for a short time the most acute mental depression which it has ever been my misfortune to encounter. I suppose that this depression was due to physical causes, but at the time it seemed to me that somewhere down there under the anesthetic, in the black abyss of unconsciousness, I had discovered a terrible secret, and the secret was that there was no God, or if there was one, He was indifferent to all human suffering.
>
> Though I had hardly reestablished my normal state of faith, still the first acuteness of that depression had faded, and only a scar of fear was left when, several days later, my bed was first wheeled out to the porch. . . .
>
> I cannot now recall whether the revelation came suddenly or gradually; I only remember finding myself in the very midst of those wonderful moments, beholding life for the first time in all its young intoxification of loveliness, . . . beauty, and importance. . . . And, as I beheld, my heart melted out of me in a rapture of love and delight. A nurse was walking past; the wind caught a strand of her hair and blew it out in a momentary gleam of sunshine, and never in my life before had I seen how beautiful beyond all belief is a woman's hair. . . . A little sparrow chirped and flew to a nearby branch, and I honestly believe that only "the morning stars singing together, and the sons of God shouting for joy" can in the least express the ecstasy of a bird's flight. I cannot express it, but I have seen it.
>
> Once out of all the gray days in my life . . . I have seen life as it really is—ravishingly, ecstatically, madly beautiful, and filled to overflowing with a wild joy, and a value unspeakable.[226]

In some mystical traditions, notably Zen Buddhism, adherents are purposefully frustrated in a variety of intellectual, as well as physical, ways. "Nonsense" questions such as "What is the sound of one hand clapping?"—known as koans—are sometimes used for this purpose. When novices finally arrive at a new way of thinking or perceiving that resolves or reduces the frustration, they often report feelings of ecstasy. In Zen Buddhism, this is known as satori. A Zen practitioner describes a satori experience—in his halting English—as follows:

> In the morning of the fifth day, I got up at five and began to sit. I returned to the state of the previous night. And unexpectedly soon a conversion came. In less than ten minutes I reached a wonderful state of mind. It was quite different from any which I had experienced in seiza (sitting quietly) or other practices. It was a state of mind, uncomparably quiet, clear and serene, without any obstruction. I gazed it. Entering this state of mind, I was filled with the feeling of appreciation, beyond usual joy, . . . and tears began to flow from closed eyes. . . . a state of mind of forgiving all, sympathizing all, and further free from all bondages. . . .[367]

In the West, conversion to Christianity is sometimes accompanied by strong mystical feelings.[336] This is not surprising since converts often view conversion as their final hope and as a solution to a wide range of serious personal problems. One convert describes his experience in this way: "I had attended a series of revival services for about two weeks off and on. Had been invited to the altar several times, all the time becoming more deeply impressed, when finally I decided I must do this, or I should be lost. Realization of conversion was very vivid, like a ton's weight being lifted from my heart; a strange light which seemed to light up the whole room (for it was dark); a conscious supreme bliss which caused me to repeat 'Glory to God' for a long time."[336]

Thus far, we have discussed how need deprivation and frustration can lead to heightened and sometimes mystical feelings as fulfillment is finally attained in fantasy or in reality. It remains for us to consider the possibility that fulfillment, in the absence of deprivation, can facilitate mystical experience. This, for example, is the position taken by Abraham Maslow, whose theory assumes that mystical experience is based on a high level of need satisfaction and a low level of frustration since infancy.[424] Although Maslow's theory may have some validity, there seems to be no satisfactory evidence to support it.

4. A final condition important in the creation of mystical experience is conditioning. We have seen that practically any stimulus

can become a conditioned stimulus able to elicit ecstatic feelings. Most stimuli, of course, have intrinsic qualities that can fulfill basic needs—for example, for stimulus input and stimulus change. As Leuba says: "[Some people] describe their transformation after a cup of tea in terms which fall little short of those fittingly used to characterize the effects of a religious ecstasy. A hot bath improves not only the general well-being but also the moral attitude: rest-lessness, mental dispersion, irritability, malevolence, pessimism, may vanish and be replaced by peace, mental unification, benevo-lence, optimism."[396]

Nevertheless, the stimuli discussed in this section undoubt-edly acquire much of their impact through conditioned associations and reinforcements of various kinds. For example, Laski found that music was the art form most frequently cited as an evoker of ecstatic feelings.[389] As one description states: "Rapt in Beethoven's music, I closed my eyes and watched a silver glow which shaped itself into a circle with a central focus brighter than the rest. . . . Swiftly and smoothly I was borne through the tunnel. . . . The light grew brighter but was never dazzling or alarming. I came to a point where time and motion ceased. . . . [I experienced the] peace that passeth all understanding. . . ."[280]

However, the fact that rock music may have little impact on a classical music buff and vice versa, although each type of music can evoke an ecstatic response in an appropriate listener, illustrates the importance of conditioning in the development of responses to music.

For many people, nature is a powerful evoker of mystical feelings, as can be seen in the following account: "Once, when walking in the wild woods and in the country, in the morning under the blue sky, the sun before me, the breeze blowing from the sea, the birds and flowers around me, an exhilaration came to me that was heavenly—a raising of the spirit within me through perfect joy. Only once in my life have I had such an experience of heaven!"[396]

Roger Bannister, the first person to run a mile in less than four minutes, seems to have acquired his love for running partly because of its association with nature. He says:

> I remember a moment [in childhood] when I stood barefoot on firm dry sand by the sea. The air had a special quality as if it had a life of

its own. The sound of breakers on the shore shut out all others. I looked up at the clouds, like great white-sailed galleons, chasing proudly inland. I looked down at the regular ripples on the sand, and could not absorb so much beauty. I was taken aback—each of the myriad particles of sand was perfect in its way . . . there was nothing to detract from all this beauty.

In this supreme moment I leapt in sheer joy. I was startled, and frightened, by the tremendous excitement that so few steps could create. . . . A few more steps—self-consciously now and firmly gripping the original excitement. The earth seemed almost to move with me. I was running now, and a fresh rhythm entered my body. No longer conscious of my movement I discovered a new unity with nature. I had found a new source of power and beauty, a source I never dreamed existed.

From intense moments like this, love of running can grow.[31]

Not surprisingly, religious settings are often mentioned as triggers for mystical feelings. The fact that this is true even for professed nonbelievers points up the unconscious nature of conditioned emotional responses.[389] For example, I find myself getting choked up and teary-eyed at religious and patriotic ceremonies, yet consciously I no longer accept the conditionings that my unconscious obviously still takes for granted.

Although many other conditioned stimuli could be cited for their effectiveness in eliciting mystical feelings, those we have just discussed are commonly mentioned. However, just as some conditions are able to facilitate mystical experience, others are noted for their ability to inhibit such responses. Many people mention that the intrusion of rational thought has the effect of dampening their ecstatic experience. They state that analyzing or evaluating the experience while it is occurring diminishes its emotional impact. In other words, concentrating our attention on intellectual matters detracts from our attending to emotional experience. Also commonly mentioned as inhibiting ecstatic experience is the presence of other people when the experience is basically a solitary one. Certainly the presence of others—a friend, a lover, an exciting crowd—often facilitates ecstatic feelings.[389] However, many ecstatic experiences involve a relationship to something nonhuman—a meadow, a sculpture, a fantasy. In these experiences, the presence of another person can constitute an unwelcome intrusion.[389]

We have mentioned that several conditions often seem to operate together to facilitate mystical experience. One example of this, perhaps, is the experience some people have reported, when on the threshold of dying, of seeing "another reality." As studied by Elisabeth Kübler-Ross,[383] Raymond Moody,[456] Karlis Osis,[489] and others,[39, 483] these visionary experiences are usually comforting and are often ecstatic, although some patients report seeing devils of which they are terrified.[396, 489] A typical example is provided by the experience of the English barrister, Sir Patrick Hastings: "Pat had a second stroke a year later. . . . It seemed that, according to the doctors, he had actually died during this attack for a time, but had managed to pull himself back into life because he felt he had one more message to deliver. Death, he told us, was nothing to fear. It was a natural culmination to life as we know it and was an experience of indescribable happiness. The release from the bondage of life—even from the bondage of love—brought with it an ecstasy and an understanding beyond anything known to living man."[287]

How can we understand such experiences in the light of what we have discussed?

The trauma of being near death probably often entails psychological and physiological effects that can significantly alter consciousness. Even though peripheral life-signs may be absent for a period, there seems to be no evidence that all parts of the brain are lifeless during the visionary experiences that have been reported. It is reasonable to expect that unconscious processes that can give rise to visions are still operating.[78] Since most people have a strong need to deny that bodily death is the end of personal existence, it is not surprising that brink-of-death visions so often portray the continued existence of souls—of the patients themselves, of departed relatives and friends, and of culturally relevant religious figures.[491] Finally, people who have had such experiences often say that they no longer fear death; this release from the dread of death is understandably often accompanied by ecstatic feelings.

Thus we see that a wide variety of conditions can lead to mystical experience. As varied as these conditions are, however, they all give rise to feelings that share much in common, as we shall see in the next section.

The Effects of Mystical Experience

The most beautiful emotion we can experience is the mystical. It is the source of all true art and science.[501]   ALBERT EINSTEIN

Let us now consider the effects of mystical experience—that is, what does the experience consist of and what are some of its enduring effects? It should be kept in mind that the mystical experience itself and most of its effects are usually reported to be short-lived, perhaps on the order of a few minutes. However, some people report that the experience, or its effect, persists for hours, days, or weeks.[17] Also, bear in mind that many people feel that a mystical experience they have undergone is ineffable—that is, it sufficiently transcends ordinary experience so that ordinary language is incapable of describing it. In view of this feeling, we must assume that many of the descriptions that follow are approximations at best.

What, then, seem to be the common elements of mystical experience and its effects?

1. One element we have already discussed is ecstasy. Of course, other terms—bliss, elation, euphoria, rapture—are often used, as can be seen in the accounts collected by Marghanita Laski: ". . . absolute ecstasy-exalted" . . . "as if being borne into heaven itself" . . . "intense joy" . . . "sensation of timeless bliss—life should be like this forever" . . . "tremendous sense of life worth living" . . . "as if nothing could ever go wrong again" . . . "wonderful feeling of peace" . . . "nearness to splendour. . . ."[389]

And here is an example from William James's study of mystical experience: "The ordinary sense of things around me faded. For the moment nothing but an ineffable joy and exhaltation remained. It is impossible fully to describe the experience. It was like the effect of some great orchestra when all the separate notes have melted into one swelling harmony that leaves the listener conscious of nothing save that his soul is being wafted upwards, and almost bursting with its own emotion"[336]

As can be seen, feelings of ecstasy relate closely to feelings of satisfaction, of problems fading into insignificance, and of the basic goodness of life.

2. Another feature of mystical experience we have mentioned is a feeling of oneness with a universal essence of goodness

and truth. For example, Rabindranath Tagore, the Indian poet, describes his feelings while watching a particularly beautiful sunrise:

> As I was watching it, suddenly, in a moment, a veil seemed to be lifted from my eyes. I found the world wrapt in an inexpressible glory with its waves of joy and beauty bursting and breaking on all sides. The thick cloud of sorrow that lay on my heart in many folds was pierced through and through by the light of the world, which was everywhere radiant. . . .
>
> There was nothing and no one whom I did not love at that moment. . . . [The movement of the people,] their forms, their countenances seemed strangely wonderful to me, as if they were all moving like waves in the great ocean of the world. When one young man placed his hand upon the shoulder of another and passed laughingly by, it was a remarkable event to me. . . . I seemed to witness, in the wholeness of my vision, the movements of the body of all humanity. . . .[280]

But why should this feeling of universal oneness and goodness so commonly accompany ecstasy? First of all, it is clear that many people, for a variety of reasons, deeply desire to feel "at one" with a universal essence, often conceived of as God. If they finally achieve this feeling, it is not surprising that they experience ecstatic feelings at the same time. However, let us see how this relationship might work the other way around.

It has been said that "all the world loves a lover." The principle of projection would imply also that "a lover loves all the world and sees the world as love," and this seems to be true for mystical experience. In other words, it is not surprising that a person in a state of ecstasy perceives goodness and love as a general state of affairs and feels, in this way, a part of a larger "whole." Of course, it is no more reasonable to assume that the *feeling* that goodness and love is everywhere is evidence of universal goodness and love than to assume that dread and despair pervade the universe because someone has these feelings.

Also, ecstasy is such a powerful out-of-the-ordinary experience that many people assume that it must come from a powerful out-of-the-ordinary source of goodness—for example, from God. In some cases, this feeling of being "touched" by God or a universal essence is accompanied by the notion of being possessed, which is certainly a variety of the feeling of "oneness." For example, F. C. Happold describes this experience while an undergraduate: "There was just the room with its shabby furniture and the fire burning in the grate and the red-shaded lamp on the table. But the room was filled by a Presence, which in a strange way was both about me and within me, like light or warmth. I was overwhelmingly possessed by Someone who was not myself. . . . I was filled with an intense happiness, and an almost unbearable joy, such as I had never known before and have never known since."[280]

The feeling that mystical experience emanates from an all-powerful source often convinces the individual that intuitions—or what are sometimes called revelations—that arise during such an experience are infallible and that ". . . all truth, all secrets of the universe [are] being revealed. . . ."[145] Although these intuitions may indeed prove to be valuable insights, many of them suffer a harsher fate, as can be seen in the following example: "Whilst under the anaesthetic for a short operation, I had a complete revelation about the ultimate truth of everything. I understood the 'entire works.' It was a tremendous illumination. I was filled with unspeakable joy. . . . When I came round I told the Doctor I understood the meaning of everything. He . . . said 'Well, what is it?' and I faltered out, 'Well, it's a sort of green light.' "[389] As William James says: "To come from [a mystical experience] is no infallible credential. What comes must be sifted and tested, and run the gauntlet of confrontation with the total context of experience, just like what comes from the outer world of sense."[336]

3. Another common accompaniment of mystical experience is perceptual and behavioral changes. An experience as profound as mystical experience might be expected to involve sensory and perceptual alterations, and that, indeed, is the case. Often mystical experience seems to involve inhibition or habituation of ordinary sensory input as the individual is wrapped up in internal fantasies or visions. Many have commented on their oblivion, during a mystical experience, to the situation around them, sometimes including insensitivity to ordinarily painful stimuli.[17, 697] This seems to be the case, for example, in the following experience: ". . . everything in time and space and form vanished from my consciousness and only the ineffable eternal things remained. . . . For a few moments of mortal time . . . all consciousness of my physical surroundings was withdrawn. . . ."[280]

The fantasies and visions that often accompany sensory withdrawal are, of course, highly varied, although, in the case of religious mystics, they usually have a religious content. That the visions that sometimes arise during mystical experience may stem from extraordinarily strong needs is illustrated by the case of a schoolgirl who was ecstatic when she saw a vision of her grandfather. As she relates:

> ... I was in the habit of discussing my school problems with my grandfather, an old man with silky white hair and a little white goatee-beard, whom I adored. . . . When he died, I was about 18, and I was desolate.

> About six months after his death, I had another big problem to resolve, and no-one to talk it over with. During that week once at about 3 a.m., my grandfather came through the outside wall of my bedroom, in a luminous circle of grey light, his head and shoulders clearly visible—and talked to me. . . .

> My "grandfather" came again some months later when I again needed his help—but he has never come again since.[258]

Also commonly mentioned in accounts of mystical experience is an ethereal light, which seems to pervade everything. As one account describes it: "All at once the glory of God shone upon and round about me in a manner almost marvelous. . . . A light perfectly ineffable shone in my soul, that almost prostrated me on the ground. . . . This light seemed like the brightness of the sun in every direction. It was too intense for the eyes."[336]

Perceiving light in mystical experience may reflect the positive connotations of light, as contrasted with darkness; this is illustrated, for example, by the word *illumination,* which can refer either to light or to an experience of perceiving the truth. However, such experiences may sometimes stem from people becoming aware of phosphenes and other optical peculiarities in the altered state of consciousness in which they find themselves. And, of course, perceiving light can occur as a direct consequence of the taking of drugs, which sometimes triggers mystical experiences.[443]

Sometimes out-of-body or levitation feelings accompany mystical experiences;[17] these feelings are probably related to sensory habituation and inhibition, which can easily result from prolonged periods of prayer or meditation. As already discussed, when our sense of body position is no longer functioning, we can perceive our bodies as free-floating or our psyche as detached from our bodies. Some people have described these feelings during ecstasy as: ". . . soaring up" . . . "floating" . . . "hovering" . . . "weightlessness" . . . "sensations of physical flying. . . ."[389] The connotations of out-of-body feelings—of floating up to heaven or of a weightless soul or spirit—are, of course, very pleasant to many people and probably encourage such imagery.

Sensory withdrawal does not always accompany mystical experience, however. Just as open meditation consists of increased receptivity to sensory input, so does mystical experience sometimes involve a heightened response to surrounding stimuli as sensory dishabituation takes place. Such an experience is described in the following:

> Two lady friends and I were out driving a few days ago. It was a lovely, perfect morning. As we passed along the shaded country road, we got out of the carriage to gather purple aster, which was blooming with all its perfection by the wayside. I was in a strangely joyous mood—all nature seemed sweet and pensive. The asters had never before seemed so beautiful to me. I looked at the large bunches we had gathered with growing amazement at their brightness, and it was some little time before I realized that this was unusual. . . . A wonderful light shone out from every little petal and flower, and the whole was a blaze of splendor. I trembled with rapture—it was a "burning bush." It cannot be described. The flowers looked like gems or stars, the color of amethysts, so clear and transparent, so still and intense, a subtle living glow. . . . What a moment that was! I thrill at the thought of it.[93]

We would also expect that heightened sensitivity to surrounding stimuli, due to dishabituation, might occur following something as unusual and powerful as a mystical experience. This is indeed the case, and comments such as ". . . our faculties . . . enhanced—keener perceptions . . . ."[389] are commonly made about the period following mystical experience. Here, for example, is how one person experienced this state of heightened awareness, which sometimes follows mystical experience: "I seemed almost to have a new pair of eyes, new ears, new abilities to taste and smell and feel. I had learned to give my full attention to whatever I was doing at any one moment and I wondered if I had ever really done this before. . . . I saw what I was doing as if I had never seen it before. And the pleasures I found in it all were something I could not have imagined."[318]

In addition to sensory and perceptual changes, overt behavior is sometimes affected in mystical experience. While some people experience inhibition of muscle movement,[17] others experience automatisms—for example, speaking in tongues or automatic writing.[697] We have already discussed how automatisms often accompany feelings of being possessed by a spirit, and so it is not surprising that many accounts of mystical experience, in which the individual feels "taken over by a higher power," should mention automatisms. Among the better-known mystics, Jakob Böhme, Mme. Guyon, Jan van Ruysbroeck, Emanuel Swedenborg, and St. Teresa are noted for their automatic writings.[17]

4. Another common element of mystical experience is physiological changes. We have already mentioned certain common physical effects of mystical experience, including crying (from happiness) and feelings of exhilaration or great calm. However, no discussion of mystical experience would be complete without a more detailed consideration of the physiological reactions that are reported.

Physiological responses that are described in accounts of mystical experience vary widely and certainly imply different basic physiological states.[17, 389] For example, heart rate is often described as becoming slower, which would indicate a parasympathetic state; on the other hand, erection of body hair is also commonly mentioned, which would indicate a sympathetic state. Respiration is sometimes described as becoming more rapid, other times as becoming slower. Sometimes increased body warmth is reported, sometimes chills. From our knowledge of autonomic nervous system states, we might expect to find such a variety of responses depending on whether the person is excited (sympathetic state), peaceful (parasympathetic state), or in the process of changing from a sympathetic to a parasympathetic state. Any of these states, except probably extreme sympathetic activation (indicative of fear or anger) could conceivably accompany ecstatic feelings. Various descriptions of mystical experiences could fit such a scheme: excitement seems to be described in accounts such as ". . . a rushing together—one swelling harmony—almost bursting," peaceful feelings by descriptions such as ". . . relaxed quietude and self-dissolving stillness," and a change from one state to another in, for example, ". . . a great climax which has built up."[389]

The general physiological states involved in mystical experience, together with other conditions—drugs, fever, oxygen-carbon dioxide imbalances—which sometimes produce ecstasy, must ultimately relate to emotional centers in the brain—for example, in the limbic system and hypothalamus. It has been known for some time that certain of these centers produce euphoric feelings when electrically stimulated.[288] Recently, natural substances called enkephalins and endorphins, which are similar to opiates, have been identified at these brain centers and have been found to produce euphoria.[635]

On the other hand, certainly higher brain centers are also involved in mystical experience. A number of studies have shown that the same general level of physiological activation is subjectively experienced quite differently depending on the prior conditioning and present surroundings of the subject.[704]

The physiological changes that take place during mystical experience might be expected to facilitate recovery from illness, particularly psychosomatic or hysterical illnesses that could be affected by alleviation of physiological stress. This is indeed the case, and Richard Bucke,[93] William James,[336] and Evelyn Underhill[697] all cite cases in which it appears that mystical experience was at least partly reponsible for recovery from, at times, serious illnesses.

5. An outcome of mystical experience sometimes reported is perceiving new meaning in life. It is not surprising that an experience as overwhelming and dishabituating as mystical experience can induce profound and creative insights. Many people have stated that their lives took on new meaning as a consequence of such an experience.[389] For example, Jack Huber, an American undergoing training in Zen Buddhism, describes a satori experience as follows:

> And then—it was late in the morning—a white, clear screen came before my eyes. In front of the screen passed, or rather, floated, simple images—faces, objects. I have no clear recollection of the images. A rush of feeling came over me.
>
> I burst into tears; the tears became quiet sobbing. . . .
>
> My feeling was that I was seeing something of great importance, as if

everything fitted together for the first time. What had all my life struggles been about? Things were very clear and simple.[318]

In the words of others: "... [the] whole world falls into place, matches, fits" ... "for the first time you're seeing things in proper proportion" ... "the world makes sense" ... "it gave me a new lease on life and taught me ... how to make use of it. ..."[389]

Sometimes a mystical experience will completely change the course of a life. St. Catherine of Siena, for example, decided to devote her life to serving the poor as a consequence of mystical experience.[697] Another religious convert describes the change that he underwent after a profound mystical experience as follows: "[I] decided to be God's child for life, and to give up my pet ambition, wealth, and social position. My former habits of life hindered my growth somewhat, but I set about overcoming these systematically, and in one year my whole nature was changed, i.e., my ambitions were of a different order."[336] And here is the way a scientist describes how his life was affected by a mystical experience resulting from a scientific insight:

> ... at the age of 23, I took a summer job in ... physics. ... I was isolated almost entirely from friends and family. ... I began, for the first time in my life, to work hard, really hard, my half-understood objective being to develop a capability for independent work in theoretical physics. ... The going was difficult at first. ... But fairly rapidly I started getting somewhere, and in the course of the summer began to get ideas ... after some two months ... after ... playing with the properties of a certain physical equation that is thought to describe the behavior of electrons, I hit upon a connection between the properties of a certain mathematical structure related to this equation with an apparently unrelated mathematical structure that has long been a curiosity in physics. ... this discovery triggered instantaneously an experience akin to a revelation in me: it was as if there had suddenly opened a door into the empyrean of physical knowledge, as it were, and I *saw,* I *knew,* what elementary particles were. ... For perhaps 10 minutes I paced the halls in a state of extreme elation and agitation as the overpowering force of this insight held me in its grip.
>
> Soon my mind returned to relative calm, but I was no longer the same person by far as I had been a few minutes earlier. It's hard to avoid sententiousness here, but I must say that my primary life's work was determined from those moments.[505]

Thus mystical experience can be more than a temporary respite from the cares and worries of our everyday lives. Sometimes, in revealing a whole new order of things, it profoundly transforms a life.

Summary

To see a World in a Grain of Sand
And a Heaven in a Wild Flower
Hold Infinity in the palm of your hand
And Eternity in an hour.[189]

WILLIAM BLAKE

In this chapter we have discussed mystical experiences—that is, experiences characterized by feelings of ecstasy and of oneness with the universe.

We have discussed various circumstances which seem to induce mystical experience. For one thing, a variety of physical conditions—drugs, fasting, fever, excitement, fatigue, and alterations in breathing—can produce altered states of consciousness and allow unconscious ecstatic feelings to emerge. Such feelings also can surface when ordinary conscious attention is superseded during reverie, fantasy, meditation, drowsiness, or dreaming.

We have seen that deprivation and frustration can produce mystical states in at least two ways. Gratification can be obtained through sublimation and fantasy; this is a route to mystical experience much favored by many great religious mystics, who deny themselves intimacy with fellow human beings but consequently feel a close intimacy and identification with the spiritual world. Or gratification can be obtained directly, physically, in which case the impact of need fulfillment after a long period of deprivation can produce mystical feelings. Such gratification can be of many kinds: reaching a mountain top after a long climb, arriving at an insight into a problem on which one has been working for a lengthy period, or falling in love after many months of feeling lonely and isolated.

We have discussed conditioning in relation to mystical experience and have seen that almost any stimulus can effectively produce mystical feelings through conditioning. Some of these experiences, reported by a great many people to elicit mystical feelings, are art and music, religious ceremonies, and scenes in nature.

Concerning the effects of mystical experience, we have seen that ecstasy and a feeling of oneness are the common denominators. However, other effects are commonly reported. Perceptual and behavioral changes—for example, visions, out-of-body feelings, automatisms—sometimes accompany mystical experience. Physiological changes—in heart rate, breathing rate, and so on—are often reported. And we have seen that some people claim that their personalities were changed significantly and permanently as a result of a mystical experience and that they subsequently found a new meaning and direction to their lives.

There is little question that mystical experience is a powerful and generally valuable experience. Although its transcendental quality leads many people to assume that mystical feelings arise from mysterious supernatural or paranormal forces, we have seen that to a large extent, we can understand mystical feelings in the light of what is known about underlying psychological processes.

Thus it is that we have the capacity to transcend our ordinary existence and to feel in touch with the infinite.

6

Psychic experience

Wonderful phenomena need wonderful evidence in their support.[561]

JOSEPH RINN

Returning once more to the hexing of Colin Turnbull, we saw that the hex might have produced sufficient stress, as well as sufficiently strong suggestion, to cause the illness. However, this does not prove that his illness actually developed in this way. It is a widespread belief that witchcraft entails paranormal effects that go beyond the natural, if not widely known, processes discussed thus far. To many people, the heart of the issue of paranormal involvement in human affairs is psychic experience, which—the belief goes—allows us to read minds, to see into the future, and to sense and influence events in ways that surpass our present conceptions of psychological and physical processes. Thus, in this chapter, we will discuss a wide range of experiences that have been thought to reflect the operation of psychic forces.

To begin, let us examine some of these extraordinary experiences in the light of the psychological processes discussed in previous chapters. Consider the following example: "In the summer of

1934, a woman in St. Louis had a sudden irrational, intuitive impression. She was riding through the park on a bus, when she suddenly felt she must leave it. She jumped up and got off at the next stop, and found herself standing there feeling very foolish, as she had to wait some time for the next one. When it came she entered, still feeling uneasy. When this bus came out of the park, a group of people were standing on the street. The fire department was there and the bus she had left was burning."[556]

Of course, any such description may largely reflect coincidence, exaggeration, or omission, but, for our present purposes, let us accept this description, and similar descriptions in this chapter, at face value.

In this example, a woman evidently had a premonition of danger. Where did it come from? We have seen that it is possible for faint stimuli—perhaps a few whiffs of smoke—to register subconsciously and to affect behavior without the person being aware of its influence. The lesson here is that it is a good idea to listen carefully to our intuitions.

Even when this intuitive impression forms a distinct conscious image, the individual may still be ignorant as to its source. Thus, in the example below, the writer may have seen the rare plants "out of the corner of his eye," without being aware of doing so, and thus formed a conscious image that appeared "psychic."

> ... I was on a geological excursion in the environs of Nice. ... I conceived a great ambition for ... *Asplenium Trichomanes,* or Common Maidenhair Spleenwort abnormally bifurcated, which I had often seen mentioned in a book, but which I had never ... been able to discover. ...
>
> Hardly was this mental picture evoked [when] my eyes ... were arrested by one amongst all the green tufts which surrounded me, and amongst all the fronds which composed it—by one alone, which, two yards off, had the exact appearance of a bifurcation. ...
>
> ... I could not believe my eyes. But the evidence was undeniable ... highly delighted, I ... plucked the fern [and] said to myself ... "Well, I only want now to find the *Cet*—." I had not finished my sentence when my gaze ... fell below the footpath on the left ... on ... *Ceterach Officinarum* (Common Scale-Fern or Scaly Spleenwort) crowded into the midst of the *Asplenium* (Spleenworts). ...
>
> Being at once led on ... I argued: "If I have found one, and even two bifurcated fronds, certainly the third is not far to seek." And in

less time than it had taken to announce this decision . . . amongst all
the attractive groups of fern, I distinguished [a third!].[475]

On occasion, intuitive images take the form of a perception
that seems to originate mysteriously from outside of oneself. In the
following case, for example, the miner might have subconsciously
picked up the first subtle sounds of collapsing timbers, which were
sufficient to trigger an appropriate image.

> I was working in a coal mine north of Pittsburg, Kansas, at the age of
> 24. I asked the mine foreman for a job at a deep mine. The foreman
> said he had a room not being worked—the man had quit.
>
> . . . As I had crawled back to work . . . I heard a voice "Stop". . . . I
> was scared. I crawled as fast as I could to the face of the room . . .
> then through the cross cut. I cannot describe the noise the falling
> rock made. . . . Hundreds of tons of rock had fallen.
>
> If it had not been for that voice "Stop" . . . I would have been cov-
> ered by that rockfall.[376]

At other times, subliminal impressions reveal themselves in
dreams, as may have happened in this example:

> . . . a young couple in New York City . . . had gone to a theater. . . .
> After the theater, this couple stopped at a candy store for an ice
> cream soda. Suddenly, with a cry of dismay, the young woman saw
> that the stone, a sky-blue opal, was missing from her ring.
>
> "It was a matrix stone and black on the underside," she says. . . . "I
> was heartbroken at the loss. . . .
>
> "Well, the next morning before breakfast [my husband] said he was
> going out for a short time. . . . In about three-quarters of an hour he
> came back and placed my opal before me on the breakfast table.
>
> "He said, 'I had a dream. I saw a large, round, black thing and lying
> next to it a small, round, black thing; and I thought of those hat
> cushions in the theater. Something inside of me said, "Go there," and
> I did. I had our seat checks; a cleaning woman let me in; and there,
> *as in my dream,* the two black things were side by side.' "[556]

Paying attention to such dreams can sometimes literally spell
the difference between life and death. For example, in the case
below, it is reasonable to think that the mother was already vaguely
aware of her child's inability to keep his head above water and that

the dream crystallized this awareness for her. The correspondence of the rest of the dream to her real experience may only indicate that her dreams tend to reflect her real-life tendencies.

> I dreamed I was bathing the children and left the bathroom a minute to run to the kitchen to get the towels, where I had placed them in the oven to warm. While in the kitchen I thought I might just as well do the breakfast dishes, while the children played a few minutes in the tub. When I got back to the bathroom I was horror-struck to find little Brad lying underwater at the bottom of the tub. I grabbed him, he was unconscious and his fingertips and lips were blue. I put him across my lap with his head down and started working feverishly over him. At this point, as dreams so often do, it faded.

> I had no recollection of this next day as I went about my chores. At lunch time I put a couple of towels in the oven to warm and then went on to the bathing of the babies. Before taking them from the tub I went into the kitchen to get the towels and did a thing I had never done before—I started tidying up and as I did a feeling came over me that I had lived this moment before. It was a strange feeling and as I tried to analyze it the memory of the dream came back. I flew into the bathroom and found Brad exactly as I feared I might; he was lying absolutely still under the water. I had him out in a flash and even though I was filled with terror I noted the blueness of his lips and fingers. I followed the same procedure of the dream and brought him around. His cry that morning was one of the most thrilling sounds I ever heard.[557]

In the final example below, we see the consequences of ignoring a dream that foretells the future.

> On Sunday, August 24, 1941, a 78-year-old man in North Carolina told his wife a dream he had the night before. He dreamed he was standing at Butler's Crossing about three miles from his house when he saw a vehicle coming toward him at great speed. . . . the vehicle struck him, as he said, hurling him into everlasting darkness.

> . . . at the time [he] was suffering from an allergy, for which twice a week he was taking treatments from a doctor in a nearby town. Three days later, he went to town for his shots. On the way back, he caught a ride to Butler's Crossing, where he got out of the car, stood a few minutes by the road lighting his pipe, and then started across the highway. He was at the center white line when a speeding car came around the curve. He stepped back, the car swerved to the left, hit him and threw him sixty feet. Fifteen minutes later he was dead.[556]

Evidently, both this man and his wife overlooked the possible significance of this dream. People who dream of dying in situations in which they have some control may be expressing suicidal tendencies. By heeding the dream's warning, the man's life might have been saved. Thus, seeing the seemingly prophetic dream as a route to self-discovery might have led to a worthwhile examination of this man's feelings about his life. In contrast, interpreting the dream as psychic would have laid stress on some mysterious "psychic energy" that he was picking up, thus overlooking the possibility of achieving enhanced self-awareness through understanding the dream.

These examples emphasize a point that was stressed previously. We can gain a great deal from transcendental experience. As we recognize and cultivate our abilities to foresee the future, to intuit events, and to be sensitive to our deepest feelings and to people around us, we can add a new and useful dimension to our lives.

Although the experiences described above make sense in the light of what we know about various psychological processes, this does not eliminate the possibility that psychic abilities might be involved. Many people believe that experiences such as these indicate human capacities that go beyond the psychological processes discussed thus far. In fact, according to polls, about half of all Americans believe that some sort of psychic force exists[204] and about half claim they have undergone a psychic experience.[739]

A major question that faces us then, is: What is the evidence for paranormal factors in various kinds of experiences that are commonly called psychic? The answer to this question is important since, if paranormal factors are involved, then the psychological processes we have considered to this point can account only in part for transcendental experience. On the other hand, if the evidence for paranormal factors is weak or lacking, then these psychological mechanisms are probably of primary importance.

For many years, I have searched for believable evidence for paranormal phenomena. My motivation has been in part academic and in part personal. Personally, I am eager to find out about any human capacity that broadens our conception of ourselves. In my search, I have supervised research studies by students (these studies are reported in the sections that follow). I have tested psychics and, in fact, anyone who claimed to possess paranormal ability. I have even advertised in newspapers, offering rewards for any demonstration of paranormal phenomena. Unfortunately, this search has not produced any evidence for such abilities. However, my studies have been conducted on a small scale and cannot be considered at all definitive. Therefore, we will spend considerable time discussing studies conducted by other investigators, which claim to provide evidence for the paranormal.

The belief in psychic (or psi) phenomena usually entails a belief in the existence of a force in humans, and perhaps other organisms, which allows communication and influence in the absence of a physical agency. The belief that this psychic force involves physical energies not yet discovered is less common, and we will not discuss it further at this point.

A broad definition of psychic phenomena, which we will use, would encompass the following:

1. Extrasensory perception (ESP)—this refers to sensing an external event without the use of the ordinary sense organs. ESP includes telepathy (extrasensory perception between individuals), clairvoyance (direct extrasensory perception of an event), and precognition (extrasensory perception of a future event).

2. Psychokinesis—this refers to psychic influence over an object, without the use of physical contact or energies.

3. Spirit communication—this refers to contact with disembodied spirits. Experiences of this kind include possession states (the feeling of being possessed by a spirit), apparitions, hauntings and poltergeists (observable manifestations attributed to a spirit), and mediumship (communication with a purported spirit through an individual known as a medium). These spirits are commonly conceptualized as spirits of human beings who have died; however, such a spirit is sometimes thought to be that of a god or devil, or of a living animal or human being.

4. Miscellaneous experiences—we will also discuss several other experiences commonly conceived of in terms of psychic forces. These include psychic healing (healing through psychic power alone), fakirs (individuals who display psychic control of their bodily processes), water witching and related phenomena (locating groundwater, etc., through psychic means), auras (a "glow" around the body that is psychic in origin), and out-of-body experience (psychically leaving one's body).

Although we will utilize these categories, it should be realized that psychic influences are, by their definition, mysterious in operation and therefore difficult to conceptualize adequately. For example, J. B. Rhine, the "father of parapsychology," has said, "We have nothing on the record that we can, without hesitation and ambiguity, call evidence of telepathy. . . ."[551] By this Rhine means that there is no way to conceptualize telepathy that clearly distinguishes its effects from other psychic effects.

The first kind of evidence for psychic phenomena is, of course, that of personal experience. However, there are so many problems with such experience that even parapsychologists do not generally believe that spontaneous experience provides conclusive evidence for psychic phenomena.[723] The following case, which was thought by many at the time to be one of the most convincing demonstrations of spontaneous psychic experience on record, illustrates many of these problems.

According to his account of the incident, Judge Edmund Hornby awakened at about 1 A.M. one morning, startled to see a local editor and acquaintance, Hugh Nivens, in his bedroom. The two then carried on a brief conversation concerning a court case. Judge Hornby stated that he discovered the next morning that Nivens had died that morning at about 1 A.M. without having left his death-bed and that Nivens was found to have a copy of the court judgment in his possession that he could only have obtained from Judge Hornby during their early morning visit. Furthermore, Hornby stated that his wife, in bed beside him at the time, verified his account of the incident.[267]

Some time later, Frederick Balfour, an acquaintance of both men, became interested in the story, made some inquiries, and reported the following:

1. Sir Edmund says Lady Hornby was with him at the time, and subsequently awoke. I reply that no such person was in existence. Sir Edmund's second wife had died two years previously, and he did not marry again till three months *after* the event he relates.

2. Sir Edmund mentions an inquest on the body. I reply, on the authority of the coroner, that no inquest was ever held.

3. Sir Edmund's story turns on the judgment of a certain case, which was to be delivered next day, the 20th of January, 1875. There is no record of any such judgment in the *Supreme Court and Consular Gazette*, of which I am now editor.

4. Sir Edmund says the editor died at one in the morning. This is wholly inaccurate: he died between eight and nine A.M. after a good night's sleep.[30]

It is impossible to know why Judge Hornby's account is so inaccurate, but psychological processes such as the following, discussed in previous chapters, are possibilities:

1. Judge Hornby may have overheard a conversation concerning Nivens' death, which registered subliminally but not consciously and which expressed itself the evening following Nivens' death in the form of a vivid dream in which Nivens visited his bedside.

2. The day after his dream, Hornby may have been informed of Nivens' death, leading to the feeling that he had had a precognitive vision the night before.

3. Consciously or subconsciously, over time Judge Hornby may have modified his recollection to fit his notion that it was a paranormal experience.

Knowledge of such psychological factors often spells the difference between interpreting an experience as paranormal, on the one hand, or gaining awareness of the operation of one's own psychological functioning, on the other hand. For example, Sigmund Freud relates the following experience of one of his colleagues, A. A. Brill:

While engrossed in conversation during our customary Sunday evening dinner at one of the New York restaurants, I suddenly stopped and irrelevantly remarked to my wife, "I wonder how Dr. R is doing in Pittsburgh." She looked at me much astonished and said: "Why, that is exactly what I have been thinking for the last few seconds! Either you have transferred this thought to me or I have transferred it to you. How can you otherwise explain this strange phenomenon?" I had to admit that I could offer no solution. Our conversation throughout the dinner showed not the remotest association to Dr. R, nor, so far as our memories went, had we heard or spoken of him for some time. Being a skeptic, I refused to admit that there was anything mysterious about it, although inwardly I felt quite uncertain. To be frank, I was somewhat mystified.

But we did not remain very long in this state of mind, for on looking toward the cloakroom we were surprised to see Dr. R. Though closer inspection showed our mistake, we were both struck by the remarkable resemblance of this stranger to Dr. R. From the position of the cloakroom we were forced to conclude that this stranger had passed our table. Absorbed in our conversation, we had not noticed him consciously, but the visual image had stirred up the association of his double, Dr. R.[227]

If spontaneous experience does not provide definitive evidence for psychic phenomena, there are still hundreds of experiments that claim to provide just such evidence. At the same time, however, many critiques of these experiments have been written; the most thorough is by C. E. M. Hansel[279] and is recommended to the interested reader. Of the criticisms raised, the four that seem most crucial are: 1. the possibility that the sensing of subtle sensory cues creates the appearance of psychic ability, 2. the possibility that favorable outcomes are a result of chance and coincidence, 3. the possibility of fraud, and 4. the failure of many researchers to obtain results that support the psi hypothesis. Let us consider these criticisms in detail.

1. First, let us discuss how the sensing of subtle sensory cues might create the appearance of psychic ability.

That sensory cues can convey information without the awareness of the individuals involved has already been discussed. Robert Rosenthal has conducted a number of studies that show how easily information can be conveyed in this way. In fact, he describes the ". . . case of unintended interpersonal influence once-removed. . . . The methodological implications . . . are clear. Simply not telling our research assistants what to expect from a given subject . . . does not insure real blindness [lack of information transfer]. In some subtle way, by tone and/or gesture, experimenters may unintentionally overinform their research assistants."[572] In other words, information sometimes may be transmitted from one person to another (for example, from experimenter to subject) through an intermediate person (a research assistant), none of the individuals involved being aware of the communication thus conveyed! Such communications, of course, can create the appearance of psi in the absence of any psi effect.

One would expect, therefore, that ESP investigators routinely would design experiments that prevented the transmission of sensory cues. Unfortunately, this is not always the case. For example, a study conducted by J. G. Pratt and J. L. Woodruff is often cited as providing strong evidence for clairvoyance.[519] J. B. Rhine states:

"Through the succeeding years a number of other experiments followed in which the standards of control required for verification were maintained. Perhaps the most elaborately controlled of these was that published by Pratt and Woodruff. . . . the scoring rate was highly significant and chance as well as all other conceivable hypotheses were ruled out, leaving only the hypothesis of ESP."[554] However, in this study, the experimenter and subject were seated at the same table with only a barrier to separate them, while the experimenter handled the stimulus cards. It is impossible to know, of course, whether subtle sensory cues in fact were communicated in this study, but reanalyses of the data reveal peculiarities that support the hypothesis that such communication did occur.[436]

2. Next, let us consider how favorable outcomes in psi research might arise from chance and coincidence.

Studies of psi typically depend on statistical analyses to reveal greater-than-chance results, which often are not evident at first inspection. With such elusive effects, extreme care must be exercised to avoid selection or manipulation of data that might produce the appearance of psi in the absence of any real psi effects.[479]

A simple example will help to illustrate. Let us say that you would like to see if the flip of a coin—heads or tails—can be communicated telepathically. You station two people in separate locations and have one subject attempt to communicate the outcome of each flip of a coin to the other subject. You know that the chance of guessing one flip correctly is one-half, the chance of guessing two flips in a row correctly is one-fourth, of guessing three flips in a row correctly is one-eighth, and so on. Further, you assume that the chance of guessing five flips correctly, which is one-thirty-second, or approximately three percent, is so small that, if your subject correctly identifies five flips in a row, you will consider this tentative evidence for telepathy.

Now let us consider the many ways in which, without realizing it, you could "pyramid the probabilities" and produce the appearance of psi even though psi is not operating.

First, you might modify conditions somewhat as you go along to streamline the experiment and to be more conducive to the operation of telepathy. You may run a series of trials of five flips each until, after a period of trying out various arrangements, you finally obtain some perfect trials of five correct identifications.

Second, if your experiment is not working out, you may decide that your subject is telepathically sensing the *next* flip or the *prior* flip. So you test alternative hypotheses such as these until you find one that yields a significant result.

Third, you may decide that your subject actually does better at making *incorrect* identifications (called psi-missing), so you analyze the data for this effect.

Fourth, you may decide that your initial subjects are not sufficiently telepathic, so you try many pairs of subjects until you find a pair that produces above-chance results.

Fifth, you may decide that your experiment is a failure and therefore decide not to publish your findings. Or, if you submit your experimental failure for publication in a parapsychology journal, the journal editor may decide not to publish it because it is a "failure."

Each of these procedures has the effect of selecting results that support the notion of psi, while rejecting negative results. In this fashion, of course, purely chance findings can result in what appears to be support for psi.

You may feel that parapsychologists are aware of these difficulties and of how to guard against them. But these problems can still be found in parapsychological research. For example, J. B. Rhine, for many years editor of one of the two leading American parapsychological journals, has had a long-standing editorial policy of refusing to publish research articles that report negative findings.[553] The British parapsychologist Donald West summarizes the situation this way: ". . . it is difficult to disprove the theory that the positive scores are mere flukes of chance counterbalanced by the large numbers of tests that yield null results."[725]

3. Now let us see how fraud can produce what appears to be evidence for psi.

Fraud is by no means a new thing in science.[296, 375, 721] However, the field of parapsychology seems to have had more than its share of fraud and accusations of fraud.[279]

Fraud, of course, can be committed by either the investigators or their subjects. Although it may seem an easy matter to prevent fraud on the part of subjects, the following account by the psychologist George Estabrooks points up how difficult this can be:

... I was once running a series of telepathic experiments with playing cards under conditions which I would have sworn were fraud-proof. The mind reader sat in one room and the agent or the individual whose mind was to be read was seated in another. The cards were shuffled after each guess and the pack cut with a knife so as to make sure of a chance selection only. The agent then concentrated on the card chosen and tried to force the mind reader in the next room to name the card. The signals that a card had been chosen were given by a clockwork apparatus which sounded an electric telegraph key. These signals came at certain definite intervals and were never interfered with in any way. I was always present with the agent—the sender—during the entire experiment.

... One particular pair [of subjects] came and engaged in the experiment. Next day this same pair returned and boldly announced that they could make the fraud-proof conditions look ludicrous. They were told they were talking nonsense, when they offered to bet the price of a supper that they could demonstrate, so we set to work.

... To my utter consternation the mind reader in the next room ... guessed the color of the cards—red or black—correctly the entire fifty-two times....

I begged for two days in which to try and solve the puzzle but could get nowhere.... Then bribery to the extent of two theater tickets revealed the secret. So simple as to be almost ridiculous, it had nevertheless been extremely effective.

... There are only two colors on the regular playing cards, red and black.... When the cards came up as expected ... no signal of any kind passed between the two. That meant that the receiver was to [mark down a] black card if it were an even number in the series of fifty-two ... and a red card if an odd number....

But that left, of course, those times when the cards did not come out this way. It was simple. The rooms adjoined each other and in spite of the double doors between them, any sound such as a cough, a voice or the scraping of a chair could be clearly heard. So when the cards did not come up as they had agreed to expect—say a black card came up on the thirteenth guess—the sender simply made some noise. He would clear his voice, or shift his chair or do anything to break the silence, but always in a perfectly natural manner so as not to attract attention. The hoax was an absolute success.[190]

If fraud committed by subjects is a potential danger, fraud on the part of investigators is also. For example, recent evidence has cast doubts on studies by the British parapsychologists S. G. Soal and K. M. Goldney, which have generally been considered the most definitive research in support of psi ever conducted.[637] Of several charges, the most serious is that the sequence of targets was tampered with and when these ". . . trials are discounted the scoring rate in the record sheets concerned falls to chance levels, leaving an insignificant 'ESP' effect."[422]

In the United States, psi researchers were recently scandalized by the detection of Walter Levy, who succeeded J. B. Rhine as head of the Institute of Parapsychology, in the act of falsifying data. Levy subsequently confessed and resigned his position.[525]

And in India, evidence has come to light which strongly suggests the tampering with data by H. N. Banerjee, director of the Seth Sohan Lal Memorial Institute of Parapsychology.[532]

In addition to these examples, there are more than a dozen lesser-known cases for which there is relatively strong evidence of fraud in parapsychological research.[550]

4. Finally, let us discuss the problem of adequate replication in psi research.

There is little question that the problems discussed above have plagued studies of psychic phenomena and raise the possibility that, taken together, they might account for the seeming "successes" that parapsychologists point to. How, then, can we avoid accepting questionable findings as legitimate?

Because such problems are characteristic of scientific inquiry in general, sciences have adopted the policy of replication as the surest means of separating legitimate findings from spurious ones. A replication is the duplication of a study by different researchers, on the principle that methodological errors vary considerably from researcher to researcher, whereas the phenomenon being studied should manifest itself no matter where it is studied. If other researchers consistently obtain the same result, this is a good indication that it is probably not a consequence of methodological error. In the case of psi research, in particular, where the potential effects are so subtle and the potential errors so serious, the question of adequate replication becomes crucial. We will examine this issue in the next section.

Extrasensory Perception and Psychokinesis

Independent replication is the best basis for judgement.[552]

J. B. RHINE

Let us consider some of the often-cited findings in parapsychological research and see if any have proved consistently replicable.

1. Of all potential psychic phenomena, telepathy is considered by many to be the most plausible. Consequently, a great deal of attention has focused on the possibility of psychic communication between individuals.

The best known of these experiments were carried out by J. B. Rhine and his associates. Soon after the publication of Rhine's first book *Extrasensory Perception*[548] in 1934, many other investigators attempted to replicate his findings. Although some replications succeeded, others involving hundreds of subjects and hundreds of thousands of trials, failed.[279] Likewise, other extensive series of studies carried out over a period of years and involving hundreds of experiments have failed to find any evidence for telepathy.[134, 658]

A more recent series of studies of great interest are the dream-telepathy tests done at the Maimonides Medical Center in New York, in which, it is claimed, dreams are influenced telepathically.[695] However, some other investigators have failed to obtain similar results.[161, 247] One unsuccessful replication used a subject who was "successful" in the Maimonides studies;[54] another was conducted by the Maimonides investigators themselves.[219]

2. Next to telepathy, clairvoyance is probably the most believable potential psi ability, and many studies have investigated the possibility that people can psychically detect the occurrence of a distant event. Studies seeking to relate clairvoyance ability to personality traits have been particularly popular. The best known, the "sheep-goat" study by Gertrude Schmeidler, claimed that believers in ESP (called "sheep") had more psi ability than nonbelievers (called "goats").[595] However, this study has given rise to many replication failures.[497] In addition, a reanalysis of Schmeidler's original study has shown her results to be nonsignificant.[96]

3. To many people, precognition seems an even less likely possibility than telepathy or clairvoyance. Yet some studies claim support for the ability of humans to predict a future event concerning which they have no ordinary knowledge. Here, research using random-generating machines to generate the targets to be guessed is particularly interesting, since such machines should reduce the element of human error. Helmut Schmidt has published perhaps

the best known and most successful of these studies.[598] Once again, however, a number of replication attempts have failed to confirm his findings in support of precognition.[53, 681]

4. Psychokinesis refers to influencing an object by psychic means. Here again, Schmidt has claimed positive results using his random generator.[599] In this case, a large number of replications of Schmidt's work have been conducted, perhaps because of the relative ease of testing psychokinesis with a machine. According to one survey, researchers other than Schmidt have published twenty articles reporting replication attempts; of these, significant results were obtained in fourteen.[306] This is certainly an encouraging replication count, even if not conclusive, and Schmidt's studies seem to provide some of the strongest support for psi.

Another interesting study of psychokinesis involves supposed psychic effects on a thermistor (a temperature measuring device).[596] Here again there are failures to replicate, including an attempt by the original investigator.[513, 597] In addition, there is evidence that the methodology of the original study was flawed.[447]

Martin Gardner points out that if psychokinesis existed, one would expect players to be able to influence the outcome of gambling games; however, in Chicago, where a game called "26" has been played for decades in bars and cabarets, the ". . . tally sheets, year after year, show precisely the percentage of house take allowed by the laws of chance."[237]

PSYCHOKINESIS

Finally, a variety of psychic abilities are said to be reflected in a series of studies known as "remote viewing," in which subjects are reported to demonstrate routinely a high level of psychic functioning. As conducted by Russell Targ and Harold Puthoff at Stanford Research Institute in California, these studies incorporate a number of design features—including using as targets natural environments chosen from a large target pool, encouraging subjects to use creative imagery when trying to picture the target, and taking subjects to see the target after every trial.[667, 668] Unfortunately, there have been serious criticisms of these studies.[420] Also, the replication count to this date is only marginally encouraging. Of eleven replication accounts by other investigators of which I am aware, evidently six[69, 70, 171, 286, 705, 735] have succeeded while five[9, 357, 537, 638, 671] have failed. In addition, a number of my own students have attempted to replicate Targ and Puthoff's work—without success.

In summary, I have been unable to find any study claiming support for psi that has proved consistently replicable. It is true that there are encouraging replication counts—for example, for Schmidt's random-generating machine studies. Hopefully, as work proceeds, the critical conditions for psi functioning will become clear so that replications will routinely succeed; at that point, explanations in terms of nonpsychic processes would no longer be tenable.

When confronted by the generally poor record of replication attempts in psi research, parapsychologists often admit that this constitutes a real barrier to the general acceptance of psi.[470] At the same time, various claims are sometimes put forward to account for such failures. Let us now consider these claims and their validity.

1. Subjects with demonstrable psi ability are few and far between, it is claimed, and experimenters who fail to get results probably are testing poor subjects. However, many psychological abilities—for example, the ability to be a good hypnotic subject—are found in only a few individuals; yet this does not prevent experimenters from locating promising subjects. Many studies that have failed to find evidence for psi have tested hundreds of people in a futile attempt to locate a few promising subjects. A separate but important point is that, if psychic ability is this rare, it is probably not a factor in the vast majority of experiences that people call psychic.

2. Subjects who score well initially on tests of psi will eventually show a

drop-off in scoring, it is claimed, since psychic ability is unpredictable and easily extinguished. This "decline effect" means that replications using subjects who have done well previously may not succeed. The problem is that decline effects would also result if chance flukes or erratic methodological errors were responsible for the initial positive results.

3. Psychic ability is subtle and temperamental, it is claimed, and replications conducted by experimenters who are skeptical, using experimental conditions that are sterile and artificial, are likely to fail. Again, this problem is not unique to psi research; many hypnotic subects, for example, are greatly affected by the emotional atmosphere of an experiment, and yet hypnotic effects are generally replicable. Thus the problem is a real one, potentially, but this hardly accounts for the common failure of parapsychologists themselves to replicate positive findings. Of course, if psi is really this tenuous, then, if it exists, it is probably a somewhat minor effect.

Of course, if these are indeed real problems, then that fact needs to be accounted for in the experimental procedure. In other words, the procedure should specify how to select high scoring subjects, how to limit or arrange testing of subjects to guard against fatigue or extinction of the response, and how to establish a conducive laboratory environment.

In general, there seems to be no good reason to excuse the field of parapsychology from the requirement of demonstrating replicability of results. Such replicability has not yet been demonstrated. As the parapsychologist John Beloff says: ". . . parapsychology . . . aspires to the status of the established sciences. . . . But to date it is an unsuccessful science, for no experiment showing the clear existence of the paranormal has been consistently repeated by other investigators in other laboratories with the same results. Often the same investigators cannot replicate their own experiments."[52] And Gardner Murphy, also a parapsychologist, acknowledges ". . . the failure of psychical research to produce any truly repeatable experiment. . . ."[469]

Concerning the demand for replicability, parapsychologists sometimes complain that the standards of proof demanded for parapsychological studies are higher than for ordinary psychological studies. They rightfully point out that research in many areas of psychology has been beset by the same problems that have plagued parapsychology—that is, problems of unintentional cueing of subjects, of biased selection of results, of fraud, and of inadequate replication.[307] However, it is also true that we should demand *more* from studies that claim to demonstrate paranormal or other processes that run counter to much of our experience.[262, 745] Donald West, the parapsychologist, puts it this way: ". . . parapsychologists need to be ultra-cautious, and critics need to be ultra-skeptical, because of the a priori improbability of the phenomena in question. . . ."[727]

It has been said that the Russians "are ahead of us" in parapsychological research and that they have come up with more definitive proof of psi than we have. Although publications such as *Psychic Discoveries Behind the Iron Curtain*[493] have conveyed this impression, other information refutes it. For example, perhaps the best-known work in parapsychology in Russia has been done by L. L. Vasiliev.[706] Yet, after his major studies in telepathy were completed, his laboratory staff made the following statement: "We have not established whether telepathy exists. We want to find out. Then we can say yes or no."[658] And J. B. Rhine commented as follows on Russian psi research in general: "I haven't heard of well-designed psi research in Russia in the last 30 years. And we've had lots of contact with researchers behind the Iron Curtain."[272]

Let us see how a noted parapsychologist, Donald West, summarizes the status of parapsychological research. Although his views are not necessarily typical, they do furnish an insight into the doubts of some researchers in this area of study.

> First, the [psi] phenomena are sporadic and uncontrollable. Except in an immediate and limited sense, experiments are not repeatable at will. Second, the phenomena often seem to retreat before too close an inquiry. Results that seem indisputable at first dwindle away to nothing when other investigators try to follow them up. Third, the nature of the phenomenon tends to change from one research to the next. For example, no one is quite sure of the limits of ESP as regards time and distance because different investigators have reported contradictory findings. . . .
>
> . . . In point of fact, all kinds of ideas have been tried out to try to bring out a reliable and repeatable ESP effect. Targets with emotional overtones, subliminal targets, conditioned responses, unconscious responses picked up on lie detectors, the use of altered states of consciousness in hypnosis, dreams and drugged conditions, the use of animals as subjects. . . . Many of these ideas appeared at first to yield promising results, but every one has tended to fade into oblivion as success dwindled with repetition.[727]

[West comments elsewhere] I have been present on occasions when persons who have worked in the field of parapsychology for years have seriously discussed whether the whole of the evidence for extrasensory perception might not be a worthless conglomeration of fraud and fallacy.[725]

In sum, it seems that we do not yet have an adequate demonstration of the existence of psychic ability. The possibility of methodological errors is all too real and the replications all too few. As a group of parapsychologists states: "[Parapsychologists] do not claim that their results compel belief in ESP, only that the results compel attention to the strong possibility of ESP."[652] Although the word "strong" seems a bit strong, this statement may be taken as a reasonable position on the question of psychic abilities.

On the other hand, it is certainly true, as C. E. M. Hansel says, that "While all the years of research into ESP have failed to provide a clear demonstration for its existence, this does not necessarily imply that it does not exist."[279]

There is no question that people have experiences that *seem* to be psychic. At present, it seems likely that these experiences usually arise from subconscious mechanisms such as we discussed in earlier chapters. There is little question that we have the capacity to be exquisitely sensitive to the feelings and thoughts of others, to tap latent memories, to influence events in many subtle ways, and to "intuit" the future to some extent. Developing these capacities allows us to deal more effectively with the world around us. It is not necessary to mystify such experiences in order to benefit from them.

However, if you know individuals who feel they are psychic, or if you yourself feel you have psychic abilities, you may want to run some tests under controlled conditions. You can start with some studies based on the following suggestions:

1. Since it is not easy to distinguish between the postulated effects of various forms of psi phenomena, you might begin with a test for general ESP ability that does not distinguish between the various forms of ESP and that also allows for the possibility of psychokinesis. Such a test has the potential advantage of revealing the existence of any kind of psi ability.

2. You will need to decide what kind of "target" you wish to use, for example, a coin (heads or tails), a regular deck of cards (four suits of thirteen cards each), an ESP card deck (twenty five cards with five cards each of circle, cross, square, star, and wavy lines), or a die (one to six dots on each of six sides). Care must be taken with coins and dice in particular to insure that they are not biased because of the way they are tossed or because of uneven weight. These common targets are listed only for the sake of simplicity. Many people feel that it is better to use a more interesting and varied set of stumuli, which you should feel free to do as long as they are different enough so that they cannot be confused with one another.

3. There are many possible procedures for testing general psi ability. Since many parapsychologists believe that a positive psychological atmosphere facilitates psi, it is best to choose a procedure that will foster confidence and enthusiasm in your subjects. One test requires a "sender" and a "receiver" who are located a sufficient distance apart so that no sensory cues can be communicated between them. The sender selects the first target by a random process (for example, by taking the top card from a thoroughly shuffled deck of cards) and attempts to send the image of the card to the receiver who attempts to "sense" the image being sent. At a prearranged signal (for example, at a certain time or at the sound of a bell rung by the receiver), both sender and receiver record their corresponding images. The sender then selects the second target, and the procedure is repeated for as many trials as previously decided on. This test allows for the operation of telepathy (the receiver senses the images of the targets as conveyed by the sender), clairvoyance (the receiver senses the target cards directly), precognition (the receiver senses the target values as they will appear in their final recorded form), and psychokinesis (the receiver influences the cards so that they are arranged in a certain order).

4. The results of such a test of psi ability will be two records of the target stimuli as recorded by sender and receiver. A certain number of hits, of course, will occur by chance: in the case of a coin, about 50 percent of the values should match; in the case of a deck of cards of four suits, about 25 percent should match, and so on. The question is, is the number of hits that you obtain sufficiently different from chance that it implies the existence of

		10	25	50	100	200
NUMBER OF TARGET VALUES	2	9	18	32	59	113
	3	7	13	23	42	79
	4	6	11	19	33	61
	5	5	9	16	28	50
	6	5	8	14	24	43

Figure 19. Probability table—number of hits required to reach 5 percent significance level.

psi? One common standard is: if the number of hits you obtain (or more) would be expected to occur by chance less than five percent of the time, it is unlikely that chance was responsible. With the help of Figure 19, you can determine the minimum number of hits required to attain this five percent significance level.[245] You will notice that the number of hits required differs for various kinds of targets (a coin has two values—heads and tails, a regular deck of cards has four suits or values, etc.) and for various numbers of trials. Of course, a greater number of trials constitutes a greater amount of evidence, but this must be balanced against the problem of fatiguing your subjects. For example, let us say you are using regular playing cards with four suits or values (spades, clubs, hearts, and diamonds) and you want to run 100 trials. For this, you can use two decks and remove one card of each suit from one of the decks to yield 100 cards total. According to Figure 19, 33 hits (suit correctly identified, or eight more than the 25 matches expected by chance, are necessary in order to reach the five percent level of significance.

If you have good success with tests of the sort described here, you should make sure that the methodological problems discussed earlier are not a factor. In addition, if you wish to develop more sophisticated methodology, you can obtain one of the books that summarizes basic experiments in parapsychology.[429, 558] You may also find it helpful to look through the basic journals in the field for ideas for experimentation: the *Journal of Parapsychology,* the *Journal of the American Society for Psychical Research,* and the *Journal of the Society for Psychical Research.*

Psychic Animals and Plants

You believe that easily which you hope for earnestly.[689]

TERENCE

Some people believe that psychic ability is a characteristic of a wide variety of animals—not just humans—and they cite numerous experiences in support of their belief. For instance, what would you conclude from the following account? "A . . . parapsychologist said that his wife, as a little girl, had a pigeon for a pet. She remembered that the pigeon had a way of finding her wherever she might be. This happened so often and under such circumstances that it did not seem possible that the pigeon was locating its owner by sight or any other ordinary sensory means. In other words, the surprising feat could only be explained by those who observed the behavior as ESP."[518]

Would you accept this experience as a demonstration of the psychic ability in animals? Or do you see the possibility that some of the processes discussed in previous chapters are important in animal, as well as human, experience? In this account, for example, it is possible that the pigeon had an acute sense of hearing, which enabled it to know where the little girl was in the house.

And what would you say about the following example: "A . . . friend told me that he once had a pet cat that would go and wait just inside the door several minutes before he reached home. He said that the members of the family came to know that the cat's behavior meant that he would be home within a few minutes, and that this did not depend upon his coming at the usual time."[518]

Here again, an acute sense of hearing might be involved. Or the cat may have found a vantage point from which it could spot its master while he was still several blocks away.

We should remember that nonhuman animals sometimes display astonishing abilities and that some of these abilities surpass our own. Not only can many animals detect stimuli outside of the range of our own senses, but also some animals can detect forms of energy—magnetic fields, for example—to which we seem to be largely insensitive.[520] And the account in the last chapter of Clever Hans, the "telepathic" horse which was able to sense subtle cues "leaked" by his questioners, indicates that animals can learn to perceive weak stimuli that untrained humans cannot detect.

As with humans, however, the issue of psychic abilities in animals cannot be settled by anecdotal accounts. Furthermore, as with human subjects, experiments with animals must be conducted with proper controls. For example, J. B. Rhine once instituted a study[555] of a horse named Lady Wonder, which appeared to many observers to be guided by cues similar to those used by Clever Hans.[120] Rhine pronounced Lady Wonder telepathic after instituting such "controls" as the following: ". . . there was no reasonable hypothesis of guidance left alternative to that of telepathy. . . . Our own eyes were screened from view and our bodies held as motionless as possible."[549] In view of the fact that Pfungst, who investigated Clever Hans, found that he could not avoid giving involuntary body cues, this hardly seems an adequate control!

After reviewing studies of psychic abilities in animals up to 1970, parapsychologist Robert Morris concluded: "None of the studies . . . can stand alone as conclusive evidence for psi in animals. In each case, either the design was lacking or the results

PSYCHIC ANIMALS

obtained were not sufficiently clear-cut."[458] In a later review, which included research up to 1977, Morris still felt the evidence to be somewhat lacking, stating that "The experimental evidence for psi in animals is encouraging but still weak."[459]

With the publication of *The Secret Life of Plants*,[686] the belief that plants possess psychic capacities has gained in popularity. The studies exciting the most interest were those conducted by Cleve Backster, a lie-detector expert whose major study contended that philodendron plants responded electrically ("emotionally?") to the killing of brine shrimp in another room.[25] With the publication of Backster's study, other experiments attempted to replicate his findings. To this date, all controlled experiments that I know of that have attempted to replicate this, or any of Backster's findings, have failed.[308, 344, 373, 601] At the same time, many of these investigators have pointed out flaws in Backster's procedure. This does not deny, of course, that plants exhibit certain forms of electrical response.[236] However, to this point, it has not been demonstrated that plants have "feelings," much less any kind of psychic capacities.

Other studies of potential psi in plants that have elicited considerable interest are those by Bernard Grad.[250, 251] Grad wanted to determine if the psychic influence of a reputed psychic healer, Oskar Estebany, would facilitate plant growth, in particular the growth of barley seeds. Thus, Estebany treated, by "laying on of hands," containers of water that were used to water the plants. In any experiment, of course, it is essential that the only difference between the experimental and control conditions is the stimulus (in this case, the "psychic energy" of the healer), the effect of which you want to measure. Although the growth of the seeds treated by Estebany seemed to be enhanced, Grad failed to provide the same physical conditions for the control plants (of temperature, agitation, etc.) that were created by the "laying on of hands" treatment by the healer. In other words, the enhanced growth may have been due to the purely physical differences in the treatment of the plants.

Students of mine have conducted a variety of studies of potential psychic sensitivity in plants; none has produced evidence in support of this notion.

In summary, there seem to be no well-replicated studies that support the belief that animals or plants possess psychic capacities of any kind. The belief that a pet or a house plant is "tuned in" to you psychically, while it may be comforting to lonely people in an alienated society, is probably more a matter of faith than a matter of fact.

Prophecy

Beware of false prophets.

Prophecy refers to the ability to foresee events that occur in the somewhat distant future. Let us consider, as examples, two prophetic dreams and see if we can learn from them anything about our potential to foretell the future.

> . . . a girl in California . . . dreamed she was walking along the street of what she knew to be a small western town. She says, "The sidewalk was of boards and the buildings overhead extended out to form a wooden roof over it. I was carrying what seemed to be a small overnight case and I knew the name of the town was 'Tomb—' "
>
> When a [future] job materialized, this girl, with two companions, was traveling through several southwestern states modeling dresses. They stopped at Tombstone, Arizona, for dinner one night and she walked down wooden sidewalks, as she says "carrying the model's inevitable makeup box, which was about the size of a small overnight case," as in the dream.[556]

In this example, if the dreamer had seen her dream as a reflection of her current state of mind, she might have realized that she had a desire to visit Tombstone, Arizona. The same wanderlust may have prompted her to accept a job which took her around the Southwest. She could then manage to visit Tombstone, among other places. Her carrying an overnight or makeup case in real life as well as in her dream may only indicate that her dreams reflect her real-life habits.

Now consider a second example:

> [A six-year-old boy] began to have nightmarish dreams: . . . he thought he "fell in a hole." For three weeks he wakened nearly every night, sweating and screaming in fright.
>
> Then, his mother says, "One day he was playing in our neighbor's yard where there was still snow on the ground. I heard terrible screams coming from what sounded like a long way off. I hurried in

the direction of my neighbor's basement. The screams sounded almost as if coming from underground. Then I saw the hole of an old septic tank with rotted cover, and Steve up to his waist in the water and sinking rapidly. But my neighbor and I got him out, though the water was up to his shoulders before we finally rescued him."[556]

In this example we see the importance of paying attention to seemingly prophetic dreams. Not all such dreams will come true, of course, but it is wise to attempt to determine what underlies the dream. In this case, if the mother had questioned the boy about his dreams, she might have learned that he had been playing with the neighbor children around the old septic tank and that he was afraid of falling in. She then might have been able to prevent what turned out to be a near tragedy.

But can people accurately foresee future, otherwise unexpected, events with which they have no connection? In other words, is there such a thing as a psychic "gift of prophecy"? There are many prophets in the news who claim to be able to do just that. But there are also a multitude of problems involved in attempting to evaluate such prophecies (we discussed many of these problems in the section on spontaneous psychic experience). One particular problem is that it is usually impossible to determine the probabilities of the occurrence of future events, in the light of which the prophecy might be evaluated. That is, if a prophet predicts an event that can be reasonably expected to occur on the basis of current knowledge, the prophecy is not particularly good evidence for precognition. On the other hand, a prophet who foretells events that are totally unexpected is worth listening to. Keeping this and other difficulties associated with spontaneous events in mind, let us consider some prophets who are currently popular.

1. Nostradamus (Michel de Notredame) was a medical doctor and prophet in sixteenth-century France. He composed a set of quatrains, which, because of their allusions to future events, are believed by many to be significant prophecies. Here are two examples from the first set of prophecies:

Quatrain 22—
That which shall live shall leave no direction,
Its destruction and death will come by strategem,
Autun, Chalons, Langres, and from both sides,
The war and ice shall do great harm.[562]

Quatrain 27—
Underneath the cord, Guien struck from the sky,
Near where is hid a great treasure,
Which has been many years a gathering,
Being found, he shall die, the eye put out by a spring.[562]

Before reading further, see if you can determine what events these quatrains predict.

Now compare your conclusions with those of Henry Roberts, author of a popular book on Nostradamus. Roberts says that Quatrain 22 is "a forecast of the use of supersonic weapons, traveling in the near absolute zero temperature above the stratosphere," and that Quatrain 27 means "paratroopers alight near the Nazi's plunder hoard and, captured, they are executed."[562]

If you disagree with Roberts, perhaps you are not sufficiently "sensitive" to Nostradamus' meaning. A fairer test might be to compare two experts on Nostradamus. A comparison of Henry Roberts with another author of a popular book on Nostradamus, Erika Cheetham, yields interesting interpretations, all from the first set of quatrains.

Quatrain 9—
ROBERTS: "A remarkably prophetic description of the role of Emperor Haile Selassie, in World War II. . . ."[562]
CHEETHAM: "Lines 1–2 . . . refer . . . to Henri IV. The man who troubles him from the East is the Duke of Parma. . . . Lines 3–4 most probably refer to the seige of Malta in 1565. . . ."[114]

Quatrain 26—
ROBERTS: "The taking over of Czechoslovakia by Hitler, the resignation of President Benes, the dissensions over the matter between France and England and the dire warning of the consequences of this betrayal, are all remarkably outlined in this prophecy."[562]
CHEETHAM: "The first three lines here may apply to the assassinations of the two Kennedy brothers."[114]

Quatrain 29—
ROBERTS: "A clear account of the D-Day invasion of the Normandy beaches, with an exact description of the amphibious tanks and ducks employed by the Allies."[562]

CHEETHAM: "This is a perfect description of a Polaris ballistic missile. . . ."[114]

In comparing the conflicting interpretations of the quatrains, it is apparent that Roberts and Cheetham are projecting into them meanings that exist in their own minds, which leads them to think that Nostradamus had great precognitive ability. In general, there seems to be no evidence that Nostradamus was a gifted prophet.

2. Edgar Cayce was a psychic who became known, in the 1930s and 1940s, for his readings given in a trance state. Cayce gave various kinds of readings, including many dealing with medical diagnosis and treatment, as well as with "reincarnations." However, it seems that no controlled study of Cayce's purported psychic abilities was ever conducted during his lifetime, and only his readings on prophecy can be evaluated at this time. According to Jess Stearn, author of the best-selling *Edgar Cayce—The Sleeping Prophet,* Cayce was ". . . perhaps, [the] most fantastically gifted prophet of all time! . . . [whose] batting average on predictions was incredibly high, close to one hundred percent."[645] So an examination of Cayce's prophecies should be worthwhile.

One of my students conducted a study of Cayce's prophecies by reading through all published material on Cayce that might contain any of his prophecies. My student compiled the prophecies concerning events prior to the time of his study in 1976, including only prophecies that were specific enough to evaluate and also not in the realm of general knowledge. For example, Cayce's prediction, in 1941, that "In the next few years, lands will appear in the Atlantic as well as in the Pacific"[112] was not included in the analysis, since it is known that volcanic and other geological mechanisms frequently create small new land masses. The prophecies included for analysis are listed below.

In 1932, Cayce spoke of ". . . the great catastrophe that's coming to the world in '36, in the form of the breaking up of many powers that now exist as factors in the world affairs. . . ." In particular, the powers that would be broken up by 1936 were ". . . Russia, U.S., Japan, and England or United Kingdom."[107] In addition, Cayce predicted that "The wars, the upheavals in the interior of the earth, and the shifting of the earth by the change in the axis as respecting the portions from the polaris center"[645] would occur in 1936.

Also in 1932, Cayce predicted the discovery of ". . . those forces in nature as make for iron to swim. Stone floats in the air in the same manner. This will be discovered in '58."[107]

The next year, Cayce predicted that ". . . that which is at present termed the death ray—or the super cosmic ray—that which many are seeking, which will give their lives much, from the stratosphere—or cosmic rays—that will be found in the next twenty-five years."[645]

Also in 1933, Cayce prophesied regarding Adolph Hitler that ". . . few does power not destroy. Yet this man unless there is material change will survive even that."[645]

In 1940, Cayce predicted ". . . Atlantis [the lost island civilization postulated by many occultists] to rise again—expect it in '68 or '69"[112] And a year later, Cayce predicted that "In the next few years . . . what is the coast line now of many a land will be bed of the ocean. Even many of the battlefields of the present will be ocean, will be the seas, the bays, the lands over which the new order will carry on their trade as one with another." In particular, Cayce predicted that ". . . much sooner [than another generation]," which works out to be sometime before 1976, ". . . the southern portions of Carolina, Georgia, these will disappear."[112]

Also in 1941, Cayce predicted that ". . . the new order of peace is to be established in '44 or '45."[107]

Then, in 1943, Cayce predicted that ". . . rule in the next twenty-five years in China is to grow towards the Christian faith . . . "and that China's leadership would tend towards "more of the democratic."[107]

To summarize Cayce's specific predictions: Russia, the United States, Japan, and England or the United Kindgom would be broken up by 1936; war and a shifting of the earth's axis would also occur in 1936; a force to make iron swim and stone float would be discovered in 1958; a death ray would be discovered before 1958; Hitler would not be destroyed by the exercise of power; Atlantis would rise again in 1968 or 1969; by the mid-1970s, many lands, including the southern portions of Carolina and Georgia, would disappear; peace would be established in 1944 or 1945; and, from 1943 to 1968, rule in China would become more Christian and democratic.

As far as we could determine, the only prophecy that was

fulfilled was the prediction that peace would be established in 1944 or 1945. However, two others deserve additional comment. First, the death ray that Cayce predicted would be discovered before 1958 might seem to refer to lasers. However, the first crude laser, which was far from being useful as a weapon, was not constructed until 1960, although lasers had been postulated theoretically long before Cayce made his prediction. The second prophecy that deserves comment is that China would become more democratic between 1943 and 1968. Although some would claim that this is so, others would dispute it.

In view of Edgar Cayce's extremely poor batting average for his prophecies that can be followed up, there seems little reason to regard him as a great prophet.

3. Criswell, although less well known than Edgar Cayce, has a considerable following who read his newspaper columns, purchase his books on prophecy, and watch his television appearances. One of my students researched his prophecies listed in his book, *Criswell Predicts*, to see if they lived up to the book's declaration that "87% of Criswell's predictions have come true."[139] Fifty-two events that Criswell predicted would occur in the ten year period following the book's publication—that is, 1969 through 1978—were judged sufficiently specific to follow up and outside the realm of general knowledge. Of these, *one* came true! It seems obvious that, whatever talents Criswell may possess, prophecy is not one of them.

4. Jeane Dixon is probably the best-known living prophet in America. In particular, her prediction of John Kennedy's assassination probably has done more than anything else to establish her in the public eye. However, a closer look at this prediction is revealing.

In 1958, the following Dixon prediction was published: "As for the 1960 election, Mrs. Dixon thinks it will be dominated by labor and won by a Democrat. But he will be assassinated or die in office 'though not necessarily in his first term." [14] Note that Kennedy's name is not mentioned. Also note the qualifiers: ". . . will be assassinated or die . . ." and " . . . not necessarily in his first term." Of course, her faulty prophecies in the same magazine article have been forgotten; these include her prediction that "[Thomas Dewey] will be assistant [sic] President in Ike's second term."[14]

When 1960 rolled around, however, she changed her mind

and predicted that a Republican, and not Kennedy, would be elected President.[87] At the time of her prediction, furthermore, three of ten presidents in this century had been assassinated or died in office, so that her odds for this kind of prediction were good in any case.

In other words, this prophecy is generally remembered as being much more specific than it actually was; her faulty predictions made at the same time and her change of heart in predicting Kennedy's defeat have been forgotten; and the good odds for such a prediction coming true in the light of recent history are not usually mentioned. Here we see distortions in memory that operate to make a commonplace prediction seem extraordinary (and, in this case, psychic).

But what of Jeane Dixon's prophecies in general?

Kurt Saxon followed up her predictions for 1971 as published in the *National Enquirer*. Of fourteen predictions, Saxon judged that one of them had come true.[590] One of my students did the same thing for Jeane Dixon's predictions for 1973; of eight predictions judged sufficiently specific to follow up and not in the realm of general knowledge, one came true. Finally, Mary Bringle has compiled:

> . . . some of the more important prophecies [of Dixon's] which have been totally wrong. . . . That Russia would move into Iran in the fall of 1953, and into Palestine in 1957. That General Douglas MacArthur would be appointed to a new post of great importance (possibly an ambassadorship) by Eisenhower in 1953. That Red China would plunge into war over Quemoy and Matsu in October, 1958. That World War III would begin in 1958. That Red China would be admitted to the United Nations in 1959. . . . That Russia and China would be ruled by a "swarthy-skinned" man who was part Oriental by 1964. That the Vietnam War would end in ninety days (the date was May 7, 1966) on terms not satisfactory to America. That Fidel Castro, although possibly in Red China, was more than likely dead in the summer of 1966. That Lyndon Johnson would be the Democratic nominee for President in 1968. That the Russians would be first to put a man on the moon.[87]

In general, it appears that there is little evidence that Jeane Dixon possesses the psychic gift of prophecy.

5. There are many other prophets in the news these days: although less well known, perhaps they fare better than Jeane Di-

xon. A number of investigators have compiled the predictions of various prophets as published at the beginning of each new year in the *National Enquirer*. Of several hundred such predictions surveyed, spanning the years 1969 to 1973, the overall success rate as determined by the investigators varied from about 10 to about 20 percent.[590, 607] Remembering that studies of this kind have many difficulties, nevertheless it seems that precognition is not proved by prophecies such as we have considered thus far.

6. Earthquake predictions by psychics have been particularly popular. To evaluate such predictions, Roger Hunter and John Derr compared quake predictions by 92 noted psychics, astrologers, and other seers, with quake predictions randomly generated by a computer. Unhappily, predictions by the seers were no more accurate than the random computer predictions.[321]

7. What about religious leaders; are their prophecies more reliable? Predictions of the end-of-the-world and the establishment of the holy kingdom (that is, the millenium) are among the most popular of religious prophecies. Some of the more recent predicted dates for the end of the world are:

1843 and 1844, by William Miller and the Millerites.[126]

1967, by Sun Myung Moon, head of the Unification Church.[405]

1975, by the Jehovah's Witnesses and by Herbert W. Armstrong, leader of the Worldwide Church of God.[149, 508]

Since the world has not yet (quite) ended, we can chalk up these prophecies as failures.

8. Finally, on the chance that ordinary people might be better predictors than the professionals, Albert Shadowitz and Peter Walsh followed up predictions deposited with the New York Premonitions Registry and found that "Of the first 3,500 premonitions received . . . only about one percent were eventually considered to have come true."[607] Donald West did the same for predictions received by the Society for Psychical Research in London and found that of ". . . 32 such cases in the S.P.R. files. . . . not one of the predictions deposited with the Society came true; even though some of the people making the predictions were supposed to be almost invariably correct in their forecasts."[723]

It is evident from our consideration of prophecies of various kinds that they do not furnish convincing evidence for the existence of precognitive abilities. Nevertheless, seemingly prophetic flashes may be useful even if they are not truly psychic. When such feelings are seen as representing fears, desires, memories, or perceptions of which we are ordinarily unaware, we may consequently learn a great deal about ourselves, and we may find that we have indeed correctly perceived and evaluated a situation, unconsciously if not necessarily psychically.

Psychic Healing

The part can never be well unless the whole is well. . . .
This . . . is the great error of our day in the treatment of the
human body.[400]

PLATO

We have seen that psychosomatic and hysterical illness can result from stress and can also be "learned," and, therefore, "unlearned." In this section we will take a deeper look at the potential effects of these factors—that is, of stress reduction and of conditioning—in approaches to healing that are variously called mental healing, psychic healing, and faith healing. Consider the following example:

> I had long been ill, and one of the first results of my illness, a dozen years before, had been diplopia (double-vision) which deprived me of the use of my eyes for reading and writing almost entirely, while a later one had been to shut me out from exercise of any kind under penalty of immediate and great exhaustion. I had been under the care of doctors of the highest standing both in Europe and America, men in whose power I had had great faith, with no or ill result. Then, at a time when I seemed to be rather rapidly losing ground, I heard some things that gave me interest enough in mental healing to make me try it. . . .
>
> I sat quietly with the healer for half an hour each day, at first with no results; then, after ten days or so, I became quite suddenly and swiftly conscious of a tide of new energy rising within me, a sense of power to pass beyond old halting-places, of power to break the bounds that, though often tried before, had long been veritable walls about my life, too high to climb. I began to read and walk as I had not done for years, and the change was sudden, marked, and unmistakable. . . . The lift I got proved permanent, and left me slowly gaining ground instead of losing it.[336]

Assuming that the mental healing did, in fact, provide the cure, what might have been involved?

Sitting quietly for half an hour each day certainly might have reduced stress, and this "training" in stress reduction could have carried over into ordinary activities. In addition, the patient consulted the mental healer when he was feeling particularly low and when his faith in traditional medicine had not borne fruit; these factors might have led him to place a great deal of faith in the novel mental-healing approach—in other words, to be open to the suggestion of healing implicit in this approach.

The powerful effects of suggestion in healing can be clearly seen, for example, in the following experience of the psychic healer, Lawrence Le Shan:

> The most dramatic single result I had occurred when a man I knew asked me to do a distance healing for an extremely painful condition requiring immediate and intensive surgery. I promised to do the healing that night and the next morning when he awoke a "miraculous cure" had occurred. The medical specialist was astounded, and offered to send me pre and post healing x-rays and to sponsor publication in a scientific journal. It would have been the psychic healing case of the century except for one small detail. In the press of overwork, I had forgotten to do the healing![394]

That such "placebo cures" are not uncommon is suggested by the following account of:

> . . . three hospitalized female patients, all in their 60s, who had not been helped by medical treatment. One woman was suffering from chronic gallbladder inflammation; the second had failed to recuperate after an operation for pancreatitis and was wasting away; and the third had inoperable cancer of the uterus, along with edema of the legs and anemia. As an experiment, the doctor called in a faith healer—who practiced his wonders on an absentee basis—without informing the patients. After 12 healing sessions there was no change in the patients' conditions. Then the doctor told the patients that the faith healer, who was described in glowing terms, would be working for them each morning for three days, when in fact he would not be. The three women experienced an immediate lessening of symptoms, and all were able to leave the hospital within a week's time.[224]

Almost all cultures make use of mental healing and, although

Figure 20. Faith healing by "laying on of hands"

the specific approaches vary, they generally incorporate procedures such as the following:[223, 365]

First, stress reduction is accomplished through body contact
(massage, "laying on of hands," etc.), through elaborate and en-
grossing rituals, which divert attention away from worries, and
through encouraging the patient to vent repressed and disturbing
emotions in a cathartic discharge.

Second, conditioned therapeutic responses are elicited in the
patient through invocations to supernatural powers, through
suggestions that the rituals (exorcism, "bloodless surgery," etc.) will
cure the condition, and through strong social approval at signs of
recovery.

Here, for example, is a description of a Navaho healing ritual
in which many of these elements are present:

> The bolstering attendance of family and friends, the authority of the
> medicine man, and the invocation for reinstated good health are
> doubtless important in healing. The patient is actively doing some-
> thing about his illness. He participates in the ceremony and its costs.

> Moreover, powerful forces are being amassed for his benefit. In the sand paintings, songs and prayers, a cultural hero makes a symbolic journey on his behalf. . . . Instead of isolating the patient all possible means of support are drawn together, the family, clan, friends, and the symbolic history they share.[163]

Unfortunately, in the West, these powerful healing processes have been largely rejected by the mainstream of medical practice, and even psychotherapeutic practice, and are now found mainly in the procedures of psychic, occult, and faith healers. As the psychoanalyst Otto Fenichel has said: "[For neurotics, the] healing power of Lourdes [the healing shrine in Lourdes, France] is of a much higher order than that of the average psychotherapist. . . ."[364] We should not be surprised, then, that psychic healers and faith healing ceremonies are often effective in alleviating illnesses that are largely psychological in origin and that some illnesses are often most effectively dealt with in this fashion. Some of the psychological impact of such healing ceremonies is evident in the photograph in Figure 20 of "laying on of hands" in a faith healing service.

Psychic healers sometimes also claim that they are able to diagnose illnesses even though they have had no medical training. Let us see if we can understand how this might occur. Consider the following example:

> A family living in a remote area of Australia included three girls and a pair of twin boys, aged two-and-a-half years.

> The father says: "One night I found my wife sitting up with one of the twins in her lap, rocking him. He had a slight fever. We agreed that it was a touch of malaria. Malaria was not uncommon there and we were always prepared to treat it, usually with success without having to call a doctor. (The nearest one was twenty miles away.) I was satisfied and went to bed and to sleep.

> "About daybreak or a little before I had a dream that our family physician came in and examined the boy and said he had diptheria. I awoke, startled, and tiptoed into the room where my son and his mother were. She was still awake, he was sleeping peacefully, breathing naturally, and his temperature was normal. I went back to my room, but not to sleep. The memory of the dream kept nagging me. I 'reasoned' with myself that isolated as we were with no contacts between my children and other children, with no case of diptheria anywhere within many miles reported, it was foolish for me to be disturbed because of the dream.

"After a while I could stand it no longer, but still I did not want to confess the reason for my concern to my wife. I went back to the room and asked my wife if the boy had indicated any pain in his throat. No. He had said it didn't hurt anywhere. Still I wanted to look at his throat. She took him up and, shining a Delco light down his throat, we made a thorough examination and found a tiny white spot about the size of a small pinhead. . . .

"It was about three hours after the spot was discovered that the doctor arrived. By that time the boy had fever again and the white spot had become a white patch and was on both sides. The doctor was satisfied it was diptheria—took a smear and injected the antitoxin into all five of the children. The boy was critically ill for two or three days. . . . The doctor told me that a few hours later would have been too late for the treatment to have saved his life."[556]

In this case, the father seemed to "know" subconsciously that his son had diptheria. It seems likely that there were some subtle symptoms that he noted. Certainly he possessed a fund of medical knowledge—living where he did—that might have provided him with the correct diagnosis. It is no surprise that the diagnosis came to him in a dream; we have seen that a variety of altered states of consciousness can provide creative and useful solutions to problems.

We can see, then, how psychic or faith healers might be adept at medical diagnoses. In a trance or other altered state, they may be able to process impressions of the patient, together with stored knowledge of many prior patients, as well as miscellaneous reading on medical subjects, and come up with diagnoses that are quite accurate.

However, just because we can understand how psychic healers and faith healers might activate curative psychological processes, and accurately "read" symptoms of disease, does not mean that there are no paranormal influences involved as well. The evidence that bears on this question of paranormal factors is of several kinds.

1. There are laboratory tests by parapsychologists that attempt to measure psychic effects in a quantitative way. Perhaps the best-known study of this kind is by Bernard Grad, who attempted to measure the effect of "laying on of hands" by the healer, Oskar Estebany, on the healing of wounds in rats. However, in this study, the influence of purely physical factors, which were part of the "laying on of hands" treatment, was not eliminated. For example,

as Grad states: ". . . it is possible that the favorable effect was due to some chemical substance or substances transpired by [Oskar Estebany] or exhaled by him and affecting either the wound locally or the animal totally."[252] The results are thus inconclusive as far as demonstrating psychic influence is concerned.

The same healer, Oskar Estebany, was the subject in a separate study by M. Justa Smith, who wanted to determine if "laying on of hands" would have an effect on enzyme reactions, which might account for psychic healing effects.[629] Unfortunately, the control beakers in this study were not subject to equivalent physical conditions, and the results, thus, are also inconclusive.

Another kind of study has involved Silva Mind Control and Mind Dynamics graduates, who claim, as a result of their training, to be able to diagnose illnesses clairvoyantly when the sick person is not present. Three separate studies have tested these graduates and have concluded that, when sensory clues are excluded, their diagnoses are not more accurate than chance guessing.[86, 333, 707]

2. Some studies of psychic healing have involved contacting persons, who have been treated by healers, in an attempt to determine the effects of the treatment on their condition. In reading about these studies, keep in mind that, since these are not experiments and therefore lack control groups, it is not possible to know definitely whether the cure rates are higher than they would be in the absence of treatment by a psychic healer. It is possible, however, to evaluate whether the cures could be accounted for in terms of known medical processes. Some of the healers studied were psychic healers; others were faith healers who view themselves as servants of God. These distinctions are not clear-cut and generally no attempt will be made to distinguish the healers in these studies on this basis.

Louis Rose contacted over 90 people who were said to have been cured by a variety of healers in England. Of these, medical records were available for 37. Of the 37, Rose determined that one had an organic condition that had definitely improved; two had organic conditions that had possibly improved; three had improved and then relapsed; four had improved only with additional medical treatment; and one had deteriorated. Four patients had improved psychologically, but not organically. An example of this outcome was Miss E. W., who wrote that it ". . . was certainly a miracle after being deformed for forty-two years.... I was able that day to throw away my stick and run into the house." Miss E. W.'s doctor commented as follows: "... *the organic bone formation is actually the same.* There is no doubt, however, that *her movements are much better than they were before,* due, I suspect, to the psychological improvement."[571]

Finally, in 22 cases, the medical records were at variance with the patient's subjective evaluation. For example, Mr. J. E. E. thought it a miracle when, as he says: "I suddenly recovered the sight in my right eye which had been completely blind for over 50 years." However, Mr. J. E. E.'s opthalmologist commented: "There is no miracle—he was a case of spontaneous dislocation of lens which was cataractous."[571]

Rose's study indicated that the healers' influence was chiefly psychological, even in those few cases in which organic conditions improved, and that no miracles were evident.

In another study, Inge Strauch contacted 538 patients of a well-known German healer, Kurt Trampler. Asked to evaluate their condition subjectively, 39 percent reported improvement in their condition, 22 percent reported temporary improvement, 29 percent reported no change, and 10 percent reported that their condition had deteriorated. However, of the 247 patients whose medical records were available, only 9 percent showed objectively verified improvements (2 percent showed temporary improvement), whereas 75 percent showed no change and 14 percent showed deterioration. Consequently, Strauch concluded that *"Trampler's influence produces in the main subjective changes,"*[660] and that no miracles had been observed.

William Nolen, a physician and surgeon, has studied a number of healers. In one study, he was able to contact six of the eight persons whom the Texas healer Norbu Chen identified as among his most successful cases. Nolen concluded that some psychosomatic ills seem to have been helped, but that no paranormal effects were required to account for these.[482]

Nolen also journeyed to the Philippines to study "psychic surgeons" who claim to penetrate patients' skin with their hands, remove tumors and foreign substances, and then close the wound, all without anesthesia, surgical instruments, pain, or loss of blood. Although similar approaches are found in many folk societies,[185] the Philippine psychic surgeons are certainly the best known to

Westerners. To Nolen, the "surgeons" appeared to be performing sleight-of-hand (all of the films and photographs of psychic surgery I have seen also appear to be sleight-of-hand). Although Nolen presents no statistics, none of the cases he followed up showed evidence of actual tumor removal or other signs of paranormal healing.[482] From hearing a dozen or so patients of psychic surgery discuss their "operations," I agree with Nolen that there were no effects that could not be accounted for in terms of psychological factors. Additional evidence that the psychic surgeons fake their operations comes from the Federal Trade Commission trial involving travel agencies that were advertising the curative powers of psychic surgeons to promote trips to the Philippines. A great deal of evidence demonstrating fraud on the part of psychic surgeons was introduced in the trial, including laboratory evidence that blood and tumors produced during the operations were from nonhuman animals.[379] In particular, Tony Agpaoa, the most popular of the psychic surgeons, has several times been detected in trickery.[570] It is worth knowing that even Harold Sherman and Tom Valentine, who have written the most popular books on the psychic surgeons, state that there is much fakery involved, although they believe that some of the "surgery" is legitimate.[620, 703]

William Nolen also contacted people who had been "healed" in services performed by Kathryn Kuhlman, probably the best-known faith healer in America in recent years. Of 23 cases who claimed they were "cured" by Kuhlman in the Minneapolis area, ". . . none of the patients who had returned to Minneapolis to reaffirm the cures they had claimed at the miracle service had, in fact, been miraculously cured of anything . . ."[482] In other words, any change in their condition was accounted for in terms of ordinary medical knowledge. In addition, Nolen contacted five alleged cancer patients who had claimed they were cured in Kuhlman's services. Of these, one did not have cancer, two were as seriously ill as before, and two had died. Nolen also contacted sixteen cases whom Kuhlman thought constituted some of the best proofs of her own faith healing. Of these, ten had psychosomatic conditions that could be expected to be affected. The remaining six were cancer cases, five of whom refused to cooperate; the single cancer patient who cooperated had received medical treatment that is often effective. Nolen finally concluded that there was no evidence for paranormal effects in Kuhlman's healing.[482]

3. In South America, some healers are reported to perform actual surgery with crude unsterilized instruments, without benefit of anesthetics and with little resultant pain, blood flow, or infection.[379] Arigo, who died in 1971, was probably the best known of such healers. Known as the "surgeon of the rusty knife," Arigo claimed to work in a trance under the guidance of a "spirit doctor," Dr. Fritz, and was felt by many to have paranormal powers.[230] However, such operations may only reflect some of the remarkable, but natural, processes we have already discussed. For example, we know that pain during surgery can be alleviated in many people through suggestion. As we shall see in the next section, blood flow and the body's resistance to infection may be affected in a similar fashion. And, concerning the possibility of performing delicate operations without benefit of Western medical training, Stephen Black reports that: "In Nigeria, I found that the 'traditional healers' of the Yoruba can effectively treat cataract—an opacity in the lens of the eye—by surgical detachment of the lens."[71]

4. Finally, let us consider perhaps the best-known place of spiritual healing in the Christian world—Lourdes, France. Ever since a girl had a vision of the Virgin Mary there in 1858, throngs of infirm pilgrims have visited Lourdes in hopes of having their health restored.

Donald West has conducted perhaps the most thorough analysis available of the Lourdes healings. He examined the eleven cases that the reactivated Catholic commissions, established to evaluate Lourdes healings, had pronounced miraculous up to the time of his research in 1957. After examining all available evidence, including the medical records, West concludes: "There are no cases of lost eyes or amputated legs sprouting anew. . . . The [miraculous] cures claimed mostly consist in a sudden tipping of the balance in favour of the patient, whose recuperative powers seemed suddenly to reassert themselves."[726]

In the light of these considerations, what accounts for the strong belief that many persons have in paranormal factors in healing? Undoubtedly many of the psychological processes we have mentioned in our previous discussions are involved. In particular, Louis Rose and Donald West make a good case for the importance of mechanisms such as the following:[571, 726]

Self-limiting diseases. Illnesses are often self-limiting as natural physiological defense and repair mechanisms are activated. Over a period of time, many such cases would be expected to coincide by chance with a visit to a psychic or faith healer. Even cancer sometimes regresses in the absence of effective medical treatment.[82, 194] Of course, the successful cases tend to be remembered, and failures can be dismissed as due to insufficient belief.

Mistaking attitude change for organic change. The subjective burden of many organic conditions can be relieved through a change of attitude, which psychic or faith healing sometimes achieves. Generally, patients thus "cured" would rather believe that the cure is organic and, perhaps, permanent and "miraculous," than to think that the cure consists of "merely" a change in attitude.

Ignorance of psychological factors. Many people are quite ignorant regarding the powerful effects of suggestion, attention, touch, and other psychological factors in almost all cases of illness, organic illness included. Consequently, they may ascribe psychic or faith healing cures to paranormal factors because they do not believe that their own minds are capable of producing such effects.

Charlatan healers. As can be expected in any field, some healers are consciously intent on duping the public. For example, the healer-evangelist Marjoe has shown that such motivations are not unknown among faith healers in the United States.[232] James Walsh makes the point that "There have been not a few instances where people wrote testimonials as to their cure that were used [by their 'healers'] for years after their death from the disease of which they had been 'cured.'"[715] To the extent that such practices exist, of course, people are likely to be seriously misled regarding the efficacy of psychic and faith "cures."

However, we have seen that psychic and faith healing are by no means total deception. It is true that there is no good evidence that paranormal factors are involved. Nevertheless, a birds-eye view of the studies summarized above indicates that psychic and faith healing can activate powerful psychological mechanisms, producing not only remarkable changes in attitude, but also organic improvement. On the other hand, some individuals, particularly those who refuse effective medical treatment in favor of what turns out to be ineffective psychic or faith healing, are undoubtedly harmed.[190] In general, the curative effects of psychological healing procedures can be enhanced, and the harmful effects largely avoided, as we develop awareness of our own psychological capacities for self-healing. As we learn to avoid stress, to find love in the world, and to have faith in the capacity of the human body to heal itself, we can gain a new level of physical health and well-being.

Fakirs

A mind equal to any undertaking that he puts it alongside of.[42]

CHARLES DICKENS
Dombey & Sons, Chapter 23

Of all cases of control over bodily processes, perhaps the most spectacular examples are furnished by practitioners of various religious and philosophical disciplines, who are known generally as fakirs. Although many fakirs claim to possess paranormal powers, not all make such claims. There is little doubt that some fakirs are able to achieve remarkable control over ordinarily involuntary responses, including pain, bleeding, and perhaps resistance to infection.[504] The following account of Indian members of the Rifa'i sect of Dervishes provides an illustration of such feats: ". . . Dr. Hunt exhibited at the Royal Anthropological Institute photographs and cinema films of men thrusting long iron skewers through the neck between the gullet and the backbone, of dislocation of the eyball outwards—it might almost be said on to the cheek—and of the hammering of a very heavy ball-headed metal spike into the top of the skull, the spike in some individuals being fixed so firmly that it was hard to withdraw."[605]

On the other hand, sometimes the feats of fakirs seem to depend on genetic abnormalities, such as the absence of a sense of pain.[561] And sometimes outright tricks of various sorts are involved; that is, fakirs are sometimes also fakers.[102] These various factors are evident in the accounts below.

D. Scott Rogo describes the following method for walking on broken glass in bare feet:

> First, the glass need not be pulverized; even large wicked-looking pieces can be used. However, the catch is that the glass must be laid

Figure 21. Walking on broken glass

evenly on a firm surface (Glass laid on *glass* will cause slippage and is extremely dangerous). If the person walks steadily, bringing his feet directly downward with no shifting, evenly and slowly, no cut will occur.... The weight is so absorbed that a one-hundred-and-twenty-pound person can be placed on the performer while he is lying on the bed of glass, with no injury.[566]

Rogo can be seen taking his own advice as he walks on broken glass in Figure 21.

According to Harry Houdini, procedures such as the following can be used to enable one to swallow poison without ill effects:

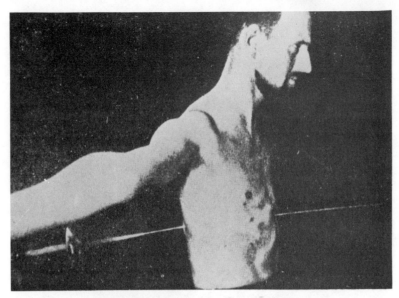

Figure 22. The remarkable Mirin Dajo

taking antidotes before or after injesting the poison, swallowing a substance to coat the stomach and dilute the poison, building up a tolerance over time, and, if all else fails, throwing up afterward![312]

Milbourne Christopher gives a remarkable account of Mirin Dajo, who, among his other feats, would run a thin unsterilized blade all the way through his abdomen, from front to back, without appreciable blood flow or infection. Figure 22 shows Dajo with such a blade through his abdomen. After observing this demonstration, Albert Bessemans found that he could insert similar blades through the abdomens of mice, guinea pigs, and rabbits without killing them.[121] This indicates that our ordinary notions of what the body can endure, without paranormal intervention of any kind, may be much too conservative.

Mayne Coe has investigated fire-walking and fire-handling feats and has himself performed the following feats:

> Touched red-hot iron with my fingers.
> Touched red-hot iron with my tongue.
> Touched molten iron with my tongue. (No sensation! Can't feel it!)
> Bent red-hot steel bars by stamping them with my bare feet.
> Run barefoot on red-hot iron.
> Walked on red-hot rocks.
> Plunged my fingers into molten lead, brass, and iron.

Taken a small quantity of molten lead in my mouth and spat it out immediately. Once I allowed it to solidify in my mouth and almost was burned. Never try this.

Carried red-hot coals around in my hands.

Popped red-hot coals into my mouth.

Chewed charcoal off burning sticks. This is easy if done fast enough.

Walked on beds of red-hot coals, taking eight steps to cross a fourteen-foot pit.[124]

Coe explains his feats as being due to a number of physical phenomena, including spheroidal states (in which moisture on the skin, turned rapidly gaseous by the heat, forms a vapor barrier between the skin and the hot object), thickness of the skin, and localized cooling of the hot object by the moisture of the skin. He concludes that "No paranormal explanation is necessary for fire-walking and related behaviors."[124]

Walking on a bed of hot coals in particular has been the subject of several other studies. Charles Darling reports on studies in London in the 1930s as follows:

Careful observation with a stop-watch having shown that the average time of contact of the walker's foot was half a second at each step and it being noted that each foot rested twice on the surface during the passage, the junction [a temperature-measuring device] was struck on to the surface twice in succession, a period of contact of half a second per impact being attempted. Actually, owing to the difficulty of working near the fire, this period was always exceeded, but a number of separate trials showed a rise of 15°–20°C. in the junction. This was conclusive evidence that the feet of the performer would not become hot enough for blistering to occur.[148]

Other accounts also indicate that a steady, rapid stride is the secret of a successful walk across hot coals and that other physical or paranormal explanations are not required.[136, 207, 388, 539, 710] Of course, the implicit or explicit suggestion that redness, blisters, and soreness will not develop helps to prevent these reactions in the case of sufficiently hot coals.

You can test your own ability to withstand high temperatures by holding a cigarette with the lighted end against one of your fingers and the other end against your thumb. Although it appears impossible, you can hold a cigarette this way for quite a

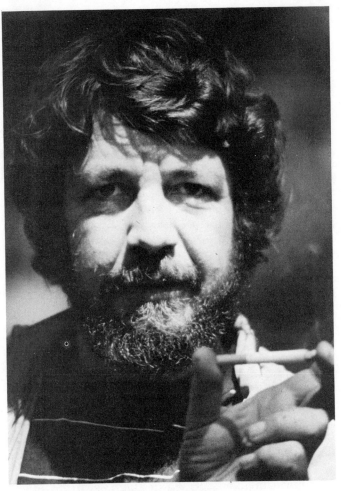

Figure 23. The cigarette test

few seconds–in other words, considerably longer than "fire walkers" leave each foot in contact with hot coals—before it begins to be painful. Even then, the temperature is not sufficient to cause a burn. A "cigarette test" of this nature is shown in Figure 23.

Although some of the feats of fakirs may seem like grotesque exhibitionism, there is an important lesson involved in their demonstrations: we do possess capacities that considerably transcend our ordinary levels of functioning. Although most of us are not interested in performing spectacular feats, we are interested in maintaining our bodies in a state of health. Fakirs demonstrate that a high level of control over bodily functions is attainable.

Water Witching and Related Phenomena

"Tell me about your stick," Adam said. "How does it work?"

Samuel stroked the fork now tied to his saddle strings. "I don't really believe in it save that it works." He smiled at Adam. "Maybe it's this way. Maybe I know where the water is, feel it in my skin. Some people have a gift in this direction or that. Suppose—well, call it humility or a deep disbelief in myself, forced me to do a magic to bring up to the surface the thing I know anyway." [647]

JOHN STEINBECK, *East of Eden*

In the last chapter, we discussed automatisms in which subconscious associations result in behaviors that are not under conscious control and that therefore often seem mysterious. In particular, automatisms are involved in a number of behaviors often interpreted as paranormal—water witching, radiesthesia, Ouija, and table levitation and table turning in seances. Automatic writing, automatic drawing, and automatic speech (glossolalia) also are automatisms that are often thought to be paranormal, but these behaviors are discussed in other sections.

Water witching (or divining or dowsing) is the practice of searching for underground water—usually for the purpose of drilling a well—by holding some kind of device that is supposed to indicate by its movement the presence of water. Although pendulums and other items are occasionally used, the most popular device is a Y-shaped branch that is held by its two ends with its point facing away from the body. The presence of water is usually indicated by a dipping of the end of the rod. Evon Vogt and Ray Hyman describe the action of the rod as follows:

Typically the diviner holds the rod under considerable compression, i.e., he pushes the two forks toward one another to create the tautness in the rod. In this case, if he just eases his grip slightly, the rod will move. It moves because the tension in the rod is now greater than the force of the grip. A second way to move the rod is to rotate your wrists slightly toward each other. Even a slight imperceptible rotation is sufficient to give quite a kick to the rod's rotation (if you rotate your wrists outward, the rod will tend to rotate upward). The remaining two ways to produce the rod's movement are to pull the hands slightly apart or to push them slightly together. Either of these movements creates greater tension in the rod than in the force of the grip. When the balance is so upset, the rod acts like a coiled spring and may straighten out with such force that the bark may literally come off in the hands of the diviner.

Each of these movements, or a combination of them, are almost always made imperceptibly and unconsciously. The subjective impression is always that the stick twists in opposition to your grasp. In a sense, this is true. The tighter your grasp, the less chance the rod will have to move.[708]

A water witcher, holding a rod in the usual fashion, can be seen in Figure 24.

There is little question that witchers can tap subconscious impressions that might otherwise be lost to consciousness. Consider the following example:

Some time ago I met a personal friend, Mr. William Brown . . . at the Board Room of the G.W.R. Company, at Bristol. . . . While we were waiting . . . my friend asked me if I had ever seen a water diviner. . . . He then introduced me to John Mullins. . . . After I had had some conversation with Mullins, my friend asked him to leave the room for a few moments. When he had done so Mr. Brown informed me that . . . he had had proof of [Mullins'] capacity to discover hidden metal, and he would test it in my presence. He then took three sovereigns from his purse and placed them in a line, and several feet apart, underneath the carpet. . . . We then called Mullins in, and asked him to use his rod along the left-hand side of the room. He took a forked twig from his pocket and proceeded up the room with it, holding it in front of him as I have described. It showed no agitation at first, but soon did so, and we marked the spot with a piece of paper. . . . We then turned up the carpet and found the sovereigns on the spots indicated by the rod.[40]

The subtle cues that the witcher was guided by in this case could have been the small subconscious muscle reactions of the two men who were watching him walk along the rug and who knew

Figure 24. Water witching

where the coins were hidden. On the other hand, the witcher may have been acutely sensitive to small wrinkles in the rug or disturbed patterns of dust where the coins were hidden. In any case, it is entirely possible that the witcher would have failed if he had not used his witching rod to tap his subconscious impressions.

Although there are many folk theories that seek to explain the movement of the rod, most serious investigators of water witching agree that automatism is involved; however, some investigators believe that psychic sensitivity to the presence of water, or other substance being sought, activates the automatism.[40] What is the evidence regarding the influence of paranormal factors in water witching? To put it another way, can witchers find water when other cues (such as features of the landscape) are eliminated? That is, we might expect an automatism to tap unconscious memories concerning environmental features found in the vicinity of productive wells. Thus water witchers might be successful for this reason.

Vogt and Hyman review both controlled field and laboratory studies of water witching and conclude that there is no good evidence that paranormal factors are involved.[708] For example, Dale and his fellow researchers conducted an extensive controlled field study of 27 witchers and found that their success in locating water was at the level of chance guessing.[146] More recent field studies have also failed to find evidence for paranormal abilities.[220] In particular, Henry Gross, perhaps the best-known witcher in the United States,[563] seems to have failed under controlled conditions, including a test conducted by J.B. Rhine.[237]

Radiesthesia encompasses a range of activities, all basically similar to water witching, if less common. Radiesthesia typically involves holding a pendulum, the motions of which are said to indicate the sex of eggs and unborn children, the presence of minerals in the ground, the identity and location of criminals, or the diagnosis of disease. There is little question that radiesthesia is based on automatism,[339] and, although I know of no test of possible paranormal factors involved, we could guess the outcome on the basis of the negative findings for water witching.

A Ouija board is a smooth-surfaced board printed with numbers, letters, and words such as *yes* and *no*. Ouija players rest their hands on a pointer, which glides easily on felt-covered legs, and concentrate on a question they want answered. Studies have shown that thinking about a certain pattern is sufficient to produce small subconscious movements of the hand in the appropriate directions.[337] Exaggerated, this movement directs the pointer to an answer, which seems to have been arrived at mysteriously since the Ouija player ordinarily has no conscious awareness of having moved the pointer and is often genuinely surprised at the answer. From my own informal experience, it seems possible to elicit memories, as well as subliminal impressions, using a Ouija board, which are otherwise lost to consciousness. Obviously, this can be very useful, as can be seen in the following account describing the use of a planchette, which is similar to a Ouija pointer except that it guides a pencil that writes out the answer.

... we asked a friend to dictate a question, the answer to which we did not know. She said, "Who is coming to breakfast tomorrow?" Miss Lay and I placed our hands upon Planchette and asked the question. It wrote "Lucas." Our friend said that was the name of the gentleman who was coming to breakfast. Neither Miss Lay nor I had ever heard of him before. Our friend said, "Ask his Christian name." We asked; it wrote "William." "Is that right?" we asked our friend. "I don't know," she answered; "I never heard his Christian name." Then somebody else, who was *not* touching Planchette, remembered that there was a song by him somewhere among the music. We looked, and at length found the song by "William Lucas"—of whom we had never heard before, nor have we heard of him since.[475]

In this example, the writers had the opportunity to observe and be guided by the small muscle reactions of their friend who was watching the planchette spell out the name of her breakfast guest. Then their friend, or someone else in the room, could have "guided" the pointer in this fashion to spell out the guest's first name—William—even though no one was consciously aware of knowing his first name, as long as one of them subconsciously "knew" the name from having seen or heard it previously.

Although the Ouija board, or the planchette, seems to be a handy device for tapping subconscious impressions, there do not seem to be any studies to indicate that Ouija is, in any way, paranormal in its operation. In fact, as with most transcendental experiences, interpreting Ouija as paranormal can lead to ludicrous outcomes, as can be seen in the following account:

A student of mine descended upon my office last fall to announce that he had been in contact with the devil. A normally sober, responsible, industrious, Methodist-turned-agnostic, the young man was visibly shaken by his experience with the diabolic. He and some of his friends had engaged in an emotionally supercharged bout with a Ouija board on Halloween night and become persuaded that the devil had taken charge of the board. As my young friend pointed out, the board knew answers to questions that nobody in the room could possibly have known. For example, the board was able to tell the assembled group the year of Plato's birth and, as my friend pointed out, he was only three years off. (What kind of devil it is who would make a mistake was an issue I did not raise with him.) I asked him what he had done with the board and he said that he and his friends had been so terrified by the experience that they brought the board to a local Roman Catholic rectory where the priest had sprinkled it with holy water and told them to break it into many different pieces and put each piece into a separate garbage can . . . [!][256]

Besides the automatisms we have already discussed, mediums and psychics sometimes utilize automatisms to create seemingly mysterious table movements, which are attributed to the presence of spirits. Although there are many ways to turn, tilt, or levitate tables by trickery, automatism is also an effective mechanism, as can be seen in the following account:

> A number of individuals seat themselves round a table, on which they place their hands, with the *idea* impressed on their minds that the table will move in a rotary direction; the direction of the movement, to the right or to the left, being generally arranged at the commencement of the experiment. The party sits, often for a considerable time, in a state of expectation, with the whole attention fixed upon the table, and looking eagerly for the first sign of the anticipated motion. Generally one or two slight changes in its place herald the approaching revolution; these tend more to excite the eager attention of the performers, and then the actual "turning" begins. If the parties retain their seats, the revolution only continues as far as the length of their arms will allow; but not infrequently they all arise, feeling themselves obliged (as they assert) to *follow* the table; and from a walk, their pace may be accelerated to a run, until the table actually spins around so fast that they can no longer keep up with it. All this is done, not merely with the least consciousness on the part of the performers that they are exercising any force of their own, but for the most part under the full conviction that they are not.[105]

Table tilting or table levitation can be accomplished similarly, with the appropriate suggestion, as long as at least some of the sitters have their thumbs hooked over the èdge of the table so that their subconscious muscle movements will lift the table. Studies have shown that automatisms can easily produce such movements, and there is no good evidence that paranormal factors are involved.[708]

Closely related to table levitation is "girl levitation," which is a slumber party tradition among adolescent girls. For this kind of levitation, several girls place one finger of each hand at various points under a lying, or sometimes sitting, subject. After the suggestion of levitation and a ritual chant, the subject will often rise into the air. The typical feeling among the "lifters" is that they are only "following" the subject as she levitates and that they exert no force of their own. Such a "levitation ritual" is shown in Figure 25.

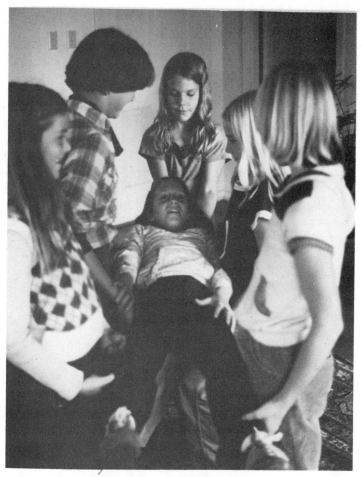

Figure 25. Levitation ritual

Of all the devices discussed in this section, perhaps the easiest for the beginner to use is the pendulum. If you would like to experience the feeling of creating movement of an object without conscious awareness, get a piece of string about eight inches long, tie a weight on one end that is just sufficient to keep the string taut, and hold the other end in one hand. You can rest your elbow on a table or not, depending on what gives you better results. Then think yes *to yourself to establish a movement for* yes; *since we are conditioned to an up-and-down movement for* yes, *from the corresponding head movement, this often trans-*

lates to a swinging of the pendulum away from the body and back toward the body. Then think no to yourself; this is often indicated by a swinging of the pendulum from left to right. These movements should occur without conscious volition as the long string of the pendulum amplifies small subconscious movements of your arm. To assure yourself that the movement is subconscious, you can close your eyes and see if you can sense in what direction the pendulum is swinging. Upon opening your eyes, you will probably find that your guess is often wrong. Once these movements are dependably established, you can ask yourself some questions that can be answered yes or no, perhaps dealing with dim memories or with unclear feelings. With practice, you can learn some interesting and useful things about your own unconscious.

Auras

Believing is Seeing.[626]

JOHN SLADEK

Have you ever noticed a region of light that seems to surround people and perhaps a variety of objects. This is called an aura and is sometimes thought to result from the emanation of "psychic energy." Before considering the evidence for the psychic origin of auras, however, let us review some physical and psychological explanations for auras.

1. Afterimages—In my experience, auras seen by myself and others I have questioned usually seem to be a result of afterimages. As discussed in Chapter 2, afterimages are the result of the constant motion of our eyes creating movement on the retina of images of objects in our field of vision. This movement produces an afterimage region surrounding any object, such as the heads of people, that we look at for extended periods. The color and brightness of this aura depend on the coloring and brightness of the object and of the background, and the size of the aura depends on the extent of movement of our eyes.[539]

2. Contrast effects—If the background is considerably brighter than the object viewed (for example, a human body), a region of intensified brightness will be perceived surrounding the object; that is, the contrast between the light and dark areas will make the light areas

immediately adjacent to the darker object appear lighter, forming a sort of aura. Also, if the colors of the object and background are complementary, the border between them—that is, the periphery of the head if you are looking at a person's face—will appear intensified in brightness.[397]

3. Imagery effects—The expectation of seeing an aura is, of course, sufficient to produce the perception of an aura in some individuals with strong imagery. Some people may have a "set" to see auras because, to them, auras are a sign of a nonphysical spiritual essence or of paranormal mental forces. The depiction of auras and halos surrounding religious figures in both Western and Eastern cultures undoubtedly both reflects and influences this "set."

4. Physical causes—M. Minnaert presents a good summary of auras arising from purely physical causes, such as reflection and refraction effects, particularly due to moisture in the air or on the ground, and refraction effects in the lens of the eye due to the brightness of the perceived object. These auras are often spectacular, but are observable only under special conditions.[452]

There are other purely physical "auras" surrounding the body, due to heat radiation and "sweating" of water and organic molecules. However, there is little evidence that we can detect these "auras," and so we will not consider them further.

But are there auras, in addition to the kinds described so far, that have purely psychic origins and how could we test for them? Generally, auras arising from purely physical and psychological causes are observable only if the person around whom the aura is seen is visible. On the other hand, a purely psychic aura should still be visible even if the person is just out of sight behind a partition. Charles Tart has proposed a test based on this distinction, which he calls the "doorway test."[669] In this test, the person around whom the aura is perceived stands on the other side of an open doorway, at times just out of sight of the perceiver so that any psychic aura would be visible extending into the doorway, and at other times a considerable distance away from the edge of the doorway so that a psychic aura would then be out of sight. A "reader" who truly is perceiving a psychic aura should detect an aura only when the person is near the edge of the doorway.

Since neither Tart nor other investigators seem to have conducted tests of this kind, we attempted to locate individuals who claimed to see auras. Through placing newspaper ads and posting notices, we contacted approximately two dozen "aura readers." Of these, only two felt that the auras they perceived were sufficiently distinct to be seen under the proposed test conditions. Unfortunately, neither of the readers passed the "doorway test." Thus it seems there is no evidence at present that auras are at all psychic in origin. If you see auras or you know someone who sees auras, you might want to conduct a doorway test of your own.

In addition to the doorway test, we made another kind of study of auras. We compared writings on auras by various authors in the belief that the degree of agreement on the characteristics of auras might indicate something about their objective versus subjective nature. That is, a low level of agreement might indicate that subjective factors were important. Although this is far from a conclusive test, it is interesting to compare some of these descriptions.

Concerning the size of auras, John Pierrakos, for example, states that the aura ". . . extends for 2 to 4 feet where it loses its distinctness and merges with the surrounding atmosphere."[511] On the other hand, Oscar Bagnall says that "Up to the age of puberty, it [the aura] protrudes only some four inches beyond the bright inside aura. From about the age of fourteen to eighteen, a woman's aura gradually widens until it attains about eight inches (nearly a foot in all). . . . This widening does not take place in the aura of man."[27] On the size of auras of males compared with those of females, Walter Kilner says: "On observing the Aura of an adult woman. . . . Above the shoulders round the head, down the arms and hands it is very similar to that of males."[366]

Comparing these quotes, we see that Pierrakos says auras are from two to six times as large as Bagnall says they are. And Bagnall says the adult female aura is some fifty percent larger than the adult male aura, whereas Kilner says that they are of comparable size, at least around the upper part of the body.

Concerning the color of auras, Pierrakos says it is generally ". . . a cloudlike, blue-gray envelope. . . ."[511] Bagnall says that "The better the intellect of the subject, the bluer the haze."[27] But Ursula Roberts says: "If the person is of a religious nature, it [the aura] changes to blue."[564] In other words, a blue color is common, according to Pierrakos, whereas Bagnall says blue is characteristic of intellectuals, and Roberts claims that blue is a sign of a religious nature.

With respect to auras that are red, Edgar Cayce says: "I knew a man who . . . became more nervous and more tired. He was working too hard and eventually he had a nervous breakdown. During this time the red had grown in prominence in his aura."[111] But Roberts says: "The colour of early love is red."[564] In other words, if you have a red aura, Cayce would say you are ill, whereas Roberts would say you are feeling "earthly love."

The lack of agreement on important points among writers on auras certainly does not bolster the notion that the auras thus perceived have an objective existence outside of the imagination of the viewer.

In recent years, there has been much interest in Kirlian photography, named after the Russian investigators, Semyon and Valentina Kirlian, who did early work with the process. Kirlian photographs are made by passing a high voltage electric current through an object in contact with photographic paper; the electrical discharge leaves an impression on the photographic paper, which appears as an "aura" around the image of the object. A Kirlian aura surrounding a hand, for example, can be seen in Figure 26. Kirlian auras have been shown to vary according to such conditions as the relative position[683] and surface moisture[502] of the object being photographed.

Many people interested in auras as a psychic phenomenon have expressed interest in Kirlian auras as a possible demonstration of their claims. Unfortunately, there seems to be little relationship between auras as perceived visually and Kirlian auras. And although there have been claims that Kirlian photographs measure psychic phenomena in various ways, there seems to be no well-controlled studies in support of these claims. Perhaps the most impressive such claim involves the so-called phantom-leaf effect, evidently first reported by Russian investigators.[493] The phantom-leaf effect refers to their observation that, when part of a leaf is cut away, the Kirlian aura extends *around* the area of the missing part as if it were still present. The major study claiming to have replicated the phantom-leaf effect, by Thelma Moss and her associates[464] has turned out to be equivocal; the experimenters now admit that faulty techniques could have produced their results.[343]

We must conclude that there is no good evidence to support the notion that auras are, in any way, psychic in origin. Nevertheless, various kinds of auras are known to exist. I am often aware of

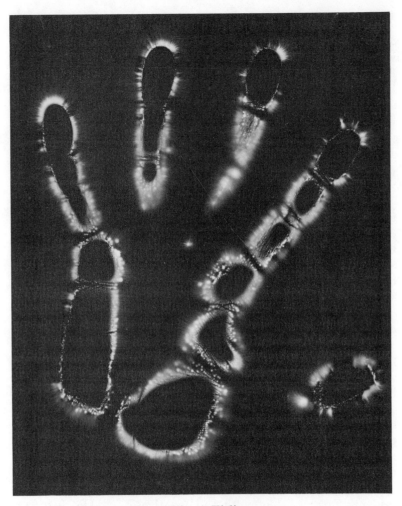

Figure 26.   A Kirlian aura

afterimage auras, for example, and I have seen most of the other
kinds of nonpsychic auras discussed.

> *If you are not ordinarily aware of auras, and would like to
> experience them, you might begin with afterimage auras because
> they are generally the easiest to observe. One of the best ways to
> observe afterimage auras is to look at someone who is against a
> bright background—the bright sky, a brightly illuminated wall.*

Look at the person's nose for a minute or so. Now look at the person's forehead, and you should see a light-colored aura extending around the head and shoulders. Once you can dependably see auras under these conditions, you should be able to see an aura without having to look at any particular part of the person's face; the ordinary movement of your eyes is sufficient to create the aura. After some practice, you should be able to see auras under a wide variety of conditions that are not optimal, but that are nevertheless sufficient, for afterimage formation.

Becoming aware of auras adds a new dimension to our perception. Since most auras are rather faint, they are excellent projective stimuli. That is, their appearance is easily affected by our current feelings regarding ourselves and the person around whom we see the aura. By becoming aware of these projections, it is possible to stay in touch with some of our feelings and intuitions about ourselves and others.

Out-of-Body Experience

To fly, float or otherwise displace oneself through thin air [through imagery] . . . is fraught with a fuller sense of exhilaration than usually befalls the aviator in his passage through the sky.[311]

LYDIARD HORTON

Have you ever suddenly realized that you were not aware of the position of your body and that you accordingly felt somewhat detached and free-floating. Such an "out-of-body" feeling is common in cultures around the world[616] and is usually reported to be an impressive and pleasurable experience.[517] Feeling free of the ordinary limitations of the physical body can take different forms: some people feel that their physical body is floating or levitating, while others feel that their consciousness leaves the body. Although these are probably basically similar experiences, only the latter is, strictly speaking, an out-of-body experience. Occasionally, in out-of-body states, people have the feeling of traveling to a distant location and sometimes the feeling of seeing their body as if from a distance.[257]

Readers who have not experienced out-of-body states may get some idea of the feelings involved from the following account:

> I . . . "awoke" early next morning being fully conscious of the real me floating near the ceiling in a prone position. The sensation was of total weightlessness and freedom, and was altogether most delightful. I observed my physical body lying on the bed sleeping peacefully, on my left side as usual, but was struck by the extreme pallor of the skin of my face which looked as if it would have been stone-cold to the touch. I next recall changing my position to the vertical and traveling around the room for some little time, thoroughly enjoying a wonderful state of well-being. . . . I felt tremendously disappointed to find myself back in a "normal" state. . . .[257]

In this example, the out-of-body feeling seems to have occurred in the hypnopompic period between sleep and wakefulness. In fact, most out-of-body feelings occur while people are lying or sitting quietly, often while they are asleep; out-of-body experiences rarely occur while people are active.[257,517] Thus two mechanisms we have already discussed are probably important in producing out-of-body experience.

OUT-OF-BODY EXPERIENCE

1. The loss of a sense of body position can arise from habituation of the body-sense receptors, which cease to convey a sense of body position after the body is quiet for a period of time, or from inhibition of these receptors. For example, Lydiard Horton observed in a laboratory study that: "Out of thirty subjects who relaxed completely and of the twenty or so who retained consciousness after they had completely relaxed, eight of them reported illusions of levitation . . . a woman gripped the chair in the momentary belief that she was floating away. . . . One other . . . reported himself 'just floating away,' the sensation being overwhelmingly real!"[310]

And, in another study, John Palmer found that relaxation, together with imagery, produced out-of-body feelings in approximately 50 percent of his subjects.[498]

Although a sinking or falling sensation is occasionally reported,[389] a feeling of levitation or floating is much more common and fits much better our conditioned associations—heaven is up, hell is down, light is above, dark is below.

2. Strong imagery may be responsible for the feeling of perceiving the world from a point outside of one's body. For one thing, feeling detached from one's physical body during relaxation probably suggests to some people that they "really" are detached and that they therefore could even see their own body as if from a distance. Also, since all of us have experienced "seeing" the world from a point outside of our (sleeping) body while we are dreaming, we should not be surprised if this universal "out-of-body" imagery is highly developed in some people and might be found in waking fantasies and visions.

Occasionally, as in the following example, out-of-body experiences seem to arise from a specific need:

> In the year 1944 I was asked to repair a very complicated book-keeping machine . . . which I hardly knew how to work with. . . . During a night in the week I was at work with the machine, I was awakened in my sleep and saw . . . on the table of our bedroom that book-keeping machine . . . and saw myself, fully dressed, take out with the fingers of my left hand a little triangle formed from the machine and give it . . . a pinch making it somewhat longer and placed that part back in the machine. . . . the day following . . . I did the same manipulation done in the preceding night and see, the machine was working. . . .[258]

In this example, the vision seemed to stem from a need to see how to solve a problem. What other needs might be involved in out-of-body imagery that is this vivid? From his experience with patients facing death, psychoanalyst Jan Ehrenwald makes the point that out-of-body feelings, when they occur, seen to relate to the need to believe that consciousness survives death.[182] Another researcher of out-of-body experiences, John Palmer, agrees, saying that: "Because of our religious upbringing (whether we accept it intellectually or not), death means the possibility, or at least the hope, that our soul is real and will leave the body to carry on in another state. Therefore, a psychological set favoring [out-of-body experience] is . . . present in these 'real-life' situations. . . ."[498] In addition, feeling outside of one's body may allow one to escape the hurts and limitations of the physical body or may provide a sense of freedom.[257]

The fulfillment of these needs—through the imagery of out-of-body experiences—is often accompanied by feelings of ecstasy, as can be seen in the experiences of various people.

> The escaped me felt absolutely wonderful, very light and full of the most wonderful vitality, in fact more well than I have ever felt before or since.
>
> A feeling of well-being as never experienced before.
>
> I only wanted to pursue and prolong this happy state of being where everything was more bright, vivid and real than anything I had previously known.
>
> I suddenly felt filled with the utmost joy and happiness. I felt such great freedom, like a bird just being let out of cage for first time in life.
>
> My mind felt so free it was ecstasy and I told myself I could now go anywhere I wished.[257]

And so it seems that out-of-body feelings can lead to ecstasy. However, this relationship probably can work the other way around. That is, we should not be surprised if feelings as overwhelming as those in the above examples could produce inhibition of competing sensory input. Restricting ordinary proprioceptive, visual, and other sensations in this way should not only encourage out-of-body imagery, but also make it seem correspondingly "real."

The convincing quality of many out-of-body experiences undoubtedly contributes to the widespread belief that the "psychic self" can actually leave the body. Under names such as astral projection and soul travel, this belief is found in a number of popular quasi-religious systems, including Eckankar, Rosicrucians, and Scientology. Most of these folk systems instruct their adherents to achieve "out-of-body" states through techniques such as relaxation, meditation, and fantasy, which fits the theory that neural habituation, inhibition, and imagery states are involved in out-of-body experiences.[498]

If you would like to read more about out-of-body experience, Celia Green's survey study of several hundred subjects is an excellent place to start.[257] In addition, there are several fascinating accounts available by individuals who provide extensive descriptions of their feelings during their out-of-body experiences.[140, 222, 454, 466]

Finally, a number of investigators have sought to determine if out-of-body experiences ever indicate *actual* projection of the psychic self so that an individual could perceive events in a distant location. In general, these studies suffer from the methodological problems discussed earlier; in particular, the few significant results that have been obtained have not been adequately replicated.[569] On the other hand, studies *have* found that the vast majority of subjects cannot perceive events in a distant place during an out-of-body experience, even though they feel certain they are doing so.[490]

If you have never had an out-of-body experience and would like to, find a quiet spot and get into a comfortable position. Keep your body relaxed and quiet for a long enough period of time to habituate your body position senses. A few minutes should suffice. As you lose your sense of body position, imagine yourself getting lighter and lighter and floating in the air higher and higher. Although not everyone will experience an out-of-body state, a great many people can. You will probably find that you lose awareness of at least part of your body. With practice, you will find that the out-of-body feeling becomes easier to attain. In this process, you should also find that you increasingly experience the relaxation and euphoria that commonly accompany out-of-body feelings.

Possession

*Exactly similar types of possession, producing exactly similar
states of intense faith, [are] explained in very different cultures
as being due to the intervention of the Holy Ghost, or perhaps
Voodoo gods, or Abyssinian "satans," or Sudanese "zars," or
Zambian "pepos."*[588]   WILLIAM SARGANT

In the last chapter, we discussed cases of multiple personality
and mentioned that the feeling of having another "personality"
take over your body could easily lead to the interpretation that you
are being "possessed" by an external spirit or agency. As William
James has said: ". . . it is one of the peculiarities of invasions from
the subconscious region to take on objective appearances, and to
suggest to the Subject an external control."[336]

One difference between multiple personality and possession
experiences seems to be that, in possession experience, ordinary
conscious awareness is usually only partly and temporarily sus-
pended. In this state, known as a trance state, the individual has at
least a transitory awareness of being "possessed" that is not usually
present in the case of multiple personality. Another difference between cases of multiple personality and possession is that possession experience is encouraged in various social contexts—seances,
healing ceremonies—whereas multiple personality usually appears
sporadically, as a result of stress, in individuals who lack a social
framework within which their experience is given an acceptable
interpretation.

The psychological importance of possession experiences is
indicated by the fact that they are fostered by a wide variety of
cultures in a wide variety of ritualistic as well as informal settings.[74]
Although possession experience has its dark side—for example, it
is sometimes seen as a cause of illness or as a punishment for
sin[74]—often it seems to have a more positive impact.[453] Socially,
possession experience appears to promote various social goals, including a common belief in, and identification with, the "spirit
world." Psychologically, possession seems to encourage the discharge of repressed feelings. Thus individuals possessed by "animal spirits" or "the devil" often engage in otherwise taboo behaviors. After all, people are not responsible for their behavior
while they are "possessed" by another personality. As Aldous Hux-

ley wrote about nuns at a convent in Loudun, France, who became possessed by "devils": "What if there never had been any devils? Then all these monstrous things they had done and said could be imputed to them as crimes. Possessed they were guiltless. Unpossessed, they would have to answer . . . for blasphemy and unchastity, for lies and malice."[322]

As Huxley indicates, the exorcism conducted to get rid of "devils" can also have certain psychological appeals.[322]

Although it may seem strange, possession by the "holy spirit" is probably similar to devil possession in allowing for release of inhibitions and repressed feelings. For example, when possessed by the "holy spirit," otherwise circumspect Christians feel free to shout and dance about; some also "speak in tongues," when ordinarily they would not talk in what most people would perceive as gibberish.

Ari Kiev summarizes some of the psychological dividends of possession as follows: "For the depressed and guilt-ridden, the sin-cathartic basis of the ideology and ceremonies provides a useful guilt-reducing device; for the hysteric, a socially acceptable model for acting out; and for the obsessional and the depressed, the encouragement of a reduction of inhibitions and an increase in emotionality. . . . Possession thus . . . offers an opportunity for the expression of much repressed and suppressed feeling and thought . . . ."[363]

William Sargant arrives at similar conclusions from his observations of possession experience in a variety of cultures. ". . . possession states provide an outlet for . . . people whose lives are one long struggle against poverty and despair. We saw them becoming gods, behaving like gods, and for a while forgetting all their troubles. After the ceremony they were quite convinced that for a time, despite their humility and poverty on earth, they had been one with the gods themselves. Life had regained purpose and dignity for them."[589]

Not surprisingly, the emotional release in such experience can be not only ecstatic, but also therapeutic.

Finally, as in cases of multiple personality, the altered state of consciousness that accompanies possession experiences can tap otherwise latent talents and memories. A number of authors, including Goethe, Charles Dickens, Rudyard Kipling, and George

POSSESSION EXPERIENCE

Eliot, have described their feelings of being "possessed" while engaged in writing.[389] For example, "George Eliot . . . declared that, in all the writings which she considered her best, there was a 'not herself' which took possession of her and made her feel 'her own personality to be merely the instrument through which the spirit acted.' "[396]

Let us now discuss a form of possession that is quite common in our culture—namely, speaking in tongues, or what is sometimes known as glossolalia. Speaking in tongues is a good example of possession experience to consider in some detail because, in contrast to most other possession states, there are studies of glossolalia that bear on the question of the paranormal nature of the experience. In particular, Christian glossolalists often believe that glossolalia is a sign of being "possessed" by the holy spirit, that it is unique to Christians, that it represents an ancient, foreign, or spiritual tongue, and that it has a spiritual meaning that can be discerned by another believer. On these issues, studies of glossolalia have shown the following:

1. Glossolalia exists in many different cultures and in many different religious contexts; it is not peculiar to Christianity.[427]

2. Attempts by linguists to ascribe meaning to glossolalic utterances, including showing that such utterances come from ancient or foreign languages, have failed. As William Samarin says: "[glossolalia is] strings of syllables, made up of sounds taken from among all those that the speaker knows, put together more or less haphazardly but which nevertheless emerge as word-like and sentence-like units because of realistic, language-like rhythm and melody. . . . it has never been scientifically demonstrated that xenoglossia [speaking in a language that the speaker never learned] occurs. . . ."[583]

3. Interpretation of glossolalic utterances by other believers has likewise been shown to be generally arbitrary and unrelated to the utterance. As William Samarin states: "Religious glossolalists claim, of course, that their utterances have meaning, and it is consistent with Pentacostal beliefs that there are 'interpretations' of such utterances; usually of 'messages' in a public context. However, when two such texts are compared—one glossolalic and the other its 'interpretation,' no covariant [related] patterns emerge."[584]

Thus, there seems to be no satisfactory evidence that glossolalia is, in any way, a paranormal or supernatural experience.

Possession beliefs are faddish to some extent. For example, devil possession increased in popularity in the 1970s, as did the corresponding frequency of exorcism. In the realm of animal possession, werewolves are now "out of fashion,"[539] but people who fancy themselves vampires are "making a comeback."[260] If you find animal possession difficult to understand, you should remember the importance of identifying with (totem) animals in our cultural tradition, in such forms as school mascots; bear, wolf, and other animal symbols in scouting; and even in "animal clubs" such as the Lions, Elks, Eagles, and Moose.

The seemingly bizarre nature of possession experience should not blind us to its uses. We have seen that, in allowing for the expression of repressed feelings, possession experience can serve a therapeutic function. And, in serving as a vehicle for latent talents, it can allow for the expression of abilities that might otherwise remain dormant. In these ways, possession experience serves to put people in touch with unexpressed parts of their own personalities. The remaining step, of course, is to integrate these repressed characteristics into the personality structure as a whole.

Apparitions, Hauntings, and Poltergeists

Ghosts were created when the first man woke in the night.[42]

JAMES MATTHEW BARRIE

Apparition refers to the sight of a ghost or spirit. Haunting refers to the frequenting of a particular place by a ghost or spirit. Poltergeist refers to a ghost or spirit that causes physical disturbances, although sometimes poltergeists are ascribed to the unconscious and rebellious "psychic spirit" of a living person.

We have already discussed psychological processes that might account for reports of ghosts and spirits, such as afterimages, phosphenes, autokinetic effects, altered states of consciousness, suggestion and expectancy effects, and need states. The role of suggestion, for example, can be seen in a description by psychologist William James of an experience, which, in another context, might have been interpreted as a visitation by a spirit.

> I was lying in my berth in a steamer listening to the sailors holystone the deck outside; when, on turning my eyes to the window, I perceived with perfect distinctness that the chief-engineer of the vessel had entered my state-room, and was standing looking through the window at the men at work upon the guards. Surprised at his intrusion, and also at his intentness and immobility, I remained watching him and wondering how long he would stand there. At last I spoke; but getting no reply, sat up in my berth, and then saw that what I had taken for the engineer was my own cap and coat hanging on a peg outside the window.[335]

And the role of hypnagogic imagery is suggested by the following description which, again in another context, could easily have been interpreted as the manifestation of a spirit:

> There was no light in the room, and it was perfectly dark; I had my eyes shut also. . . . I was suddenly conscious of looking at a scene of singular beauty. . . . The moon was shining upon the water, which rippled slowly on to the beach . . . and the sea and the gleam of the moonlight on the rippling water was just as if I had been looking out upon the actual scene. It was so beautiful that I remembered thinking that if it continued I should be so interested in looking at it that I should never go to sleep. . . . Then suddenly . . . the scene changed. The moonlit sea vanished, and in its place I was looking right into the interior of a reading room. . . . I remember seeing one

GHOSTS

reader . . . hold up a magazine or book in his hand and laugh. It was not a picture . . . it was there. . . . [I] saw the play of the muscles, the gleaming of the eye, every movement of the unknown persons in the unnamed place. . . .[390]

However, drowsy or dreamlike states are not necessary in order to see "apparitions." In the account that follows, for example, Mr. A. describes a figure that he saw in his left-side field of vision, the only unusual circumstance being that he is blind in his left eye.

He then saw as distinctly as he had ever seen anything in his life the figure of a female walking so closely in front of him, that he could scarcely avoid treading on her skirt. "The skirt was of red cloth with groups of white lines (a broad line with two very thin lines on each side of it) crossing each other at frequent intervals, as in a tartan, and over this was a black silk jacket or short cloak. The dress was beautifully illuminated with sunlight and moved naturally in response to the motion of the figure, while the light silk jacket was occasionally lifted as if by a breeze." Mr. A. realized that the figure was hallucinatory when told by his companion that no one was there. On crossing to the shady side of the street, Mr. A. still saw the figure with the sun still shining on it.[694]

Experiences with "spirits" should not necessarily be dismissed lightly; sometimes they tell us important things about subconscious impressions to which we should pay attention. In the case below, for example, it seems likely that the landlord sensed that his tenant was depressed or anguished and that his subconscious accordingly created a suitable perceptual experience. Unfortunately the landlord did not consciously connect the two experiences until the next morning.

> . . . a landowner, on terms of acquaintance but not of friendship with his tenant, is asked by the latter to come in one evening and smoke a cigar with him. The landlord refuses, and, as they separate, the tenant exclaims, "Then, if you will not come, good-bye." The landlord . . . went into the breakfast-room . . . and about 10 o'clock. . . . [he says] "I distinctly heard the front gate opened . . . and shut again with a clap, and footsteps advancing at a run up the drive . . . [then] I was conscious that someone or something stood close to me outside. . . . I could hear the quick panting laboured breathing. . . . Suddenly, like a gunshot . . . there broke out the most appalling shriek—a prolonged wail of horror, which seemed to freeze the blood. . . . My fright and horror . . . increased tenfold when I walked into the dining-room and found my wife sitting quietly at her work. . . . *She had heard nothing.*

> In the morning an examination of the ground under the window showed no footsteps in the snow, which was still there, either on the grass or in the drive.

> About 10 o'clock that evening, the tenant had committed suicide by taking poison in his own house.[694]

Similarly, in the following example, the daughter, Mary, may have been sensitive to signs of her sister's condition—for example, labored breathing or absence of breathing—which was expressed in the form of a vision of her sister standing beside her bed. Unfortunately, her mother did not consider that the vision might have been Mary's way of telling her mother that her sister needed help.

> . . . in a family in Ohio some years ago several young daughters slept in one room in different beds. One night ten-year-old Mary wakened her mother in an adjoining room to complain that her older sister Nancy was standing by her bed and wouldn't go away. The mother went to the girl's room, and saw that Nancy was asleep in her own bed, and she thought Mary was just imagining things. . . . Throughout the night at intervals Mary kept talking to Nancy, asking her to please go over to her own bed.

The next morning, as was their custom, the family arose, leaving Nancy asleep, for she was not a strong child and needed extra rest. Later, at bedmaking time, her mother called her and getting no response, came closer and discovered that Nancy was dead. The doctor's opinion was that she must have died soon after retiring.[556]

But are there accounts that cannot be explained in terms of psychological mechanisms? After conducting an extensive survey of people who claimed they had seen apparitions, Celia Green and Charles McCreery concluded that neither their accounts nor historical accounts provided adequate proof of ghosts or spirits.[258] In addition, Trevor Hall has reviewed the evidence for some of the best-known haunting and poltergeist cases in England, including Borley Rectory, Epworth Rectory, the Bealings House Bells, the Leeds Library Ghost, and the Cock Lane Ghost. In each case, Hall concludes that the evidence supports explanations based on normal, rather than paranormal, phenomena.[274] In the case of Borley Rectory, possibly the best-known case of haunting in recent history, Hall and his coworkers conclude that deception was involved in the investigation and publicizing of events to make them appear paranormal in nature.[167]

Coming to the most highly publicized haunting episode of recent times—*The Amityville Horror*[16]—a number of investigators declare that the account is riddled with errors and discrepancies.[460, 568] For example, the Catholic priest whose experiences are cited throughout the book denies that he witnessed anything supernatural, the weather records do not substantiate the reports of storms in the book, and there is no evidence of damage or repairs in the house, which supposedly sustained serious physical damage during the episode.

In many haunting and poltergeist cases that have been investigated, trickery has been discovered. To understand how such trickery can be accomplished, it will help to consider some specific cases.

From the eighteenth century comes the following account concerning poltergeist phenomena in the household of Mrs. Mary Pain: "An egg flew across the kitchen and cracked on the head of a cat. A mortar and pestle, brassware, and candlesticks jumped from their places. To protect the glass and chinaware, Mrs. Pain had her maid and Ann Robinson [the neighbor's maid] place them flat on the floor. Despite this they were soon breaking in pieces. . . . A kettle, a tray, and a silver tankard were as active as the glasses and plates. Two hams dropped from their hooks by the sides of the chimney, a side of bacon followed."[120]

Before reading further, see if you can arrive at an explanation for these incidents.

Now compare your explanation with that given by Ann Robinson, the neighbor's maid, who confessed that: "She had pelted the cat with an egg, hung the hams and bacon so they would fall when their weight caused the hooks to tear through their skins. She had dropped a chemical in the pail of water to make it bubble. Rows of plates were dislodged when she yanked a wire she had earlier arranged behind them. Long horse-hairs were attached to other objects to give them sudden life. They seemed to jump or fall when she pulled the ends."[120]

For readers who are interested in learning how to produce poltergeist phenomena, Milbourn Christopher provides directions for quite a number of them.[120]

From the nineteenth century comes the following account of an evening spent in a haunted house:

> ... I soon heard certain extraordinary sounds.... shrieks and groans were heard from various parts of the mansion.... a curious string of light burned around the room.... Then the jangling of bells and the clanking of chains, and flashes of light; then thumpings and knockings of all sorts came along, interspersed with shrieks and groans. I sat very quiet. I had two of Colt's best pistols in my pocket, and I thought I could shoot anything spiritual with these machines made in Connecticut. I took them out and laid them on the table. One of them suddenly disappeared! ... at this moment the candle went out.... No person was visible, but the noises began again, and they were infernal. I then took one of my ... candles out and went to unlock the door. I attempted to take the key out of my pocket; it was not there! Suddenly the door opened, I saw a man or a somebody about the size of a man, standing straight in front of me![37]

The man at the door was:

> ... an old family servant, and ultimately a gardener in charge of the place, [who] had been employed by an enemy of the gentleman who owned the property to render it so ... that the estate should be sold for much less than its value; ... he had got an ingenious machinist and chemist to assist him in arranging such contrivances as would make the house so intolerable that they [the owner's family] could

not live there. A galvanic battery with wires were provided, and every device of chemistry and mechanism was resorted to in order to effect this purpose.

One by one the family left, and they had remained away for nearly two generations under the terror of such forms, and appearances, and sights and sounds, as frightened them almost to death.[37]

The reader may be interested to know that, for a time at least, a "haunting service" was available whereby, for a fee, the haunting of a house could be arranged.[658] A magician friend of mine, who is also an electronics buff, has told me how he has rigged houses for the presence of spirits. In one particularly clever installation, he hid a row of speakers in the woodwork of a staircase so that, when a hidden tape recorder fed each speaker in turn, "ghosts" could be heard descending the staircase, stair by stair!

From the mid-twentieth century comes this poltergeist account:

In the Wild Plum School, near Richardton, N. Dak., Teacher Pauline Rebel and her eight pupils were droning through a dull school day when It began.

In a coal scuttle near the stove, the lignite coal began to stir. Soon lumps of coal popped spontaneously from the bucket and flew about the room. They hit the walls and Pupil Jack Steiner's head. The bucket capsized. The window shades began to smolder. A dictionary, touched by no human hand, started moving. The bookcase suddenly burst into flame.[746]

The cause of these incidents remained a mystery until some of her pupils confessed that they had: ". . . stuck lighted matches in the bookcase and behind the window shades to stimulate spontaneous combustion. They juggled the coal bucket with long pointers, threw lumps of coal around the room. Their sleight of hand was so skillful that it fooled not only the teacher but suggestible parents, one of whom swore that coals jumped out of his hand."[737]

As can be seen, some of the trickery involved in haunting and poltergeist cases is clever enough that even a determined investigator, much less a casual observer, might have difficulty uncovering the deception.

Before leaving the topic of apparitions, hauntings, and poltergeists, we should consider the claim, put forward by Konstantin

Raudive[536] and others[47] that a tape recorder, when disconnected from a microphone or other device for ordinary recording, will pick up sounds that are claimed to be voices of the dead. Others have disputed this interpretation, saying that radio or electrical signals or amplifier noise are responsible for what are very indistinct sounds on the tapes and that the meaning ascribed to the sounds by Raudive and others is a product of unconscious projection and is not to be found in the sounds themselves.[187, 628] As one observer of the "Raudive phenomenon" puts it:

> The problem is that different individuals listening to the recordings seldom hear the same words. Often the listener has to be told what the voice allegedly is saying before he can make out the words. This subjective factor is well illustrated in a message that Raudive claimed came from Sir Winston Churchill. Raudive wrote down the message as "Te Mac-Cloo, mej dream, my dear, yes"—a combination of Latvian, Swedish, and English words. Two British researchers thought the message was entirely in English, which is more plausible inasmuch as Churchill did not speak either Swedish or Latvian. One of them thought he said, "Hear, Mark you, make believe, my dear, yes," while the other thought the British leader was saying, "Mark you, make thee mightier yet." In either case the message is something of a stylistic deterioration for a man who was arguably the greatest master of rhetoric of our time.[648]

I have heard some of these tapes, together with Raudive's interpretation of them, and I would agree that the sounds are indistinct and that Raudive appears to "read in" meaning that I, at any rate, could not perceive.

The ease with which meaning can be ascribed to random sounds was brought home forcefully the other day while I was driving a tractor in my orchard for the first time. Over the various noises of the tractor, I heard voices of my wife and my neighbor calling to me to be careful and to watch what I was doing. I looked around for them and then realized they were nowhere near the orchard. There are two possible interpretations of this experience. One interpretation is that, just as "spirits" imprint their voices on tape recorders, so did my wife and neighbor paranormally cause the noises of the tractor to "speak" to me. However, the more likely interpretation is that my unconscious apprehensions caused me to project meaning into random noises. As a consequence of realizing that the "voices" reflected my unconscious feelings, I became aware of my apprehensions and, after that, drove more carefully. "Hearing voices," in this case, provided useful insights that I would not have gained if I had assumed that the voices were paranormal.

Likewise, although there is no satisfactory evidence that experiences involving "ghosts" or "spirits" are truly paranormal, we have seen that much can be learned if one regards such experiences as reflecting one's own feelings and sensitivities that are perhaps otherwise difficult to bring to consciousness.

Mediums and Psychics

Glendower: "I can call spirits from the vasty deep!"

Hotspur: "Why, so can I, or so can any man;
But will they come when you do call for them?" *

WILLIAM SHAKESPEARE

It is sometimes difficult to distinguish between mediums and psychics. Mediums claim to be able to contact spirits, who manifest themselves through physical signs (physical mediumship) or through revelations expressed through the medium (mental mediumship). Psychics, on the other hand, claim to produce their effects through their own psychic powers. With regard to these distinctions, there seem to be two long-term trends. First, there is a trend away from the idea of "spirit influence," so that psychics are common today whereas mediums were in vogue 100 years ago. Second, there is a trend away from physical mediumship, which is subject to physical tests of various kinds, in favor of mental mediumship, which is more difficult to investigate.

There is little question that some mediums and psychics display extraordinary abilities and that these abilities are often the result of altered states of consciousness, called trance states. As William Sargant says: "In [trance] states people can remember languages which they have consciously long forgotten, or they can construct new languages. They can act or give impersonations or produce art or music with a degree of skill which is not normally available to them. They may also feel convinced that they are in touch with divine powers or with the spirits of the dead. . . ."[589]

King Henry IV (Part 1), Act 111, Scene 1

For example, Rosemary Brown is a British medium who claims that the spirits of dead composers act "through" her, enabling her to compose and play compositions on the piano that are beyond her own abilities. Her compositions are certainly pleasant and in the style of various dead composers, and, if she had had no prior contact with such music, her compositions would certainly seem mysterious. However, according to Rosemary Brown, she loved music as a child, there was a piano in her home while she was growing up, her mother played the piano, and she herself took piano lessons.[91] All of this, together with the enhanced skill often displayed in altered states of consciousness, seems sufficient to account for her musical compositions. My own experience in playing the piano is somewhat similar, if less spectacular; in certain states of consciousness, I am able to improvise "automatically" and unusually well and even in the style of various composers. That Rosemary Brown is probably denying her own music-making ability should not detract from the real skill she is displaying as a result of achieving an altered state of consciousness.

Having discussed some of the achievements of mediums, let us now consider what it is like to attend a "seance" of a physical medium. Such seances are noted for their occasionally powerful psychological impact.

Carl Jung writes: ". . . I was once at a spiritualistic seance where four of the five people present saw an object like a moon floating above the abdomen of the medium. They showed me, the fifth person present, exactly where it was, and it was absolutely incomprehensible to them that I could see nothing of the sort. I know of three more cases where certain objects were seen in the clearest detail (in two of them by two persons, and in the third by one person) and could afterwards be proved to be non-existent. Two of these cases happened under my direct observation."[354]

Eric Dingwall relates that he attended a seance in which participants reported the following experiences: "Music as if by a full orchestra filled the seance room; full form phantoms stood between the curtains of the cabinet presenting chalices out of which the sitters drank; materialized but invisible dogs lay on the laps of favoured sitters and were fondled by them."[165] Dingwall adds that, as far as he could detect: "There were no phenomena whatsoever,"[165] all of these experiences being purely objective.

And Harlow Gale describes a seance at which many attenders reported the following:

> After the Master [Jesus], as usual, appeared "a little Italian girl playing a harp," a Jewish girl for a Mr. Lazarus, Zacchaeus for quite a stay, and then the Table of the Lord's Supper was described by Dr. S. as before us and administered spiritually, Mrs. B. indicating the position of the Master in his service around the circle. Then "Sophie," Mr. A's wife, was announced, accompanied by a historical Minnesota Indian squaw, "Old Betz," who brought frogs' legs to Mr. A. as she had formerly done in real life. A dove also brought herbs in an envelope to Mr. A. from his wife.[234]

> [Gale states:] "Mrs. Gale and I saw nothing except the streaks and patches of light which came through the blinds and cracks, and the changing coloured patches of the retina's own light. . . ."[234]

In other words, Jung, Dingwall, and Gale attended seances in which other attenders saw, heard, and felt things that evidently had no objective existence. That seances can indeed produce such strong imagery, as well as many other effects, is known from a number of sources. Aside from attending ordinary seances, several investigators have arranged phony seances in order to observe how individuals respond, under controlled conditions, to various factors present in seances.[66, 298, 299, 561] Other investigators, as a consequence of years of informal acquaintanceship with mediums, have developed a good understanding of their methods.[244, 346, 467] Two conclusions emerge from this work.

1. First, a variety of psychological processes (discussed in previous chapters) are undoubtedly involved in creating the psychological effects of seances. For example:

Seances are typically held in the dark; darkness facilitates imagery—of ghosts, spirits, whatever is suggested by the setting—based on phosphenes, autokinetic effects, and hypnagogic states.

Mediums sometimes go into trance; in this state, they may appear "possessed" and—perhaps through automatisms—may convey information they cannot consciously tap. In addition, attenders can project their own meaning into the messages of the medium, further enhancing their appearance as "revelations." Of course, some of the revelations may be quite accurate, since some mediums are probably acutely sensitive (that is, hyperesthesia may be a factor) in picking up revealing cues from attenders.

The impact of a seance can, of course, be reinforced by the strong need that many people have to believe in paranormal phenomena. This need is evident particularly in cases in which individuals refused to believe confessions of fraud by mediums. Gustav Jahoda describes such an experience as follows:

> I found myself in the company of six other people after dinner, and the conversation veered toward the supernatural. An impromptu seance was proposed, and all of us settled around a large circular table. The idea was that questions would be asked, and the spirits would answer by rapping once for "yes" and twice for "no." The first question was asked, but nothing happened. We sat for several minutes in the semi-darkness, with tension rising. Getting rather stiff, I shifted in my chair, accidentally knocking the table, and was staggered to find that this was taken as the expected answer. After a brief struggle with my conscience, the desire to experiment gained the upper hand; I told myself that after a while I would reveal the deception and pass it off as a joke. For another half-hour or so I knocked the table quite blatantly with the tip of my shoes, without arousing the slightest suspicion. I was just about to summon my courage to come clean, when one of the persons present asked the spirit to materialize. Another long tense silence followed, then one person whispered, "He's there, in the corner—a little grey man." It was said with such conviction that I almost expected to see something when I looked. There was in fact nothing except a faint shadow cast by a curtain moving in a slight breeze. Two others claimed to see the homunculus quite clearly. . . . About a year after the seance I met one of the participants. Recalling the evening, he said that he had previously been sceptical about the occult, but this experience had convinced him. On hearing this my guilt feelings were thoroughly aroused, and I decided to make a clean breast of it. Once more I had badly miscalculated—he just would not believe me.[334]

And Rawcliffe discusses the case of the famous spirit photographer, Buguet: "One of the most striking examples of the spiritualist's capacity for self-deception occurred during the trial of the French photographer Buguet. Buguet admitted that he faked [spirit] photographs, used a draped doll or lay figure for his purpose. Yet witness after witness testified that Buguet had given them photographs of their dead loved ones, refusing even to accept the photographer's explanation of how he made them."[539]

2. The second conclusion that emerges from observations of mediums, as well as from their confessions, is that mediums have been known to make use of a broad range of techniques of decep-

tion, including sleight-of-hand, misdirection, accomplices, codes, networks to gather information on clients, electronic devices, and mechanical tricks of all sorts—in other words, as wide a variety of methods of deception as magicians are known to use. In fact, there are supply houses that stock a wide assortment of materials for use by mediums. The catalog of one such supplier states:

> Our experience during the past thirty years in supplying mediums and others with the peculiar effects in this line enable us to place before you only those which are practical and of use, nothing that you have to experiment with. . . . while we do not, for obvious reasons, mention the names of our clients and their work (they being kept in strict confidence, the same as a physician treats his patients), we can furnish you with the explanation and, where necessary, the materials, for the production of any known public "tests" or "phenomena" . . . our effects are being used by nearly all prominent mediums, entertainers, and others of the entire world. . . .[467]

Effects available from such suppliers include spirit-rapping, levitating tables, materializations, sealed letter writing, slate writing, psychic readings, psychometry, ectoplasm, ghosts, and spirit faces.[658] The reader who would like to know how such effects are produced should consult one of the books on the subject by Harry Houdini,[313] Joseph Rinn,[561] Joseph Dunninger,[172] or Milbourne Christopher;[120] all of these writers, at some point in their careers, were mentalists—that is, magicians who specialize in magic that appears to be "psychic." The trick described below by Joseph Rinn gives an idea of how clever, and difficult to detect, some of these effects can be.

> During one seance I attended, . . . Madame [Diss Debar] announced that her spirit guides had promised to have the spirits of some of the great painters of the past produce paintings for her on perfectly blank canvases. . . . In a moment, General Diss Debar entered with a framed blank canvas which he placed on an easel in the middle of the room.
>
> Madame urged us to examine the canvas and assure ourselves that it was, as she said, a plain, unpainted artist's canvas.
>
> After we had passed our hands over it, Marsh said, "It seems to be an ordinary canvas free and clean of any picture," to which Creelman and I, after examination, agreed. . . .
>
> "Now let all be passive and watch the canvas," commanded Madame.

> As we watched the canvas, we were amazed to see something appearing on it. The outline of a head was seen developing and it became clearer and clearer until a perfect head was visible.
>
> "It's an oil painting all right," said Marsh after feeling the canvas, and he showed us paint on his fingers.
>
> What we had witnessed stumped both Creelman and me. It seemed as if a miracle had been performed.[561]

Before reading further, see if you can figure out how this painting was made to materialize on a blank canvas.

Here is how it was, in fact, accomplished, as described by Rinn: "A freshly painted oil portrait was inserted in a deep frame and about an inch in front of this was placed a blank canvas of some thin material like cheesecloth. Inside the frame was a gadget or spring which, when pressed, drew the two canvasses together. When the front blank piece of cheesecloth rested against the oil painting, it attached itself to the painting, which, being freshly painted and wet, seeped through the blank piece, on which the second painting was gradually developed from the one underneath."[561]

However well these factors can account for effects experienced in seances, this, of course, does not prove that paranormal factors are not involved as well. Although this issue cannot be settled conclusively, it will help to consider some of the evidence concerning the incidence of deception on the part of mediums. If this incidence is high, this leaves less "room," as it were, for the operation of paranormal effects. For this purpose, we will discuss some of the noted mediums of the last 100 years or so and the evidence concerning their exposures and confessions. Our discussion will encompass only the better-known personalities; literally dozens of lesser-known mediums and psychics who have confessed or been exposed will not be discussed.[121, 132, 180, 521, 561]

Let us first discuss physical mediums, who claim to summon spirits, usually of departed souls, who make their presence known by physical signs of various kinds. Then we will discuss mental mediums, but bear in mind that many mediums employ elements of both approaches. We will conclude with a discussion of psychics, who, although differing somewhat in techniques and rationale, share many methods in common with mediums.

1. Modern mediumship is generally considered to have been ushered in, in the late 1800s, by Margaret and Catherine Fox. These two sisters discovered, as children, that their family and neighbors interpreted sounds that they made, chiefly by rapping their toes, as communications from spirits. The girls played along with this idea and the hoax mushroomed until the Fox sisters were famous and much in demand as mediums. The methods of deception used by the Fox sisters are known chiefly through the public confession of Margaret Fox, although Catherine Fox and a relative to whom the sisters had told their secret also revealed the hoax.[150] The relative, Ruth Culver, stated that: "The raps are produced with the toes. All the toes are used. After nearly a week's practice, with Catherine showing me how, I could produce them perfectly myself. At first it was very hard work to do. . . . She told me that all I should have to do to make the raps heard on the table would be to put my foot against the bottom of the table when I rapped; and that, when I wished to make the raps sound distant on the wall, I must make them louder, and direct my own eyes earnestly to the spot where I wished them to be heard."[329]

Ruth Culver was also instructed in how to rap the correct answer. "Catherine told me how to manage to answer the questions. She said it was generally easy enough to answer right if the one who asked the questions called the alphabet. She said the reason why they asked people to write down several names on paper, and then point to them till the spirit rapped at the right one, was to give them a chance to watch the countenances and motions of the persons, and that in that way they could nearly always guess right."[329]

In her confession, Margaret Fox stated:

My sister Katie was the first to observe that by swishing her fingers she could produce certain noises with her knuckles and joints, and that the same effect could be made with her toes. Finding that we could make raps with our feet—first with one foot and then with both—we practiced until we could do this easily when the room was dark. No one suspected us of any trick because we were such young children. . . .

. . . The rappings are simply the result of a perfect control of the muscles of the leg below the knee which govern the tendons of the foot and allow action of the toe and ankle bones that are not commonly known. . . . With control of the muscles of the foot the toes may be brought down to the floor without any movement that is perceptible to the eye.[329]

After her confession, Margaret gave a demonstration of the power of her rapping in front of an audience in a large auditorium: "On the surface of a plain little wooden stool she 'produced those mysterious sounds which for forty years frightened and bewildered hundreds of thousands of people in this country and Europe.' "[217] "Then all heard loud, distinct rappings that seemed to be now in the aisles, now behind the scenes."[561] Margaret's confession and demonstration were so detailed and persuasive that her effort to retract them at a later date was not very convincing.[329]

Thus it is instructive to know that William Crookes, the noted English physicist, had endorsed Catherine Fox as genuine. Crookes wrote that:

> . . . for power and certainty I have met with no one who at all approached Miss Kate Fox. For several months I enjoyed almost unlimited opportunity of testing the various phenomena occurring in the presence of this lady, and I especially examined the phenomena of these sounds. . . . I have had these sounds proceeding from the floor, walls, etc., when the medium's hands and feet were held—when she was standing on a chair—when she was suspended in a swing from the ceiling, when she was enclosed in a wire cage—and when she had fallen fainting on a sofa, I have heard them on a glass harmonicon—I have felt them on my own shoulder and under my own hand. I have heard them on a sheet of paper, held between the fingers by a piece of thread passed through one corner. . . . I have tested them in every way that I could devise, until there has been no escape from the conviction that they were true objective occurrences not produced by trickery or mechanical means.[141]

Crookes also endorsed several other mediums who were later exposed,[750] including Anna Eva Fay (who was exposed more than once[561] and who eventually explained how she duped Crookes[313]), Florence Cook (who was the subject of more than one exposé[273, 750]), and D. D. Home.

2. D. D. Home has a reputation in some quarters as an honest medium who was never exposed and who did not have to darken the room to produce his effects.[750] However, as Horace Wyndam demonstrates in his book, *Mr. Sludge, the Medium,*[756] none of these

assumptions withstands scrutiny. In particular, at least four people claimed to have detected Home in fraud on different occasions.[41, 313, 515, 750] Home's best-known feat, in which he reportedly floated out of one window and into another, is known only through accounts that hopelessly disagree on such matters as the building in which the event occurred, on what floor it occurred, and whether there was a ledge or balcony outside the windows.[626]

3. Ira and William Davenport were brothers and well-known mediums who specialized in the production of "spirit music" while seemingly bound securely with rope and seated in a cabinet. Ira Davenport has admitted that both he and his brother were fakes and that they themselves created the music after freeing themselves from their bonds.[313]

4. Madame Helena Blavatsky was the founder of the cult of Theosophy and was a self-proclaimed medium.[740] Among other things, she claimed she had obtained certain writings from spirits she called the Mahatmas. Because of her claims, the Society for Psychical Research investigated and came to the conclusion that Madame Blavatsky ". . . has achieved a title to permanent remembrance as one of the most accomplished, ingenious, and interesting imposters in history."[297] Later in her life, Blavatsky confessed to many of her deceptions,[193] explaining their necessity as follows: "What is one to do when, in order to rule men, you must deceive them, when, in order to catch them and make them pursue whatever it may be, it is necessary to promise them and show them toys? Suppose my books and *The Theosophist* were 1000 times more interesting and serious, do you think that I would have anywhere to live and any degree of success, unless behind all this there stood 'phenomena'? I should have achieved absolutely nothing. . . ."[271]

5. Henry Slade was celebrated for his ability to produce "spirit writings" on slates. However, he failed to impress the Seybert Commission on Spiritualism, which investigated him,[544] and, toward the end of his life, he wrote a confession in which he admitted that all of his manifestations were done by trickery.[313]

6. Nino Pecoraro specialized in producing physical manifestations of spirits of the departed while he was "tied up" in a cabinet. Toward the end of his life, Pecoraro related how he had deceived many famous people, including the novelist Sir Arthur Conan Doyle[561] (who was easily fooled[313]); he also wrote a confession in which he admitted that all his phenomena were faked.[172]

7. Eusapia Palladino never confessed, but she was exposed on several occasions.[147, 313, 561] One of these observers describes her method of table levitation as follows: "A foot came from underneath the dress of the medium and placed the toe underneath the leg of the table on the left side of the medium, and pressing upward, gave it a little chuck into the air. Then the foot withdrew and the leg of the table dropped suddenly to the floor. . . . I was lying with my face on the floor within *eight inches* of the left leg of the table; and each time that the table was lifted, whether in a partial or complete levitation, the medium's foot was used as a propelling force upward."[338]

8. Margery Crandon was studied by at least half a dozen different sets of investigators,[561] all of whom reached the conclusion that there was no substantial evidence that any of her phenomena was paranormal and some of whom detected her in outright deception; once, she displayed some "spirit fingerprints" impressed on wax, which turned out to be those of her dentist.

9. William Roy was a well-known medium in England in recent years who specialized in producing voices of departed spirits. However, he confessed that all of his performances were fraudulent and revealed his methods in his confession.[19] He stated that his revelations would: ". . . shock and distress the 100,000 and more people who came to my private and mass-audience seances and learned to regard me as one of the world's most capable and trustworthy mediums. . . . My victims were the dazed and griefstricken people who believed that I could put them in touch with the spirits of their loved ones from the world beyond the grave."[180]

10. M. Lamar Keene was a medium at Camp Chesterfield, Indiana, the largest spiritualist camp in the United States. Not long ago he confessed to being a fraud and exposed some of the trickery used at the camp and at the spiritualist church of which he was pastor. In one case, as Lamar Keene describes it:

> . . . Rose Johnson was attending the Sunday evening service of the church where I was then co-pastor, the New Age Assembly in Tampa, Florida. She heard me say from the pulpit, "People are always misplacing things. Who here has lost something?"
>
> Most of the 250 people in the church raised their hands, including Rose Johnson who had lost her library card a couple weeks before. . . .

"Mrs. Johnson," I said, pointing to her, "would you come forward?"

"I was overwhelmed," she wrote later in a formal statement (which I have before me) "and wondered what on earth or in heaven was going to happen to me.

"Mr. Keene asked me in front of the congregation what I had lost and I told him my library card.

"He requested that the congregation sing a hymn of faith to help raise the power. I stood watching Mr. Keene, who had his eyes half-shut in a semi-trance.

"Suddenly, as quick as that, something fell at my feet. It just seemed to come right out of the air. I picked it up. It was my lost library card!"

A loud "Oh!" rose from the congregation, followed by applause.[358]

In case you have not guessed it by now, Lamar Keene had stolen Rose Johnson's library card a few weeks previously; he was then able to "materialize" it by sleight of hand in the church service.

Having reviewed some exposés and confessions, it would seem that the possibility of paranormal factors in physical mediumship is slim. Let us now discuss some noted mental mediums and see if they fare any better. Mental mediums claim that spirits possess them while they themselves are in trance, so that their utterances and actions are actually communications from the spirits.

1. Helene Smith lived in Switzerland at the turn of this century. She exhibited a "spirit" personality during trance, which, among other things, related stories of Martians, including their living conditions, customs, and language. Through a lengthy study of Helene Smith, Theodore Flournoy showed that the knowledge she displayed during trance probably stemmed from personal experiences that were retained subconsciously and then expressed in a trance.[215] For example, the "Martian language" she described had exactly the same grammatical structure as French, the only language she knew.

2. Leonore Piper lived in the United States around the turn of the century. Through her, a number of "spirits" related stories of persons and events concerning which Leonore Piper denied any knowledge. However, a number of incidents cast doubt on her ability to contact the dead. For example, she gained some degree of fame with a "spirit" revelation about the circumstances of the death of a man named Dean Connor. However, when the revelation was

finally checked out, it turned out to be grossly unreliable.[561] In another incident, the family of George Pellew—whose departed spirit supposedly conveyed much of the news of the "other world" to Leonore—was shown the information furnished by "Pellew" about himself; they judged it to be highly inaccurate.[279] On another occasion, Leonore claimed to have contacted the spirit of Bessie Beals, who was a fictitious person invented on the spur of the moment by the psychologist G. Stanley Hall.[284] Later in her life, Leonore Piper made the following statement: "I cannot see but that it must have been an unconscious expression of my subliminal self. . . . it seems to me that there is *no* evidence of sufficient scientific value to warrant acceptance of the spiritistic hypothesis."[561]

3. Pearl Curran was a medium around the time of World War I, who "gave birth," through working a Ouija board, to a spirit personality named Patience Worth. This spirit claimed to be that of an English woman of the 1600s. After the appearance of a popular book on her experience, Patience Worth clubs sprouted across the country. Eventually, investigation revealed that Pearl Curran's own experience was adequate to account for the knowledge she displayed as Patience Worth.[120, 156]

4. Virginia Tighe, in the 1950s, revealed a personality under hypnosis that claimed to have lived a prior existence in Ireland.[64] Bridie Murphy, as the "past life" personality was called, became a household word before a reporter discovered that Virginia Tighe, as a child, was a good friend of a neighbor whose life was very similar to Bridie Murphy's.[237] In other words, cryptomnesia appeared to account for the information that "Bridie Murphy" possessed of which Virginia Tighe was not consciously aware.[372]

I have "regressed" several subjects to "past lives" under hypnosis. In most cases, the "past lives" they described could be accounted for in terms of impressions—for example, acquired during childhood—that emerged during hypnosis, but that they had largely consciously forgotten. In some cases, the "past life" was obviously a repressed—sometimes a very creative—part of the individual's personality, which, when seen as such, was on its way to being integrated into the person's total personality structure.

5. Arthur Ford—described as ". . . the world's greatest medium"[642] by his biographer—is best known for two of his "readings."

First, in a sitting with Harry Houdini's wife, Ford correctly identified the message that the magician had said he would attempt to communicate to his wife after his death. Afterward, however, evidence came to light indicating that Ford could have obtained knowledge of the message through devious means.[538, 561, 642]

Second, Arthur Ford was, in part, responsible for converting Episcopal Bishop James Pike to belief in spiritualism by conveying information, through his "trance personality," about Pike's dead son, which Bishop Pike considered too personal and obscure for Ford to know about.[327] As Pike stated: ". . . we were fully satisfied that the explanation wasn't fraud. . . . Any theoretical doubts about Arthur Ford's integrity were completely allayed by that sitting."[512] After Ford's death, however, his biographer discovered ". . . every one of these supposedly unresearchable items. . . ." among news clippings in Ford's files. In addition: "Among his papers we found certain material, in the form of handwritten notes, which strongly suggested that in one instance Ford was aided and abetted in fraudulent clairvoyance by a psychical researcher with whom he had been friends for years." Ford's biographer concludes: "The evidence is disquietingly strong that Ford cheated—deliberately as well as unconsciously. . . ."[642]

To my knowledge, Ford submitted to a formal test of his powers only once, when he attempted to identify, through psychic means, the owners of various objects (this is called psychometry). In this test, he failed completely.[415]

Although mental mediums do not provide good evidence for paranormal phenomena, some demonstrate that, as in cases of multiple personality, subconscious talents and memories can be tapped in altered states of consciousness. Particularly if recognized for what it is, this capacity is potentially very useful. In contrast to physical mediums who resort to conscious trickery, many mental mediums are undoubtedly sincere, as well as naive, about the basis of their abilities.

Now let us look at some psychics who, unlike mediums who are mainly vehicles for spirit influences, claim to personally possess psychic powers.

1. Soon after the Society for Psychical Research was established in England in the late 1800s, it set up a committee to investigate the reputed psychic abilities of the Creery sisters. After many

sittings, the committee endorsed the sisters as genuine psychics. Several years later, the sisters admitted they had deceived the committee.[279]

2. G. A. Smith and Douglas Blackburn were likewise endorsed as genuine psychics by a Society for Psychical Research committee. Many years later, Blackburn confessed his deception in the following words:

> For nearly thirty years the telepathic experiments conducted by Mr. G. A. Smith and myself have been accepted and cited as the basic evidence of the truth of Thought Transference. . . .
>
> . . . the whole of those alleged experiments were bogus, and originated in the honest desire of two youths to show how easily men of scientific mind and training could be deceived when seeking for evidence in support of a theory they were wishful to establish.
>
> . . . if two youths, with a week's preparation, could decieve trained and careful observers like Messrs. Myers, Gurney, Podmore, Sidgwick, and Romanes, under the most stringent conditions their ingenuity could devise, what are the chances of succeeding inquirers being more successful against "sensitives" who have had the advantage of more years experience than Smith and I had weeks?[279]

Although Smith continued to proclaim his innocence, Blackburn's detailed description of methods he said he and Smith had used in their deception is persuasive.

3. Nina Kulagina and Rosa Kuleshova are Russians who have a reputation, not unique but nonetheless noteworthy, for being able to "see" with their fingertips. However, their "eyeless vision" is now in question, inasmuch as Kulagina has been caught cheating and the conditions under which Kuleshova has been tested seem now to have been inadequately controlled.[196] Incidentally, being able to see while the eyes seem to be effectively blindfolded is the stock in trade of many magicians, and there are literally dozens of methods used.[121, 135, 666]

4. Peter Hurkos is a Dutch psychic who has made many claims, including being able to locate missing persons and to solve crimes. However, his failures are so numerous that Milbourne Christopher devotes a whole chapter to them in his book, *Mediums, Mystics, and the Occult.*[121] I know of only one test, under controlled conditions, of Hurkos' abilities. In this test, dealing with his reputed ability to do psychometry—that is, to identify the absent owner

of an object from the object alone—he failed to score above chance guessing.[672]

5. Gerard Croiset is another Dutch psychic who claims to have used his psychic powers to help police apprehend criminals. One of his better-known claims is that he helped solve a case of an assault on a young girl in Wierden, Holland. However, the Chief of Police of Wierden has stated that: "The police could do nothing with these communications [from Croiset]"[279] and that the description of the suspect and other information conveyed by Croiset were grossly inaccurate. Although some psychic researchers believe that Croiset has demonstrated psychic ability,[675] the Belgian Committee for the Scientific Investigation of Phenomena Reputed to be Paranormal has tested Croiset under controlled conditions and has found no evidence of psychic ability.[658]

With regard to criminal cases in Holland in general, the Chief of Police of Amsterdam has stated: "There are no Dutch crime cases known here which were solved by clairvoyants."[658] And F. Brink, a Dutch police investigator who has researched the claims of psychics to have aided the Dutch police in solving crimes, concludes that ". . . while such persons were sporadically consulted, the police had . . . never derived any help from their supposed powers of clairvoyance." Brink also personally tested the crime-solving ability of four of these psychics over a period of time and states that ". . . the results invariably proved to be nil. . . ."[279]

In the United States also, stories have circulated that psychics have helped police departments solve crimes.[691] In an effort to track down these stories, Richard Guarino sent questionnaires to the 100 largest police departments in the United States. Of the 68 departments that responded, seven had in fact consulted psychics. However, none reported that the psychics had provided any substantial help; at the same time, many failures were described. For example: "Despite the use of psychics on many occasions, the New York Police Department [stated] that no substantial results were ever achieved by their consultation. More than this, they believe that in some instances, investigators were sidetracked because wrong leads provided by the psychic diverted the police from concentrating on more established methods of investigation."[266]

What conclusions can we draw from these examples of mediums and psychics? First, the prevalence of deception, as indicated by the confessions and exposures of so many, means that fraud must be considered a likely hypothesis in evaluating claims of paranormal feats by mediums and psychics. Second, there is no conclusive evidence that mediums or psychics have produced phenomena that are not explainable in terms of either deception or ordinary psychological processes. This does not, of course, prove that no mediums or psychics have paranormal abilities; it does mean that this is still an open issue.

What about Uri Geller, the young Israeli who in the 1970s excited so much interest because of his supposed psychic powers? Memory is short, and the deceptions and confessions of mediums and psychics of the past are easily forgotten. But is Uri Geller any different?

Uri Geller and Magic

If you believe everything, you are not a believer in anything at all.[609]

SUFI SAYING

One problem in evaluating the performance of a self-proclaimed psychic such as Uri Geller is that it is almost impossible to be sure that tricks of some kind are not used. The following account is a good illustration of this problem:

> Edward Saint ... once used a simple demonstration of "psychic" power to prove to interested scientists that they were not qualified as psychic investigators. A set of precision scales were set on a table under a glass covering. Saint announced that through the power of his mind, he would cause the scales to unbalance. ... After the scientists had examined the apparatus, Saint then concentrated—and sure enough, the scales suddenly went off balance. The scientists, impressed, thought of every possible solution: atmospheric pressure, vibrations, preset machinery, and so on.[658]

Before reading further, see if you can think of a method by which the scales could have been unbalanced.

Here is how Saint managed to fool these scientists: ". . . Saint explained: just before he placed the glass jar over the scales, he released a *number of fleas* into the space from the hollow end of a fake pencil. With the glass jar over the scales, one or more of the fleas, invisible at even a few feet, would land on one side of the scale and upset the balance while Saint was concentrating."[658]

As we saw in the previous section, the line dividing mediums and psychics from mentalists (magicians who specialize in illusions that appear "psychic") is exceedingly fine. Many magicians, including Harry Houdini, Joseph Dunninger, James Randi, David Hoy, and George Kreskin, have billed themselves, at some point in their careers, as genuine psychics.[102, 530, 693] If you are interested in learning how mentalists perform their tricks, you should read some of the literature on the subject.[15, 35] Nevertheless, this will not insure that you will always be able to detect trickery when it occurs; even magicians are sometimes fooled by other magicians.[313] But is Uri Geller a magician? There is little doubt that he is. For one thing, Geller has been detected in trickery.[121,419] But there are two other kinds of evidence that also support this conclusion.

1. Friends and associates of Geller have confessed to helping him with his tricks. Hannah Shtrang, a former girlfriend, says "I used to help him with his tricks during appearances [and] my brother used to sit in the audience and pass signals to Uri that they had practiced beforehand." Danny Pelz, a showman and friend of Geller's, says: "We, from our side know all the lies. . . . And we also helped him to perpetuate some of these lies!" And Itzhaak Saban, Uri's chauffeur and close friend, says, "I know all of his tricks very well, and I can even appear in his place if I wish to." A reporter wrote, "Saban succeeded during the interview in moving the hands of my wristwatch without touching it in any way. After doing it he explained that it was done by means of sleight of hand. . . . This trick, which at the moment is driving the world crazy, he learned from Geller." Saban said that "Uri confessed, in a heart-to-heart talk with him, that everything in the act was just bluff."[530] More recently, Geller's ex-manager, Yasha Katz, has explained how many of Geller's favorite tricks are done.[531]

2. Magicians have duplicated the majority of Geller's feats. James Randi, in particular, has shown that he can duplicate Geller's major feats using trickery.[530] For example, one observer relates how Randi bent a nail.

> He handed me a carton of sturdy four-inch nails. "Pick any six that you think are perfectly straight." I did. I also looked to make sure

they were all real nails. "Now put a rubber band around that bunch and set them aside." I did so. [later] He picked up the bunch of six nails. "Let's find one that's absolutely straight." He rolled each one back and forth on the table, keeping up a constant patter while eliminating any nails that had "little woggily-woggilies," as Randi called them—slight irregularities which kept them from rolling smoothly. He ended up with one nail he liked, holding it between thumb and forefinger, midway along the shaft. "Now, keep your eye on it," he said, "I'm going to try to bend it." He moved it back and forth slowly and gently between his thumb and forefinger. I hardly knew what to expect.

Suddenly the nail began to bend before my eyes. "Look at that," Randi chuckled. Sure enough, it was bent about 30 degrees, and by a stage magician.

I shook my head in astonishment.[720]

And an editor of the British magazine, *Psychic News,* relates an incident in which Randi presented himself as a genuine psychic under the assumed name of Zwinge.

I collected a teaspoon. . . . As he stroked it lightly Zwinge told me he "gets a stickly feeling. It's like running your finger over clear glass."

I touched the spoon ends as he stroked it. Suddenly it seemed to shudder. Then it broke cleanly in two.

I was impressed. Next we were summoned into the adjoining "Two Worlds" office. We found the occupants, Lilian and Mary, excitedly proclaiming, "Look at the paper knife."

Lilian had used it that morning to open the mail. It was perfectly straight then. Now its handle had curved an astonishing 45 degrees.

All could vouch Zwinge had not been near it. Up to that point he had not entered their office.

Later another "Two Worlds" employee, Mona Bethune, announced, "My tea spoon has bent!"

It was perfect when she stirred the tea a few minutes earlier. . . .

By now, further manifestations were discovered. Mary noticed her clock had suddenly gained two hours. It had been correct earlier.

A glance at my office clock showed it fast by 2½ hours! Certainly Zwinge had no opportunity to interfere with them. He had been under constant surveillance.

I had not left his side, or taken my eyes from him, for one second. I was determined to be an objective reporter. I was fully alert to any suspicious moves. But Zwinge made none.[530]

In addition, James Randi has duplicated Geller's feats—activating a Geiger counter and making a compass needle deflect while standing several feet away—that puzzled scientists at the University of London.[530]

Randi also describes several other performers who have pretended to be "psychics" and have suggested on television shows, in imitation of Geller, that viewers will experience their metal objects bending, their mirrors cracking, and their stopped watches starting, and have thereby elicited floods of phone calls verifying their "psychic powers."[530]

David Marks and Richard Kammann, psychologists at the University of Otago in New Zealand, have found that you do not have to be a magician to imitate Uri Geller. After an appearance by Geller in New Zealand, Marks and Kammann obtained the double, sealed envelopes containing drawings that Geller had "clairvoyantly" duplicated in one performance. Noting that the outline of the drawings could be seen even through the two thicknesses of envelopes that held each one, Marks and Kammann gave the envelopes to students and found that "good renditions of Rachel's drawing, some much better than Geller's, were obtained from six students, none of whom claim any paranormal abilities whatsoever."[419]

> [Then, investigating Geller's feat of starting "broken watches," Marks and Kammann:] . . . interviewed six jewellers in Dunedin. It turns out that many or most stopped watches and clocks are not really broken, but are jammed in some way. Perhaps the oil has flowed to one side, or there is some other minor fault that only requires a cleaning and overhaul. The watch-men told us that a little winding, shaking, rotating, and especially warming the oil by holding the watch in your hand may be all that is needed to get it going again—temporarily. . . .
>
> . . . We sent out a few students to "fix" broken watches, and out of 16 watches tried, 14 of them started, and seven have kept going for at least four to five days.[419]

Other duplications of Geller's feats could be mentioned.[546]

The reader who is interested in learning how to perform these feats should consult a booklet by Uriah Fuller, which provides instructions for most of them.[231]

Interestingly, after Geller's performances became widely known, some children began to claim that they could also perform feats such as bending objects without touching them. Some of these "mini-Gellers" have now been studied by several different investigators and have been caught cheating.[51, 305, 500, 567]

Of course, demonstrating that trickery can produce the effects Geller achieves does not prove that Geller uses trickery. But these demonstrations, combined with reported observations of cheating and with confessions by Geller's associates, seem to point to the conclusion that Geller does indulge in trickery. The question is whether he also possesses psychic ability. Obviously, this question cannot be answered by relying on observations of his parlor or stage performances; it requires tests done under controlled conditions.

Unfortunately, Geller has been reluctant to submit to controlled experiments, and, to my knowledge, only two such studies have been done. The first was conducted in Israel by psychologist Ariel Merari. Three testing sessions yielded what Merari describes as "absolutely negative" results.[739] These findings, however, have been eclipsed in the public eye by a study conducted by Russell Targ and Harold Puthoff at the Stanford Research Institute.[667] In this study, Geller reportedly was able to determine, by psychic means alone, what target pictures had been chosen and displayed in another location. However, this study can be criticized on a number of grounds. In particular, there is some debate over whether targets were really chosen "randomly," whether the criteria for "passes" (that is, for not counting certain trials) were always legitimate, and, perhaps most importantly, whether Geller's talent for trickery was sufficiently guarded against.[328, 654, 739]

All in all, although the case is certainly not proved one way or the other, I must agree with the statement by Joseph Hanlon, an English physicist, who summarizes his investigation of Geller, including Geller's Stanford Research Institute performance, as follows: ". . . every Geller event that I could investigate in detail had a normal explanation that was more probable than the paranormal one."[278]

Summary

No testimony is sufficient to establish a miracle unless the testimony be of such a kind that its falsehood would be more miraculous than the fact which it endeavors to establish.[48]

DAVID HUME

In this chapter we have discussed the evidence for the existence of psychic abilities, through which communication and influence, in humans and perhaps other organisms, might occur by unknown nonphysical means. We have seen that spontaneous cases do not provide satisfactory evidence for psychic ability and that controlled studies are necessary to eliminate other possible explanations. We have seen, however, that studies of psychic abilities have often failed to eliminate the possibility that sensory cues, chance and coincidence, or fraud is responsible for what appears to be psychic phenomena.

Because of these potential problems, replications by independent investigators of studies favorable to psi are necessary before such studies can be accepted as evidence for psi effects. Unfortunately, we were unable to find any studies claiming support for psychic phenomena that have proved consistently replicable. At this point, therefore, the most reasonable conclusion seems to be that psychic phenomena have not yet been conclusively demonstrated.

We then discussed a variety of experiences often regarded as psychic in nature, namely prophecy, psychic healing, fakirs, water witching, auras, out-of-body feelings, and a number of experiences—apparitions, mediumship, etc.—often thought to be due to the influence of spirits. We saw that, in each case, the evidence favors a naturalistic, and not a paranormal, explanation of the experience.

At the same time, we examined the psychological processes—hyperesthesia, automatisms, projections, etc.—that seem to be involved in experiences that are so often considered to be psychic. We saw that, by becoming aware of these processes, it is possible to develop our capacity for such experiences and, in this way, transcend our usual sensitivities and capabilities. In other words, we saw that we need not mystify transcendental experiences in order to benefit from them.

7

Occult Experience

*How many strange cults and odd philosophies seem to be
established and flourishing, how many imposing titles that imply
transcendent powers of mind and body, how many opportunities
for the development of one's hidden capacities!*[547]

J. B. RHINE

An occult belief can be defined as one that claims to explain observable events, but that is generally considered ill-founded, particularly by experts in relevant fields of knowledge. That is, an
occult belief is a "fringe" belief that is usually based on faulty notions of evidence. A related characteristic of occult beliefs is that
they usually postulate the existence of some kind of paranormal
phenomenon. In addition, occult beliefs often entail a corresponding procedure or practice thought to be effective in the prediction
or control of events. Originally, occult meant "hidden," which can
be taken to mean either that the forces envisioned were hidden
from view or that the belief or practice itself was shrouded in se-
crecy; however, few occultisms have remained hidden in today's
world.

By this definition, belief in psychic phenomena is an occult
belief. Because of its importance, we devoted the whole of the last
chapter to some of the postulated forms of pyschic experience. In

this chapter, we will consider a variety of other kinds of occult beliefs of interest to transcendental psychology.

First, however, it is important to realize that sometimes what was once considered an occult belief comes to be validated and accepted by the public and the scientific community alike.[32, 384] For example, the idea that "stones fall out of the sky" was dismissed by scientists as superstition until meteorites came to be accepted as a natural phenomenon early in the nineteenth century.[440] And Kepler's theory that the tides were due to the gravitational pull of the moon was labeled an "occult fancy" by Galileo.[374] Likewise, what is accepted as a legitimate scientific belief or practice sometimes is later seen to be invalid. For example, astrology and alchemy, during certain periods, were widely viewed as legitimate pursuits.

This should alert us to the danger of using general acceptance as a criterion for judging the validity of a belief. A wiser procedure is to examine the evidence that exists in its support. Therefore, in our consideration of various occult beliefs, we will note the evidence that bears on each. Of course, this is not an infallible procedure; judgment of evidence varies and what lacks sufficient evidence today may be supported by sufficient evidence tomorrow. But it is the best procedure we have.

Finally, consideration of the evidence bearing on various occult systems is important because it allows us to evaluate the significance of the psychological processes discussed in earlier sections. That is, if a belief is unsupported by evidence, then psychological processes are probably important in maintaining commitment to the belief and in producing the effects ascribed to the occult practice. At the same time, we will see that many of these effects are quite useful, particularly if the psychological mechanisms that underlie them are understood and cultivated.

Astrology and Other "Readings"

A king who was also an astrologer read in his stars that on a certain day and at a particular hour a calamity would overtake him.

He therefore built a house of solid rock and posted numerous guardians outside.

*One day, when he was within, he realized that he could still see
daylight. He found an opening which he filled up, to prevent
misfortune entering. In blocking this door he made himself a
prisoner with his own hands.*

And because of this, the king died.[610]

SUFI TALE

Have you ever read your horoscope in the newspaper and
found that it rather mysteriously fits you? If so, you have some
notion of the appeal of the beliefs discussed in this section—
astrology, numerology, palmistry, Tarot, and the *I Ching*. All of
these can be considered "readings," by which, their adherents
claim, the study of some external event can reveal your personality,
life experiences, or future destiny. Such practices are sometimes
called "divination," "sooth saying," or "fortune telling," but "readings" seems a more neutral term. It is clear that many people receive guidance from readings that is useful to them. To understand
how this is possible, we need to consider some of the psychological
processes involved in readings as they are commonly used.

Many readings are conducted by a reader for a client who is
present at the reading. This allows the reader to interpret the fall
of the cards or the pattern of the stars to fit the character of the
client as this is expressed by the client's demeanor, speech, and so
on. My own observations of readers leads me to think that they
often are astute, sensitive individuals who pick up subtle cues
"leaked" by the client. Usually neither the reader nor the client is
consciously aware of this communication process, which therefore
can result in a reading that seems mysteriously perceptive. For
example, some readers use a glass ball ("crystal ball") to tap subconscious impressions in the form of imagery. One reader describes
how, in this manner, she was able to elicit a memory that was lost to
consciousness: "I had carelessly destroyed a letter without preserving the address of my correspondent. I knew the county, and
searching in a map recognized the name of the town. . . . But I had
no clue to the name of house or street, till at last it struck me to test
the value of the Crystal as a means of recalling forgotten knowledge. A very short inspection supplied me with [the address, so] I
risked posting my letter. . . . A day or two brought me an answer. . . ."[540] Similarly, a reader's subconscious impressions of a

client can be projected and made conscious through the use of tea leaves, a deck of cards, and so on.

In addition, readers sometimes train themselves to look for revealing cues, and manuals are available that provide instructions for developing such sensitivity. One of these manuals advises readers to be aware of:

> The client's sex, probable age, dress and physical appearance and condition, actions, facial indications, jewelry such as wedding rings (or, by close inspection of the fingers the previous removal of a ring), condition of the hands, fingernails, hair and shoes. . . . The client's grammar, nervous mannerisms, manner of sitting are important indicators. . . .
>
> Reactions will be revealed by word of mouth, facial expressions, movement of the hands, figiting [sic] in the chair, posture in chair, breathing, relaxation or tenseness of the body and a million and one SIGNIFICANT signs made by the client SUBCONSCIOUSLY.[480]

To the extent that readers are accurate in their insights, of course, clients may benefit greatly from the understanding they thus gain of themselves. However, many people consult their daily horoscope, for example, and interpret their own readings without the help of a reader. To understand how this process can result in helpful insights, we need to consider some additional psychological mechanisms that are involved in readings of all kinds, whether or not a reader is consulted. It will help us to understand these mechanisms if we first discuss some studies of how subjects respond to personality evaluations.

A number of studies have shown that people will tend to perceive a generalized personality description as an accurate description of themselves, particularly if they believe that the description is derived from a valid method of personality evaluation.[634] In these investigations, a single personality description is drawn up that is broad enough to be true of most people. The description usually contains insightful statements that typical subjects will realize are true of themselves, but will not realize are also true of most people. One of these descriptions, originally taken from an astrology publication, reads as follows:

> You have a strong need for other people to like you and for them to admire you. You have a tendency to be critical of yourself. You have

a great deal of unused capacity which you have not turned to your advantage. While you have some personal weaknesses, you are generally able to compensate for them. Your sexual adjustment has presented some problems for you. Disciplined and controlled on the outside, you tend to be worrisome and insecure inside. At times, you have serious doubts as to whether you have made the right decision or done the right thing. You prefer a certain amount of change and variety and become dissatisfied when hemmed in by restrictions and limitations. You pride yourself on being an independent thinker and do not accept others' opinion without satisfactory proof. You have found it unwise to be too frank in revealing yourself to others. At times, you are extroverted, affable, sociable, while at other times you are introverted, wary, and reserved. Some of your aspirations tend to be pretty unrealistic.[696]

To determine subjects' responses to this personality description, all subjects in a group were given this same description, presented as the outcome of a personality test, and were asked to rate its accuracy as a portrayal of themselves. The comments of a few of the subjects provide an insight into some of the ways such descriptions are interpreted.

It appears to me that the results of this test are unbelievably close to the truth. For a short test of this type, I was expecting large generalizations for results, but this was not the case. . . .

The interpretation is surprisingly accurate and specific in description. I shall take note of many of the things said.

For the first time things that I have been vaguely aware of have been put into concise and constructive statements which I would like to use as a plan for improving myself.[696]

A similar study was conducted as follows:

A horoscope was drawn up which was complete but false—that is, established by chance and without reference to the sky at the time of birth—and which was confined to fairly vague statements like "You have two personalities which are in conflict . . . your character upsets those around you . . . beware of road accidents . . ." etc. We . . . received enthusiastic congratulations from deceived victims. "I admire your knowledge of astrology and I envy you it!" one wrote, and another went even further: "My father has till now been dubious about astrology, but after reading your analysis of my character he is convinced that it is true!"[242]

Likewise, still another investigator, who gave each of a group of subjects identical personality evaluations, received comments such as: "What you have told me of my past and character is the absolute truth," and "You seem able to read my life like a book."[242]

Such studies demonstrate that people often will accept, as a highly accurate description of their own personalities, a set of highly general statements that are the same for all subjects. To some extent, this undoubtedly occurs because any generalized personality evaluation is not only a good description of most people, but is also a particularly accurate description of some people. However, there is evidence that subjects accept such general statements as an accurate portrayal of themselves as readily as they accept the results of a valid personality test.[663] How can we make sense of this finding?

A moment's thought will reveal that a generalized personality description is an ideal stimulus for the operation of projection. Projection, you will recall, is the ascription of our own characteristics to an external stimulus. Furthermore, the less defined the stimulus, the more easily we can project. That is, given the description of *any* personality trait, all of us could think of how it applies to ourselves, in some ways, under some circumstances. Thus a generalized personality description can operate in the same fashion as any projective personality measure, as a mirror to our inner selves. Likewise, of course, projection occurs when we interpret readings concerning past events or future happenings. People who are not sufficiently aware of their own tendency to project may be mystified by what thus appears to be a strangely perceptive reading and consequently may ascribe some kind of "power" to the stars, a deck of cards, or other objects.

Compared to a highly general personality description, a description derived from a valid personality test is likely to be sufficiently specific, as well as threatening to our preconceived image of ourselves, so that we fail to "project" ourselves into it and thus fail to see its greater validity.

Studies also indicate that another process, known as the "self-fulfilling prophecy," is involved in the use of readings.[159] People who believe that they are destined to undergo a certain experience in the future, because a reading has predicted it, may subconsciously bring about the experience, thus "fulfilling the prophecy."

Or if individuals learn, through a reading, that they "should" have certain personality traits, they may accentuate those aspects of their personalities. Obviously, belief in the particular type of reading employed can be strongly reinforced in these ways. At the same time, however, these individuals are "disowning" some of their own responsibility and capacity to make decisions as they project responsibility onto the stars or a deck of cards. Feeling that "the stars" or "the cards" can be counted on for direction may, of course, be comforting to some people, who thus are relieved of the burden of having only themselves to depend on. Likewise, in the realm of human relationships, some people undoubtedly rely on astrology or other readings to provide a framework for categorizing people, which is quicker or easier than the lengthy, and sometimes threatening, process of getting to know others through personal interaction.

The potentially destructive effects of placing "faith" in a reading was brought home forcefully when a friend gave a Tarot reading to a client in which the "death" card figured prominently. A few days later, the client drove her car off a cliff. There is no way of knowing, of course, if her "faith" in Tarot caused her to live out its prediction, but this, unfortunately, is a possibility.

Our consideration of how projection can make readings appear remarkably accurate and perceptive, however, has revealed the potential utility of such readings. Just as a Rorschach inkblot can serve as a "psychological mirror" into which we project ourselves in order to see our inner selves more clearly, so also a symbolic system such as astrology or Tarot can be an excellent means of self-discovery. The usefulness of this process, of course, will be enhanced if we are sufficiently aware of our projections to call them our own.

The question still remains however, whether there are paranormal factors involved in readings that go beyond the psychological processes we have discussed so far. In our attempt to answer this question, we will now consider several kinds of readings that enjoy considerable popularity.

1. Astrology is without question one of the most popular occult beliefs. According to various surveys, anywhere from 10 to 30 percent of the population express some belief in astrology.[235, 334]

Although fascination with the heavens probably dates from

ASTROLOGY

the dawn of humankind on earth, astrology as we know it originated in the time of the Babylonians, was further developed by the Greeks, and was systematized in its most influential form by the noted astronomer and astrologer, Ptolemy.[403] The central tenet of astrology is that one's life experiences can be predicted from a knowledge of the positions of the heavenly bodies at the time of one's birth. The sun, the moon, each of the planets, and certain constellations of stars (Aries, Taurus, etc.) are thought to represent different kinds of influences in one's life, depending on the characteristics ascribed to them and on their relative positions in the sky. For example, the constellation closest to the sun's position at the time of birth is called the sun-sign and is one of the factors taken into account in the development of an individual's horoscope.

Many studies have been conducted to test the validity of astrology. The concept of sun-sign, probably owing to its popularity, has given rise to many such tests. Geoffrey Dean summarizes approximately three dozen studies that have sought to determine if sun-signs are related, as astrologers believe they are, to personality characteristics, occupational success, or marriage success.[153] In addition, there are at least half a dozen studies on sun-signs that

Dean does not mention.[44, 58, 73, 320, 345, 431] Of a total, then, of more than 40 studies, about the only ones that show promising results report that—as astrology postulates—people born under odd-numbered signs (Aries, Gemini, etc.) are more extroverted than people born under even-numbered signs (Taurus, Cancer, etc.). Although three studies have reported this finding, two other studies have reported conflicting results.[153, 632] Obviously, at this point, more research is needed.

One fact casts doubt on the concept of sun-sign in general, however; because of precession of the earth's axis, the constellations on which sun-signs are based have shifted about one sun-sign since the system currently in use was codified by Ptolemy in the second century. In other words, people now considered Taurians by astrologers actually were born under Aries, Geminians are actually Taurians, and so on through the sun-signs. A few astrologers, in fact, compensate for precession (this is called sidereal, in contrast to traditional tropical astrology). However, results using the sidereal system are generally no more consistent or successful than results of traditional studies.[153]

Geoffrey Dean also summarizes approximately 60 tests of astrological concepts other than sun-sign, including houses, aspects, rulership, and angularity. Except for a very few findings, which need to be replicated before they can be accepted, these studies provide little support for astrology.[153]

A different kind of test of astrology has entailed giving the birth times and places of subjects, together with descriptions of their personal characteristics, to astrologers, who are then asked to use any and all astrological indicators to match the birth charts with personal characteristics. Vernon Clark has reported significant results using this method, and two other studies support his conclusion. However, three other investigators, and several of my students, have attempted to replicate Clark's results—without success.[153] At this point, it seems that Clark's studies cannot be considered definitive support for astrology.

Of all of the studies of astrology summarized thus far, one deserves particular mention because of its popularity and its dangerous implications. This is a study by Eugen Jonas, which claims to show that effective birth control—as well as determination of a child's sex—can be achieved by paying attention to astrological indicators. A half dozen or so replication studies now clearly indicate that astrological birth control does not work and that Jonas' system is founded on faulty research.[153]

In contrast to studies of traditional astrology, other studies have sought to determine if there are *any* relationships—whether predicted by astrologers or not—between significant life experiences and the positions of the heavenly bodies at birth. If successful, these studies would support the general notion of astrology, but not its specific predictions.

First, several investigators have wondered if people born at different times of the year—in other words, under different sunsigns—differ in their life experiences in any way, whether congruent with astrology or not. Generally, these studies reveal few consistent differences, which, in any case, show little correspondence to astrological beliefs.[153] Any such difference, of course, could arise from purely seasonal influences.

Second, John Addey has developed an astrological system using "harmonics," which is complex and, in contrast to much of traditional astrology, not intuitive. Although Addey claims promising results, it is too early to say if "harmonics" will stand up to long-term testing.[6]

Third, Michel Gauquelin claims to have found some relationships—which show little agreement with traditional astrology—between occupational success and the position of planets at the time of birth.[243] However, there is much dispute about his results.[128, 129, 340, 341, 753, 754] As Gauquelin himself points out: ". . . the surprising result may be due to peculiarities in the data, and not to an intrinsic dependence of profession on planetary configurations."[3] At present, the final word on the significance of Gauquelin's research is not yet in.

Thus we see that, of 100 or so studies of various kinds of astrological predictions, none has produced convincing evidence in support of astrology, either as traditionally conceived or as modified according to various systems. In particular, the few promising findings that do exist have not been adequately confirmed by means of successful replications.

The poor showing that astrology makes in these research studies, however, should not blind us to the fact that there are behaviors—the sleeping-waking cycle is an obvious example—that are basically related to astronomical events and that we are only beginning to investigate in a thorough manner.[406, 407] As we continue to discover relationships between astronomical events and human behavior, however, we should not make the error of assuming that the causal mechanisms are as obvious as the correlations. For example, did you know that when Venus appears in the night sky, your activity level probably changes! This conceivably could affect the personality of babies born during this period when the mother's body experiences this change. However, if this were so, it would be a mistake to assume—as most astrologers would—that Venus had anything to do with it. The fact is that Venus, being close to the sun, appears in the sky around the time the sun sets or rises, and these are the times when our activity level typically changes—from active to passive, or vice versa. Judging from the poor showing that astrology makes in tests of its validity, any such relationships that are discovered between astronomical events and life experiences will probably bear little resemblance to astrology as traditionally conceived.

Lack of evidence, however, is not the only problem with astrology. Many other questions arise that astrologers have failed to answer satisfactorily. For example:

> How is it that the characteristics and relative positions of particular heavenly bodies, many of them billions upon billions of miles away, can predict the specific experiences of individual human beings?

> What about events that affect masses of people: must we conclude that victims of floods and earthquakes all have tragedy written into their horoscopes?

> Why is the configuration of the heavenly bodies at the time of birth more important than at the time of conception?

> Why are the various constellations, the planets, and the sun and moon thought to represent the particular psychological influences that are ascribed to them?

> Why is the particular pattern of stars in a constellation thought to be more important than their relative distance from the earth?

> Why are constellations that are near the sun's position considered more important than other constellations?

> Why is the constellation Ophiuchus, which is even more closely related to the path of the sun than some of the constellations traditionally considered important by astrologers, not thought to have any influence?

The poor showing that astrology makes in the light of critical scrutiny points up the wisdom of Shakespeare's words: "The fault, dear Brutus, is not in our stars, But in ourselves."

Although interest in astrology is widespread, other types of readings are also often in the news. Let us take a look at some other approaches to understanding ourselves.

2. Numerology is the study of the numbers in your life. Such features as your name and your birthdate are reduced to single digits by the process of converting letters into numerals (A=1, B=2, etc.) and by adding the digits in numbers of more than one digit until a single digit results (for example, 52 reduces to 7). The exception is the number "9," which sometimes is regarded as too "spiritual" and may be omitted in the assigning of numbers to letters.

The single numerals that result are said to represent different influences in your life. For example: "1" indicates a person who is single-minded and a potential leader; "2" indicates a person who is internally divided, second-rate, but a good follower, and so on.

In addition, it is best if the key numbers in your life are harmonious and complementary rather than in conflict. Sometimes adding or dropping a middle initial, for example, is sufficient to create harmony out of chaos.

Perhaps because of its relatively low level of popularity compared with astrology, I know of no published study that tests the validity of numerology. However, a student of mine conducted a small-scale study in which he compiled personality descriptions for a number of subjects based on the numerology system of Louis Hamon (otherwise known as Cheiro).[276] He then asked subjects to pick out their own description from all the descriptions for all subjects. He found that subjects could not identify their own personality description with any greater accuracy than chance guessing would produce.

There seems no evidence, then, that numerology is a valid method for determining personality characteristics.

3. A number of reading systems are based on body characteristics—that is, on physiognomy. Of these, palmistry is the most popular. Palmists believe that the various features of your palms—the fate, heart, and life lines, the mounds—are indications

of particular life experiences. Now some features of the hands do, in fact, indicate significant life experiences; for example, certain diseases affect the condition of the nails. However, these features generally are not noted by palmists.

Is there any evidence that the features palmists esteem are psychologically significant? The only study of palmistry I was able to locate was an investigation of the relationship between the lifeline and age at death of 51 individuals. Palmists would say that longer-lived individuals should have longer, unbroken lifelines. The study found no such relationship.[744]

As a general test of palmistry, a student of mine derived personal descriptions from the palms of a number of subjects, using a standard system of palmistry as described by Louis Hamon.[275] Subjects then were asked to identify the description that was derived from characteristics of their own palms. Subjects were unable to do so with greater than chance accuracy.

In sum, there seems to be no evidence in support of palmistry as a valid method of determining personal characteristics.

4. The type of reading we have discussed so far is based on events and characteristics that are relatively unchanging over time. Let us now consider readings based on the notion that a random process conducted at the time of the reading can relate to the life experience of the subject. Although many different forms of divination by random events are found in different cultures, we will discuss two popular varieties—Tarot and the *I Ching*.

Tarot readings are based on a deck of cards, each picturing a different figure (King, Devil, Hermit, etc.). Some of the Tarot cards are pictured in Figure 27. The cards are shuffled in the presence of the subject and then dealt according to one of a variety of methods. The final arrangement of cards is then interpreted according to the particular method used. The fact that there is a wide variety of conflicting methods is an indication—although not a proof—that Tarot, as ordinarily conceived, is either invalid or arbitrary.

One of my students tested Tarot by conducting readings for a number of subjects, according to the system described in *The Aquarian Tarot*.[253] She then compiled the readings and asked subjects to identify their own readings from among all of them. She found they could not identify their own readings with better than chance accuracy.

Figure 27. Tarot cards

The *I Ching* consists of 64 ancient Chinese proverbs, of which the following is an example:

Horse and wagon part
Strive for union
To go brings good fortune
Everything acts to further.[325]

A number of these proverbs are selected by one of several possible random processes, which also indicates how the proverbs should be viewed in relationship to one another.

A student of mine tested the *I Ching* by presenting a number of subjects with three sets of proverbs, one that was chosen by the accepted method and two chosen beforehand that were the same for all subjects. The subjects could not identify the correctly chosen set of proverbs with greater than chance accuracy.

In general, it seems that there is no adequate evidence in support of paranormal processes in readings such as we have considered. However, this does not mean that readings are worthless; we have seen that, viewed as "tools" for the projection and understanding of the content of our own unconscious, readings can be very useful. In the case of the *I Ching*, for example, Carl Jung states that it is not difficult to: ". . . show how I have projected my subjective contents into the symbolism of the hexagrams. Such a critique . . . does no harm to the function of the *I Ching*. On the contrary, the Chinese sage would smilingly tell me: 'Don't you see how useful the *I Ching* is in making you project your hitherto unrealized thoughts into its abstruse symbolism?' "[353]

You might enjoy obtaining a reading to see what you can gain from it. The personality description on pages 231–32 will serve or you can look at any daily horoscope column; as we have seen, the reading for a sign chosen at random probably will work as well as the reading for your own sign. Feel free to interpret liberally and see if you can obtain some useful insights from the reading. Note what seems particularly accurate, and ask yourself whether you were previously aware of the importance of that aspect of your life. If not, you will have learned something without, however, ascribing occult powers to the reading itself.

However, you may feel that some particular type of reading has an intrinsic validity that does not depend on the psychological processes discussed above. In that case, you may want to conduct your own validity test of the reading. In one such test, using astrology as an example, subjects are chosen who have had little or no contact with astrology (subjects who have had much contact with astrology may, perhaps subconsciously, have conformed in some ways to its predictions). Subjects are asked to submit the time and place of their birth, on the basis of which a reading is developed for each subject. Next, all of the subjects are given all of the readings and are asked to identify their own. Obviously, in this process it is important that no readings contain references to place or time of birth that would allow subjects to identify their readings on that basis. The number of subjects who can identify their own readings is then noted. To evaluate your results, a good rule of thumb is that no matter how many subjects you have in your study, at least four of them must identify their own readings for the results to be significantly better than what chance guessing would produce. [245]

If you feel that your subjects are not sufficiently self-aware to be able to identify their own readings, you can ask friends of the subjects to match subjects with their readings. In all other respects, the procedure remains the same as described above.

If you would rather test the ability of a particular reader more directly, you can use an alternative procedure, at least for readings such as astrology and numerology, where the subject need not be present at the reading. Again using astrology as an example, subjects who are naive concerning astrology are asked to furnish their birth time and place, from which the astrologer develops their horoscopes. In addition, the astrologer draws up a questionnaire on which subjects submit personal information that the astrologer feels will relate most closely to their horoscopes. The astrologer then tries to match the horoscopes with the questionnaires. Of course, it is important to insure that the astrologer has no other clues, such as handwriting or indications of age or place of birth in the questionnaires, which would allow the possibility of matching on those grounds. The astrologer's success is then evaluated in the manner already described—regardless of the number of subjects in the study, the astrologer must correctly match at least four questionnaires with their corresponding horoscopes for the results to be considered significant. [200]

Although you should have at least four subjects in your study to determine if your results are significant, more subjects are better up to a point. This point, which is somewhere between six and twelve subjects, is reached when the subjects are frustrated by the number of different readings they have to compare.

Health and Healing Systems

Oz, left to himself, smiled to think of his success in giving the Scarecrow and the Tin Woodman and the Lion exactly what they thought they wanted. "How can I help being a humbug," he said, "when all these people make me do things that everybody knows can't be done? It was easy to make the Scarecrow and the Lion and the Woodman happy, because they imagined I could do anything." [46] FRANK BAUM, *The Wizard of Oz*

In the last chapter, we noted that in psychic healing the healer is assumed to possess some kind of psychic capacity that facilitates healing. Now we will evaluate some occult approaches to healing and health that do not necessarily assume that psychic influences are involved. In spite of this theoretical distinction between psychic healing and other forms of occult healing, the same psychological processes are undoubtedly involved in both. You will remember that healers who rely on psychological mechanisms for healing generally use two approaches: first, stress reduction, accomplished through touch, massage, and personal concern and support; and, second, conditioning effects, accomplished through the use of placebos and suggestion as well as through reinforcement of positive patient attitudes and practices. The following experience, for example, illustrates the importance of suggestion in the occult healing of various conditions:

> The ... Africans, among whom I have spent many years ... make large use of charms, worn on the person, in cases of illness. Missionaries and traders ... occasionally derive great benefit from this "superstition. ..."
>
> I was curious to know whether any evidence could be obtained pointing to the probable cause for their effect.
>
> In order to do this I imitated the African. ... I prepared a "charm," consisting of a few hieroglyphics written on paper. This was wrapped up and sewn into a piece of tape, and tied firmly on the bare arm of the subject of the experiment. It was to be worn night and day for a few days, no time limit being given. I gave the subjects to understand that I was only asking them to assist in an experiment; that the charm was only paper with writing on it; that they were not to expect any improvement, but simply to tell me if such happened. ... Now for the results in detail: ... Myself, age 46. I have, all my life, been subject to some nervous ... twitching of a muscle; sometimes of the

face, the head, the shoulder, etc. . . . I . . . tried earnestly to suppress it, but without effect. I wore a charm, and it immediately disappeared. Some few days after I found myself at it again, and found that the charm had slipped from *where I could feel it* to the elbow. On replacing it the annoyance ceased. The same lapse occurred two or three times, but I always found the charm had slipped. After a few weeks I discontinued its use, and the bad habit has not recommenced.

Another case lately occurring to myself is the following:—I have for the last two months been very weak and ill—slight valvular affection of the heart, on the occasion I mention accompanied by severe pain in the back and sides. I was visiting my sister, having a rest, but did not seem to improve. One night she tied me a charm on the left arm, and I passed a good night. The following morning . . . I felt well, though weak. I had no pain whatever, and for the first time in many months was not conscious that I had a heart. This freedom from pain has remained for about three weeks, up to the present time. . . .

L. H., 78, chronic sufferer from rheumatism. I gave him a charm. . . .

I did not see him for some time, but he told me that, from whatever cause, he had been very free from pain, and had discontinued the charm. He then had a fatiguing journey in Holland, and on his return told me he was going to look for his charm, as he had had a recurrence of the pain. A week or so after he told me he was wearing it [and] had no pain. . . .[510]

Once again, the power of our subconscious healing processes is clearly shown. We will obviously benefit to the extent that we learn to develop these potentials for healing that are latent in us all.

Now let us consider some occult health and healing systems, including the evidence that bears on the occult beliefs underlying each. If you keep in mind the psychological mechanisms we have discussed, you can probably make your own judgment concerning the validity of these beliefs.

The first approaches we will consider share the assumption that various kinds of manipulation of the external body are an effective approach to healing. These manipulations include massage, stimulation of body pressure points, and adjustment of various bones and muscles. Insofar as many conditions, especially psychosomatic ones, can be helped by such means, many body therapies are undoubtedly effective. In particular, body therapies often involve implicit processes that can be highly therapeutic psychologically, but that are usually not acknowledged explicitly. Some of these implicit processes are:

1. Touch and massage, which can lessen anxiety, promote relaxation, provide distraction, and produce an "alive" feeling as tactual nerves are stimulated.
2. Release, or catharsis, of feeling and tension, which can result from manipulation in an area of the body that is associated with traumatic experiences and which can be highly therapeutic.
3. Discomfort, and even pain, which can result from manipulation of various kinds and which can alleviate guilt feelings, draw attention from other problems, foster pride in being able to "take it," and produce assurance that the procedure is "powerful."

Perhaps it is not surprising that body therapies do not explicitly acknowledge these psychological processes. For example, we have seen that touch and the need for touch are, to some extent, taboo subjects in our culture. Many people probably find it easier to believe that an occult body treatment is rearranging their "energy flow" than to acknowledge that they are seeking human touch because they feel alienated and under stress. In spite of the potential effectiveness of body therapies of various kinds, however, the particular approaches we will now discuss unfortunately entail highly occult notions that undermine most of the legitimacy they might otherwise enjoy.

1. Chiropractic is a healing procedure based on the belief that illness results from dislocations in the bones of the spinal column, which cause pinching of the spinal nerves. These spinal subluxations, as they are called, are assumed to create disease in the area or organs of the body that the spinal nerves serve. The basic cure for illness in general, therefore, is manual manipulation of the spine to correct subluxations.[138]

At one time or another, chiropractors have claimed that subluxations cause almost every conceivable type of illness, including appendicitis, deafness, diabetes, epilepsy, eye disorders, polio, encephalitis, and cancer.[630] It has never been demonstrated, however, that such subluxations are ever a factor in these illnesses, or in most illnesses for that matter.[630]

First, there is some question whether subluxations, as defined by chiropractors, can cause pinched nerves.[249] For example, R. R. Bensley, director of the Department of Anatomy at the University of Chicago, states that: "In a period of twenty-nine years, during which time I have been Director of this Department, we have never found in our dissecting rooms a single instance in which the foramen or aperture between the vertebrae through which the nerve branches issue from the spinal cord have been so narrowed as to cause pressure upon nerves!"[630] And Edmund Crelin, testing spinal columns from fresh cadavers, tried to pinch spinal nerves by extreme displacement of spinal vertebrae, but found that it was impossible; the spinal columns would break first.[138]

At most, it seems that subluxations, as defined by chiropractors, might occasionally cause limited or localized problems, but not the variety of conditions that they propose.[249]

Second, although there is some question whether pinched nerves result from subluxations, they can result from other conditions, which, however, chiropractors generally do not treat.[630] And when they occur, pinched nerves do not have the effects that chiropractors expect. For one thing, partial blockage of nerve impulses generally has little effect. Total blockage, of course, can have serious effects; quadriplegics, whose spinal nerves are useless from the neck down, certainly suffer severe incapacities, but they typically do not suffer from the range of illnesses that chiropractic theory would predict as a consequence of totally blocked nerves.[117]

Third, of the 43 major nerve tracks serving the body, only 26 are potentially subject to chiropractic manipulation.[117] The remainder either exit directly from the brain without going through the spinal column or pass through the spinal column at fused immobile vertebrae at the base of the spine. In other words, many nerves serving the "... head, senses of smell, taste, hearing and sight, organs of the neck, respiratory apparatus, heart, stomach, small intestine, part of large intestine, pancreas, gall bladder, liver, spleen, kidneys, pelvic organs, and part of lower limbs"[630] are not subject either to subluxation or to chiropractic manipulation.

Although the basic tenet of chiropractic seems to be faulty, chiropractors might facilitate recovery from illness through their implicit reliance on many of the psychological processes we have already discussed, such as the effects of touch and suggestion.[662] Also, for some conditions, muscle and bone manipulation, and advice in such matters as nutrition, may be directly beneficial.[118]

However, there are risks in chiropractic treatment. Occasionally, patients receive serious injuries as a result of manipulation. In addition, there are indirect risks resulting from overuse of x-rays, which are taken to reveal "subluxations," and from the failure to seek proper medical treatment for conditions for which chiropractic is ill-suited.[118, 630]

2. A number of therapies are based on the theory that certain points on the body surface are linked with organs and other regions of the body in such a way that stimulation of these points will have a therapeutic effect on the related organs and regions. By and large, these therapies do not postulate relationships that are known to exist as a result, for example, of neural connections. Rather, the nature of the postulated connections is generally vaguely defined and unsupported by anatomical or physiological evidence. These therapies are particularly intriguing because one of them, acupuncture, began to attract much attention in the 1970s and may prove to be one of those practices, initially considered occult by many, that eventually enjoys general acceptance. It is too early to say whether the effectiveness of acupuncture depends primarily on such factors as suggestion and counterirritation[85, 113, 123, 381] or on physiological relationships only now beginning to be studied.[50, 142, 438, 711]

Unlike acupuncture, however, there is no evidence that pressure-point therapies, such as zone therapy and foot reflexology, have any intrinsic therapeutic effects.

Zone therapy was developed in the early part of the twentieth century by William Fitzgerald and his associate Edwin Bowers,[210] who postulated that the body was divided into ten vertical zones. Zone therapy assumes that a stimulus applied to an area remote from a diseased organ or region of the body, but at the proper point in the proper zone, will have a therapeutic effect. According to its advocates, zone therapy is effective in the treatment of such conditions as appendicitis, cancer, diabetes, epilepsy, heart disease, tuberculosis, and ulcers.[60,210] For hearing problems, for example, the following approaches are recommended:

> One of the handiest methods of curing hearing problems is to place a wad of absorbent lint in the space between the last tooth and the angle of the jaw, so that one is able to bite down hard. . . .
>
> Another method that has worked for some people is to squeeze the joints of the ring fingers or the toes corresponding to the ring fingers. . . .

> Some cases of deafness have been cured by pressing the teeth of an aluminum comb against the tips of the fingers of the hand . . . five minutes at a time, and then following this up with pressure against the floor of the mouth for six or seven minutes, then against the hard palate, and lastly against the tongue.

> [Or if these fail:] Hearing may generally be improved by the following procedure: lift the end of the third fingernail of the left hand and do this forcibly for a few minutes at a time. Then do the same with the ring fingers.[60]

We thought it might be instructive to compare the zone designations in zone therapy with the meridian lines in acupuncture. Discrepancies between the two systems would be some indication, although certainly not proof, that at least one of these approaches is basically arbitrary. Such a comparison indicates that the zone designations and meridian lines show essentially no correspondence.

Using the same rationale, we undertook a comparison of the pressure points in foot reflexology—a branch of zone therapy that stresses the role of the feet in treatment[60]—with the acupuncture points for the same conditions. We found that the treatment points in the two systems differ markedly.[108, 417] For example, for tonification (rejuvenation) and sedation of the gall bladder, acupuncture points are located just above the small toe of the left foot and above the ankle of the right leg respectively. On the other hand, foot reflexology recommends pressure on the right side of the sole of the right foot for gall bladder conditions. And for tonification and sedation of the lungs, acupuncture points are found at the base of the thumb of the left hand and near the elbow of the left arm, respectively. However, for lung problems, foot reflexology recommends pressure near the toes on the soles of both feet. Other acupuncture points likewise show essentially no correspondence with pressure points in foot reflexology.

Some foot reflexologists also claim that disease can be diagnosed by exerting pressure on various points of the soles of the feet; soreness or tenderness at a point supposedly indicates disease in the organ to which the point is "connected." To test this belief, my students did reflexology diagnoses of this kind on a series of subjects, who then filled out questionnaires regarding their bodily ills. When diagnoses were matched with questionnaires, we found that there was no significant correspondence between the reflexology diagnosis and the subjects' ills.

In sum, there seems to be no evidence that zone therapy or foot reflexology has any diagnostic or therapeutic value other than placebo and other psychological effects already discussed.

3. Polarity therapy is a multifaceted approach, developed by Randolph Stone and popularized by Pierre Pannetier. Stone's system incorporates a wide range of notions, including those of zone therapy and bloodletting (particularly recommended in cases of rheumatism and low back pain). However, polarity therapy is noted for postulating an energy field in the body that differs from those ordinarily recognized and that is characterized by its polarities. It is postulated that therapists can treat bodily ills by modifying the field through the action of their hands over certain locations on the patient's body. For example, Stone recommends that: "In all cases of *Eye Trouble*, line up the *Navel* to the exact median line, and work the hypersensitiveness out of it [manually] by correlating it to the *thighs*, the *perineum*, and the *upper cervical tensions, in relation to its center in the hands and on the soles of the feet.*"[656]

Stone explains the basis of his approach as follows: "But the body as a whole has an energy field of vital force that is so similar to the sleeping energy in the gold and in the sun that its *real value* points to the *exchange and stimulation* of that *energy field direct by means of its radiating action,* rather than through its digestive function."[657]

As you can see, Stone's own words give an insight into polarity therapy that would be hard to convey otherwise.

Since we were unable to locate any studies of polarity therapy, one of my students decided to conduct his own. He selected from Stone's books two treatments for headache and head congestion, since these conditions could be expected to respond relatively quickly to treatment. To test whether Stone's approaches have specific effects over and above placebo and other effects that would result from almost any manipulation, my student devised control treatments as follows.

The manipulation Stone recommends for headache is a "neck pull" with the therapist's left hand on the forehead and right hand at the top of the neck in back.[655] The control treatment, with which the specified treatment was compared, was a neck *push* with the therapist's right hand under the chin and left hand on top of the head. The treatment Stone suggests for head congestion is to lie on your stomach with your knees bent and lower legs raised. Then you are directed to move your lower legs out and to "scissor" them across one another, and to repeat this motion for several minutes (according to Stone, this exercise acts on ". . . the serpent force of the sun and moon energies [and then cuts] the electro-magnetic lines of force. . . .").[655] The control treatment in this case was to lie on your *back* and, with your legs *straight*, open and close them for a few minutes.

My student did the recommended treatments with a group of subjects with headaches and head congestion and the control treatments with a comparable group. Self-reports of relief obtained showed that, while both groups reported some improvement, there was no significant difference in therapeutic value between the recommended and the control treatments. This indicates that these particular polarity treatments, at any rate, owe any effectiveness achieved to placebo and other nonspecific effects.

To my knowledge, there exists no evidence in support of Stone's notion of energy fields of the human body that can be therapeutically modified in the manner he suggests. In fact, the characteristics of the energy field that Stone proposes,—its electromagnetic nature, its sustained polarities, and its curved lines of force—are internally inconsistent and logically impossible.[655] Although it is true that direct current electrical fields that relate closely to basic growth processes have been discovered in a variety of organisms by Robert Becker[49] and Harold S. Burr,[98] the characteristics of these fields show little correspondence to the notions of polarity therapy.

4. As an approach to health, nutrition is closely related to the body therapies we have been discussing. Without denying the importance of good nutrition to health, we can recognize that there are numerous occult notions concerning nutrition. Of these, one of the most extreme is macrobiotics. Although macrobiotics postulates a number of occult principles concerning food, its most distinctive and dangerous notion is that an ideal diet consists entirely of cereals—in particular, rice.[1] As Georges Ohsawa, the foremost proponent of macrobiotics, says concerning his all-cereal diet: "[It] is the easiest, simplest, and wisest. . . . Try Diet No. 7 [all-cereal

diet] for . . . even months." According to Ohsawa, Diet 7 will cure detachment of the retina, glaucoma, meningitis, peritonitis, and poliomyelitis. Concerning syphilis, Ohsawa says it is "Easy to cure since the spirochete that causes syphilis is very Yin, therefore weak and vulnerable to salt. Try Diet No. 7." Concerning cancer, Ohsawa states: "No illness is more simple to cure than cancer . . . through . . . Diet No. 7." And, concerning leprosy, Ohsawa says: "Like cancer, this is very easy to cure. . . . Take Diet No. 7."[486]

Of course, a diet consisting solely of cereals lacks essential nutrients and is likely to result in such conditions as scurvy, anemia, protein deficiency, calcium deficiency, and loss of kidney function. At least one death has been directly attributed to the practice of macrobiotics.[8]

Macrobiotics provides a good example of the dangers of occultism. It is not hard to imagine how someone could derive psychological benefits from adherence to a new diet, no matter how unsound nutritionally. The dishabituating effects of such a change, the pride that results from self-control, and, possibly, altered consciousness states from lack of nutrients—these can be potent psychological effects. Someone who interprets these effects as demonstrating the diet's validity may pursue a deadly diet to its logical conclusion.

We now leave therapies that involve direct physical interventions of one kind or another to discuss some other systems of occult therapy.

5. Wilhelm Reich, a psychoanalyst, postulated the existence of a universal "life energy" that he called orgone.[543] Reich claimed that orgone energy could be used to run motors, to change the weather, and to shoot down UFOs, among other things.[261] The orgone theory is of particular interest in this section because Reich constructed orgone boxes (called "energy accumulators"), orgone blankets, and orgone shooters, which he claimed could concentrate orgone energy and thereby facilitate recovery from a wide variety of illnesses.

However, there is no satisfactory evidence that orgone energy exists or that Reich's devices have any intrinsic therapeutic effects.[237] As Charles Rycroft says: "From a scientific point of view, there is something pathetic about Reich's accounts of his experiments and theories. The experiments seem to have been designed and carried out in a hopelessly amateurish and gimcrack manner with, in particular, no understanding of the need for adequate controls, while his theorizing is full of the most elementary mistakes in biology and physics."[581]

For example, consider Reich's instructions and rationale for the construction of his orgone box: "The orgone energy is collected by a certain arrangement of organic and metallic material. . . . Organic matter absorbs and holds, while metal attracts and reflects orgone energy quickly. It is, therefore, obvious that by layering the accumulator always with organic matter toward the outside and metallic toward the inside, a direction is given to the orgone energy directed from the outside toward the inside."[261] For organic matter, Reich recommends cotton, glass wool, or rock wool.

In the statements above, Reich's naivete is clearly seen.

According to Reich, ". . . metal attracts and reflects orgone energy. . . ." However, if metal does reflect orgone energy, then incoming orgone energy will be reflected away from, not into, the orgone box.

Reich says that "Organic matter absorbs and holds . . . orgone energy . . ." However, if this is so, no orgone energy will pass to the interior of the orgone box.

Reich recommends for organic matter the use of cotton, glass wool, or rock wool.[261] However, neither glass wool nor rock wool is organic.

Even trying to read between the lines, there seems to be no conceivable way that an orgone box, constructed according to Reich's directions, will have the effect he intends.

Although Reich's ability as an investigator is certainly in doubt, the question arises whether other researchers have conducted valid studies that support some of his notions. In fact, although there has been a considerable outpouring of writings on orgone energy in recent years, there have been very few attempts at controlled studies. In looking through the recent literature on orgone energy, I have not found a single well-controlled study that supports the notion of orgone energy. Unfortunately, few non-Reichians have attempted to test Reich's beliefs. The Food and Drug Administration did sponsor some research by non-Reichians, which yielded no evidence in support of orgone energy. However, these studies have been criticized, perhaps justly in some cases, as biased or at least not sufficiently thorough.[261]

Mention of Food and Drug Administration-sponsored studies

of orgone energy brings us to the matter of Reich's death. The FDA studies were part of an effort to prosecute Reich for interstate shipment of a medical device, the orgone box, which was promoted by false therapeutic claims. After a lengthy legal battle, Reich was sent to prison, where he died a few months afterward, in 1957. His imprisonment is a sad example of the costs of occultism and seems, at first glance, an unnecessarily harsh punishment. However, Reich's refusal to stop promotion of orgone boxes constituted a real problem for the FDA. As we have seen, almost any procedure, including an orgone box, can have therapeutic effects if the patient has sufficient faith. However, occult medical procedures can also exact a price in human suffering, as patients with treatable medical conditions are sometimes persuaded to postpone effective medical treatment until it is too late.

On the other hand, it is important to note that, unlike his orgone theory, Reich's work in the early part of his career, on character analysis and the muscular rigidities involved in neuroses, has proved valuable and, in fact, was the forerunner of several contemporary body therapies.[542]

6. L. Ronald Hubbard is the founder of a movement initially called dianetics but more recently converted into a religion known as Scientology. Although Hubbard expounds many traditional occult beliefs, such as astral travel and reincarnation,[316] some of his claims, of visiting heaven and of being on the threshold of learning how to bring the dead back to life,[192] are less common. However, Hubbard's most unique and interesting notions deal with the cause of mental distress.

According to Hubbard, the origin of mental disturbance, including psychosomatic conditions, is traumatic experiences recorded as engrams (memory traces) in the "reactive" (unconscious) mind. Many psychologists would agree with this. Hubbard maintains, however, that the most bothersome engrams are those laid down before birth.[237] These prenatal engrams can develop in the embryo or fetus, in the sperm or egg, in a prior life as another human being, or in a prior life as a clam or sloth. For example, according to Hubbard, the reason humans have a crying reflex is because one of our primeval ancestors was a clamlike creature that developed the protective behavior of "crying-out" sand that kept hitting it in the face on ocean beaches.[317]

An important characteristic of these engrams is that they are extremely literal representations. According to Hubbard, for example, if a pregnant woman habitually exclaims "Oh, shoot!" when under stress, her fetus may interpret "shoot" literally and grow up to be a murderer. In fact, Hubbard believes that most criminality can be traced to such prenatal impressions.[315]

It perhaps needs to be stated that, although the human fetus can be conditioned in the womb,[640] there is no evidence that higher forms of learning, as Hubbard proposes, are possible or that memories can be implanted before the nervous system is formed— that is, during the sperm, egg, or embryo stages. The notion of engrams from prior lives is, of course, even more fanciful.

Hubbard's technique for erasing engrams is a process originally called auditing, and now known as confessional, in which the individuals being processed are connected to a galvanometer, called an E meter. They are then encouraged to talk about their troublesome past experiences until the E meter shows that the negative feelings evoked by the memories have dissipated. Again, many psychologists would support such a procedure, except that the E meter readings are probably frequently spurious since Scientologists generally do not seem to take the precautions required to obtain valid readings on such a device.[133, 192]

In spite of its basically occult orientation, however, Scientology may achieve some real therapeutic results in its "confessional" process. Even if the individual conjures up fantasies of sperm memories and past-life experiences in this process, these fantasies may well represent actual feelings and conflicts in symbolic form, which may then be worked through in the confessional. For example, the psychiatrist William Sargant has found that for many of his patients ". . . the release of great anger or fear could be more effectively produced around incidents which were entirely imaginary and had never happened to the patient at all, and such abreactions of imaginary events could have remarkably beneficial effects."[589]

The story of Scientology is truly a fascinating one and cannot be adequately told here. Interested readers should consult one of the publications that discusses this subject at greater length.[714, 732]

In discussing occult therapies, we have considered a variety of approaches. We have seen that the various occult theories that are proposed to account for the healing effects of these therapies have little in the way of evidence to support them. On the other hand, it is likely that various psychological processes definitely contribute to occult healing. Thus occult healing may be truly effective. However, as with any occultism, there are risks involved in such therapies that stem from lack of psychological awareness; for example, people who seek occult treatment for serious organic conditions that are resistant to such treatment sometimes pay with their lives for their naivete.[482] We see again the importance of becoming aware of our own psychological functioning. Through such awareness, we can enhance our potential for self-healing and also avoid the risks that occult beliefs entail.

Theories of a "Golden Age"

[The Atlantis theme] strikes a responsive chord by its sense of the melancholy loss of a beautiful thing, a happy perfection once possessed by mankind. Thus it appeals to that hope that most of us carry around in our unconscious, a hope so often raised and as often disappointed, for assurance that somewhere, some time, there can exist a land of peace and plenty, of beauty and justice, where we, poor creatures that we are, could be happy.[155]

L. Sprague de Camp

The occult theories discussed in the next few sections share one feature in common. They all constitute attempts to explain various features of our physical world, which, at first glance, seem mysterious—for example, huge ancient monuments, UFOs, and the Bermuda Triangle. In various ways, these phenomena transcend our ordinary understanding of the world we live in. Thus they all serve as projective stimuli in terms of which we can evaluate some of our beliefs about our role as observers. That is, in the face of a strange experience, can we accept that, to a large extent, its "strangeness" is a product of our background and expectations and that, to this extent, we are the creators of the world that we perceive? In this view, the attempt to understand an extraordinary experience provides an opportunity to understand ourselves better. Or do we prefer to believe that experiences "are" what they seem and that our role as observer is a passive one? In this view, for example, the fact that an object in the sky *"looks* like a UFO from outer space" is sufficient grounds for believing that it is. Let us see how we feel about these two views as we consider the occult theories below.

We begin our discussion with a consideration of "golden age" theories. The idea that there was, in a time long ago, a "golden age" more inspiring and wonderful than what exists today is a common theme of the myths of many lands.[184] In our society, the Garden of Eden story is probably the best known of such myths. In this section, we will examine several "golden age" theories, namely those of the lost civilization of Atlantis, the pyramids as the embodiment of highly advanced esoteric knowledge, and the ancient astronaut theory of Erich von Daniken. Let us begin with the story of the ancient island civilization of Atlantis.

1. In the fourth century B.C., Plato wrote two dialogues, *Timaios and Kritias,* in which he described a great civilization called

THEORIES OF A GOLDEN AGE

Atlantis. According to Plato, Atlantis was an island the size of a continent in the Atlantic Ocean, west of the Mediterranean Sea and possessed, among other things, extensive canals, parks, and gold- and silver-covered buildings. As a result of a geological catastrophe long before Plato's time, Atlantis sank beneath the ocean waters, its civilization destroyed.

Plato's dialogues constitute the earliest surviving story of Atlantis from which many subsequent elaborate accounts are derived. Therefore, it is important to understand, as far as possible, the origin of Plato's account. L. Sprague de Camp, in a thorough evaluation of the Atlantis story, makes the following points:[155]

First, there is no geological evidence that a land mass the size of a continent disappeared into the Atlantic Ocean or, for that matter, anywhere in the world since humans evolved on earth.

Second, although it is conceivable that Plato derived the inspiration for his story from accounts of the actual destruction of a Mediterranean island by a volcano,[233] the story line, complete with descriptions of the affairs of gods and goddesses, seems to have been Plato's own fantasy. For example, according to Plato, Poseidon, the sea god, populated Atlantis by mating with mortals, after which Zeus sank the island because it was becoming corrupt.

Third, Plato's Atlantis tale is in the style and tradition of mythical storytelling of the time, in which a favorite theme consisted of accounts of far-off continents and islands that rose out of the sea only to sink again into oblivion.

In spite of the generally mythical nature of Plato's story of Atlantis,[529] many writers since his time have preferred to interpret his account as literal. These writers have misconstrued geological, biological, and cultural evidence in their attempt to support the notion of the lost island civilization. Atlantis, they claim, could account for the origin of the human race, the peopling of the world, and the spread of civilization. Among modern works on Atlantis, Ignatius Donnelly's *Atlantis: The Antediluvian World*,[169] published in 1882, probably has been the most influential. Concerning this work, de Camp concludes that: "Most of Donnelly's statements of fact . . . either were wrong when he made them, or have been disproved by subsequent discoveries."[155]

Since Donnelly's time, many other writers, notably Madame Blavatsky, the Theosophist, have embellished the myth with further flights of fantasy. As a result, a wide range of occultists today accept Plato's Atlantis as veritable truth rather than as the basically mythical tale that it was.

Plato's Atlantis is not the only account of a fictional place that has been taken seriously by readers, but it certainly has succeeded in this regard beyond all others. For example, the notion of a lost island civilization, Lemuria or Mu,[122] in the region of the Pacific Ocean, has enjoyed less popularity.

2. In contrast to Atlantis, which is obscured by the mists of time and fantasy, the pyramids—as can be seen in the photograph of the Great Pyramid of Khufu, or Cheops, in Figure 28—are overwhelmingly tangible. Here the question is "how did the ancient Egyptians manage to construct what are perhaps the most spectacular of ancient archaeological wonders?" Many occultists believe that their builders must have been aided by paranormal or supernatural forces of some kind.

The modern cult of Pyramidology dates back to the nineteenth century, after Howard Vyse made the first extensive measurements of the Great Pyramid in the 1830s. John Taylor, in his book *The Great Pyramid. Why Was it Built? And Who Built It?*,[673] was the first to expound the notion that the dimensions of the Pyramid embodied scientific and mathematical concepts, such as the length of the earth's axis, which were beyond the knowledge of the ancient Egyptians. Taylor concluded that the Great Pyramid had been divinely inspired, having been built, in fact, by Noah of Old Testament fame.

Taylor's theories did not gain widespread attention, however, until they were adopted and greatly elaborated by Charles Piazzi Smyth, the Scottish astronomer. In addition, Smyth popularized the notion, originally proposed by Robert Menzies, that various dimensions of the internal passageways of the Great Pyramid embodied the dates of significant events, such as the creation of the world and the birth of Christ. Smyth published these theories, in 1880, in his widely read work, *Our Inheritance in the Great Pyramid.*[633]

Unfortunately for Taylor, Smyth, and the cult of Pyramidology, however, their elaborate calculations and theories are undermined by several considerations.

First, many of the measurements upon which the theories are based have been determined, by the Egyptologist Flinders Petrie and others, to be inaccurate. For example, the casing stone, the width of which Smyth used to compute his basic unit of measure-

Figure 28. The Great Pyramid of Cheops

ment, the "pyramid inch," was later found to be atypical. Many other casing stones, with quite different measurements, have since been unearthed. Petrie even reports that he once caught a pyramidologist filing down a stone of the "wrong dimensions" to better fit his theories![237]

Second, many of the scientific truths that the Great Pyramid was supposed to embody, such as the distance from the earth to the sun, were not accurately known in the days of Taylor and Smyth. Thus many of the "relationships" they discovered are now known to be faulty.[237]

Third, with dozens of measurements to manipulate, many "relationships" can be discovered that exist only in the minds of the believer.[240] As Martin Gardner points out: "If you set about measuring a complicated structure like the Pyramid, you will quickly have on hand a great abundance of lengths to play with. If you have sufficient patience to juggle them about in various ways, you are certain to come out with many figures which coincide with important historical dates or figures in the sciences."[237]

Using this same technique of juggling figures until you find some coincidences, Martin Gardner has shown how it can be "proved" that William Shakespeare took time out from his plays and sonnets to help compile the King James version of the Bible! "Shakespeare was 46 when the King James translation was completed in 1610. The 46th word of Psalm 46 is 'shake,' and the 46th word from the end (the terminal 'Selah' is not part of the psalm) is 'spear.' [Obviously] Shakespeare helped in the translating and deliberately arranged to conceal his name in the psalm.[!]"[239]

Fourth, the following dates, derived from pyramid measurements, which pyramidologists have set for the occurrence of events associated with the Second Coming of Christ and "the end of the world" as we know it, have come and gone: 1882, 1914, 1928, 1936, 1957, 1960, and 1978.[151, 179, 580, 633] The world, alas, continues in its old ways.

All in all, we must conclude that the evidence does not support the notion that the pyramids reflect knowledge, however highly advanced, that was beyond the capabilities of the Egyptians or that the pyramids embody predictions of future events.

In more recent years, a new pyramid cult has proposed that the secret of altering fundamental physical processes was known during the "golden age" of ancient Egypt. According to the "pyramid power" cult, this is accomplished by the shape and geographical orientation of the pyramids. These features are said to affect energy fields so that, inside the pyramids, dehydration is arrested, the taste of food is improved, and razor blades remain sharp, among other effects.[212] Originated by a Frenchman, Antoine Bovis, elaborated by a Czech, Karl Drbal, and popularized in the United States by Pat Flanagan and others, the pyramid power theory states that a miniature pyramid, even one constructed of cardboard, will have these effects, provided it has the proper dimensions and geographical orientation.[212, 493, 688] Evidently, little thought has been given by the pyramid power advocates to the fact that the proposed effects of pyramids are contradictory. For example, pyramids are supposed to speed up life processes—as in the case of enhancing the growth of plants, and at the same time slow them down—as in the case of retarding the growth of microorganisms that spoil meat.

Realizing that the observations on which pyramid power advocates based their claims had not been well controlled, Allen Alter and Dale Simmons conducted controlled studies of the effects of model pyramids on preserving and dehydrating food, on preserving flowers, and on maintaining the sharpness of razor blades. These investigators concluded: "Extensive tests involving controls show that pyramidal containers are no more effective than those of other shapes . . ."[11] and that ". . . model pyramids have no effects which can be related to their particular shape."[623] In another study, Ib Nonnecke, a horticulturalist at the University of Guelph in Canada, conducted controlled tests to see if, as pyramid power advocates claim, pyramid-shaped structures would produce healthier plants than nonpyramid-shaped structures. He states that ". . . [in] a controlled experiment . . . there was no response difference. Both experimental and control groups of plants proved subject to the same insects and disease and there was no difference in growth rate."[402]

Some of my students have tested the postulated effects of pyramids on fermentation and on the taste of wine and beer. None of these tests showed any effects due to "pyramid power."

After reviewing some 30 additional reports on pyramid power, Gary Null and Judith Wildenberg conclude that most of them are based on poorly conducted or poorly reported studies.[484] The only well-controlled study that produced significant results—in which bean plants placed under pyramid-shaped structures grew better than plants placed under nonpyramid-shaped structures—has not yet been validated by independent replication.

We must conclude that there is no satisfactory evidence to support the theory of pyramid power. Although the pyramids are impressive structures, their particular construction—their shape and geographical orientation—does not seem to be capable of altering fundamental physical processes.

3. In recent years, a new notion has arisen to explain the architectural wonders of the ancient world. According to Erich von Daniken, the foremost proponent of the theory, visiting astronauts from outer space were responsible for these wonders, since our ancestors were not up to the task. Since the pyramids are generally considered the most spectacular of ancient monuments, let us see what von Daniken has to say about them.[709]

First, (according to von Daniken), the Egyptians did not possess sufficient resources for handling the blocks used in the construction of the Great Pyramid. In particular, they lacked sufficient wood for rollers, rope, worker's quarters, and supplies of food for the workers.

Second, von Daniken claims the Egyptians did not possess the manpower required to quarry, transport, and erect 2,600,000 blocks weighing, as von Daniken seems to think, 12 tons each.

Third, says von Daniken, the Egyptians did not possess the technology required to cut and fit these blocks together ". . . to the thousandth of an inch" or to ". . . carefully and accurately level. . . ." the ground upon which the pyramid sits.

Fourth, von Daniken thinks that the dimensions of the pyramid, as well as the site chosen for its construction, reveal knowledge the Egyptians did not possess. In particular, von Daniken claims that ". . . the height of the pyramid of Cheops multiplied by a thousand million—98,000,000 miles—corresponds approximately to the distance between the earth and sun." He also marvels that ". . . the area of the base of the pyramid divided by twice its height gives the celebrated figure $\pi=3.14159$," that ". . . a meridian running through the pyramids divides continents and oceans into two exactly equal halves," and that ". . . the pyramid . . . lies at the center of gravity of the continents."

Let us now compare von Daniken's statements with what is known about the pyramids.

First, the Egyptians did possess sufficient resources for the construction of the pyramids. They imported vast quantities of wood sufficient for making huge rollers, and by the time of the building of the pyramids, they had centuries of experience in manufacturing several kinds of rope sufficient to haul blocks weighing many tons. Food for the workers was supplied from the Nile Valley nearby, which is noted for its fertility and productivity, and the workers were housed in quarters that have been found near the pyramids.[29, 314]

Second, the pyramid blocks weigh an average of about two and one-half tons each, which reduces the weight problem to about one-fifth of what von Daniken estimates.[314] However, the Egyptians were well able to move extremely heavy objects, as attested by a figure, dating from several centuries before the pyramids, which depicts a statue weighing about 60 tons, being transported on a sledge pulled by workmen. With regard to getting the blocks to the proper location on the pyramid, the remains of ancient earthen ramps suitable to the task can still be seen around Egypt.[29]

Third, copper saws and chisels adequate for cutting the pyramid blocks have been found dating to before the time of the pyramids. Wedge marks have been found on huge quarry rock faces, indicating the use of wedges to split off large blocks. And sawn blocks, as large as pyramid blocks and dating from several centuries before the pyramids, have been found in the quarries; the Egyptians, in building the pyramids, could draw on several hundred years of experience in working with huge blocks.[29]

With regard to the precision with which the blocks were fitted together, "The core stones [which constitute the great bulk of the Great Pyramid] were only roughly fitted together, and the joints between the blocks were often quite pronounced."[742] The exterior blocks, mostly relatively easily worked limestone, were more carefully joined, although not to a thousandth of an inch.

Leveling the ground on which the pyramid stands was probably the easiest of all. Flooding the ground with water would quickly reveal high and low spots, which could then be eliminated.

Fourth, if von Daniken is right that ". . . the height of the pyramid of Cheops multiplied by a thousand million [equals] 98,000,000 miles," this hardly supports the claim that its builders intended it to represent the distance from the earth to the sun, which is *93*,000,000 miles. In addition, von Daniken is mistaken when he says that ". . . the area of the base of the pyramid divided by twice its height gives the celebrated figure $\pi=3.14159$." Although it is conceivable that the value of pi was incorporated into the dimensions of the pyramid, this particular calculation does not give the value of pi using any standard of measurement known then or now.[291]

As for the meridian of the pyramids dividing ". . . continents and oceans into two exactly equal halves," if this is true they are similarly divided by millions of other locations on that meridian in Europe, Africa, the Arctic, Antarctica, North America, and the South Pacific, which weakens von Daniken's argument considerably.

Finally, von Daniken's claim that the Great Pyramid lies on the center of gravity of the continents is meaningless since it depends entirely on what land areas are included on what side of the balance, which is an arbitrary matter. What does seem to have been important in the location of the pyramids is that they were positioned near suitable sources of stone used in their construction.[291]

So we see that von Daniken's major arguments concerning the pyramids are based on faulty information and that his theory that astronauts from outer space must have been responsible for their construction is not supported by the evidence.

But do von Daniken's arguments hold up any better when he discusses other ancient constructions that are also spectacular and impressive, if somewhat less so than the pyramids? A number of writers have analyzed his arguments concerning other archaeological wonders[659, 741] and generally conclude that, as E. C. Maclaurin puts it, von Daniken's ". . . chief weakness is sheer ignorance. . . ."[414]

But perhaps von Daniken, to judge from his own statements, is putting us on. For example, he has admitted that, in spite of his elaborate description in his book, *The Gold of the Gods,* of his visit to caves in Ecuador, he was never in the caves and that his description of the gold artifacts contained within rests on the unsubstantiated claims of a single man, Juan Moricz.[13]

How is it, then, that so many people read, and evidently believe, von Daniken? Aside from citing faulty information, von Daniken uses a style of writing that stretches possibilities into proofs. This can be appreciated in a passage in which another writer uses von Daniken's brand of logic to prove that Santa Claus was really a spaceman!

> Santa Claus, as far as can be determined, has never been thoroughly investigated by orthodox antiquarians, anthropologists and archaeologists, obsessed as they are by their own vested interests in what they call the truth. . . . And yet, as soon as the most obvious elements of his legend are mentioned—those elements which are known even to the smallest children in our civilization—it becomes clear that "Santa Claus" is nothing else than a folk memory of just such an inter-stellar visitor as Erich [von Daniken] has described.
>
> He is, to begin with, a technological wonder-worker. Popular account endows him with a workshop in which he, with the help of 'gnomes' (surely cybernetic devices of some kind) manufactures children's toys in incredible quantities. By the same popular account, his workshop is stationed at the North Pole. Considering that the North Pole is "up" on a map, and that the North Pole was to earlier Man the ultimate in remoteness, it is not the least fanciful to see "the North Pole" as *really* being some sort of orbiting space vehicle.
>
> As to the way Santa Claus is said to travel, it is plain that . . . we have a naive description of some sort of rocket. Santa's vehicle travels at unbelievable speed . . . he must . . . be able to make a complete circuit of the earth, visiting every major population centre, within the space of one night. The only workable explanation of the legend is that there was once a visiting space man who regularly did this.[718]

What can we conclude from our consideration of the legend of Atlantis, the theories of Pyramidology and pyramid power, and von Daniken's ancient astronauts theory? We have seen that none of these theories is supported by the evidence. Why, then, do occultists continue to perpetuate them?

All of these theories postulate the existence of a "golden age," more wonderful in some respects than the present day. All of these theories also postulate superhuman influences to account for the wonders they seek to explain. Accordingly, all of these theories belittle the role played by humankind in the events they describe. Why, then, does this kind of theory appeal to so many people? There are many possible answers.

In folk cultures, theories of a "golden age" may develop to account for wonders of nature and cultural developments that otherwise seem inexplicable. In our culture, where archaeological knowledge at least is available, perhaps it is individuals who are dissatisfied with their lives in the present who find inspiration in tales of wonders from some other age. In particular, the notion that God or spacepeople have intervened to help out humans in the past might appeal to people who feel alone and inadequate in dealing with the frustrations of their own lives and who, therefore, gain some comfort from the thought that superhuman beings might again intervene to save us all.

Certainly the pyramids and other wonders of the ancient world transcend our notions of what humans can ordinarily accomplish.[154, 181] However, denying the capacity of humans to transcend the ordinary has the effect of denying one's own capacities for extraordinary achievement. Certainly the thought that humankind can create such awesome structures as the pyramids can be more inspiring than the notion that gods or astronauts must have done it because our ancestors were not sufficiently intelligent or ingenious.

So we see that we can view the pyramids and similar structures as stimuli for the projection of our attitudes regarding ourselves and others. Do we see ourselves as capable of extraordinary feats or do we feel the need to invoke supernatural or paranormal explanations to account for such accomplishments?

Unidentified Flying Objects

Nothing is so firmly believed as that which is least known.[507]

MICHEL DE MONTAIGNE

We have discussed theories that postulate a "golden age" that existed sometime in the past and that came about through the intervention of supernatural or paranormal forces. These theories are essentially modern myths that meet the psychological needs of a large number of people.

Closely related to such theories is the belief that even now creatures from outer space are visiting our planet in what are known generally as unidentified flying objects, or UFOs. Ever since Kenneth Arnold, piloting a private plane in 1947, reported seeing a group of objects that were subsequently dubbed "flying saucers," popular interest in UFOs has remained strong.[192, 237]

An obvious question that arises in a consideration of this topic is—"Do UFOs exist?" However, this turns out to be the wrong question, since few people dispute the existence of unidentified flying objects. That is, there is little question that certain people have perceived "something in the sky" that neither they nor others can conclusively identify. The right question is—"What interpretation of these perceptions is justified by the evidence at hand?" In answer to this question, a number of general theories have been proposed, namely that:

1. UFOs are spaceships from other regions of the universe (the extraterrestrial origins theory).
2. UFOs are highly advanced devices being developed and tested secretly by some government or group on earth.
3. UFOs are terrestrial phenomena as yet unknown to science.
4. UFOs are natural and known physical phenomena that appear mysterious because the observer is unaware of the phenomenon involved.
5. UFO reports arise from psychological anomalies of misperception and misreporting and thus represent states of mind more than states of nature.

Let's examine these theories.

1. Although the "extraterrestrial origins" theory, more than any other, has captured the popular imagination, it is least supported by hard evidence. For example, Philip Klass, after examining the most convincing photographs of UFOs, has concluded that ". . . there is not a single photo showing a craft-like UFO which can withstand close analysis. . . ."[369] And John Sladek, reviewing cases claiming direct physical evidence for extraterrestrial UFOs—for example, metal fragments claimed to be nonterrestrial in origin—has found no evidence that would withstand scrutiny.[626] Finally, there are reports of "close encounters" with UFOs, complete with descriptions of the creatures who pilot them; however, none of these reports has been substantiated. As Robert Sheaffer has shown, "close encounter" reports can be expected whenever belief in a certain phenomenon is widespread. For example, in the early part of this century, when belief in fairies was more popular than it

is today, many people reported encountering little fairies who danced merrily through the countryside.[615] After reviewing the major writings on UFOs, I must agree with the conclusion of the Condon Committee, established by the Air Force to evaluate the wisdom of continuing to support research on UFOs, which concluded that ". . . no convincing evidence exists for the [extraterrestrial origin of UFOs]."[131]

2. Likewise, there seems to be no satisfactory evidence that UFOs are advanced, but secret, terrestrial developments. Such manufactured devices as balloons and satellites have certainly given rise to UFO reports, but most people are familiar, at least in a general way, with these objects.

3. It is possible that some UFOs arise from terrestrial phenomena that are presently unknown to science. For example, some UFO reports seem to have arisen from sightings of ball lightning, yet until relatively recently many scientists doubted its existence.[624] The hard core of UFO sightings that investigating committees have been unable to explain constitutes possible evidence for this hypothesis,[607] although inaccuracies in the original observations and reports could also be responsible.

The best case for the "unknown terrestrial phenomena" hypothesis is made by J. Allen Hynek, astronomer and long-time consultant on UFOs to the Air Force, who, however, does not necessarily restrict his hypothesis to terrestrial phenomena. Hynek believes that ". . . the body of data points to an aspect or domain of the natural world not yet explored by science."[324] In fact, Hynek and others have proposed that UFOs may signify the presence of a "separate reality" quite different from our everyday reality. But the Condon Committee concluded that ". . . further extensive study of UFOs probably cannot be justified in the expectation that science will be advanced thereby."[130] At present, the hypothesis of yet-to-be-discovered terrestrial phenomena is highly debatable.

4. In contrast to the above hypotheses, there is little question that many UFO sightings arise from natural and known physical phenomena, which, nevertheless, are not recognized as such by the observer. Consider the following example:

> . . . an extraordinary UFO event—hard evidence objectively recorded on photographic film—was displayed on television programs several years ago. . . . It was accompanied by a statement by Charles

Gibb-Smith of the Institute of Aeronautics Museum in Kensington in London, who is a scholarly and precise historian of aircraft over the entire span of aeroengineering. After having seen the motion picture film, he submitted that it was a picture of a metallic object, that it was some sort of aircraft, that it resembled no aircraft that he knew of in the history of aeronautical engineering, and that its rate of recession [its velocity away from the observer] exceeded anything that anyone had seen before. . . . There were many good arguments, which I shall not give, which made people feel that the film was in fact not a hoax, not deliberately produced to deceive. What the photograph showed was a view from the inside of a passenger aircraft, looking out. Outside the window was a tiny metallic ellipsoid, whose . . . texture and illumination resembled very strongly the metal construction of an airplane; then rapidly the image disappeared . . . in a few seconds going from invisible to [an image occupying 10% of the field of view] and back again. A very striking observation indeed, and certified by a legitimate expert not to be any kind of aircraft anyone has ever seen![461]

Before reading further, ask yourself what conclusion you would draw on the basis of such a report.

A little investigation revealed that the UFO: ". . . was in fact the tail of the very aircraft in which the camera was riding, perceived through the extraordinarily astigmatic lens of the thick edge of one of those round plastic windows set into the pressure cabins in some aircraft. The image was not merely distorted but topologically distorted. As the aircraft tilted, a piece of the tail structure came in view of the lens, rapidly grew, and rapidly went out of view again."[461]

Another example of the difficulty even trained observers sometimes have in interpreting unusual perceptions is the experience of astronomer Donald Menzel aboard an airplane: ". . . suddenly I saw a bright object shoot in at a tremendous speed from the horizon, directly toward the plane. At first I thought it was a meteor or a fire-ball and I instinctively ducked, but the object came to a sudden skidding stop about 300 feet away, thereafter riding along with our plane and keeping pace with our speed. I could scarcely believe my eyes. The thing possessed green and red signal lights that flashed back and forth, and something that looked like a lighted propeller on the top."[440]

Menzel finally identified the phenomenon as follows: "It was a mirage of Sirius, the brightest star in the heavens. Actually, Sirius was slightly below the horizon at this time, but the bending of the light had raised the image above the horizon and had diffused the beam into a saucerlike form. The flashing red and green lights were common phenomena associated with star twinkling and the apparent structure, including the whirling propeller, resulted from distortion by the earth's atmosphere."[440]

When scientists such as Menzel have difficulty in identifying natural phenomena, we can expect that many untrained observers will be completely mystified by such experiences and, having heard of "flying saucers," may interpret them as craft from outer space.

In addition to unusual optical effects, many other natural physical phenomena seem to have given rise to UFO reports—for example, meteors, balloons, bright planets, aircraft, unusual cloud formations, ball lightning, formations of birds, swamp gas, animal luminescence, searchlights, missiles, satellites, and radar "phantoms."[369, 441]

5. The psychological component is extremely important in many UFO reports and, of course, is of particular interest here. Consider the following reports of a UFO sighting:

> All . . . observers saw a long jet airplane-looking vehicle without any wings. It was on fire both in front and behind. All observers also saw many windows. . . . If there had been anybody in the UFO near the windows I would have seen them.[285]

> It appeared to have square-shaped windows along the side that was facing us. . . . It appeared to me that the fuselage was constructed of many pieces of flat sheets of metal-like material with a 'riveted together look'. . . .

> I listened intently for some sound from the 'thing,' but I didn't hear a whisper of a sound! This was the most eerie part of my whole experience! Certainly, there should be some sound from an aircraft that looks so near! . . .

> I was impressed with what looked to me like low altitude of the craft at this point of my sighting—I thought around 1,000 feet or less.[439]

Such reports seem to constitute strong evidence for the existence of craftlike UFOs, perhaps of extraterrestrial origin. However, these reports arose from sightings of the flaming re-entry of a satellite on March 3, 1968. When observed, the satellite was approximately 75 miles high, much too distant for any details of its construction to be perceived. In other words, the perceptions of windows, riveted fuselage, general shape, and distance to the object are all faulty. What could account for such inaccuracies?

We have previously discussed how suggestion, particularly group suggestion, can give rise to highly inaccurate perceptions. We have also discussed the mechanism of projection, in which we project our hopes and fears onto the outside world. In these ways, popular discussion, as well as widespread hopes or fears, concerning UFOs are likely to produce illusory perceptions of UFOs, especially when an unusual phenomenon, such as a re-entering satellite, provides a suitable impetus for such perceptions. Add to this the possibility of purely sensory illusions, such as phosphenes, afterimages, and autokinetic movement, and we should realize that UFO reports are highly subject to error because of psychological processes.

The notion of psychological error in UFO reports is also supported by accounts of UFOs from the latter part of the nineteenth century.[330] In this period, many observers described craft with sails, flapping wings, and thoroughly human pilots who, allegedly, sometimes explained that they were conducting secret trials of newly invented aircraft. These descriptions matched popular speculations of the day concerning flying machines that were expected to be developed in the near future. The weight of the evidence indicates that these reports resulted from psychological mechanisms such as we have discussed, rather than from actual sightings of strange aircraft.

A final factor demonstrating the importance of psychological processes in UFO beliefs is the number of hoaxes that many believers have accepted without question. UFO hoaxes date back at least as far as the last century, and many hoaxes of the more current UFO craze have found their way into bestsellers.[330, 369] To demonstrate the ease with which a UFO hoax can be perpetrated, three high school students in Iowa:

> . . . burned a circular area about ten feet in diameter, to indicate the purported landing site of a UFO, together with the added nice touch of four smaller circles, meant to suggest some kind of ancillary gear on each landing leg. . . . The students activated the scheme the next morning by reporting the "sighting" to fellow students and to a local radio station. Before nine o'clock one of the student perpetrators had been interviewed by someone from the radio station and by ten o'clock a UFO expert had arrived at the school. Public reaction to the experiment escalated rapidly . . . the students . . . noted in their re-

port: "Within a few hours a relatively small burned patch near a little country church and a statement by a few high-school boys had gained state-wide and finally nation-wide attention." . . . the report appearing in the local newspaper saying that "the boys have pictures to *prove* some sort of *'unidentified flying object'* really *did* touch down." [italics added] . . . other observers in nearby towns stated that they, too, had seen the UFO![441]

In fact, for people who like their hoaxes ready-made, UFOs can be ordered by mail, as the following ad indicates: "FOR SALE: SIMULATED SAUCER. Be the first in your block to create a real scare. Breaks down quickly and packs in an ordinary station wagon for fast getaway. Glows in many colors and provides simulated radiation effect. Built-in static generator creates radio and TV interference in one-mile radius. . . . Set up saucer beside a road and watch for fast results! Then be the first on the scene to "investigate" the sighting and get fat interviews with newspapers and big-time UFO researchers."[441]

We have seen that UFO reports probably arise predominantly from misinterpreted natural phenomena and/or from psychological effects. A few reports may result from observations of natural phenomena that are not generally known to science. The belief that UFOs are extraterrestrial in origin is least supported by the evidence, yet enjoys a wide popularity. Important psychological needs must therefore be involved in the development of this belief.

We have compared beliefs in extraterrestrial origins of UFOs to "golden age" myths; they share in common a belief in superior beings that have the capacity to accomplish marvelous feats, including, perhaps, the capacity to intervene to save us from ourselves. Carl Jung presents this argument as follows: "We have here a golden opportunity to see how a legend is formed, and how in a difficult and dark time for humanity a miraculous tale grows up of an attempted intervention by extra-terrestrial 'heavenly' powers. . . . Anything that looks technological goes down without difficulty with modern man. The possibility of space travel makes the unpopular idea of a metaphysical intervention much more acceptable."[354]

In fact, most UFO accounts emphasize the helpful intentions of the visitors from outer space. However, people project fears as well as hopes, and some accounts affirm that the creatures from space have evil motives indeed.[369]

Hopefully as we gain an appreciation of and confidence in, our own ability to transcend the ordinary, we will have less need to project our faith and fears onto mysterious alien forces.

The story of the UFO controversy is indeed fascinating and instructive. Readers who would like to explore the topic further will find David Jacobs' book, *The UFO Controversy in America*,[330] the most complete historical study. On the other hand, the best compilation of original writings expressing the most prominent conflicting viewpoints is probably Carl Sagan's and Thornton Page's book, *UFOs—A Scientific Debate*.[582]

The Bermuda Triangle

As science and history, mythology is absurd.[101]

JOSEPH CAMPBELL

Just as myths of a "golden age" express the yearnings of humans for superhuman intervention, so the myth of the Bermuda Triangle expresses fears of such intervention. The Bermuda Triangle is the name popularly given to an area of the Atlantic Ocean roughly bounded by Florida, Puerto Rico, and the island of Bermuda (see Figure 29). According to the myth, an unaccountably large number of ships and planes have disappeared or have been abandoned under mysterious circumstances in this region. Offered in explanation are a wide variety of occult theories, from sea monsters to time warps.

Perhaps the most popular of the many books on the subject is *The Bermuda Triangle* by Charles Berlitz,[61] which topped the best seller lists. To determine the accuracy of the Bermuda legend as related by Berlitz, I compared his descriptions of lost or abandoned ships with the original newspaper and other accounts of the incidents as compiled by Lawrence Kusche.[385]

Of the 26 incidents listed by both Berlitz and Kusche, and which Berlitz considers mysterious, Kusche demonstrates that only three incidents deserve the designation "mysterious" in relationship to the Bermuda Triangle. In two of these incidents, the ships *Carroll Deering* and *Vagabond* were found abandoned with little in-

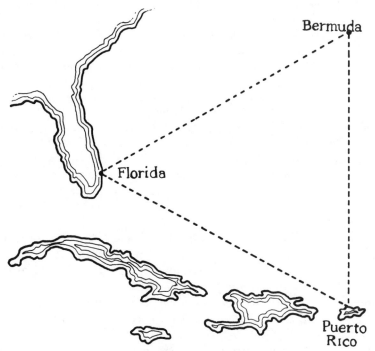

Figure 29. The Bermuda Triangle

dication of what might have caused their abandonment. In the
third incident, after achieving fame as the first man to sail alone
around the world, Joshua Slocum and his ship, the *Spray,* set out
from Martha's Vineyard bound for South America. He was never
heard from again. However, it is not certain that Slocum met his
end in the Bermuda Triangle. In general, such mysteries are not
unique to the Bermuda Triangle; similar unexplained incidents
have been reported from other well-traveled ocean routes.

Of the 23 remaining incidents, Kusche demonstrates that:

1. Twelve ships (*Atalanta, Cyclops, Raifuku Maru, Cotopaxi, Suduffco,
   Rubicon, Sandra, Connemara IV, Revonoc, Marine Sulpher Queen, Witchcraft,* and *Norse Variant*) were the probable victims of heavy seas and
   storms that are substantiated by survivors and/or weather reports.

2. One ship (*Sno' Boy*) was severely overloaded.

3. No adequate records are available for three ships (*Rosalie, Ellen Austin,* and *Stavenger*).

4. Six of the ships (*Mary Celeste, Freya, John and Gloria Colita, Scorpion,* and *Anita*) were not in the Bermuda Triangle.

5. One ship (*Maplebank*) is obviously misidentified by Berlitz, as it was neither lost nor abandoned.

It is instructive to compare some of Berlitz's claims with the original accounts concerning these ships as gathered by Kusche.

Concerning the *Suduffco,* Berlitz states that "Most of the ships have disappeared in good weather. . . . These vanishing ships have included . . . the *Suduffco.* . . ." However, Kusche quotes the *New York Times* of April 8, 1926 (page 2) as saying: "The *Suduffco* was proceeding down the coast at a time when the coast was swept by storms."[385]

Concerning the *Witchcraft,* Berlitz says: "They proceeded through calm seas to about one mile from the shore. . . ."[61] Kusche quotes the *Miami Herald* of December 24, 1967 (page B1), as follows: "Stiff winds blowing from the north and northeast whipped the surface of the Atlantic into a carpet of foam against which a white boat like *Witchcraft* would have been well camouflaged."[385]

Concerning the *Sno' Boy,* Berlitz states that ". . . the *Sno' Boy* . . . was lost without a trace or explanation in 1963. . . ."[61] Here, Kusche quotes the *Miami Herald* of July 7, 1963 (page 1) as follows: "A tabletop identified as coming from the *Sno' Boy* was recovered Friday by the fishing vessel *Marsutana*. The debris was scattered over an area several miles wide. . . . The Coast Guard expressed amazement at the volume of passengers and cargo, calling the vessel 'tremendously overloaded.' "[385]

As Kusche well demonstrates, the Bermuda Triangle myth has been sustained through fabrication, omission, exaggeration, and ignorance. In general, there seems to be no convincing evidence that mysterious forces are attacking ships in the Bermuda Triangle. As the Coast Guard explains:

The majority of disappearances can be attributed to the area's unique environmental features.

[One] environmental factor is the character of the Gulf Stream. It is extremely swift and turbulent and can quickly erase any evidence of a disaster. The unpredictable Caribbean-Atlantic weather pattern also plays its role. Sudden local thunder storms and water spouts often spell disaster for pilots and mariners. And finally, the topography of the ocean floor varies from extensive shoals around the islands to some of the deepest marine trenches in the world. With the interaction of the strong currents over the many reefs, the topography is in a state of constant flux and development of new navigational hazards is swift.[61]

There has been nothing discovered, in a review of many aircraft and vessel losses in the so-called "triangle" area over the years that would indicate that the casualties were the result of anything other than physical causes. No extraordinary factors have ever been identified.

The very location of the so-called "triangle" is probably the greatest single factor responsible for the relatively high level of losses in the western Atlantic over the years. . . .

Within the area described above converge the ocean currents known as the Antilles Current, the Florida Current, the North Equatorial Current (all three combine to make up the Gulf Stream) and the Labrador Current. The first three great rivers of water within the Atlantic are considerable warmer than the surrounding water while the latter is much colder. The interface of these thermal energy transfer conduits with the continental land and air mass sometimes creates micro-weather systems of small size, having great energy and violence which can and do inflict serious damage to vessels or aircraft caught up in them. . . .

The area encompassed within the semi-circle is heavily traveled by surface vessels and aircraft as it includes within it highly attractive recreational areas, busy commercial trade routes, and rich fishing grounds. These factors alone increase greatly the possibility of increased accidents simply by reason of the greater than normal number of vessels and aircraft in transit within the area.[62]

We are forced to conclude that the myth of the Bermuda Triangle is perpetuated not so much by mysterious incidents as by the need of some people to believe in mysterious forces that can sabotage our best laid plans. There are undoubtedly many psychological reasons for such a belief; one reason may be that the burden of responsibility for the course of one's own life is lightened if the intervention of mysterious and uncontrollable external influences is thought likely.

Mystery Houses

There is nothing in an experience that testifies to its corre-
spondence with "reality," nothing in a perception that guaran-
tees its truth. Judgments of reality and truth must come from
sources other than the experience or perception.[377]

In California, there are at least three locations that boast of
"mystery houses"—Knott's Berry Farm in the southern part of the
state, and Santa Cruz County and the Redwood Highway in the
north. Similar mystery houses are scattered across the country. At
these locations, visitors experience a number of striking illusions:
balls appear to roll uphill; people appear to lean noticeably and
seem unable to stand straight up; and, as they move from one area
to another, people seem to shrink or grow taller. The mystery
house guides explain these perceptions according to a variety of
occult theories postulating strange energy vortexes or antigravity
fields.

Indeed, what can account for these odd and seemingly unique
experiences? You will recall our discussion of the proprioceptive
sense—in our muscles, tendons, joints, and inner ear—which informs us of the position of our bodies. This sense tells us how
gravity is acting on our bodies and thus lets us know how much we
deviate from an upright position. However, in spite of this
physiological sense of the vertical, studies indicate that we usually
are even more dependent on our prior conditioning in arriving at
our perceptions of whether we and objects around us are vertical,
horizontal, or somewhere in-between.[22, 747] Therefore, let us consider what kinds of conditioning we have acquired with respect to
structures such as houses.

Most of us spend most of our lives in and around houses and
other kinds of buildings. Almost all of these houses have level
floors and vertical walls. Thus we have learned to expect that
"houses are level and straight up and down." We have seen that a
perception that is reinforced over a period of time becomes a set—
that is, it becomes automatic, subconscious, and resistant to change.
Thus our assumption that "houses are level and straight up and

Figure 30. A mystery house—people appear to stand at an angle.

down" becomes a set that can bias our interpretation of our environment without our being aware of it.

How does this help us understand the mystery houses? All of these houses have one feature in common: they are all tilted. This, together with the fact that we have a subconscious set to see a house as vertical and level even though consciously we know it is not, is sufficient to explain all of the illusions experienced. These illusions can be understood by referring to Figures 30 through 32, which are photographs taken at the Mystery Spot in Santa Cruz. Although photographs do not convey the full impact of the illusions, they do illustrate the mechanisms involved.

Figure 30 shows a group of people standing by the tilted cabin at the Mystery Spot. Although they appear to be leaning, they are actually standing straight up. The illusion that they are leaning is created by the tilt of the cabin and of the ground on which they are standing, as well as by the odd camera angle, which helps to convey the impact of the illusion.

Figure 31 shows two girls on either side of a level plank. Notice that the girl on the right appears somewhat taller than the one on the left. Figure 32 shows the same two people who have now exchanged places. Note that the girl on the left, who previously appeared taller, now seems shorter. Again, this illusion results from using the cabin as a frame of reference. In this case, we are judging heights in terms of how high the two girls stand in relation to the cabin. That is, in both photos, the girl on the right seems

Figure 31.   A mystery house—girl on the right appears taller.

Figure 32. A mystery house—the same girl now appears shorter.

taller because she stands higher in relationship to the cabin. That the illusion is due to the background of the cabin against which the people are viewed can be demonstrated by blocking out the background or by measuring the heights of the girls in each photograph; you will see that they are practically identical in height.

Although other illusions can be produced by means of a tilted house, these examples give some idea of the range of possibilities.

However, it should not be concluded that tilted houses are necessary to achieve these illusions. Many surroundings that give a false sense of what is vertical and level produce similar, if usually less spectacular, effects. For example, certain stretches of road in some areas have the reputation of seeming to "go uphill" when they actually "go downhill." When I was a teenager, we used to impress dates by taking them to such a road where we would stop the car, turn off the engine, and coast "uphill!"

Mystery houses are a good example of phenomena that appear mysterious and therefore give rise to occult explanations, but which are understandable when their psychological bases are examined. The striking perception that is produced at the mystery houses, then, arises from the nature of our own perceptual processes, not from some mysterious external energy field.

In the realm of perception, we seem to have the power to modify drastically the face that the world presents to us. Nevertheless, many people prefer to deny this capacity and to ascribe such powers to external agencies.

Occult Metaphysics

A number of philosophers had banded themselves together and were traveling from one country to another engaging local sages in learned disputation. When they arrived in Nasrudin's town, the local Governor sent for the Mulla to confront them, for all the intellectuals who he had produced were regularly routed by these strangers.

Mulla Nasrudin presented himself. "You had better first speak to those who have faced the philosophers," the Governor told him, "so that you can get some idea of their methods."

"Not at all," said the Mulla, "the less I know about their methods of thought the better, for I do not think like them, nor will I become imprisoned by their artificialities."

The contest was staged in a large hall, before an enormous gathering from far and near.

The first philosopher stepped forward to start the disputation.

"What," he asked the Mulla, "is the centre of the earth?"

The Mulla pointed with his pen. "The exact centre of the earth is the centre of the spot upon which my donkey, yonder, has his foot."

"How can you prove it?"

"On the contrary, you disprove it. Get a measuring tape!"

The second philosopher asked: "How many stars are there in the sky?"

Nasrudin immediately replied: "Exactly the same number as there are hairs in the coat of my donkey. Anyone who disbelieves this is at liberty to count both."

The third philosopher said: "How many avenues of human perception are there?"

"Not at all difficult," said Nasrudin. "There are exactly as many as there are hairs in your beard, and I will demonstrate them if you like, one by one, as I pluck those hairs for you!"[611]

SUFI TALE

Occult beliefs, as we have defined them, are beliefs that claim to explain observable events, but which are generally considered ill-founded by experts in relevant fields of knowledge. Such a definition excludes most religious and ethical beliefs, which do not usually involve explanations of observable events. Consideration of metaphysics stretches this definition of occultism, since metaphysics involves speculation about the ultimate nature of the world around us. Such speculations often, although not always, extend beyond the realm of observable events. Nevertheless, it will be useful to consider briefly occult metaphysics as illustrating the extreme edge of occult speculation.

However, metaphysics is a broad field and, by presenting a few of the more occult metaphysical speculations, I do not want to imply that these examples are typical of metaphysical speculations in general.

The following gives the flavor of many occult metaphysical statements:

> . . . the all-world is threefold, the sphere of man, the sphere of nature, and the sphere of God; or, as is laid down by the ancient sages, microcosm, the macrocosm, and the super-mundane emanations. The evolution of life is perpetually from the macrocosm into the microcosm and is the third physical emanation. The microcosm is *one* in its end, viz: the attainment of the spiritual and the final co-association with the En-soph: it is several in its growth, viz: in the gradual elimination of the mundane, and the macrocosmic bonds.
>
> The lowest life is the microcosmic bird, and is self-locked, seeing naught, knowing naught of its illusive environment; the higher life, the microcosmic flower, be it of the beast, or of the swarming millions of men, dimly sees and knows itself and the other self; but, purblind, reckons these the end-all and the be-all, here and now, as well as yonder and forever. . . .[213]

Actually composed as a spoof by several authors under the pseudonym "Hiraf," the article from which this selection comes was taken seriously by Madame Blavatsky, editor of *Spiritual Scientist,* the magazine in which the article appeared. Blavatsky praised the article as follows: ". . . the author needs fear few rivals, still less superiors. . . . The weapons he seems to hold in reserve, in the arsenals of his wonderful memory, his learning and his readiness to give any further information that inquirers may wish for, will undoubtedly scare off every theorist, unless he is perfectly sure of himself, which few are."[213]

You will notice that the selection by Hiraf is either meaningless or ambiguous when analyzed, although it has an impressive ring at first reading. Nonsense statements such as these are known as amphigory and are characteristic of much occult metaphysics. Amphigory, of course, allows readers to project their own meaning into such statements, since there is little inherent meaning to begin with. Readers who are unaware of their own tendency to project are likely to assume that the insightful meanings that they "read into" such statements originated with the author of those statements.

One of the major exponents of occult metaphysics is Georges Gurdjieff. Let us examine just one of Gurdjieff's subjects of speculation—namely, the moon and its relationship to the earth.

Gurdjieff believes that the earth and moon depend on one another in several respects. For one thing, the moon receives, from organisms on earth, energy it needs to evolve toward its destiny as a warm planetlike body, complete with a moon of its own. In fact, the moon's very existence depends on the energy it attracts, like an electromagnet, from life on earth. (Can we conclude, therefore, that the moon gradually grew from nothing as life developed on earth?) Even after organisms die, they give up their souls to the moon to nourish its growth.

While the moon, nourished on earth's life, is becoming a planet, the earth, nourished by the rest of the solar system, is evolving into a sun! But the moon does more than *attract* the energy of earth's life; it also *controls* it, so that all happenings on earth—all crime, all good deeds—are actually done by the moon! Gurdjieff concludes that humans, in developing their potential for freedom of action, are actually engaged in a struggle to free themselves from the moon's influence.[495]

What can we make of these speculations that go against almost everything we know about the world? Are they nonsense statements into which followers of Gurdjieff read meaning that makes sense to them? If so, perhaps they serve as projective stimuli that reveal the psychological state of the interpreter. Gurdjieff's scheme seems well suited for the projection of personal meanings: it is lively and of manageable scope, filled with "souls" and with heavenly bodies that "need" each other but also "feed off" each other in their evolution torward higher levels of existence. Fertile fields for the projection of psychological meaning! In contrast, a scientific view of the world is less "personal," less accessible, and certainly more demanding in its emphasis on rigorous observation and reasoning. Little wonder that occult metaphysicians continue to attract followers. An unfortunate consequence, however, is that occult theorists seem blinded to the wonders of nature as they now present themselves to us. The awesome immensity of the universe, the fascinations of subatomic particles, the intricate workings of our nervous systems, and our surpassing capacity to discover and comprehend these marvels—all of this is lost on occult metaphysicians, wrapped up as they are in their solitary theorizing.

Summary

A belief is not true because it is useful. [5]
HENRI-FREDERIC AMIEL

In this chapter, we have discussed a variety of occult beliefs and practices. We have seen that occult beliefs constitute attempts to understand the workings of nature, but that they arise more from personal needs and biases than from valid methods of observation. Although occult practices thus generally lack intrinsic validity, we saw that, because of subtle psychological processes, of which occult practitioners are generally unaware, such practices are sometimes psychologically effective and can produce experiences that transcend ordinary levels of functioning.

We first discussed astrology and other readings which claim to reveal one's personal destiny and characteristics through the study of some external event. We saw that, although many studies of astrology have been conducted, there is very little evidence to support its basic tenets. We also examined studies that bear on the validity of other readings, such as numerology, palmistry, Tarot, and the *I Ching* and found no evidence that these practices have any intrinsic validity. At the same time, however, we saw that, thanks to processes such as projection and the self-fulfilling prophecy, such readings can seem mysteriously accurate and can, as a consequence, be useful for understanding ourselves.

We then examined various occult health and healing practices, including chiropractic, zone therapy and reflexology, polarity therapy, macrobiotics, orgone therapy, and Scientology. Although there is no satisfactory evidence to support the occult theories connected with these practices, we saw that suggestion effects and the effects of love and concern are commonly involved and that these can indeed be powerful healing agents.

We saw that a number of occult theories postulate a "golden age" that existed some time in the past, when marvelous and magical events were commonplace. However, when we examined the evidence for the lost civilization of Atlantis, for the mysterious power of the pyramids, and for von Daniken's ancient astronaut theory, we found only flimsy evidence in each case. Thus such theories probably arise from psychological needs—for example, to believe in the possibility that magical powers might again appear on earth and come to the aid of us lowly mortals.

Similar psychological needs—for magical intervention—may also underlie the belief that UFOs in the news are actually emissaries of an extraterrestrial power that is watching over us; certainly the evidence in support of this belief is rather weak.

Hopefully, as we become more familiar with our own capacities to transcend the ordinary, we will no longer need to project such capacities onto mysterious external forces.

We also discussed the belief that a mysterious force in a region of the Atlantic Ocean known as the Bermuda Triangle is responsible for the loss of a large number of ships. However, we saw that, according to the original accounts of the ships involved, the reasons for the loss of the vast majority are known and are not mysterious. On the other hand, the belief that mysterious forces, rather than we ourselves, might be responsible for the tragedies in our lives is undoubtedly a comforting thought to many.

We have seen that the strange happenings at mystery houses, where the force of gravity seems to be violated, is an illusion based on our tendency to misperceive the vertical when we are surrounded by objects that are tilted. However, rather than becoming aware of their own capacity to alter perceptually the appearance of their surroundings, some people prefer to ascribe their experience in mystery houses to mysterious external forces.

Finally, we examined occult metaphysics as illustrated by the theories of Georges Gurdjieff. We saw that such theories are essentially pure speculation with almost a total lack of evidence to support them. Unfortunately, in their solitary gropings for an understanding of the world around us, occult metaphysicians have cut themselves off from the beauty of the wonders of nature as they are now revealing themselves to us.

In general, we have seen that occult beliefs are based on powerful psychological needs and processes that operate outside of conscious awareness. Consequently, occult practices can have psychological effects that transcend ordinary experience. Finally, we have seen that we can reap the benefits of such effects, and at the same time avoid the dangers of occultism, through a more highly developed awareness of our own psychological functioning.

8

Conclusion

The one who knows his self knows God.[476]
MOHAMMED

Let us summarize what we have discussed, set it in perspective, and touch on the importance of furthering, through competent research, our understanding of transcendental experience.

Transcendental experiences in general arise from psychological processes that operate outside of our ordinary awareness. Given the subconscious nature of these processes, it is not surprising that transcendental experience is often considered mysterious and even paranormal or supernatural. Unfortunately, these labels can steer us away from an awareness of the role of our own psychological functioning in such experiences. This is a shame, because transcendental states—heightened sensitivities, creative imagery, control of bodily processes, increased memory capacity—can be enhanced if the psychological processes involved are recognized and cultivated. In this endeavor, we can gain a greatly expanded vision of human potential. Certainly the greatest creative minds have known how to tap these inner resources.

In contrast, a naive view of these same experiences can produce a superficial occultism with potential dangers that arise whenever powerful psychological mechanisms are misinterpreted and misunderstood.

Of course, some transcendental experiences may indeed be paranormal, but, as we have seen, conclusive evidence does not exist at present. When and if paranormal mechanisms are demonstrated in adequately replicated studies, they should take their rightful place alongside other transcendental processes. On the other hand, the difficulty of demonstrating paranormal processes suggests that they would account for only a small portion of experiences that appear to be paranormal.

Until paranormal mechanisms are shown to exist, we need to account for the strong belief that many people have in such phenomena. Certainly the tendency to formulate such theories stems, in part, from psychological needs—for example, to explain and intellectualize our experience, even when evidence to support our explanation is lacking. However, cultural characteristics are also important; certainly our culture creates insecurities that foster belief in hidden forces we can count on even though we no longer have much faith in ourselves or our fellow human beings.

Everything considered, it is sometimes difficult to develop the self-awareness and self-confidence needed to recognize and develop transcendental potentials in ourselves. However, the rewards of such self-awareness and self-confidence are well worth the effort.

On the Other Hand

Light—more light.[303]
GOETHE

When light is brought to bear on any subject, dark corners are often illuminated that were previously hidden from view. In the case of transcendental experience, close scrutiny reveals some dark corners that need to be examined.

First, transcendental experiences are so powerful that it is not surprising that they have their counterpart in mental disturbance.[80] The scientist's vision, the artist's automatic drawing—in another context, in another individual, might be taken as a sign of mental disturbance;[173] it is no secret that the psychedelic drug that leads some to heaven can lead others to hell.

Mystical experience, in particular—powerful and overwhelming as it is—has sometimes been compared with psychosis,[18] and various features of mystical experience given psychiatric labels— for example, hallucination, delusion, mania, and dissociation. The similarity of mystical experiences to some forms of psychosis can be seen in the following account written by someone who was, at the time of the experience, in the throes of a psychotic breakdown:

> I felt alive and vital, full of energy. My senses seemed alive, colors were very bright, they hit me harder. Things appeared clear-cut, I noticed things I had never noticed before. There was a feeling of exhilaration, a sense of union with the whole world. Time slowed down, much more experience could be crowded into a brief time span. Sexually I felt awakened, competent, responsive. I seemed to notice symmetry and harmony and I wanted to experience everything. I could concentrate on a speck of something and just stare at it. A whole new world opened up, and I felt more secure than ever before.[79]

Furthermore, the ecstatic peaks of mystical experience occasionally seem to be followed by depths of depression,[389, 697] or what some mystics have called "the dark night of the soul." As Georgia Harkness states: "Its theme is the sense of spiritual desolation, loneliness, frustration, and despair which grips the soul of one who, having seen the vision of God and been lifted by it, finds the vision fade and the presence of God recede."[282]

We also know that various states of consciousness that can accompany mystical experience have their counterpart in specific neurological disorders. For example, immediately preceding both migraine and epileptic attacks, some people experience visions or out-of-body feelings;[411] others experience euphoria,[18, 400] which has been variously described as "transported to heaven" and "the most overwhelming ecstatic state it is possible for the human to conceive of."[396] How these disorders trigger such transcendental feelings is not well understood; perhaps they activate certain areas of the brain that we know can produce similar states—that is, euphoria, visions, out-of-body feelings, and déjà vu experiences—when artificially stimulated.[160, 487]

If mystical experiences sometimes arise from mental disorders, how, then, can we distinguish between the mystic and the psychotic?

Probably there are important differences—in how the individual interprets the experience (Is it so overwhelming it is frightening?) and in the acceptance of the experience by others (Is it interpreted as mental breakdown rather than transcendence?).[719] Certainly one important difference is the preparation and the readiness for the experience, which the mystic has usually cultivated and the psychotic has not.[717] As Ben-Ami Scharfstein states: ". . . psychosis is involuntary and inescapable, while the mystic state tends to be voluntary. . . . The mystic does not suffer his internal ecstasy, infinity, or truth, but creates it. His sanity is his control, for he is, when sane, sure at the very least that he can emerge from his mystic state. It can be his release only because it is not his prison."[592]

Here we return to a point we have stressed previously—preparation and understanding are the best guarantees, not only that transcendental states can be experienced and enjoyed, but that such experiences will prove beneficial and not detrimental.

A second reservation sometimes expressed about transcendental experience is that it is a selfish indulgence. This point of view was often voiced during recent periods of social activism, when activists were known as "wheelies" and those interested in personal development and mysticism were called "feelies." The wheelies said that the feelies were self-centered and lacked a social conscience, while the feelies replied that the wheelies were placing their faith in external social changes when an internal change in values and outlook was needed. Hopefully, we are past the stage when this distinction is adhered to. Although mystics, in particular, have sometimes turned their backs on society in their search for transcendence, most transcendental experiences we have discussed are very much social acts: the ecstasy of a mother holding her baby for the first time, the exquisite sensitivity of some people to the thoughts and feelings of others, the euphoria of joining with a group in a common effort of great significance, the healing of suffering people through love and kindness, the thrill of artistic and scientific creation. Certainly social involvement is part and parcel of most transcendental experiences as well as of healthy personal growth and development in general.

The Significance of Transcendence

Occurrences which, according to received theories, ought not
to happen, are the facts *which serve as clues to new discoveries.*[67] SIR JOHN HERSCHEL.

Hopefully, by this time most readers agree that transcendental experience is not only potentially significant for our personal lives, but that it also serves important functions in our society as a whole. Hopefully, most readers also agree that transcendental experience is worthy of significant research efforts. Although the extent of such research has increased considerably in recent years, there are important areas still neglected. Taking psychic and occult healing as an example, many questions remain unanswered.

Can the blood constituents that combat infection be influenced by the suggestions of a healer? If so, can people train themselves, through biofeedback, to increase their resistance to infection?

What body cues does a psychic or occult healer utilize in diagnosing disease and could we learn anything about the physiological processes of disease from research on this question?

Does ecstasy facilitate healing? If so, what specific physiological mechanisms are involved?

Unfortunately, we have not completely learned our lesson about the potential usefulness of folk wisdom. In case we need reminding, here is an account of how vaccination was discovered: ". . . when Edward Jenner, the discoverer of vaccination, was an apprentice in his teens he heard about a local belief in Gloucestershire that people infected by cow-pox from cattle were thereafter immune from smallpox. Contemporary physicians refused to pay any attention to such tales, but these probably inspired Jenner's later experiments. He kept them secret at first, rightly suspecting that his colleagues were not inclined to take them seriously. . . ."[334]

Although some 200 years have passed since Jenner's experiments, the attitude of the scientific community of that day still persists to some extent today. For example, although we have traveled to far corners of the world to collect and test drugs from exotic cultures to add to our medicine chests, we still sometimes overlook the potential value of folk practices in our own culture—

Eskimo shamans are fascinating; occult healers on Main Street are disreputable.

It is not even necessary to go out into the field to get some initial research ideas from folk beliefs and practices; many have been collected and catalogued in various publications.[738] Also available are collections—for example, by Charles Fort[218] and William Corliss[137]—of odd, unusual, and seemingly inexplicable experiences that people have reported over the years. Somewhere in these accumulations of folk experience may be research possibilities that are worth following up.

A less obvious source of research ideas is the studies conducted by parapsychologists themselves. For example, we discussed the research of Bernard Grad[252] and M. Justa Smith[629] concerning the influence of the healer, Oskar Estebany, on the healing of rat wounds and on enzyme reactions. There seemingly was an effect, which could have been due to purely physical factors. But what specifically produced the effect? Nobody knows. Neither researcher followed up these leads. So here is a possibly unknown, and potentially significant, effect, which parapsychologists were not interested in pinning down—possibly because they felt that you cannot "pin down" a paranormal process. And nonparapsychologists are not generally interested in the outcome of fringe "occult" studies. So no one picks up the ball, and a potentially valuable lead is neglected.

Following up leads in these ways should not be expected to yield results immediately. Most seemingly inexplicable effects probably stem from errors of observation or reporting. There undoubtedly are, however, a few nuggets among the dross. After all, drug companies test thousands of compounds in their search for a few that prove useful.

In this search, there is always a chance that truly paranormal processes will turn up. Certainly many scientists, past and present, have believed in paranormal events or thought them likely—for example, among psychologists, Sigmund Freud,[229] William James,[471] William McDougall,[430] Carl Jung,[351] Sir Cyril Burt,[99] Gardner Murphy,[472] Hans Eysenck,[197] Carl Rogers,[565] and Karl Pribram;[202] among biologists, Alfred Russell Wallace,[712] Charles Richet,[560] Sir Alister Hardy,[281] and John Eccles;[178] among physical scientists, Sir William Crookes,[141] Johann Zollner,[755] Camille

Flammarion,[211] Lord John Raleigh,[661] Sir William Barrett,[38] Sir Oliver Lodge,[404] Sir Joseph John Thomson,[680] and Henry Margenau.[418] The opinions of such eminent scientists should not be taken lightly; certainly we should continue our search for the paranormal.

At this point, however, we need to take a closer look at the meaning of *paranormal;* the word has led to much confusion.

First of all, we will undoubtedly continue to discover human sensitivities and abilities that have previously only been guessed at. Quite recently, for example, it was discovered that humans can hear microwave radiation even at relatively low energy levels.[355] To most people, however, paranormal does not refer to such obviously physical abilities, but rather—among other things—to human communication and influence through nonphysical means. Theoretically, there is little new about the concept of nonphysical energies. After all, both gravity and magnetism are nonphysical, or are they? That, of course, depends on your definition of *physical.* Perhaps the dualist's rigid distinction between physical and nonphysical has lost its usefulness in today's world.

Thus, perhaps, the concern of most parapsychologists with proving nonphysical channels of communication has retarded the development of our understanding of extraordinary experience. Although this perspective is understandable—for example, it ties in with deep desires for proof of a soul or spirit that exists distinct from our physical bodies[549]—it has kept most parapsychologists from being interested in "physical" capacities such as discussed in this book, except as contaminating influences to be controlled and eliminated in their research.

A related problem has to do with the sense of mystery that pervades most research into the paranormal and that is seemingly so attractive to parapsychologists. As soon as knowledge accumulates concerning a previously inexplicable experience, parapsychologists seem to lose interest—evidently because the mystery has waned. For example, as our knowledge accumulated concerning the processes involved in hypnosis, the interest of paranormal researchers faded away.

Parapsychologists have thus put themselves in a double bind. If they look very hard for a causal mechanism, they might find one and be disappointed. If they fail to look at all, they cannot view themselves as scientists. The result is a stalemate that has retarded the development of a sound understanding of many transcendental processes.

Parapsychologists need to realize that successful research efforts on their part will sooner or later turn the paranormal into the normal, the mysterious into the known. In a sense, like good social workers, their business is to put themselves out of business. But that is an unpleasant prospect, and just as many social workers have a stake in poverty, so do many parapsychologists have a stake in mystery. That parapsychologists have moved very slowly to clear up the mysteries they study is therefore understandable, but it is also unfortunate.

In a larger sense, of course, we never completely understand any phenomenon, and true scientists need never worry about putting themselves out of business. What happens is that understanding a phenomenon at one level only shifts the mystery to another level. For example, although we can now understand hypnosis, in part, as a conditioning phenomenon, the physiological processes involved remain almost a total mystery. However, parapsychologists show little interest in such mysteries, perhaps because they are potentially solvable and thus not sufficiently mysterious.

It seems that it would help revitalize and legitimize parapsychological research if emphasis were shifted to following up all leads—even if they result in "physical" or "nonmysterious" explanations—that might be helpful in understanding extraordinary and seemingly inexplicable experiences. Certainly there is nothing in the prefix *para* that excludes physical phenomena or phenomena that are potentially understandable. *Parapsychology* merely means "alongside of" or "of a different order than" the mainstream of psychology. Some parapsychological researchers have, in fact, always accepted the possibility that physical and potentially understandable processes underlie what is now called paranormal experience.[528]

However, it is not just the meaning of *paranormal* that has been a problem. It is not possible to use a number of terms—for example, out-of-body experience, radiesthesia, aura, possession—without implying to most people some kind of mysterious, nonphysical process. Unfortunately, there are no substitute terms available. Perhaps we would be better off if we used such terms to refer to the experiences themselves and not to any assumed mechanism that underlies them. Hopefully, one result of such a change in thinking would be that researchers who have shied away from studying such experiences because of their psychic or occult connotations could become involved in relevant research without fear of being branded an occultist.

Thus researchers have, for various reasons, neglected many kinds of processes that are undoubtedly involved in transcendental experience and that we have discussed here. The true believers have neglected these processes because they have their sights set on the paranormal; the debunkers have neglected them because they have failed to see their usefulness. In other words, believers have overlooked pearls while searching for diamonds, while debunkers have never spent much time searching for either.

The truth is that transcendental experience is of great importance to us all. We can better use the energy now expended in bitter argument over the possibility of paranormal influence to design and conduct research that will clarify the properties—paranormal or not as they may be—of transcendental experience. As our understanding of transcendental experience develops, we can look forward to the day when we will all reap the benefits of deepened awareness of our latent potentials.

References

References

Note: Numbers following each reference refer to page numbers in the following manner—the italicized numbers to the left of the colon refer to pages in this book (*The Psychology of Transcendence*); numbers to the right of the colon refer to pages in the reference cited. For example, "*47*:112" indicates that page 47 in *The Psychology of Transcendence* cites material found on page 112 of the reference.

[1] ABEHSERA, MICHEL, *Zen Macrobiotic Cooking.* New Hyde Park, N.Y.: University Books, 1968; *251*:77.

[2] ABELL, ARTHUR, *Talks with Great Composers.* New York: Philosophical Library, 1955; *39*:141.

[3] ABELL, G. O., and others, "A Test of the Gauquelin 'Mars Effect,'" *The Humanist,* 36 (September-October 1976), pp. 40–45; *237*:44.

[4] ABSE, D. WILFRED, *Hysteria and Related Mental Disorders.* Bristol: John Wright, 1966: *74*: all.

[5] ADAMS, FRANKLIN P., *F.P.A.'s Book of Quotations.* New York: Funk & Wagnalls, 1952; *285*:95.

[6] ADDEY, JOHN, *Harmonics in Astrology.* Green Bay, Wis.: Cambridge Circle Press, 1976; *237*:all.

[7] AGNEW, MARIE, "The Auditory Images of Great Composers," *Psychological Monographs,* 31, 1922, pp. 279–87; *41*:280, 285, *110*:284, *116*:285.

[8] ALEXANDER, GEORGE, "Brown Rice as a Way of Life," *New York Times Magazine,* March 12, 1972, pp. 87–104; *252*:all.

[9] ALLEN, STEVE, and others, "A Remote Viewing Study Using a Modified Version of the SRI Procedure," in *Research in Parapsychology, 1975,* eds. J. D. Morris, W. G. Roll, and R. L. Morris. Metuchen, N.J.: Scarecrow Press, 1976, pp. 46–48; *147*:all.

[10] ALLPORT, GORDON, and LEO POSTMAN, *The Psychology of Rumor.* New York: Russell & Russell, 1965; *46*:all.

[11] ALTER, ALLEN, "The Pyramid and Food Dehydration," *New Horizons,* 1, (Summer 1973), pp. 92–94; *262*:92.

300   *References*

  [12] ANAND, B. K., G. S. CHHINA, and BALDEV SINGH, "Some Aspects of Electroencephalographic Studies in Yogis," *Electroencephalography & Clinical Neurophysiology*, 13, 1961, pp. 452–56; *25*:all.

  [13] "Anatomy of a World Best-seller," *Encounter*, 41 (August 1973), pp. 8–17; *265*:all.

  [14] ANDERSON, JACK, and FRED BLUMENTHAL, "Washington's Incredible Crystal-Gazer," *Parade*, May 13, 1956, pp. 10–12; *161*:12, *161*:12.

  [15] ANNEMANN, THEODORE, *Practical Mental Effects*. New York: Tannen, 1963; *223*:all.

  [16] ANSON, JAY, *The Amityville Horror*. Englewood Cliffs, N.J.: Prentice-Hall, 1977; *203*:all.

  [17] ARBMAN, ERNST, *Ecstasy or Religious Trance* (Vol. 2). Uppsala: Svenska Bokforlaget, 1968; *108*:75, *113*:345, *113*:457, *122*:96–99, *124*:33–39, 133–89, 150–54, *125*:239–74, *127*:209–38, *127*:17–29, *127*:190–91.

  [18] ARBMAN, ERNST, *Ecstasy or Religious Trance* (vol. 3). Uppsala: Svenska Bokforlaget, 1970; *290*:375–90, *290*:367–74.

  [19] ARCHER, TED, *Exploring the Psychic World*. New York: William Morrow, 1967; *216*:97–103.

  [20] ARONSON, ELLIOT, "The Effect of Effort on the Attractiveness of Rewarded and Unrewarded Stimuli," *Journal of Abnormal and Social Psychology*, 63, 1961, pp. 375–80; *50*:all.

  [21] ASCH, SOLOMON, *Social Psychology*. Englewood Cliffs, N.J.: Prentice-Hall, 1965; *68*:450–501.

  [22] ASCH, SOLOMON, and HERMAN WITKIN, "Studies in Space Perception: I. Perception of the Upright with Displaced Visual Fields," *Journal of Experimental Psychology*, 38, 1948, pp. 325–37; *278*:all.

  [23] ASSAGIOLI, ROBERTO, *Psychosynthesis*. New York: Viking, 1965; *106*:17–19.

  [24] BACK, KURT, *Beyond Words*. Baltimore: Penguin, 1973; *102*:all.

  [25] BACKSTER, CLEVE, "Evidence of a Primary Perception in Plant Life," *International Journal of Parapsychology*, 10, 1968, pp. 329–48; *155*:all.

  [26] BACON, MARGARET, IRVIN CHILD, and HERBERT BARRY, "A Cross-Cultural Study of Correlates of Crime," *Journal of Abnormal and Social Psychology*, 66, 1963, pp. 291–300; *100*:all.

  [27] BAGNALL, OSCAR, "The Appearance of the Normal Aura," in *The Human Aura*, ed. Nicholas Regush. New York: Berkley Medallion, 1974, pp. 44–54; *188*:45, *188*:45.

  [28] BAKAN, PAUL, "The Right Brain is the Dreamer," *Psychology Today*, 10 (November 1976), pp. 66–68; *36*:all.

  [29] BAKER, CHRISTOPHER, "Ancient Egypt Without Astronauts," in *Some Trust in Chariots*, eds. Barry Thiering and Edgar Castle. New York: Popular Library, 1972, pp. 7–22; *264*:68–70, *264*:70–72, *264*:68.

  [30] BALFOUR, FREDERICK, Letter to the Editor, *Nineteenth Century*, 16, 1884, p. 851; *139*:all.

[31] BANNISTER, ROGER, *The Four Minute Mile.* New York: Dodd, Mead, 1962; *120*:11–12.

[32] BARBER, BERNARD, "Resistance by Scientists to Scientific Discovery," *Science,* 134, 1961, pp. 596–602; *229*:all.

[33] BARBER, T. X., *Hypnosis: A Scientific Approach.* New York: Van Nostrand/Insight, 1969; *67*:133–34.

[34] BARBER, T. X., *LSD, Marihuana, Yoga, and Hypnosis.* Chicago: Aldine, 1970; *74*:115–32, *77*:164–91.

[35] BARBER, T. X., and WILLIAM MEEKER, "Out of Sight, Out of Mind," *Human Behavior,* 3 (August 1974), pp. 56–60; *223*:all.

[36] BARD, MORTON, and RUTH DYK, "The Psychodynamic Significance of Beliefs Regarding the Cause of Serious Illness," *Psychoanalytic Review,* 43, 1956, pp. 146–62; *101*:all.

[37] BARNUM, P. T., *The Humbugs of the World.* Detroit: Singing Tree Press, 1970; *204*:215–17, *205*:217–18.

[38] BARRETT, WILLIAM, *On the Threshold of the Unseen; An Examination of the Phenomena of Spiritualism and the Evidence for Survival After Death.* New York: Dutton, 1918; *294*:all.

[39] BARRETT, WILLIAM, *Death-Bed Visions.* London: Methuen, 1926; *121*:all.

[40] BARRETT, WILLIAM, and THEODORE BESTERMAN, *The Divining Rod.* London: Methuen, 1926; *180*:256–57, *181*:all.

[41] BARTHEZ, E., *The Empress Eugénie and Her Circle.* London: T. Fisher Unwin, 1912; *215*:164–65.

[42] BARTLETT, JOHN, *Familiar Quotations.* Boston: Little, Brown, 1955; *79*:670, *174*:578, *200*:791.

[43] BASMAJIAN, J. V., "Control & Training of Individual Motor Units," *Science,* 141, 1963, pp. 440–41; *76*:all.

[44] BASTEDO, RALPH, "An Empirical Test of Popular Astrology," *The Skeptical Inquirer,* 3 (Fall 1978), pp. 17–38; *236*:all.

[45] BAUER, STEPHEN, "The Function of Hallucinations," in *Origin and Mechanims of Hallucinations,* ed. Wolfram Keup. New York: Plenum Press, 1970, pp. 191–203; *35*:202.

[46] BAUM, L. FRANK, *The Wizard of Oz.* Chicago: Rand McNally, 1956; *89*:all, *244*:188

[47] BAYLESS, RAYMOND, Letter to the Editor, *Journal of the American Society for Psychical Research,* 53, 1959, pp. 35–38; *206*:all.

[48] BEAUREGARD, LAURENT, "Skepticism, Science, and the Paranormal," *Zetetic Scholar,* 1, 1978, pp. 3–19; *227*:5.

[49] BECKER, ROBERT, "Electromagnetic Forces and Life Processes," *Technology Review,* 75 (December 1972), pp. 32–38; *251*:all.

[50] BECKER, ROBERT, and others, "Electrophysiological Correlates of Acupunctural Points and Meridians," *Psychoenergetic Systems,* 1, 1976, pp. 105–12; *248*:all.

⁵¹ BELOFF, JOHN, personal communication; 226:all.

⁵² BELOFF, JOHN, "Why Parapsychology is Still on Trial," *Human Nature*, 1 (December 1978), pp. 68–74; 148:70.

⁵³ BELOFF, JOHN, and DAVID BATE, "An Attempt to Replicate the Schmidt Findings," *Journal of the Society for Psychical Research*, 46, 1971, pp. 21–31; 146:all.

⁵⁴ BELVEDERE, EDWARD, and DAVID FOULKES, "Telepathy and Dreams: A Failure to Replicate," *Perceptual and Motor Skills*, 33, 1971, pp. 783–89; 145:all.

⁵⁵ BENDER, HANS, "The Case of Ilga K," *Journal of Parapsychology*, 2, 1938, pp. 5–22; 34:7, 34:20.

⁵⁶ BENDER, LAURETTA, "The Maturation Process and Hallucinations in Children," in *Origin and Mechanisms of Hallucinations*, ed. Wolfram Keup. New York: Plenum Press, 1970, pp. 95–101; 39:all.

⁵⁷ BENEDICT, PAUL, and IRVING JACKS, "Mental Illness in Primitive Societies," *Psychiatry*, 17, 1954, pp. 377–89; 100:all.

⁵⁸ BENNETT, JAMES, and JAMES BARTH, "Predicting Human Behavior: A Spirited Approach," *Journal of Irreproducible Results*, 20 (June 1973), pp. 5–6; 236:all.

⁵⁹ BENSON, HERBERT, *The Relaxation Response*. New York: William Morrow, 1975; 27:all.

⁶⁰ BERGSON, ANIKA, and VLADIMIR TUCHACK, *Zone Therapy*. New York: Pinnacle, 1974; 248:all, 249:71–73, 249:22.

⁶¹ BERLITZ, CHARLES, *The Bermuda Triangle*. New York: Avon, 1974; 274:all, 276:74, 276:74, 276:75, 277:115–16.

⁶² "The 'Bermuda Triangle,' " Washington, D.C., U.S. Coast Guard paper (November 1975); 277:all.

⁶³ BERNE, ERIC, "The Nature of Intuition," *Psychiatric Quarterly*, 23, 1949, pp. 203–26; 30:221, 30:all.

⁶⁴ BERNSTEIN, MOREY, and WILLIAM BARKER, *The Search for Bridey Murphy*. New York: Doubleday, 1956; 218:all.

⁶⁵ BERTINI, M., HELEN LEWIS, and HERMAN WITKIN, "Some Preliminary Observations with an Experimental Procedure for the Study of Hypnagogic & Related Phenomena," in *Altered States of Consciousness*, ed. Charles Tart. New York: Doubleday/Anchor, 1972, pp. 95–114; 42:104.

⁶⁶ BESTERMAN, THEODORE, "The Psychology of Testimony in Relation to Paraphysical Phenomena," *Proceedings of the Society for Psychical Research*, 40, 1932, pp. 363–87; 209:all.

⁶⁷ BEYNAM, LAURENCE, "Quantum Physics and Paranormal Events," in *Future Science*, eds. John White and Stanley Krippner. New York: Doubleday/Anchor, 1977; 292:309.

⁶⁸ BHARATI, AGEHANANDA, *The Light at the Center*. Santa Barbara, Calif.: Ross-Erikson, 1976; 106:15–31, 106:142.

[69] BISAHA, J. P., and B. J. DUNNE, "Multiple Subject and Long Distant Precognitive Remote Viewing of Geographical Locations," *Proceedings of the International Conference on Cybernetics and Society,* 1977, pp. 512–16; *147*:all.

[70] BISAHA, J. P., and B. J. DUNNE, "Precognitive Remote Viewing in the Chicago Area," in *Research in Parapsychology,* 1976, eds. J. D. Morris, W. G. Roll, and R. L. Morris. Metuchen, N.J.: Scarecrow Press, 1977, pp. 84–86; *147*:all.

[71] BLACK, STEPHEN, *Mind and Body.* London: William Kimber, 1969; *54*:all, *172*:14.

[72] BLONDLOT, RENÉ PROSPER, *"N" Rays: A Collection of Papers Communicated to the Academy of Sciences,* trans. J. Garcin. London: Longmans, Green, 1905; *65*:all.

[73] BOK, BART, and MARGARET MAYALL, "Scientists Look at Astrology," *Scientific Monthly,* 52, 1941, pp. 233–44; *236*:all.

[74] BOURGUIGNON, ERIKA, "World Distribution and Patterns of Possession States," in *Trance and Possession States,* ed. Raymond Prince. Montreal: R. M. Bucke Memorial Society, 1968, pp. 3–34; *196*:all, *196*:all.

[75] BOURGUIGNON, ERIKA, ed., "Introduction," in *Religion, Altered States of Consciousness, and Social Change.* Columbus: Ohio State University Press, 1973, pp. 3–35; *96*:9, 11.

[76] BOURQUE, LINDA, "Social Correlates of Transcendental Experiences," *Sociological Analysis,* 30, 1969, pp. 151–63; *107*:all.

[77] BOURQUE, LINDA, and KURT BACK, "Language, Society, and Subjective Experience," *Sociometry,* 34, 1971, pp. 1–21; *106*:all, *107*:all.

[78] BOWERS, KENNETH, "Hypnosis and Dissociation," in *Consciousness,* eds. Daniel Goleman and Richard Davidson. New York: Harper, 1979, pp. 151–54; *121*:152–53.

[79] BOWERS, MALCOLM, "Pathogenesis of Acute Schizophrenic Psychosis," *Archives of General Psychiatry,* 19, 1968, pp. 348–55; *290*:350.

[80] BOWERS, MALCOLM, and DANIEL FREEDMAN, "Psychedelic Experiences in Acute Psychoses," *Archives of General Psychiatry,* 15, 1966, pp. 240–48; *290*:all.

[81] BOWLBY, JOHN, *Attachment and Loss* (2 vols.). New York: Basic Books, 1969; *51*:all.

[82] BOYD, WILLIAM, *The Spontaneous Regression of Cancer.* Springfield, Ill.: Thomas, 1966; *173*:all.

[83] BRADLEY, RICHARD, *The Costs of Urban Growth.* Washington, D.C.: Department of Housing and Urban Development, 1973; *99*:all.

[84] BRECHER, EDWARD, *Licit and Illicit Drugs.* Boston: Little, Brown, 1972; *19*:all.

[85] BRESLER, DAVID, and RICHARD KROENING, "Acupuncture: A Multidetermined Phenomenon," *Psychoenergetic Systems,* 1, 1976, pp. 137–39; *248*:all.

⁸⁶ BRIER, BOB, GERTRUDE SCHMEIDLER, and BARRY SAVITS, "Three Experiments in Clairvoyant Diagnosis with Silva Mind Control Graduates," *Journal of the American Society for Psychical Research*, 69, 1975, pp. 263–71; *169*:all.

⁸⁷ BRINGLE, MARY, *Jeane Dixon: Prophet or Fraud?* New York: Tower, 1970; *162*:36, *162*:42–43.

⁸⁸ BROWN, BARBARA, *New Mind, New Body*. New York: Harper, 1974; *47*:168–69, *76*:164–65.

⁸⁹ BROWN, BARBARA, *Stress and the Art of Biofeedback*. New York: Harper, 1977; *75*:all.

⁹⁰ BROWN, JUDSON, "A Behavioral Analysis of Masochism," *Journal of Experimental Research in Personality*, 1, 1965, pp. 65–70; *78*:all.

⁹¹ BROWN, ROSEMARY, *Unfinished Symphonies*. New York: Bantam, 1971; *208*:all.

⁹² BROWNFIELD, CHARLES, *Isolation*. New York: Random House, 1965; *22*:13–31.

⁹³ BUCKE, RICHARD, *Cosmic Consciousness*. New York: Dutton, 1969; *106*:90, *126*:259, *128*:362.

⁹⁴ BUCKHOUT, ROBERT, "Eyewitness Testimony," *Scientific American*, 231 (December 1974), pp. 23–31; *47*:all.

⁹⁵ BURANELLI, VINCENT, *The Wizard From Vienna*. New York: Coward, 1975; *6*:all.

⁹⁶ BURDOCK, E. I., "A Case of ESP: A Critique of 'Personal Values and ESP Scores' by Gertrude Schmeidler," *Journal of Abnormal and Social Psychology*, 49, 1954, pp. 314–15; *145*:all.

⁹⁷ BURKE, OMAR MICHAEL, "Travels and Residence with Dervishes," in *Documents on Contemporary Dervish Communities*, ed. Roy Davidson. London: Hoopoe, 1966, pp. 9–14; *109*:11.

⁹⁸ BURR, HAROLD S., *The Fields of Life*. New York: Random House/Ballantine, 1973; *251*:all.

⁹⁹ BURT, CYRIL, *ESP and Psychology*. New York: Wiley, 1975; *293*:all.

¹⁰⁰ CAGE, JOHN, *Silence*. Cambridge, Mass.: M.I.T. Press, 1966; *107*:175.

¹⁰¹ CAMPBELL, JOSEPH, *The Hero with a Thousand Faces*. Cleveland: World, 1949; *274*:249.

¹⁰² CANNELL, J. C., *The Secrets of Houdini*. New York: Dover, 1973; *174*:115–31, *223*:22–23.

¹⁰³ CANNON, WALTER, *The Wisdom of the Body*. New York: Norton, 1960; *53*:227.

¹⁰⁴ CANTRIL, HADLEY, *The Invasion From Mars*. New York: Harper/Torchbooks, 1966; *68*:all.

¹⁰⁵ CARPENTER, W. B., *Mental Physiology*. London: Kegan Paul, 1874; *184*:292–93.

¹⁰⁶ CARRINGTON, PATRICIA, *Freedom in Meditation*. New York: Doubleday/Anchor, 1977; *28*:157–74, *30*:all.

[107] CARTER, MARY, *Edgar Cayce on Prophecy.* New York: Paperback Library, 1968; *159*:86, *160*:112, *160*:34, *160*:89.

[108] CARTER, MILDRED, *Helping Yourself with Foot Reflexology.* West Nyack, N.Y.: Parker, 1969; *249*:6, 8.

[109] CATANIA, A. CHARLES, and DAVID CUTTS, "Experimental Control of Superstitious Responding in Humans, *Journal of the Experimental Analysis of Behavior,* 6, 1963, pp. 203–8; *46*:all.

[110] CAVAN, RUTH, and JORDAN CAVAN, *Delinquency and Crime: Cross-Cultural Perspectives.* Philadelphia: Lippincott, 1968; *99*:227, 231.

[111] CAYCE, EDGAR, "Auras," in *The Human Aura,* ed. Nicholas Regush. New York: Berkley Medallion, 1974, pp. 67–74; *189*:73.

[112] CAYCE, EDGAR E., *Edgar Cayce on Atlantis.* New York: Paperback Library, 1968; *159*:159, *160*:157, *160*:159.

[113] CHAVEZ, JOHN, and T. X. BARBER, "Hypnotic Procedures and Surgery: A Critical Analysis with Applications to Acupuncture Analgesia," *American Journal of Clinical Hypnosis,* 18, 1976, pp. 217–36; *248*:all.

[114] CHEETHAM, ERIKA, *The Prophecies of Nostradamus.* New York: Putnam's/Capricorn Books, 1974; *158*:25, *158*:33, *159*:35.

[115] CHILD, CHARLES, "Statistics of 'Unconscious Cerebration,' " *American Journal of Psychology,* 5, 1892, pp. 249–59; *37*:all.

[116] CHIPP, HERSCHEL, *Theories of Modern Art.* Berkeley: University of California Press, 1968; *84*:370–71.

[117] "Chiropractors: Healers or Quacks? (Part 1)," *Consumer Reports,* 40 (September 1975), pp. 542–47; *247*:546, *247*:546.

[118] "Chiropractors: Healers or Quacks? (Part 2)," *Consumer Reports,* 40 (October 1975), pp. 606–10; *247*:607, *248*:608–10.

[119] CHOUINARD, YVON, "Muir Wall-El Capitan, *"American Alpine Journal,* 15, 1966, pp. 46–51; *112*:50.

[120] CHRISTOPHER, MILBOURNE, *ESP, Seers, and Psychics.* New York: Crowell, 1970; *31*:55–77, *33*:76–77, *83*:39–54, *154*:39–54, *204*:161–62, *204*:163, *204*:142–63, *211*:174–212, *218*:128–29.

[121] CHRISTOPHER, MILBOURNE, *Mediums, Mystics, and the Occult.* New York: Crowell, 1975; *176*:151–53, *212*:180–91, *220*:77–103, *220*:66–76, *223*:31.

[122] CHURCHWARD, JAMES, *The Lost Continent of Mu.* New York: Paperback Library, 1968; *259*:all.

[123] CLARK, W. CRAWFORD, "Acupunctural Analgesia? Evaluation by Signal Detection Theory," *Science,* 184, 1974, pp. 1096–97; *248*:all.

[124] COE, MAYNE, JR., "Fire-Walking and Related Behaviors,"*Psychological Record,* 7, 1957, pp. 101–10; *177*:107, *177*:110.

[125] COGWILL, DONALD, and LOWELL HOLMES, *Aging and Modernization.* New York: Appleton, 1972, *100*:all.

[126] COHEN, DANIEL,*Voodoo, Devils, and the New Invisible World.* New York: Dodd, Mead, 1972; *163*:158–92.

[127] COLLINS, RANDALL, "Toward a Modern Science of the Occult," in *Consciousness and Creativity*, ed. John-Raphael Staude. Berkeley, Calif.: Pan/Proteus, 1977, pp. 43–58; *49*:47.

[128] "The Committee Para Replies to Gauquelin," *The Humanist*, 36 (January-February 1976), p. 31; *237*:all.

[129] "The Committee Para's Reply to M. Gauquelin," *The Humanist*, 36 (May-June 1976), pp. 32–33; *237*:all.

[130] CONDON, EDWARD, "Conclusions and Recommendations," in *Scientific Study of Unidentified Flying Objects*, ed. Edward Condon. New York: Bantam, 1969, pp. 1–6; *269*:1.

[131] CONDON, EDWARD, "Summary of the Study," in *Scientific Study of Unidentified Flying Objects*, ed. Edward Condon. New York: Bantam, 1969, pp. 7–50; *269*:26.

[132] *Confessions of a Medium*. New York: Dutton, 1882; *212*:all.

[133] COOPER, PAULETTE, *The Scandal of Scientology*. New York: Tower, 1971; *255*:147.

[134] COOVER, JOHN, *Experiments in Psychical Research*. Palo Alto, Calif.: Stanford University Press, 1917; *145*:all.

[135] CORINDA, TONY, *13 Steps to Mentalism*. London: Accuba, 1964; *220*:129–58.

[136] CORLISS, WILLIAM, *Strange Minds*. Glen Arm, Md.: Sourcebook Project, 1976; *177*:231–38.

[137] CORLISS, WILLIAM, *The Unexplained*. New York: Bantam, 1976; *293*:all.

[138] CRELIN, EDMUND, "A Scientific Test of the Chiropractic Theory," *American Scientist*, 61, 1973, pp. 574–80; *246*:574, *247*:all.

[139] CRISWELL, *Criswell Predicts*. New York: Grosset, 1969; *161*:back cover.

[140] CROOKALL, ROBERT, *The Study and Practice of Astral Projection*. Secaucus, N.J.: University Books, 1966; *195*:all.

[141] CROOKES, WILLIAM, *Researches in the Phenomena of Spiritualism*. London: Burns, 1874; *214*:87, *293*:all.

[142] CROZE, S., C. ANTONIETTI, and R. DUCLAUX, "Changes in Burning Pain Threshold Induced by Acupuncture in Man," *Brain Research*, 104, 1976, pp. 335–40; *248*:all.

[143] CSIKSZENTMIHALYI, MIHALY, *Beyond Boredom and Anxiety*. San Francisco: Jossey-Bass, 1975; *17*:41.

[144] CUMBERLAND, STUART, *A Thought-Reader's Thoughts*. London: Sampson Low, 1888; *31*:all.

[145] CUSTANCE, JOHN, *Wisdom, Madness, and Folly*. New York: Pellegrini & Cudahy, 1952; *124*:52.

[146] DALE, L. A., and others, "Dowsing: A Field Experiment in Water Divining," *Journal of the American Society for Psychical Research*, 45, 1951, pp. 3–16; *182*:all.

147 DANA, CHARLES, and others, "Report of an Investigation of the Phenomena Connected with Eusapia Palladino," *Science*, 31, 1910, pp. 776–80; *216*:all.

148 DARLING, CHARLES, "Firewalking," *Nature*, 136, 1935, p. 521; *177*:521.

149 DART, JOHN, "Best News Yet This Year," *San Francisco Chronicle*, February 25, 1975, pp. 1, 20; *163*:all.

150 DAVENPORT, REUBEN, *The Death-Blow to Spiritualism: Being the True Story of the Fox Sisters, as Revealed by Authority of Margaret Fox Kane and Catherine Fox Jencken*. New York: Dillingham, 1888; *213*:all.

151 DAVIDSON, DAVID and HERBERT ALDERSMITH, *The Great Pyramid: Its Divine Message* (vol. 1). London: Williams & Norgate, 1927; *261*:458–60.

152 DAVIES, JOHN, *Phrenology: Fad and Science*. New Haven, Conn.: Yale University Press, 1955; *103*:all.

153 DEAN, GEOFFREY, *Recent Advances in Natal Astrology*. Kent, Eng.: Astrological Association, 1977; *235*:85–88, 113–17, 123–25, 128–35, *236*:123–25, *236*:51–52, *236*:all, *236*:544–54, 563, *237*:477–82, *237*:88–95.

154 DE CAMP, L. SPRAGUE, *The Ancient Engineers*. New York: Doubleday, 1963; *267*:all.

155 DE CAMP, L. SPRAGUE, *Lost Continents: The Atlantis Theme*. New York: Random House/Ballantine, 1975; *256*:287, *258*:all, *258*:12–17, *258*:44.

156 DE CAMP, L. SPRAGUE, and CATHERINE DE CAMP, *Spirits, Stars, and Spells*. New York: Canaveral, 1966; *218*:247.

157 DE CAMP, L. SPRAGUE, and WILLY LEY, *Lands Beyond*. New York: Rinehart, 1952; *259*:all.

158 DEIKMAN, ARTHUR, "Experimental Meditation," *Journal of Nervous and Mental Disease*, 136, 1963, pp. 329–43; *26*:all.

159 DELANEY, JAMES, and HOWARD WOODYARD, "Effects of Reading an Astrological Description on Responding to a Personality Inventory," *Psychological Reports*, 34, 1974, p. 1214; *233*:all.

160 DELGADO, JOSE, *Physical Control of the Mind*. New York: Harper/Colophon, 1969; *290*:150–54.

161 DEMENT, WILLIAM, *Some Must Watch While Some Must Sleep*. San Francisco: Freeman, 1974; *145*:58–59.

162 DEREN, MAYA, *Divine Horsemen: The Living Gods of Haiti*. New York: Thames & Hudson, 1953; *18*:260.

163 DICK, JOHN, "The Importance of Psychic Medicine: Training Navaho Medicine Men," in *Mental Health Program Reports (#5)*, ed. Julius Segal, Washington D.C., HEW (December 1971), pp. 20–43; *167*:29–30.

164 DIMOND, STUART, *The Double Brain*. Baltimore: Williams & Wilkins, 1972; *36*:all.

165 DINGWALL, ERIC, *Some Human Oddities*. London: Home & van Thal, 1947; *208*:128, *208*:128.

¹⁶⁶ DINGWALL, ERIC, "Gilbert Murray's Experiments: Telepathy or Hyperaesthesia?" *Proceedings of the Society for Psychical Research,* 56, 1973, pp. 21–39; *33*:all.

¹⁶⁷ DINGWALL, ERIC, KATHLEEN GOLDNEY, and TREVOR HALL, *The Haunting of Borley Rectory.* London: Duckworth, 1956; *203*:all.

¹⁶⁸ DIXON, NORMAN, *Subliminal Perception.* New York, McGraw-Hill, 1971; *30*:12–13.

¹⁶⁹ DONNELLY, IGNATIUS, *Atlantis: The Antediluvian World.* New York: Harper, 1949; *258*:all.

¹⁷⁰ DOWNEY, JUNE, "Muscle-reading," *Psychological Review,* 16, 1909, pp. 257–301; *31*:all.

¹⁷¹ DUNNE, B. J., and J. P. BISAHA, "Multiple Channels in Precognitive Remote Viewing," in *Research in Parapsychology, 1977,* ed. William Roll. Metuchen, N.J.: Scarecrow Press, 1978, pp. 146–51; *147*:all.

¹⁷² DUNNINGER, JOSEPH, *Inside the Medium's Cabinet.* New York: David Kemp, 1935; *211*:all, *215*:119–30.

¹⁷³ EARLE, BRIAN and FREDERICK THEYE, "Automatic Writing as a Psychiatric Problem," *Psychiatric Quarterly,* Supplement 42, 1968, pp. 218–22; *290*:all.

¹⁷⁴ EARLY, LORETTA and JOSEPH LIFSCHUTZ, "A Case of Stigmata," *Archives of General Psychiatry,* 30, 1974, pp. 197–200; *77*:all.

¹⁷⁵ EBON, MARTIN, "The Occult Temptation," *The Humanist,* 37 (January-February 1977), pp. 27–30; *4*:all.

¹⁷⁶ ECCLES, JOHN, "The Physiology of Imagination," *Scientific American,* 199 (September 1958), pp. 135–46; *36*:all, *37*:146.

¹⁷⁷ ECCLES, JOHN, *The Understanding of the Brain.* New York: McGraw-Hill, 1973; *36*:188–225.

¹⁷⁸ ECCLES, JOHN, "The Human Person in Its Two-way Relationship to the Brain," in *Research in Parapsychology, 1976,* eds. J. D. Morris, W. G. Roll, and R. L. Morris. Metuchen, N.J.: Scarecrow Press, 1977, pp. 251–62; *293*:all.

¹⁷⁹ EDGAR, JOHN, and MORTON EDGAR, *The Great Pyramid Passages and Chambers* (vol. 1). Glasgow: Bone & Hulley, 1910; *261*:81.

¹⁸⁰ EDMUNDS, SIMEON, *Spiritualism: A Critical Survey.* London: Aquarian Press, 1966; *212*:all, *216*:119.

¹⁸¹ EDWARDS, I. E. S., *The Pyramids of Egypt.* Baltimore: Penguin, 1961; *267*:all.

¹⁸² EHRENWALD, JAN, "Out-of-the-Body Experience and the Denial of Death," *Journal of Nervous and Mental Disease,* 159, 1974, pp. 227–33; *194*:all.

¹⁸³ "Eleanor Rigby," Revolver Album, Columbia Records ST 2576; *96*:all.

¹⁸⁴ ELIADE, MIRCEA, *Myths, Dreams, and Mysticism.* New York: Harper, 1960; *257*:59–72.

[185] ELIADE, MIRCEA, *Shamanism: Archaic Techniques of Ecstasy*, trans. Willard Trask. New York: Random House/Pantheon, 1964; *170*:256–57.

[186] ELLIOTT, JAMES, "The Nude Marathon-A Conversation with Paul Bindrim," in *Confrontation*, eds. Leonard Blank, Gloria Gottsegen, and Monroe Gottsegen. New York: Macmillan, 1971, pp. 223–44; *51*:all.

[187] ELLIS, DAVID, "Tape Recordings From the Dead," *Psychic*, 5 (January-February, 1974), pp. 44–49; *206*:all.

[188] ELLSON, DOUGLAS, "Hallucinations Produced by Sensory Conditioning," *Journal of Experimental Psychology*, 28, 1941, pp. 1–20; *64*:all.

[189] ERDMAN, DAVID, *The Poetry and Prose of William Blake*. New York: Doubleday, 1968; *130*:484.

[190] ESTABROOKS, GEORGE, *Spiritism*. New York: Dutton, 1947; *143*:123–25, *173*:190–91.

[191] ESTABROOKS, GEORGE, *Hypnotism*. New York: Dutton, 1957; *7*:86.

[192] EVANS, CHRISTOPHER, *Cults of Unreason*. New York: Farrar, 1973; *96*:all, *254*:1–134, *255*:63–66, *268*:137–75.

[193] EVANS, HENRY, *The Spirit World Unmasked*. Chicago: Laird & Lee, 1902; *215*:258–62.

[194] EVERSON, TILDEN, and WARREN COLE, *Spontaneous Regression of Cancer*. Philadelphia: Saunders, 1966; *173*:all.

[195] "The Exorcist," *Newsweek* (September 10, 1973), p. 31; *5*:all.

[196] " 'Eyeless Vision' Unmasked," *Scientific American*, 212 (March 1965), p. 57; *220*:all.

[197] EYSENCK, HANS, *Sense and Nonsense in Psychology*. Baltimore: Penguin, 1964; *293*:106–41.

[198] FARADAY, ANN, *Dream Power*. London: Pan Books, 1972; *45*:3–9.

[199] FARADAY, ANN, *The Dream Game*. New York: Harper/Perennial, 1974; *45*:all.

[200] FELLER, WILLIAM, *An Introduction to Probability Theory and Its Applications* (vol. 1). New York: Wiley, 1957; *243*:97–99.

[201] FERGUSON, MARILYN, *The Brain Revolution*. New York: Bantam, 1973; *56*:248, *70*:20.

[202] FERGUSON, MARILYN, "Karl Pribram's Changing Reality," *Human Behavior*, 7 (May 1978), pp. 28–33; *293*:all.

[203] FIELDS, HOWARD, "Secrets of the Placebo," *Psychology Today*, 12 (November 1978), p. 172; *74*:all.

[204] "53% of Americans Believe in Psychic Phenomena," *National Enquirer* (November 26, 1974), p. 2; *136*:all.

[205] FINDLAY, ALEX, *A Hundred Years of Chemistry*. London: Duckworth, 1948; *41*:36–37.

[206] FINIFTER, ADA, "Dimensions of Political Alienation," *American Political Science Review*, 64, 1970, pp. 389–410; *99*:all.

207 "Fire-walking Ceremonies in India," *Journal of the Society for Psychical Research*, 9, 1900, pp. 312–21; *177*:all.

208 FISCHER, ROLAND, "State-Bound Knowledge," *Psychology Today*, 10 (August 1976), pp. 68–72; *88*:all.

209 FISH, JEFFERSON, *Placebo Therapy*. San Francisco: Jossey-Bass, 1973; *73*:all.

210 FITZGERALD, WILLIAM, and EDWIN BOWERS, *Zone Therapy*. Mokelumne Hill, Calif.: Health Research, 1972; *248*:all, *248*:961, 966, 981.

211 FLAMMARION, CAMILLE, *Mysterious Psychic Forces*. Boston: Small, Maynard, 1907; *294*:all.

212 FLANAGAN, G. PAT, *Pyramid Power*. Santa Monica, Calif.: DeVorss, 1973; *262*:66, 83–88, *262*:all.

213 FLINT, CHARLES, *Memories of an Active Life*. New York: Putnam's, 1923; *283*:123–24, *284*:129.

214 FLOREY, ERNST, ed., *Nervous Inhibition*. New York: Macmillan/Pergamon, 1961; *15*:all.

215 FLOURNOY, THEODORE, *From India to the Planet Mars*. New Hyde Park, N.Y.: University Books, 1963; *217*:all.

216 FLOYD, H. HUGH, and DONALD SOUTH, "Dilemma of Youth: The Choice of Parents or Peers as a Frame of Reference for Behavior," *Journal of Marriage and the Family*, 34, 1972, pp. 627–34; *99*:all.

217 FORNELL, EARL, *The Unhappy Medium*. Austin: University of Texas Press, 1964; *4*:84–85; *214*:179.

218 FORT, CHARLES, *The Complete Books of Charles Fort*. New York: Dover, 1975; *293*:all.

219 FOULKES, DAVID and others, "Long-distance 'Sensory Bombardment' ESP in Dreams: A Failure to Replicate," *Perceptual and Motor Skills*, 35, 1972, pp. 731–34; *145*:all.

220 FOULKES, R. A., "Dowsing Experiments," *Nature*, 229, 1971, pp. 163–68; *182*:all.

221 FOWLER, HARRY, *Curiosity & Exploratory Behavior*. New York: Macmillan, 1965; *22*:all, *27*:all, *110*:all.

222 FOX, OLIVER, *Astral Projection*. New Hyde Park, N.Y.: University Books, 1962; *195*:all.

223 FRANK, JEROME, *Persuasion and Healing*. New York: Schocken, 1963; *166*:all.

224 FRANK, JEROME, "The Medical Power of Faith," *Human Nature*, 1 (August 1978), pp. 40–47; *165*:45.

225 FREEBORN, HENRY, "Temporary Reminiscence of a Long-Forgotten Language During Delirium," *Journal of the Society for Psychical Research*, 10, 1902, pp. 279–83; *88*:all.

226 FREMANTLE, ANNE, *The Protestant Mystics*. New York: New American Library/Mentor, 1964; *117*:260–61.

²²⁷ FREUD, SIGMUND, *The Psychopathology of Everyday Life*. New York: New American Library/Mentor, 1951; *140*:148–49.

²²⁸ FREUD, SIGMUND, *Collected Papers* (vol. 1). New York: Basic Books, 1959; *50*:264–71.

²²⁹ FREUD, SIGMUND, "Psychoanalysis and Telepathy," in *Psychology and Extrasensory Perception*, ed. Raymond Van Over. New York: New American Library/Mentor, 1972, pp. 109–26; *293*:all.

²³⁰ FULLER, JOHN, *Arigo: Surgeon of the Rusty Knife*. New York: Crowell, 1974; *172*:all.

²³¹ FULLER, URIAH, *Confessions of a Psychic*. Teaneck, N.J.: Karl Fulves, 1975; *226*:all.

²³² GAINES, STEVEN, *Marjoe*. New York: Dell, 1974; *173*:all.

²³³ GALANOPOULOS, A. G., and EDWARD BACON, *Atlantis: The Truth Behind the Legend*. Indianapolis, Ind.: Bobbs-Merrill, 1969; *258*:all.

²³⁴ GALE, HARLOW, "A Study in Spiritistic Hallucinations," *Proceedings of the Society for Psychical Research*, 15, 1900–1901, pp. 65–89; *209*:71–72.

²³⁵ "Gallup Poll Indicates 32 Million Believe in Astrology," *New York Times*, October 19, 1975, p. 46; *234*:all.

²³⁶ GALSTON, ARTHUR, "The Limits of Plant Power," *Natural History*, 84 (April 1975), pp. 22–24; *155*:all.

²³⁷ GARDNER, MARTIN, *Fads and Fallacies in the Name of Science*. New York: Dover, 1957; *146*:307, *182*:106–13, *218*:315–20, *252*:250–62, 343–45, *254*:269–70, *260*:176–78, 184, *261*:178, *261*:177, *268*:55–68.

²³⁸ GARDNER, MARTIN, "Mathematical Games: The Amazing Feats of Professional Mental Calculators, and Some Tricks of the Trade," *Scientific American*, 216 (April 1967), pp. 116–19; *10*:all.

²³⁹ GARDNER, MARTIN, "Mathematical Games: Dr. Matrix Finds Numerological Wonders in the King James Bible," *Scientific American*, 233 (September 1975), pp. 174–76, 179–80; *261*:179.

²⁴⁰ GARDNER, MARTIN, *The Incredible Dr. Matrix*. New York: Scribner's, 1976; *261*:all.

²⁴¹ GARFIELD, PATRICIA, *Creative Dreaming*. New York: Simon & Schuster, 1974; *45*:all.

²⁴² GAUQUELIN, MICHEL. *The Scientific Basis of Astrology*, trans. James Hughes. New York: Stein & Day, 1969; *232*:150, *233*:150.

²⁴³ GAUQUELIN, MICHEL, and FRANCOISE GAUQUELIN, "The Zelen Test of the Mars Effect," *The Humanist*, 37 (November-December 1977), pp. 30–35; *237*:all.

²⁴⁴ GIBSON, WALTER, *Houdini's Magic*. New York: Harcourt, 1932; *209*:all.

²⁴⁵ GILBERT, NORMA, *Statistics*. Philadelphia: Saunders, 1976; *152*:89–92, *243*:89–92, 344–47.

²⁴⁶ GLASS, DAVID, and JEROME SINGER, *Urban Stress*. New York: Academic Press, 1972; *99*:all.

²⁴⁷ GLOBUS, GORDON, and others, "An Appraisal of Telepathic-Communication in Dreams," *Psychophysiology*, 4, 1968, p. 365; *145*:all.

²⁴⁸ GLOCK, CHARLES, and ROBERT BELLAH, eds., *The New Religious Consciousness*. Berkeley: University of California Press, 1976; *102*:all.

²⁴⁹ GOLDSTEIN, MURRAY, ed., *The Research Status of Spinal Manipulative Therapy*. Bethesda, Md., National Institute of Neurological and Communicative Disorders and Stroke, Monograph 15, DHEW Publication (NIH) 76–998, 1975; *246*:all, *247*:all.

²⁵⁰ GRAD, BERNARD, "A Telekinetic Effect on Plant Growth (I)," *International Journal of Parapsychology*, 5, 1963, pp. 117–33; *155*:all.

²⁵¹ GRAD, BERNARD, "A Telekinetic Effect on Plant Growth (II)," *International Journal of Parapsychology*, 6, 1964, pp. 473–98; *155*:all.

²⁵² GRAD, BERNARD, "Some Biological Effects of the 'Laying on of Hands,'" *Journal of the American Society for Psychical Research*, 59, 1965, pp. 95–127; *169*:121, *293*:all.

²⁵³ GRAVES, F. D., *The Aquarian Tarot*. New York: Morgan Press, 1970; *240*:all.

²⁵⁴ GRAY, CYNTHIA, and KENT GUMMERMAN, "The Enigmatic Eidetic Image," *Psychological Bulletin*, 82, 1975, pp. 383–407; *10*:all.

²⁵⁵ GREELEY, ANDREW, *Ecstasy: A Way of Knowing*. Englewood Cliffs, N.J.: Prentice-Hall/Spectrum, 1974; *105*:65, *107*:11.

²⁵⁶ GREELEY, ANDREW, "Implications for the Sociology of Religion of Occult Behavior in the Youth Cult," in *On the Margin of the Visible*, ed. Edward Tiryakian. New York: Wiley, 1974, pp. 295–302; *183*:302.

²⁵⁷ GREEN, CELIA, *Out-of-the-Body Experiences*. New York: Random House/Ballantine, 1973; *25*:44, *191*:33–43, *192*:122, *192*:44–45, *194*:9–15, 90–94, *194*:92–94, *195*:all.

²⁵⁸ GREEN, CELIA, and CHARLES MCCREERY, *Apparitions*. Oxford: Institute of Psychophysical Research, 1975; *125*:66, *193*:77, *203*:all.

²⁵⁹ GREEN, ELMER, ALYCE GREEN, and E. DALE WALTERS, "Voluntary Control of Internal States," *Journal of Transpersonal Psychology*, 2, 1970, pp. 1–26; *53*:3.

²⁶⁰ GREENE, DANIEL, "Real Vampires," *National Observer*, June 1, 1974, pp. 1, 16; *199*:all.

²⁶¹ GREENFIELD, JEROME, *Wilhelm Reich vs. the U.S.A.* New York: Norton, 1974; *252*:all, *253*:372, *253*:368, *253*:125–29, 343–67.

²⁶² GREENWALD, ANTHONY, "Significance, Nonsignificance, and Interpretation of an ESP Experiment," *Journal of Experimental Social Psychology*, 11, 1975, pp. 180–91; *149*:all.

²⁶³ GREGORY, RICHARD, and E. H. GOMBRICH, *Illusion in Nature and Art*. New York: Scribner's, 1974; *60*:all.

²⁶⁴ GRIFFITH, FRED, "Meditation Research," in *Frontiers of Consciousness*, ed. John White. New York: Avon, 1974, 139–61; *26*:142, *26*:143.

²⁶⁵ GRUEN, WALTER, "Composition and Some Correlates of the American Core Culture," *Psychological Reports*, 18, 1966, pp. 483–86; *99*:all.

²⁶⁶ GUARINO, RICHARD, "The Police and Psychics," *Psychic*, 6 (June 1975), pp. 9, 14–15; *221*:15.

²⁶⁷ GURNEY, EMUND, and FREDERIC MYERS, "Visible Apparitions," *The Nineteenth Century*, 16, 1884, pp. 68–95; *138*:89–91.

²⁶⁸ HADAMARD, JACQUES, *The Psychology of Invention in the Mathematical Field*. New York: Dover, 1954; *37*:all.

²⁶⁹ HAER, JOHN, "Alterations in Consciousness Induced by Sensory Overload," *The Journal for the Study of Consciousness*, 3, 1970, pp. 160–69; *22*:all.

²⁷⁰ HAKE, HAROLD, and RAY HYMAN, "Perception of the Statistical Structure of a Random Series of Binary Symbols," *Journal of Experimental Psychology*, 45, 1953, pp. 64–74; *48*:all.

²⁷¹ HALL, ANGUS, *Strange Cults*. Danbury, Conn.: Danbury Press, 1976; *215*:112.

²⁷² HALL, MARY, "A Conversation with J. B. Rhine," *Psychology Today*, 2 (March 1969), pp. 20–25, 68; *149*:23.

²⁷³ HALL, TREVOR, *The Spiritualists: The Story of Florence Cook and William Crookes*. New York: Helix, 1963; *214*:all.

²⁷⁴ HALL, TREVOR, *New Light on Old Ghosts*. London: Duckworth, 1965; *203*:all.

²⁷⁵ HAMON, LOUIS, *Cheiro's Language of the Hand*. New York: Arco/Arc Books, 1968; *240*:all.

²⁷⁶ HAMON, LOUIS, *Cheiro's Book of Numbers*. New York: Arco/Arc Books, 1976; *239*:all.

²⁷⁷ HANAWALT, NELSON, "Recurrent Images: New Instances and a Summary of the Older Ones," *American Journal of Psychology*, 67, 1954, pp. 170–74; *43*:all.

²⁷⁸ HANLON, JOSEPH, "Uri Geller and Science," *New Scientist*, 64, 1974, pp. 170–85; *226*:178.

²⁷⁹ HANSEL, C. E. M., *ESP: A Scientific Evaluation*. New York: Charles Scribner's Sons, 1966; *140*:all, *142*:all, *145*:59–60, *150*:184, *218*:225–27, *220*:27, *220*:30–31, *221*:200, *221*:202.

²⁸⁰ HAPPOLD, F. C., *Mysticism*. Baltimore: Penguin, 1973; *119*:133, *123*:140, *124*:133–34, *124*:137–38.

²⁸¹ HARDY, ALISTER, and ROBERT HARVIE, "Telepathy or Not-Or What?" in *The Challenge of Chance*, eds. Alister Hardy, Robert Harvie, and Arthur Koestler. New York: Random House, 1973, pp. 1–120; *293*:all.

²⁸² HARKNESS, GEORGIA, *The Dark Night of the Soul*. New York: Abingdon, 1945; *290*:9.

²⁸³ HART, HORNELL, *Living Religion*. New York: Abingdon, 1937; *41*:169.

[284] HART, HORNELL, *The Enigma of Survival*. Springfield, Ill.: Thomas, 1959; *218*:128–29.

[285] HARTMANN, WILLIAM, "Process of Perception, Conception, and Reporting," in *Scientific Study of Unidentified Flying Objects*, ed. Edward Condon. New York: Bantam, 1969, pp. 567–90; *271*:576.

[286] HASTINGS, ARTHUR, and DAVID HURT, "A Confirmatory Remote Viewing Experiment in a Group Setting," *Proceedings of the IEEE*, 64, 1976, pp. 1544–45; *147*:all.

[287] HASTINGS, PATRICIA, *The Life of Sir Patrick Hastings*. London: Cresset Press, 1959; *121*:229–30.

[288] HEATH, ROBERT, "Electrical Self-stimulation of the Brain in Man," *American Journal of Psychiatry*, 120, 1963, pp. 571–77; *128*:all.

[289] HEBB, DONALD, *A Textbook of Psychology*. Philadelphia: Saunders, 1966; *15*:276–77, *108*:246.

[290] HENDRICKS, GAY, and JAMES FADIMAN, eds., *Transpersonal Education*. Englewood Cliffs, N.J.: Prentice-Hall, 1976; *8*:vii.

[291] HENNESSY, BASIL, "Archaeology of the Ancient Near East," in *Some Trust in Chariots*, eds. Barry Thiering and Edgar Castle. New York: Popular Library, 1972, pp. 7–22; *265*:12, *265*:10.

[292] HEPBURN, RONALD, "Nature and Assessment of Mysticism," in *The Encyclopedia of Philosophy* (vol. 5), ed. Paul Edwards. New York: Macmillan/ Free Press, 1967, pp. 429–34; *107*:all.

[293] HERON, WOODBURN, W. H. BEXTON, and DONALD HEBB, "Cognitive Effects of a Decreased Variation in the Sensory Environment," *American Psychologist*, 8, 1953, p. 366; *6*:all.

[294] HILGARD, ERNEST, *The Experience of Hypnosis*. New York: Harcourt, 1968; *65*:95–208.

[295] HIRAI, TOMIO, *Psychophysiology of Zen*. Tokyo: Igaku Shoin, 1974; *26*:all.

[296] HIXSON, JOSEPH, *The Patchwork Mouse*. New York: Doubleday/ Anchor, 1976; *142*:all.

[297] HODGSON, RICHARD, "Report of the Committee Appointed to Investigate Phenomena Connected with the Theosophical Society," *Proceedings of the Society for Psychical Research*, 3, 1885, pp. 201–400; *215*:207.

[298] HODGSON, RICHARD, "The Possibilities of Mal-Observation and Lapse of Memory," *Proceedings of the Society for Psychical Research*, 4, 1887, pp. 381–495; *209*:all.

[299] HODGSON, RICHARD, "Mr. Davey's Imitations by Conjuring of Phenomena Sometimes Attributed to Spirit Agency," *Proceedings of the Society for Psychical Research*, 8, 1892, pp. 253–310; *209*:all.

[300] HOLLINGWORTH, H. L., "The Psychology of Drowsiness," *American Journal of Psychology*, 22, 1911, pp. 99–111; *45*:109, 111.

[301] HOLLINGWORTH, H. L., "General Laws of Redintegration," *Journal of General Psychology*, 1, 1928, pp. 79–90; *58*:all.

302 HOLMES, THOMAS, and MINORU MASUDA, "Psychosomatic Syndrome," *Psychology Today*, 5 (April 1972), pp. 71–72, 106, 118; *98*:all.

303 HOME, D. D., *Lights and Shadows of Spiritualism*. London: Virtue, 1878; *289*:title page.

304 HONIGFIELD, GILBERT, "Non-specific Factors in Treatment," *Diseases of the Nervous System*, 25, 1964, pp. 145–56, 225–39; *71*:all.

305 HONORTON, CHARLES, personal communication; *226*:all.

306 HONORTION, CHARLES, "Replicability, Experimenter Influence, and Parapsychology," paper presented at the AAAS Annual Meeting, Washington, D.C., 1978; *146*:all.

307 HONORTON, CHARLES, "Science Confronts the Paranormal," in *Research in Parapsychology, 1975*, eds. J. D. Morris, W. G. Roll, and R. L. Morris. Metuchen, N.J.: Scarecrow Press, 1976, pp. 199–223; *149*:205–6.

308 HOROWITZ, KENNETH, DONALD LEWIS, and EDGAR GASTEIGER, "Plant 'Primary Perception': Electrophysiological Unresponsiveness to Brine Shrimp Killing," *Science*, 189, 1975, pp. 478–80; *155*:all.

309 HOROWITZ, MARDI, "The Imagery of Visual Hallucinations," *Journal of Nervous & Mental Disease*, 138, 1964, pp. 513–23; *12*:all.

310 HORTON, LYDIARD, "The Illusion of Levitation," *Journal of Abnormal Psychology*, 13, 1918, pp. 42–53; *193*:49–50.

311 HORTON, LYDIARD, "Levitation Dreams: Their Physiology," *Journal of Abnormal Psychology*, 14, 1919, pp. 145–72; *191*:145.

312 HOUDINI, HARRY, *Miracle Mongers and Their Methods*. New York: Dutton, 1920; *176*:all.

313 HOUDINI, HARRY, *A Magician Among the Spirits*. New York: Harper, 1924; *4*:181–82, *21*:all, *211*:all, *214*:204–5, *215*:41–42, *215*:36–37, *215*:99, *215*:138–65, *216*:50–65, *223*:244–65.

314 HOULSBY, CLIVE, "An Engineer's Opinion," in *Some Trust in Chariots*, eds. Barry Thiering and Edgar Castle. New York: Popular Library, 1972, pp. 83–86; *264*:84, *264*:84.

315 HUBBARD, L. RONALD, *Dianetics: The Modern Science of Mental Health*. New York: Hermitage House, 1950; *255*:212.

316 HUBBARD, L. RONALD, *Have You Lived Before This Life?* Los Angeles: American Saint Hill, 1968; *254*:all.

317 HUBBARD, L. RONALD, *Scientology: A History of Man*, Los Angeles: American Saint Hill, 1968; *254*:30–31.

318 HUBER, JACK, *Through an Eastern Window*. Boston: Houghton-Mifflin, 1967; *127*:64–65, *129*:52–53.

319 HULL, CLARK, *Hypnosis and Suggestibility*. New York: Appleton, 1933; *32*:23–24, *62*:all.

320 HUME, NICHOLAS, and GERALD GOLDSTEIN, "Is There an Association Between Astrological Data and Personality?" *Journal of Clinical Psychology*, 33, 1977, pp. 711–13; *236*:all.

[321] HUNTER, ROGER and JOHN DERR, "Prediction Monitoring and Evaluation Program," *Earthquake Information Bulletin*, 10, 1978, pp. 93–96; *163*:all.

[322] HUXLEY, ALDOUS, *The Devils of Loudun*. New York: Harper/ Colophon, 1952; *197*:142, *197*:109–20.

[323] HUXLEY, ALDOUS, *The Doors of Perception*. New York: Harper/ Colophon, 1956; *i*:62.

[324] HYNEK, J. ALLEN, *The UFO Experience*. Chicago: Henry Regnery, 1972; *269*:214.

[325] *The I Ching, or Book of Changes*, trans. Richard Wilhelm and Cary Baynes. Princeton, N.J.: Princeton University Press, 1967; *241*:19.

[326] INGHAM, GEOFFREY, "Plant Size: Political Attitudes and Behavior," *Sociological Review*, 17, 1969, pp. 235–49; *99*:all.

[327] "Interview:Arthur Ford," *Psychic*, 2 (September-October 1970), pp. 5–7, 32–36; *219*:32.

[328] "Investigating the Paranormal [editorial]," *Nature*, 251, 1974, pp. 559–60; *226*:559.

[329] JACKSON, HERBERT, *The Spirit Rappers*. New York: Doubleday, 1972; *6*:all, *213*:111–12, *213*:112, *214*:206–7, *214*:212.

[330] JACOBS, DAVID, *The UFO Controversy in America*. Bloomington: University of Indiana Press, 1975; *272*:5–34, *272*:5–34, 58–59, *274*:all.

[331] JACOBSON, EDMUND, "Electrophysiology of Mental Activities," *American Journal of Psychology*, 44, 1932, pp. 677–94; *80*:all.

[332] JACOBSON, EDMUND, *You Must Relax*. New York: McGraw-Hill, 1957; *75*:all.

[333] JACOBSON, NILS, and NILS WIKLUND, "Investigation of Claims of Diagnosing by Means of ESP," in *Research in Parapsychology, 1975*, eds. J. D. Morris, W. G. Roll, and R. L. Morris. Metuchen, N.J.: Scarecrow Press, 1976, pp. 74–76; *169*:all.

[334] JAHODA, GUSTAV, *The Psychology of Superstition*. Baltimore: Penguin, 1969; *46*:144, *46*:82, *210*:50–51, *234*:30–32, *292*:13.

[355] JAMES, WILLIAM, *The Principles of Psychology* (vol. 2). New York: Holt, 1890; *200*:101–2.

[336] JAMES, WILLIAM, *The Varieties of Religious Experience*. New York: New American Library/Mentor, 1958; *1*:298, *6*:all, *78*:238, *78*:244, *106*:204, *107*:all, *108*:297, *109*:30, *114*:27–28, *118*:157–206, *118*:202, *122*:67, *124*:326, *125*:201, *128*:all, *129*:202, *164*:109, *196*:386.

[337] JASTROW, JOSEPH, *Fact and Fable in Psychology*. Boston: Houghton Mifflin, 1900; *182*:307–36.

[338] JASTROW, JOSEPH, *Wish and Wisdom*. New York: Appleton, 1935; *216*:145

[339] JASTROW, JOSEPH, "Chevreul as Psychologist," *Scientific Monthly*, 44, 1937, pp. 487–96; *182*:all.

[340] JEROME, LAWRENCE, "Astrology: Magic or Science?" *The Humanist,* 35 (September-October 1975), pp. 10–16; *237*:all.

[341] JEROME, LAWRENCE, "Planetary 'Influences' Versus Mathematical Realities," *The Humanist,* 36 (March-April 1976), pp. 52–53; *237*:all.

[342] JOHNSON, DONALD, "The 'Phantom Anesthetist' of Mattoon," *Journal of Abnormal & Social Psychology,* 40, 1945, pp. 175–86; *71*:all.

[343] JOHNSON, KENDALL, *The Living Aura.* New York: Hawthorn, 1975; *189*:127–32.

[344] JOHNSON, REX, Letter to the Editor, *Journal of Parapsychology,* 36, 1972, pp. 71–72; *155*:all.

[345] JOURARD, SIDNEY, "Astrological Sun Signs and Self-disclosure," *Journal of Humanistic Psychology,* 18 (Winter 1978), pp. 53–56; *236*:all.

[346] JUNG, CARL, *Collected Papers on Analytical Psychology,* ed. Constance Long. New York: Moffat Yard, 1917; *209*:1–93.

[347] JUNG, CARL, *Psychology and Alchemy,* trans. R. F. C. Hull. New York: Random House/Pantheon, 1953; *89*:218.

[348] JUNG, CARL, "Synchronicity: An Acausal Connecting Principle," in *The Interpretation of Nature and the Psyche,* Carl Jung and Wolfgang Pauli. New York: Random House/Pantheon, 1955, pp. 1–146; *49*:all, *91*:all.

[349] JUNG, CARL, *Psychiatric Studies,* trans. R. F. C. Hull. New York: Random House/Pantheon, 1957; *88*:95–106.

[350] JUNG, CARL, *Archetypes and the Collective Unconscious,* trans. R. F. C. Hull. New York: Random House/Pantheon, 1959; *91*:all.

[351] JUNG, CARL, *The Structure and Dynamics of the Psyche,* trans. R. F. C. Hull. New York: Random House/Pantheon, 1960; *293*:318.

[352] JUNG, CARL, *Memories, Dreams, Reflections.* New York: Random House/Vintage, 1963; *91*:39, *91*:37, 47.

[353] JUNG, CARL, "Foreword," *The I Ching, or Book of Changes,* trans. Richard Wilhelm and Cary Baynes. Princeton, N.J.: Princeton University Press, 1967; *242*:xix–xx.

[354] JUNG, CARL, *Flying Saucers,* trans. R. F. C. Hull. New York: New American Library/Signet, 1969; *208*:20, *273*:27, 33.

[355] JUSTESEN, DON, "Microwaves and Behavior," *American Psychologist,* 30, 1975, pp. 391–401; *294*:all.

[356] KAMIYA, JOE, "Operant Control of the EEG Alpha Rhythm and Some of Its Reported Effects on Consciousness," in *Altered States of Consciousness,* ed. Charles Tart. New York: Doubleday/Anchor, 1972, pp. 519–29; *6*:all.

[357] KARNES, EDWARD, and ELLEN SUSMAN, "Remote Viewing: A Response Bias Interpretation," research report presented at the American Psychological Association Annual Meeting, San Francisco, 1977; *147*:all.

[358] KEENE, M. LAMAR (as told to Allen Spraggett), *The Psychic Mafia.* New York: Dell, 1976; *217*:21.

³⁵⁹ KEMENY, JOHN, J. LAURIE SNELL, and GERALD THOMPSON, *Finite Mathematics*. Englewood Cliffs, N.J.: Prentice-Hall, 1956; *49*:125.

³⁶⁰ KENISTON, KENNETH, *The Uncommitted*. New York: Harcourt, 1965; 97:1–20, 209–310.

³⁶¹ KERCKHOFF, ALAN, and KURT BACK, *The June Bug: A Study of Hysterical Contagion*. New York: Appleton, 1968; *71*:all.

³⁶² KEYS, ANCEL, and others, *The Biology of Human Starvation* (vol. 2). Minneapolis: University of Minnesota Press, 1950; *50*:767–918.

³⁶³ KIEV, ARI, "The Psychotherapeutic Value of Spirit-Possession in Haiti," in *Trance and Possession States*, ed. Raymond Prince. Montreal, R. M. Bucke Memorial Society, 1968, pp. 143–48; *197*:147–48.

³⁶⁴ KIEV, ARI, *Transcultural Psychiatry*. New York: Free Press, 1972; *167*:136.

³⁶⁵ KIEV, ARI, ed., *Magic, Faith, and Healing*. New York: Macmillan/Free Press, 1974; *166*:all.

³⁶⁶ KILNER, WALTER, "The Aura Made Visible by the Aid of Chemical Screens," in *The Human Aura*, ed. Nicholas Regush. New York: Berkley Medallion, 1974, pp. 33–43; *188*:40.

³⁶⁷ KITAHARA, SHUI'CHI, "August Training Session and Afterwards," *Psychologia*, 6, 1963, pp. 188–89; *118*:188–89.

³⁶⁸ KLAPP, ORRIN, *Currents of Unrest*. New York: Holt, 1972; *22*:47, *69*:119.

³⁶⁹ KLASS, PHILIP, *UFOs Explained*. New York: Random House, 1974, *65*:349–50, *268*:139, *271*:267–77, *272*:134–37, 143, *273*:134–37.

³⁷⁰ KLAUSNER, SAMUEL, *Why Man Takes Chances*. New York: Doubleday/Anchor, 1962; *27*:all.

³⁷¹ KLEITMAN, NATHANIEL, "Patterns of Dreaming," *Scientific American*, 203 (November 1960), pp. 82–88; *6*:all.

³⁷² KLINE, MILTON, ed., *A Scientific Report on "The Search for Bridey Murphy."* New York: Julian Press, 1956; *218*:all.

³⁷³ KMETZ, JOHN, "An Examination of Primary Perception in Plants," *Parapsychology Review*, 6, 1975, p. 21; *155*:all.

³⁷⁴ KOESTLER, ARTHUR, *The Act of Creation*. London: Hutchinson, 1964; *229*:48.

³⁷⁵ KOESTLER, ARTHUR, *The Case of the Midwife Toad*. New York: Random House, 1971; *49*:135–43, *142*:all.

³⁷⁶ KOESTLER, ARTHUR, "Anecdotal Cases," in *The Challenge of Chance*, eds. Alister Hardy, Robert Harvie, and Arthur Koestler. New York: Random House, 1973, pp. 167–224; *134*:186–87.

³⁷⁷ KOLERS, PAUL, "The Illusion of Movement," *Scientific American*, 211 (October 1964), pp. 98–106; *278*:99.

³⁷⁸ KRIPPNER, STANLEY, and WILLIAM HUGHES, "Dreams & Human Potential," *Journal of Humanistic Psychology*, 10 (Spring 1970), pp. 1–20; *39*:11, *44*:11, *44*:13.

³⁷⁹ KRIPPNER, STANLEY, and ALBERTO VILLOLDO, *The Realms of Healing,* Millbrae, Calif.: Celestial Arts, 1976; *171*:1–23, *172*:124–28.

³⁸⁰ KRISHNA, GOPI, "The Aims of Meditation," in *What Is Meditation?,* ed. John White. New York: Doubleday/Anchor, 1974, pp. 7–13; *28*:9–10.

³⁸¹ KROGER, WILLIAM, "Acupunctural Analgesia," *American Journal of Psychiatry,* 130, 1973, pp. 855–60; *248*:all.

³⁸² KROGER, WILLIAM, *Clinical and Experimental Hypnosis.* Philadelphia: Lippincott, 1977; *65*:212–21.

³⁸³ KÜBLER-ROSS, ELISABETH, "Death Does Not Exist," *The Co-evolution Quarterly,* 14 (Summer 1977), pp. 100–107; *121*:all.

³⁸⁴ KUHN, THOMAS, *The Structure of Scientific Revolutions.* Chicago: University of Chicago Press, 1971; *229*:all.

³⁸⁵ KUSCHE, LAWRENCE, *The Bermuda Triangle Mystery-Solved.* New York: Harper, 1975; *274*:all, *276*:78, *276*:217, *276*:198–99.

³⁸⁶ LABOVITZ, SANFORD, "Variations in Suicide Rates," in *Suicide,* ed. Jack Gibbs. New York: Harper, 1968, pp. 57–73; *100*:60.

³⁸⁷ LACHMAN, SHELDON, *Psychosomatic Disorders: A Behavioristic Interpretation.* New York: Wiley, 1972; *73*:all, *74*:52–53.

³⁸⁸ LANG, ANDREW, "The Fire Walk," *Proceedings of the Society for Psychical Research,* 15, 1900, pp. 2–15; *177*:all.

³⁸⁹ LASKI, MARGHANITA, *Ecstasy.* Bloomington: University of Indiana Press, 1961; *90*:305, *107*:all, *107*:135, *108*:249, *108*:26–27, *109*:255, *110*:256, *116*:138–44, *166*:444, *116*:443, *119*:190, *120*:173, *120*:177, 182, *120*:196–97, 205, *122*:451, 453, 454, 465, 467, *124*:261, *126*:462, 496, *126*:86, *127*:77, 247, *128*:32, *128*:279–368, *129*:87, 453, *193*:68, *198*:306, *290*:162–63.

³⁹⁰ LEANING, F. E., "An Introductory Study of Hypnagogic Phenomena," *Proceedings of the Society for Psychical Research,* 35, 1925, pp. 289–411; *201*:295–96.

³⁹¹ LE CRON, LESLIE, *Self Hypnotism.* Englewood Cliffs, N.J.: Prentice-Hall, 1964; *66*:all.

³⁹² LEE, JAMES, personal communication; *116*:all.

³⁹³ LEROY, OLIVIER, *Levitation: An Examination of the Evidence and Explanations.* London: Burns Oates & Washbourne, 1928; *25*:all.

³⁹⁴ LE SHAN, LAWRENCE, *The Medium, the Mystic, and the Physicist.* New York: Viking, 1974; *165*:125.

³⁹⁵ LESTER, DAVID, "Voodoo Death," *American Anthropologist,* 74, 1972, pp. 386–90; *77*:all.

³⁹⁶ LEUBA, JAMES, *The Psychology of Religious Mysticism.* New York: Harcourt, 1929, *43*:275, *52*:all, *107*:all, *112*:139, 141, *116*:256, *119*:261–62, *119*:207, *121*:259, *198*:241, *290*:205–6.

³⁹⁷ LEUKEL, FRANCIS, *Introduction to Physiological Psychology.* St. Louis: Mosby, 1972; *187*:249–50.

³⁹⁸ LEVI, LENNART, *Stress.* New York: Liveright, 1967; *54*:all.

399 LEVIN, MURRAY, *The Alienated Voter*. New York: Holt, 1960; *99*:all.

400 LEWIS, HOWARD, and MARTHA LEWIS, *Psychosomatics*. New York: Pinnacle Books, 1975; *164*:278, *290*:177.

401 LEWIS, IOAN, *Ecstatic Religion*. Baltimore: Penguin/Pelican, 1975; *99*:195, *100*:20.

402 LILLEY, WAYNE, "The Pyramid Pushers," *Financial Post Magazine* (April 1976), pp. 19–24; *262*:22.

403 LINDSAY, JACK, *Origins of Astrology*. London: Frederick Muller, 1971; *235*:all.

404 LODGE, OLIVER, *The Survival of Man*. New York: Moffat, Yard, 1909; *294*:all.

405 LOFLAND, JOHN, *Doomsday Cult*. Englewood Cliffs, N.J.: Prentice-Hall, 1966; *163*:267–68.

406 LUCE, GAY, *Biological Rhythms in Human and Animal Physiology*. New York: Dover, 1971; *237*:all.

407 LUCE, GAY, *Body Time*. New York: Bantam, 1971; *38*:115, *237*:all.

408 LUCKMANN, THOMAS, and PETER BERGER, "Social Mobility and Personal Identity," *Humanitas*, 8 (Spring 1971), pp. 93–109; *98*:all.

409 LUDWIG, ARNOLD, "An Historical Survey of the Early Roots of Mesmerism," *International Journal of Clinical Hypnosis*, 12, 1964, pp. 205–17; *73*:all.

410 LUDWIG, ARNOLD, "Altered States of Consciousness," *Archives of General Psychiatry*, 15, 1966, pp. 225–34; *19*:all.

411 LUKIANOWICZ, N., "Autoscopic Phenomena," *Archives of Neurology and Psychiatry*, 80, 1958, pp. 199–220; *290*:all.

412 LURIA, ALEXANDER, *The Mind of a Mnemonist*. New York: Basic Books, 1968; *10*:all, *10*:all.

413 LUTHE, WOLFGANG, "Autogenic Training," *American Journal of Psychotherapy*, 17, 1963, pp. 174–95; *75*:all.

414 MACLAURIN, E. C., "Chariots in the Land Flowing with Milk and Honey," in *Some Trust in Chariots*, eds. Barry Thiering and Edgar Castle. New York: Popular Library, 1972, pp. 31–47; *265*:37.

415 MAC ROBERT, ALAN, "Proxy Sittings: A Report of the Study Group Series with Arthur Ford," *Journal of the American Society for Psychical Research*, 48, 1954, pp. 71–73; *219*:all.

416 MAHESH YOGI, MAHARISHI, *Transcendental Meditation*. New York: Plume, 1975; *27*:all, *28*:52.

417 MANN, FELIX, *Acupuncture*. New York: Random House/Vintage, 1973; *249*:108–13.

418 MARGENAU, HENRY, "ESP in the Framework of Modern Science," *Journal of the American Society for Psychical Research*, 60, 1966, pp. 214–28; *294*:all.

419 MARKS, DAVID, and RICHARD KAMMANN, "Uri Geller: Is This How

It's Done?" *New Zealand Listener*, May 17, 1975, pp. 10–12; *223*:11, *225*:11, *225*:11–12.

[420] MARKS, DAVID, and RICHARD KAMMANN, "Information Transmission in Remote Viewing Experiments," *Nature*, 274, 1978, pp. 680–81; *147*:all.

[421] MARKS, LAWRENCE, "Synesthesia: The Lucky People with Mixed-up Senses," *Psychology Today*, 9 (June 1975), pp. 48–52; *10*:all.

[422] MARKWICK, BETTY, "The Soal-Goldney Experiments with Basil Shackleton: New Evidence of Data Manipulation," *Proceedings of the Society for Psychical Research*, 56, 1978, pp. 250–77; *144*:253.

[423] MARSH, ROBERT, *Comparative Sociology*. New York: Harcourt, 1967; *98*:all.

[424] MASLOW, ABRAHAM, *Motivation and Personality*. New York: Harper, 1954; *50*:80–154, *118*:115–16.

[425] MASLOW, ABRAHAM, *Toward a Psychology of Being*. New York: D. Van Nostrand, 1968; *106*:71–114, *107*:71–114.

[426] MATIN, LEONARD, and G. ERNEST MAC KINNON, "Autokinetic Movement," *Science*, 143, 1964, pp. 147–48; *14*:all.

[427] MAY, L. CARLYLE, "A Survey of Glossolalia and Related Phenomena in Non-Christian Religions," *American Anthropologist*, 58, 1956, pp. 75–96; *198*:all.

[428] MC CLELLAND, DAVID, *The Achieving Society*. Princeton, N.J.: Van Nostrand, 1961; *99*:all.

[429] MC CONNELL, R. A., *ESP Curriculum Guide*. New York: Simon & Schuster, 1971; *153*:all.

[430] MC DOUGALL, WILLIAM, "Psychical Research as a University Study," in *The Case For and Against Psychical Belief*, ed. Carl Murchison. Worcester, Mass.: Clark University Press, 1927, pp. 149–62; *293*:all.

[431] MC GERVEY, JOHN, "A Statistical Test of Sun-Sign Astrology," *The Zetetic*, 1 (Spring-Summer 1977), pp. 49–54; *236*:all.

[432] MC GREGOR, DOUGLAS, "The Major Determinants of the Prediction of Social Events," *Journal of Abnormal and Social Psychology*, 33, 1938, pp. 179–204; *49*:all.

[433] MC GUIGAN, FRANK, ed., *Thinking: Studies of Covert Language Processes*. New York: Appleton, 1966; *80*:all.

[434] MC KELLAR, PETER, *Imagination and Thinking*. New York: Basic Books, 1957; *5*:113.

[435] MEDALIA, NAHUM, and OTTO LARSEN, "Diffusion and Belief in a Collective Delusion," *American Sociological Review*, 23, 1958, pp. 180–86; *68*:all.

[436] MEDHURST, R. G. and CHRISTOPHER SCOTT, "A Re-examination of C. E. M. Hansel's Criticism of the Pratt-Woodruff Experiment," *Journal of Parapsychology*, 38, 1974, pp. 163–84; *141*:all.

[437] MEHRABIAN, ALBERT, *Silent Messages*. Belmont, Calif.: Wadsworth, 1971; *30*:all, *35*:all.

[438] MELZACK, RONALD, "How Acupuncture Works," *Psychology Today*, 7 (June 1973), pp. 28–38; *248*:all.

[439] MENZEL, DONALD, "UFOs—The Modern Myth," in *UFOs—A Scientific Debate*, eds. Carl Sagan and Thornton Page. Ithaca, N.Y.: Cornell University Press, 1972, pp. 123–82; *271*:156.

[440] MENZEL, DONALD, and LYLE BOYD, *The World of Flying Saucers*. New York: Doubleday, 1963; *229*:89, *270*:60, *271*:61.

[441] MENZEL, DONALD and ERNEST TAVES, *The UFO Enigma*. New York: Doubleday, 1977; *271*:all, *273*:181–83, *273*:218.

[442] MERTON, ROBERT, "The Self-Fulfilling Prophecy," *The Antioch Review*, 8, 1948, pp. 193–210; *104*:193.

[443] METZNER, RALPH, *The Ecstatic Adventure*. New York: Macmillan, 1968; *125*:all.

[444] MEYER, DONALD, *The Positive Thinkers*. New York: Doubleday, 1965; *73*:all.

[445] MILGRAM, STANLEY, "The Small-World Problem," *Psychology Today*, 1 (May 1967), pp. 60–67; *49*:all.

[446] MILGRAM, STANLEY, "The Experience of Living in Cities," *Science*, 167, 1970, pp. 1461–68; *99*:all.

[447] MILLAR, BRIAN, "Thermistor PK," in *Research in Parapsychology, 1975*, eds. J. D. Morris, W. G. Roll, and R. L. Morris. Metuchen, N.J.: Scarecrow Press, 1976, pp. 71–73; *146*:all.

[448] MILLER, DANIEL, and GUY SWANSON, *The Changing American Parent*. New York: Wiley, 1958; *99*:217–20.

[449] MILLER, GEORGE, "The Magical Number Seven, Plus or Minus Two: Some Limits on Our Capacity for Processing Information," *Psychological Review*, 63, 1956, pp. 81–97; *20*:all.

[450] MILLER, NEAL, "Learning of Visceral & Glandular Responses," *Science*, 163, 1969, pp. 434–45; *75*:all.

[451] MILLER, S. M., "Comparative Social Mobility," *Current Sociology*, 9, 1960, pp. 34–36; *98*:all.

[452] MINNAERT, M., *Light and Colour in the Open Air*. New York: Dover, 1954; *187*:206–7, 224–25, 230–33, 259, 333–34.

[453] MISCHEL, WALTER and FRANCES MISCHEL, "Psychological Aspects of Spirit Possession," *American Anthropologist*, 60, 1958, pp. 249–60; *196*:all.

[454] MONROE, ROBERT, *Journeys Out of the Body*. New York: Doubleday, 1971; *195*:all.

[455] MONTAGU, ASHLEY, *Touching*. New York: Harper, 1971; *51*:all.

[456] MOODY, RAYMOND, *Life After Life*. New York: Bantam, 1976; *121*:all.

[457] MOORE, WILBERT, "Industrialization and Social Change," in *Industrialization and Society*, eds. Berthold Hoselitz and Wilbert Moore. The Hague: Mouton, 1966, pp. 299–370; *98*:all.

[458] MORRIS, ROBERT, "Psi and Animal Behavior," *Journal of the American Society for Psychical Research*, 64, 1970, pp. 242–60; *155*:253.

⁴⁵⁹ MORRIS, ROBERT, "Parapsychology, Biology and ANPSI," in *Handbook of Parapsychology*, ed. Benjamin Wolman. New York: Van Nostrand, 1977, pp. 687–715; *155*:702.

⁴⁶⁰ MORRIS, ROBERT, "Review of *The Amityville Horror*," *The Skeptical Inquirer*, 2 (Spring-Summer 1978), pp. 95–102; *203*:all.

⁴⁶¹ MORRISON, PHILIP, "The Nature of Scientific Evidence: A Summary," in *UFOs—A Scientific Debate*, eds. Carl Sagan and Thornton Page. Ithaca, N.Y.: Cornell University, 1972, pp. 276–90; *270*:281–82, *270*:282.

⁴⁶² MOSES, ROBERT, "Entoptic and Allied Phenomena," in *Adler's Physiology of the Eye*, ed. Robert Moses. St. Louis: Mosby, 1975, pp. 545–57; *12*:549–51.

⁴⁶³ MOSS, C. SCOTT, *Hypnosis in Perspective*. New York: Macmillan, 1965; *7*:all.

⁴⁶⁴ MOSS, THELMA, *The Probability of the Impossible*. New York: New American Library, 1974; *189*:54–58.

⁴⁶⁵ MUHL, ANITA, *Automatic Writing*. Dresden & Leipzig: Theodor Steinkopff, 1930; *85*:all.

⁴⁶⁶ MULDOON, SYLVAN, and HEREWARD CARRINGTON, *The Projection of the Astral Body*. New York: Samuel Weiser, 1970; *195*:all.

⁴⁶⁷ MULHOLLAND, JOHN, *Beware Familiar Spirits*. New York: Scribner's, 1938; *209*:all, *211*:231–32.

⁴⁶⁸ MULLER, HERBERT, *The Children of Frankenstein*. Bloomington: University of Indiana Press, 1970; *95*:4.

⁴⁶⁹ MURPHY, GARDNER, "Lawfulness Versus Caprice: Is There a Law of Psychic Phenomena?" in *Journal of the American Society for Psychical Research*, 58, 1964, pp. 238–49; *148*:239.

⁴⁷⁰ MURPHY, GARDNER, "The Problem of Repeatability in Psychical Research," *Journal of the American Society for Psychical Research*, 65, 1971, pp. 3–16; *147*:all.

⁴⁷¹ MURPHY, GARDNER, and ROBERT BALLOU, eds., *William James on Psychical Research*. New York: Viking, 1960; *293*:all.

⁴⁷² MURPHY, GARDNER (with LAURA DALE), *Challenge of Psychical Research*. New York: Harper, 1961; *293*:all.

⁴⁷³ MURRAY, JANET, "Living Arrangements of People Aged 65 and Older," *Social Science Bulletin*, 34, 1971, pp. 3–14; *100*:all.

⁴⁷⁴ MYERS, FREDERIC, *Human Personality* (vol. 1). New York: Longmans, Green, 1954; *6*:all.

⁴⁷⁵ MYERS, FREDERIC, *Human Personality* (vol. 2). New York: Longmans, Green, 1954; *6*:all, *134*:411–12, *183*:145.

⁴⁷⁶ NARANJO, CLAUDIO, *The One Quest*. New York: Viking, 1972; *288*:124.

⁴⁷⁷ NEHER, ANDREW, "Auditory Driving Observed with Scalp Electrodes in Normal Subjects," *Electroencephalography & Clinical Neurophysiology*, 13, 1961, pp. 449–51; *17*:all.

⁴⁷⁸ NEHER, ANDREW, "A Physiological Explanation of Unusual Behavior In Ceremonies Involving Drums," *Human Biology,* 34, 1962, pp. 151–60; *17*:all.

⁴⁷⁹ NEHER, ANDREW, "Probability Pyramiding, Research Error, and the Need for Independent Replication," *Psychological Record,* 17, 1967, pp. 257–62; *141*:all.

⁴⁸⁰ NELSON, ROBERT, *The Art of Cold Reading.* Calgary, Canada: Hades, 1971; *231*:6, 37.

⁴⁸¹ NEWBOLD, WILLIAM, "Sub-conscious Reasoning," *Proceedings of the Society for Psychical Research,* 12, 1896–97, pp. 11–20; *39*:11–13.

⁴⁸² NOLEN, WILLIAM, *Healing: A Doctor In Search of a Miracle.* New York: Random House, 1974; *170*:139–52, *171*:155–262, *171*:90, *171*:41–101, *256*:32–34.

⁴⁸³ NOYES, RUSSELL, "The Experience of Dying," *Psychiatry,* 35, 1972, pp. 174–84; *121*:all.

⁴⁸⁴ NULL, GARY, and JUDITH WILDENBERG, "Pyramid Structures: Are They Energy Centers?" privately circulated paper, Institute of Applied Biology, New York; *262*:all.

⁴⁸⁵ OESTERREICH, TRAUGOTT, *Possession.* New Hyde Park, N.Y.: University Books, 1966; *113*:188–89.

⁴⁸⁶ OHSAWA, GEORGES, *Zen Macrobiotics.* Los Angeles: Ohsawa Foundation, 1965; *252*:27–28, 59–70.

⁴⁸⁷ OLDS, JAMES, "Pleasure Centers in the Brain," *Scientific American,* 195 (October 1956), pp. 105–16; *6*:all, *290*:all.

⁴⁸⁸ ORNSTEIN, ROBERT, "The Techniques of Meditation and Their Implications for Modern Psychology," in *On the Psychology of Meditation,* Claudio Naranjo and Robert Ornstein. New York: Viking, 1972, pp.137–234; *16*:178, *26*:193.

⁴⁸⁹ OSIS, KARLIS, *Deathbed Observations by Physicians and Nurses.* New York: Parapsychology Foundation, 1961; *121*:all, *121*:73.

⁴⁹⁰ OSIS, KARLIS, "Out-of-Body Research at the ASPR," *ASPR Newsletter,* 22 (Summer 1974), p. 1; *195*:all.

⁴⁹¹ OSIS, KARLIS, and ERLENDUR HARALDSSON, "Deathbed Observations by Physicians and Nurses: A Cross-Cultural Survey," *Journal of the American Society for Psychical Research,* 71, 1977, pp. 237–59; *121*:all.

⁴⁹² OSTER, GERALD, "Phosphenes," *Scientific American,* 222 (February 1970), pp. 83–87; *13*:all.

⁴⁹³ OSTRANDER, SHEILA, and LYN SCHROEDER, *Psychic Discoveries Behind the Iron Curtain.* New York: Bantam, 1971; *149*:all, *189*:216, *262*:367–69.

⁴⁹⁴ OUSPENSKY, PETER, *New Model of the Universe.* London: Kegan Paul, 1938; *97*:2–3.

⁴⁹⁵ OUSPENSKY, PETER, *In Search of the Miraculous.* New York: Harcourt, 1949; *284*:83–85.

⁴⁹⁶ PACKARD, VANCE, *A Nation of Strangers*. New York: Simon & Schuster/Pocket Books, 1974; *98*:7–8.

⁴⁹⁷ PALMER, JOHN, "Scoring in ESP Tests as a Function of Belief in ESP," *Journal of the American Society for Psychical Research*, 65, 1971, pp. 373–408; *145*:all.

⁴⁹⁸ PALMER, JOHN, "ESP and Out-of-Body Experiences: An Experimental Approach," in *Mind Beyond the Body*, ed. D. Scott Rogo. New York: Penguin, 1978, pp. 193–217; *193*:206, *194*:214, *195*:198.

⁴⁹⁹ PALMORE, ERDMAN, and FRANK WHITTINGTON, "Trends in the Relative Status of the Aged," *Social Forces*, 50, 1951, pp. 84–91; *100*:all.

⁵⁰⁰ PAMPLIN, BRIAN, and HARRY COLLINS, "Spoon Bending: An Experimental Approach," *Nature*, 257, 1975, p. 8; *226*:all.

⁵⁰¹ PAYNE, BURYL, *Getting There Without Drugs*. New York: Viking, 1973; *122*:xi.

⁵⁰² PEHEK, JOHN, HARRY KYLER, and DAVID FAUST, "Image Modulation in Corona Discharge Photography," *Science*, 194, 1976, pp. 263–70; *189*:all.

⁵⁰³ PELLETIER, KENNETH, *Mind as Healer, Mind as Slayer*. New York: Delacorte, 1977; *53*:39–81, *100*:82–114.

⁵⁰⁴ PELLETIER, KENNETH, and ERIK PEPER, "The *Chutzpah* Factor in the Psychophysiology of Altered States of Consciousness," *Journal of Humanistic Psychology*, 17 (Winter 1977), pp. 63–73; *174*:all.

⁵⁰⁵ Personal communication, *129*:all.

⁵⁰⁶ PERVIN, LAWRENCE, "The Need to Predict and Control Under Conditions of Threat," *Journal of Personality*, 31, 1963, pp. 570–87; *101*:all.

⁵⁰⁷ PETER, LAURENCE, *Peter's Quotations*. New York: William Morrow, 1977; *267*:69.

⁵⁰⁸ PETERSEN, WILLIAM, *Those Curious New Cults*. New Canaan, Conn.: Keats, 1973; *163*:120.

⁵⁰⁹ PFUNGST, OSKAR, *Clever Hans*, ed. Robert Rosenthal. New York: Holt, 1965; *33*:106–7, *82*:18–22, *82*:253, *83*:47, *83*:xii, *83*:177–80.

⁵¹⁰ PHILLIPS, R. C., "Experiments on the Efficacy of Charms," *Journal of the Society for Psychical Research*, 6, 1893, pp. 152–54; *245*:152–53.

⁵¹¹ PIERRAKOS, JOHN, "The Energy Field," in *The Human Aura*, ed. Nicholas Regush. New York: Berkley Medallion, 1974, pp. 55–62; *188*:56, *188*:56.

⁵¹² PIKE, JAMES (with DIANE KENNEDY), *The Other Side*. New York: Doubleday, 1968; *219*:335–36.

⁵¹³ PLACER, JOHN, and others, "Stable System Psychokinesis Studies Using Temperature Differential Between Thermistors," in *Research in Parapsychology, 1975*, eds. J. D. Morris, W. G. Roll, and R. L. Morris. Metuchen, N.J.: Scarecrow Press, 1976, pp. 69–71; *146*:all.

⁵¹⁴ PLOG, STANLEY, "Urbanization, Psychological Disorders and the Heritage of Social Psychiatry," in *Changing Perspectives in Mental Illness*, eds., Stanley Plog and Robert Edgerton. New York: Holt, 1969, pp. 288–312; *100*:301, 304.

515 PODMORE, FRANK, *The Newer Spiritualism*. London: Unwin, 1910; *215*:45–46.

516 PORAC, CLARE, and STANLEY COREN, "The Dominant Eye," *Psychological Bulletin*, 83, 1976, pp. 880–97; *61*:all.

517 POYNTON, J. C., "Results of an Out-of-the-Body Survey," in *Parapsychology in South Africa*, ed. J. C. Poynton. Johannesburg: South African Society for Psychical Research, 1975, pp. 109–23; *191*:119, *192*:111.

518 PRATT, J. G., *Parapsychology: An Insider's View of ESP*. New York: Dutton, 1966; *153*:209, *153*:209.

519 PRATT, J. G., and J. L. WOODRUFF, "Size of Stimulus Symbols in Extrasensory Perception," *Journal of Parapsychology*, 3, 1939, pp. 121–58; *140*:all.

520 PRESMAN, ALEKSANDR, *Electromagnetic Fields and Life*, ed. Frank Brown. New York: Plenum, 1974; *154*:206–15.

521 PRICE, HARRY, and ERIC DINGWALL, *Revelations of a Spirit Medium*. New York: Dutton, 1922; *212*:all.

522 PRINCE, MORTON, *The Dissociation of a Personality*. New York: Meridian Books, 1957; *87*:all.

523 PRINCE, RAYMOND, and CHARLES SAVAGE, "Mystical States and the Concept of Regression," *Psychedelic Review*, 8, 1966, pp. 59–75; *113*:all.

524 PRITCHARD, ROY, "Stabilized Images on the Retina," *Scientific American*, 204 (June 1961), pp. 72–78; *15*:all.

525 "The Psychic Scandal," *Time*, August 26, 1974, pp. 74–75; *144*:all.

526 PURCELL, EDWARD, "Research in Nuclear Magnetism," *Science*, 118, 1953, pp. 431–36; *111*:431.

527 PURDY, D. M., "Eidetic Imagery and Plasticity of Perception," *Journal of General Psychology*, 15, 1936, pp. 437–54; *40*:444–46.

528 PUTHOFF, HAROLD, and RUSSELL TARG, "A Perceptual Channel for Information Transfer Over Kilometer Distances: Historical Perspective and Recent Research," *Proceedings of the IEEE*, 64, 1976, pp. 329–54; *295*:all.

529 RAMAGE, EDWIN, ed., *Atlantis: Fact or Fiction?* Bloomington: University of Indiana Press, 1978; *258*:all.

530 RANDI, JAMES, *The Magic of Uri Geller*. New York: Random House/ Ballantine, 1975; *223*:262, *223*:210–15, *223*:166–71, *225*:259–60, *225*:253–55, *225*:191–96.

531 RANDI, JAMES, "Geller a Fake, Says Ex-manager," *New Scientist*, 78, 1978, p. 11; *223*:all.

532 RAO, K. RAMAKRISHNA, "Review of 'Five Years Report of Seth Sohan Lal Memorial Institute of Parapsychology,' " *Journal of Parapsychology*, 28, 1964, pp. 59–62; *144*:all.

533 RAPAPORT, DAVID, *Organization & Pathology of Thought*. New York: Columbia University Press, 1951; *44*:249–87.

534 RASMUSSEN, KNUD, *The Intellectual Culture of the Iglulik Eskimos*. Copenhagen: Gyldendalske Boghandel Nordisk Forlag, 1929; *107*:118–19.

⁵³⁵ RATNOFF, OSCAR, "Stigmata: Where Mind and Body Meet," *Medical Times,* 97, 1969, pp. 150–63; *77*:all.

⁵³⁶ RAUDIVE, KONSTANTIN, *Breakthrough: An Amazing Experiment in Electronic Communication with the Dead.* New York: Taplinger, 1971; *206*:all.

⁵³⁷ RAUSCHER, E. A., and others, "Remote Perception of Natural Scenes, Shielded Against Ordinary Perception," in *Research in Parapsychology, 1975,* eds. J. D. Morris, W G. Roll, and R. L. Morris. Metuchen, N.J.: Scarecrow Press, 1976, pp. 41–45; *147*:all.

⁵³⁸ RAUSCHER, WILLIAM (with ALLEN SPRAGGETT), *The Spiritual Frontier.* New York: Doubleday, 1975; *219*:179–85.

⁵³⁹ RAWCLIFFE, D. H., *Occult and Supernatural Phenomena.* New York: Dover, 1959; *80*:379–425, *84*:144, *177*:291–96, *186*:107–8, *199*:261–71, *210*:306.

⁵⁴⁰ "Recent Experiments in Crystal Vision," *Proceedings of the Society for Psychical Research,* 5, 1889, pp. 486–521; *230*:507.

⁵⁴¹ RECHTSHAFFEN, ALLAN, and SARNOFF MEDNICK, "The Autokinetic Word Technique," *Journal of Abnormal and Social Psychology,* 51, 1955, p. 346; *46*:all.

⁵⁴² REICH, WILHELM, *Character Analysis.* Vienna: published by author, 1933; *254*:all.

⁵⁴³ REICH, WILHELM, *An Introduction to Orgonomy.* New York: Farrar, 1960; *252*:all.

⁵⁴⁴ *The Report of the Seybert Commission on Spiritualism.* Philadelphia: Lippincott, 1920; *215*:all.

⁵⁴⁵ REPS, PAUL, *Zen Flesh, Zen Bones.* New York: Doubleday/Anchor, 1961; *29*:207.

⁵⁴⁶ REYNOLDS, CHARLES, and JOEL YALE, "Uri Geller's Mental Photos-Real or Fake?" *Popular Photography,* 74 (June 1974), pp. 73–77, 135–38, 174; *225*:all.

⁵⁴⁷ RHINE, J. B., *New Frontiers of the Mind.* New York: Farrar, 1937; *228*:230.

⁵⁴⁸ RHINE, J. B., *Extrasensory Perception.* Boston: Bruce Humphries, 1964; *145*:all.

⁵⁴⁹ RHINE, J. B., *New World of the Mind.* New York: Sloane, 1968; *154*:185, *294*:217–39.

⁵⁵⁰ RHINE, J. B., "Security vs. Deception in Parapsychology," *Journal of Parapsychology,* 38, 1974, pp. 99–121; *144*:all.

⁵⁵¹ RHINE, J. B., "Telepathy and Other Untestable Hypotheses," *Journal of Parapsychology,* 38, 1974, pp. 137–53; *138*:145.

⁵⁵² RHINE, J. B., "A New Case of Experimenter Unreliability," *Journal of Parapsychology,* 38, 1974, pp. 215–25; *144*:217.

⁵⁵³ RHINE, J. B., "Publication Policy Regarding Nonsignificant Results," *Journal of Parapsychology,* 39, 1975, pp. 135–42; *142*:all.

⁵⁵⁴ RHINE, J. B., and J. G. PRATT, *Parapsychology: Frontier Science of the Mind*. Springfield, Ill.: Thomas, 1957; *141*:47.

⁵⁵⁵ RHINE, J. B., and LOUISA RHINE, "An Investigation of a 'Mind-Reading' Horse," *Journal of Abnormal and Social Psychology*, 23, 1929, pp. 449–66; *154*:all.

⁵⁵⁶ RHINE, LOUISA, *Hidden Channels of the Mind*. New York: Sloane, 1961; *133*:184, *134*:20–21, *135*:163, *156*:103, *157*:153, *168*:207–8, *203*: 263.

⁵⁵⁷ RHINE, LOUISA, *ESP in Life and Lab*. New York: Macmillan/Collier, 1969; *135*:95–96.

⁵⁵⁸ RHINE, LOUISA, *Manual for Introductory Experiments in Parapsychology*. Durham, N.C.: Institute for Parapsychology; *153*:all.

⁵⁵⁹ RICHARDSON, ALAN, *Mental Imagery*. New York: Springer, 1969; *11*:121, *12*:122, *14*:13–28, *40*:45–53, *41*:21–24.

⁵⁶⁰ RICHET, CHARLES, *Thirty Years of Psychical Research*, trans. Stanley De Brath. New York: Macmillan, 1923; *293*:all.

⁵⁶¹ RINN, JOSEPH, *Sixty Years of Psychical Research*. New York: Truth Seeker, 1950; *4*:402, *33*:22, 24, *132*:244, *174*:125–27, 151–55, *209*:200–205, 297–305, 343–52, *211*:all, *212*:32, *212*:47, *212*:16, 28–29, 72, 88–92, *214*:62–63, *214*:141–42, 244, *215*:404, *216*:278–82, *216*:566–76, *218*:161–63, *218*:197, *219*:547–49.

⁵⁶² ROBERTS, HENRY, *The Complete Prophecies of Nostradamus*. Great Neck, N.Y.: Nostradamus, 1969; *157*:16, *158*:18, *158*:16, 18, *158*:12, *158*:17, *158*:18.

⁵⁶³ ROBERTS, KENNETH, *Henry Gross and His Dowsing Rod*. New York: Doubleday, 1951; *182*:all.

⁵⁶⁴ ROBERTS, URSULA, "Types of Auras," in *The Human Aura*, ed. Nicholas Regush. New York: Berkley Medallion, 1974, pp. 75–79; *188*:77, *189*:77.

⁵⁶⁵ ROGERS, CARL, "Some New Challenges," *American Psychologist*, 28, 1973, pp. 379–87; *293*:385–86.

⁵⁶⁶ ROGO, D. SCOTT, "Fakers and Fakirs," *Psychic*, 5 (November-December 1973), pp. 50–53; *175*:51–52.

⁵⁶⁷ ROGO, D. SCOTT, "A Critical Examination of the 'Geller Effect,'" *Psychoenergetic Systems*, 2, 1977, pp. 39–43, *226*:all.

⁵⁶⁸ ROGO, D. SCOTT, "Amityville Horror or Hoax?" *Human Behavior*, 7 (June 1978), p. 55; *203*:all.

⁵⁶⁹ ROGO, D. SCOTT, *Mind Beyond the Body*. New York: Penguin, 1978; *195*:all.

⁵⁷⁰ ROGO, D. SCOTT, and RAYMOND BAYLESS, "Psychic Surgery," *Journal of the Society for Psychical Research*, 44, 1968, pp. 426–28; *171*:all.

⁵⁷¹ ROSE, LOUIS, "Some Aspects of Paranormal Healing," *Journal of the Society for Psychical Research*, 38, 1955, pp. 105–21; *170*:115–16, *170*:112, *172*:all.

⁵⁷² ROSENTHAL, ROBERT, *Experimenter Effects in Behavioral Research.* New York: Appleton, 1966; *140*:369.

⁵⁷³ ROSETT, JOSHUA, *The Mechanism of Thought, Imagery, and Hallucination.* New York: Columbia University, 1939; *66*:214.

⁵⁷⁴ ROTTER, JULIAN, "Generalized Expectancies for Internal versus External Control of Reinforcement," *Psychological Monographs,* 80, 1966, #609; *90*:all.

⁵⁷⁵ RUDIN, S. A., "What Price Glory? Psychosomatic Death Rates and Motivation in 17 Countries," *Acta Psychologia,* 23, 1964, p. 107; *99*:all.

⁵⁷⁶ RUDIN, S. A., "National Motives Predict Psychogenic Death Rates 25 Years Later," *Science,* 160, 1968, pp. 901–3; *99*:all.

⁵⁷⁷ RUGG, HAROLD, *Imagination.* New York: Harper, 1963; *37*:all.

⁵⁷⁸ RUSSELL, BERTRAND, *Omni,* 1 (June 1979), p. 39; *93*:all.

⁵⁷⁹ RUSSELL, JOHN, *Max Ernst: Life and Work.* New York: Abrams, 1967; *11*:14.

⁵⁸⁰ RUTHERFORD, ADAM, *Pyramidology* (Book 1). Harpenden, Hertfordshire: The Institute of Pyramidology, 1968; *261*:193–219.

⁵⁸¹ RYCROFT, CHARLES, *Wilhelm Reich.* New York: Viking, 1972; *253*:99.

⁵⁸² SAGAN, CARL, and THORNTON PAGE, eds., *UFOs—A Scientific Debate.* Ithaca, N.Y.: Cornell University Press, 1972; *274*:all.

⁵⁸³ SAMARIN, WILLIAM, *Tongues of Men and Angels.* New York: Macmillan, 1972; *199*:227.

⁵⁸⁴ SAMARIN, WILLIAM, "Glossolalia as Regressive Speech," *Language and Speech,* 16, 1973, pp. 77–89; *199*:78.

⁵⁸⁵ SAMUELS, MIKE, and NANCY SAMUELS, *Seeing With the Mind's Eye.* New York: Random House, 1975; *19*:5, *40*:59.

⁵⁸⁶ SANTORA, PHIL, "Life and Death in Africa," *New York Sunday News,* May 28, 1972, pictorial section, pp. 21–25; *2*:21–22, *2*:22.

⁵⁸⁷ SARBIN, THEODORE, and WILLIAM COE, *Hypnosis.* New York: Holt, 1972; *62*:140–72.

⁵⁸⁸ SARGANT, WILLIAM, "The Physiology of Faith," *British Journal of Psychiatry,* 115, 1969, pp. 505–18; *196*:505.

⁵⁸⁹ SARGANT, WILLIAM, *The Mind Possessed.* Baltimore: Penguin, 1975; *197*:176, *207*:36, *255*:5.

⁵⁹⁰ SAXON, KURT, *Keeping Score on Our Modern Prophets.* Eureka, Calif.: Atlan Formularies, 1974; *162*:18–19, *163*:18–47.

⁵⁹¹ SCHACTER, DANIEL, "The Hypnagogic State," *Psychological Bulletin,* 83, 1976, pp. 452–81; *42*:all.

⁵⁹² SCHARFSTEIN, BEN-AMI, *Mystical Experience.* Baltimore: Penguin, 1974; *112*:4–25, 99–121, *112*:108, *291*:166.

⁵⁹³ SCHEIDT, FREDERICK, "Deviance, Power and the Occult: A Field Study," *Journal of Psychology,* 87, 1974, pp. 21–28; *101*:all.

[594] SCHEIDT, RICK, "Belief in Supernatural Phenomena and Locus of Control," *Psychological Reports*, 32, 1973, pp. 1159–62; *90*:all.

[595] SCHMEIDLER, GERTRUDE, "Personal Values and ESP Scores," *Journal of Abnormal and Social Psychology*, 47, 1952, pp. 757–61; *145*:all.

[596] SCHMEIDLER, GERTRUDE, "PK Effects Upon Continuously Recorded Temperature," *Journal of the American Society for Psychical Research*, 67, 1973, pp. 325–40; *146*:all.

[597] SCHMEIDLER, GERTRUDE, JOHN GAMBALE, and JANET MITCHELL, "PK Effects on Temperature Recordings: An Attempted Replication and Extension," in *Research in Parapsychology, 1975*, eds. J. D. Morris, W. G. Roll, and R. L. Morris. Metuchen, N.J.: Scarecrow Press, 1976, pp. 67–69; *146*:all.

[598] SCHMIDT, HELMUT, "Quantum Processes Predicted?", *New Scientist*, 44, 1969, pp. 114–15; *146*:all.

[599] SCHMIDT, HELMUT, "A PK Test with Electronic Equipment," *Journal of Parapsychology*, 34, 1970, pp. 175–81; *146*:all.

[600] SCHREIBER, FLORA, *Sybil*. New York: Warner Paperback, 1973; *88*:all.

[601] SCHWEBS, URSULA, "Do Plants Have Feelings?" *Harpers* (June 1973), pp. 75–76; *155*:all.

[602] SCOTT, BYRON, *How the Body Feels*. New York: Ballantine, 1973; *51*:all.

[603] SEABROOK, WILLIAM, *Doctor Wood*. New York: Harcourt, 1941; *65*:234–39.

[604] SEGAL, SYDNEY, "Assimilation of a Stimulus in the Construction of an Image," in *The Function and Nature of Imagery*, ed. Peter Sheehan. New York: Academic Press, 1972, pp. 203–30; *90*:all.

[605] SELIGMAN, C. G., "Ritual and Medicine," in *Inquiry Into the Unknown*, ed. Theodore Besterman. London: Methuen, 1934, pp. 48–62; *174*:57.

[606] SELYE, HANS, *The Stress of Life*. New York: McGraw-Hill, 1956; *9*:261, *54*:all.

[607] SHADOWITZ, ALBERT, and PETER WALSH, *The Dark Side of Knowledge*. Reading, Mass.: Addison-Wesley, 1976; *163*:117, *163*:117, *269*:201–02.

[608] SHAH, IDRIES, *The Sufis*. New York: Doubleday, 1964; *7*:58.

[609] SHAH, IDRIES, *Reflections: Fables in the Sufi Tradition*. Baltimore: Penguin, 1968; *222*:60.

[610] SHAH, IDRIES, *The Way of the Sufi*. New York: Dutton, 1969; *230*:74.

[611] SHAH, IDRIES, *The Pleasantries of the Incredible Mulla Nasrudin*. New York: Dutton, 1971; *283*:77–78.

[612] SHAH, IDRIES, *The Subtleties of the Inimitable Mulla Nasrudin*. New York: Dutton, 1973; *67*:171.

[613] SHAPIRO, ARTHUR, "Psychological Aspects of Medication", in *The Psychological Basis of Medical Practice*, eds. Harold Lief, Victor Lief, and Nina Lief. New York: Harper, 1963, pp. 163–78; *72*:167–68.

[614] SHAPIRO, JR., DEANE and STEVEN ZIFFERBLATT, "Zen Meditation and Behavioral Self-Control," *American Psychologist*, 31, 1976, pp. 519–32; *59*:all.

⁶¹⁵ SHEAFFER, ROBERT, "Do Fairies Exist?" *The Zetetic*, 2 (Fall-Winter 1977), pp. 45–52; *269*:all.

⁶¹⁶ SHEILS, DEAN, "A Cross-cultural Study of Beliefs in Out-of-the-Body Experiences, Waking and Sleeping," *Journal of the Society for Psychical Research*, 49, 1978, pp. 697–741; *191*:all.

⁶¹⁷ SHEPARD, JON, *Automation and Alienation: A Study of Office and Factory Workers*. Cambridge, Mass.: MIT Press, 1971; *100*:all.

⁶¹⁸ SHEPARD, ROGER, "Externalization of Mental Images and the Act of Creation," in *Visual Learning, Thinking, and Communication*, eds. B. S. Randhawa and W. E. Coffman. New York: Academic Press, 1978; *39*:all.

⁶¹⁹ SHERIF, MUZAFER, "A Study of Some Social Factors in Perception," *Archives of Psychology*, 27, 1935, #187; *68*:all.

⁶²⁰ SHERMAN, HAROLD, "Foreword," in *Psychic Surgery* by Tom Valentine. New York: Simon & Schuster/Pocket Books, 1975; *171*:all.

⁶²¹ SHWEDER, RICHARD, "Likeness and Likelihood in Everyday Thought," *Current Anthropology*, 18, 1977, pp. 637–58; *47*:all.

⁶²² SILVERMAN, JULIAN, "On the Sensory Bases of Transcendental States of Consciousness," in *Psychiatry and Mysticism*, ed. Stanley Dean. Chicago: Nelson Hall, 1975, pp. 365–98; *31*:all.

⁶²³ SIMMONS, DALE, "Experiments on the Alleged Sharpening of Razor Blades and the Preservation of Flowers by Pyramids," *New Horizons*, 1 (Summer 1973), pp. 95–101; *262*:95.

⁶²⁴ SINGER, STANLEY, *The Nature of Ball Lightning*. New York: Plenum, 1971; *269*:18–22.

⁶²⁵ SIZEMORE, CHRIS, and ELEN PITTILLO, *I'm Eve*. New York: Doubleday, 1977; *87*:all.

⁶²⁶ SLADEK, JOHN, *The New Apocrypha*. New York: Stein & Day, 1973; *186*:324, *215*:193, *268*:43–47.

⁶²⁷ SLOCUM, JOSHUA, *Sailing Alone Around the World*. New York: Sheridan House, 1954; *22*:39–42.

⁶²⁸ SMITH, E. LESTER, "The Raudive Voices—Objective or Subjective?" *Journal of the American Society for Psychical Research*, 68, 1974, pp. 91–100; *206*:all.

⁶²⁹ SMITH, M. JUSTA, "The Influence on Enzyme Growth by the 'Laying-on-of-hands,'" *The Dimensions of Healing*. Los Altos, Calif.: The Academy of Parapsychology and Medicine, 1972, pp. 110–20; *169*:all, *293*:all.

⁶³⁰ SMITH, RALPH, *At Your Own Risk*. New York: Simon & Schuster/Pocket Books, 1969; *246*:22–24, *246*:148–49, *247*:144–45, *247*:148–49, *247*:150, *248*:101–22.

⁶³¹ SMITH, THEODATE, "Paramnesia in Daily Life," *American Journal of Psychology*, 24, 1913, pp. 52–65; *30*:all.

⁶³² SMITHERS, A. G., and H. J. COOPER, "Personality and Season of Birth," *Journal of Social Psychology*, 105, 1978, pp. 237–41; *236*:all.

[633] SMYTH, CHARLES P., *Our Inheritance in the Great Pyramid*. London: William Isbister, 1880; *259*:all, *261*:546–48, 572, 586.

[634] SNYDER, C. R., and RANDEE SHENKEL, "The P. T. Barnum Effect," *Psychology Today*, 8 (March 1975), pp. 53–54; *231*:all.

[635] SNYDER, SOLOMON, "Opiate Receptors and Internal Opiates," *Scientific American*, 236 (March 1977), pp. 44–56; *128*:all.

[636] SOAL, S. G., "A Case of Pseudo-ESP," in *Ciba Foundation Symposium on Extrasensory Perception*, eds. G. E. W. Westenholme and Elaine Millar. Boston: Little Brown, 1956, pp. 131–40; *33*:all.

[637] SOAL, S. G., and K. M. GOLDNEY, "Experiments in Precognitive Telepathy," *Proceedings of the Society for Psychical Research*, 47, 1943, pp. 21–150; *144*:all.

[638] SOLFVIN, GERALD, WILLIAM ROLL, and JOAN KRIEGER, "Meditation and ESP: Remote Viewing," in *Research in Parapsychology, 1977*, ed. William Roll. Metuchen, N.J.: Scarecrow Press, 1978, pp. 151–57; *147*:all.

[639] SPARKS, LAURENCE, *Self-hypnosis*. New York: Grune & Stratton, 1962; *66*:all.

[640] SPELT, DAVID, "The Conditioning of the Human Fetus *in Utero*," *Journal of Experimental Psychology*, 38, 1948, pp. 338–46; *255*:all.

[641] SPERRY, ROGER, "Cerebral Organization and Behavior," *Science*, 133, 1961, pp. 1749–57; *6*:all.

[642] SPRAGGETT, ALLEN (with WILLIAM RAUSCHER), *Arthur Ford: The Man Who Talked with the Dead*. New York: New American Library/Signet, 1974; *218*:cover, *219*:142–65; *219*:246, 249, 261.

[643] STACEY, B. G., "Psychological Consequences of Intergeneration Mobility: An Overview," *Acta Psychologia*, 31, 1969, pp. 261–76; *98*:all.

[644] STAHL, SIDNEY, and MORTZ LEBEDUN, "Mystery Gas: An Analysis of Mass Hysteria," *Journal of Health & Social Behavior*, 15, 1974, pp. 44–50; *71*:all.

[645] STEARN, JESS, *Edgar Cayce—The Sleeping Prophet*. New York: Bantam, 1968; *159*:intro., 81, *159*:35, *160*:14, *160*:86.

[646] STEIN, MORRIS, *Stimulating Creativity* (vol. 1). New York: Academic Press, 1974; *36*:6.

[647] STEINBECK, JOHN, *East of Eden*. New York: Bantam, 1967; *179*:148.

[648] STEMMAN, ROY, *Spirits and Spirit Worlds*. Danbury, Conn.: Danbury Press, 1975; *206*:94–95.

[649] STENGEL, ERWIN, *Suicide and Attempted Suicide*. Baltimore: Penguin, 1969; *100*:22–23.

[650] STEPHENS, WILLIAM, *The Family in Cross-Cultural Perspective*. New York: Holt, 1963; *99*:357–60.

[651] STEVENS, JOHN, "Hypnosis, Intention, and Wake-fullness," in *Gestalt Is*, ed. John Stevens. New York: Bantam, 1977, pp. 258–69; *61*:258.

References

652 STEVENSON, IAN, and others, "ESP—A Scientific Evaluation," letter to the editor, *British Journal of Psychiatry*, 115, 1969, pp. 743–45; *150*:745.

653 STEWART, KILTON, "Dream Theory in Malaysia," in *Altered States of Consciousness*, ed. Charles Tart. New York: Doubleday/Anchor, pp. 161–70; *44*:all.

654 STOKES, DOUGLAS, "Review: Mind-Reach," *Journal of the Society for Psychical Research*, 71, 1977, pp. 437–42; *226*:all.

655 STONE, RANDOLPH, *A Course in Manipulative Therapy*. Chicago: published by author, 1953; *250*:58, *251*:61, *251*:10–15.

656 STONE, RANDOLPH, *Energy: The Vital Polarity in the Healing Arts*. Chicago: published by author, 1957; *250*:64.

657 STONE, RANDOLPH, *Vitality Balance*. Chicago: published by author, 1957; *250*:99.

658 STONE, W. CLEMENT, and NORMA BROWNING, *The Other Side of the Mind*, Englewood Cliffs, N.J.: Prentice-Hall, 1964; *5*:103–4; *145*:83–84, *149*:19, *205*:114–16, *211*:114–16, *211*:83–84, *221*:85, *222*:118, *223*:118.

659 STORY, RONALD, *The Space-Gods Revealed*. New York: Harper, 1976; *265*:all.

660 STRAUCH, INGE, "Medical Aspects of 'Mental' Healing," *International Journal of Parapsychology*, 5, 1963, pp. 135–65; *170*:149.

661 STRUTT, ROBERT, *John William Strutt, Third Baron Rayleigh*. London: Edward Arnold, 1924; *294*:379–91.

662 SULZER, JEFFERSON, "Chiropractic Healing as Psychotherapy," *Psychotherapy: Theory, Research, and Practice*, 2 (Winter 1965), pp. 38–41; *247*:all.

663 SUNDBERG, NORMAN, "The Acceptability of 'Fake' versus 'Bonafide' Personality Test Interpretations," *Journal of Abnormal and Social Psychology*, 50, 1955, pp. 145–47; *233*:all.

664 SUPA, MICHAEL, MILTON COTZIN, and KARL DALLENBACH, "Facial Vision: The Perception of Obstacles by the Blind," *American Journal of Psychology*, 57, 1944, pp. 133–83; *31*:all.

665 SZASZ, KATHLEEN, *Petishism*. New York: Holt, 1968; *99*:all.

666 TARBELL, HARLAN, *The Tarbell Course in Magic* (vol. 6). New York: Tannen, 1954; *220*:251–61.

667 TARG, RUSSELL, and HAROLD PUTHOFF, *Mind-Reach*. New York: Delacorte, 1977; *147*:1–119, *226*:135–65.

668 TARG, RUSSELL, HAROLD PUTHOFF, and EDWIN MAY, "State of the Art in Remote Viewing Studies at SRI," *Proceedings of the International Conference on Cybernetics and Society*, 1977, pp. 519–29; *147*:all.

669 TART, CHARLES, "Concerning the Scientific Study of the Human Aura," *Journal of the Society for Psychical Research*, 46, 1972, pp. 1–21; *187*:all.

670 TART, CHARLES, "Introduction to Section 2: Between Waking and Sleeping," in *Altered States of Consciousness*, ed. Charles Tart. New York: Doubleday/Anchor, 1972, pp. 75–76; *43*:75.

[671] TART, CHARLES, *Psi*. New York: Dutton, 1977; *147*:173–76.

[672] TART, CHARLES, and JEFFREY SMITH, "Two Token Object Studies with Peter Hurkos," *Journal of the American Society for Psychical Research*, 62, 1968, pp. 143–57; *221*:all.

[673] TAYLOR, JOHN, *The Great Pyramid. Why Was It Built? And Who Built It?* London: Longman, Green, 1859; *259*:all.

[674] TAYLOR, JOHN, *The Shape of Minds to Come*. Baltimore: Penguin, 1971; *54*:66.

[675] TENHAEFF, W. H. C., "Some Aspects of Parapsychological Research in the Netherlands," *International Journal of Neuropsychiatry*, 2, 1966, pp. 408–19; *221*:all.

[676] TEXTOR, ROBERT, *A Cross-Cultural Summary*. New Haven, Conn.: HRAF Press, 1967; *98*:all.

[677] THERA, NYANAPONIKA, *The Heart of Buddhist Meditation*. London: Rider, 1969; *26*:32, 33, 35.

[678] THIGPEN, CORBETT, and HERVEY CLECKLEY, *The Three Faces of Eve*. New York: McGraw-Hill, 1957; *87*:all.

[679] THOMPSON, RICHARD, "The Search for the Engram," *American Psychologist*, 31, 1976, pp. 209–27; *9*:all.

[680] THOMSON, JOSEPH JOHN, *Recollections and Reflections*. New York: Macmillan, 1937; *294*:147–63.

[681] THOULESS, ROBERT, "Experiments on Psi Self-Training with Dr. Schmidt's Pre-cognitive Apparatus," *Journal of the Society for Psychical Research*, 46, 1971, pp. 15–21; *146*:all.

[682] TIGHE, THOMAS, and ROBERT LEATON, *Habituation*. New York: Wiley, 1976; *15*:all.

[683] TILLER, WILLIAM, "Are Psychoenergetic Pictures Possible?" *New Scientist*, 62, 1974, pp. 160–63; *189*:all.

[684] TOCH, HANS, *The Social Psychology of Social Movements*. Indianapolis, Ind.: Bobbs-Merrill, 1965; *101*:43.

[685] TOFFLER, ALVIN, *Future Shock*. New York: Random House, 1970; *98*:all.

[686] TOMPKINS, PETER, and CHRISTOPHER BIRD, *The Secret Life of Plants*. New York: Avon, 1973; *155*:all.

[687] TORRANCE, E. PAUL, "What is Honored in a Country will be Cultivated There," *Gifted Children Quarterly*, 10, 1968, pp. 16–21; *103*:all.

[688] TOTH, MAX, and GREG NIELSEN, *Pyramid Power*. New York: Warner Destiny, 1976; *262*:all.

[689] *Treasury of Familiar Quotations*. New York: Avenel/Crown, 1963; *4*:80, *23*:163, *49*:131, *59*:119, *153*:29.

[690] TRIPLETT, NORMAN, "The Psychology of Conjuring Deceptions," *American Journal of Psychology*, 11, 1900, pp. 439–510; *61*:all.

[691] TRUBO, RICHARD, "Psychics and the Police," *Psychic*, 6 (June 1975), pp. 8–12; *221*:all.

⁶⁹² TRUZZI, MARCELLO, "The Occult Revival as Popular Culture," *The Sociological Quarterly*, 13, 1972, pp. 16–36; *96*:all.

⁶⁹³ TRUZZI, MARCELLO, "A Postscript," *Explorations*, 2 (November 1973), p. 11; *223*:all.

⁶⁹⁴ TYRELL, G. H. M., *Apparitions*. New York: Macmillan/Collier, 1963; *201*:109, *202*:59–60.

⁶⁹⁵ ULLMAN, MONTAGUE, and STANLEY KRIPPNER, *Dream Telepathy*. Baltimore: Penguin, 1973; *145*:all.

⁶⁹⁶ ULRICH, ROGER, THOMAS STACHNIK, and N. RANSDELL STAINTON, "Student Acceptance of Generalized Personality Interpretation," *Psychological Reports*, 13, 1963, pp. 831–34; *232*:832, *232*:833.

⁶⁹⁷ UNDERHILL, EVELYN, *Mysticism*. New York: World/Meridian, 1972; *39*:272, *111*:301–2, *113*:392, *113*:292, *115*:223–26, *124*:258–60, *127*:66, 293–97, *128*:363, *129*:174, *290*:380–412.

⁶⁹⁸ U. S. Bureau of Statistics, *Statistical Abstract*, Washington, D.C., U.S. Gov't. Print. Off., 1910; *99*:78.

⁶⁹⁹ U. S. Bureau of the Census, *1970 Census of Population, Characteristics of the Population, United States Summary*, Washington, D.C., U. S. Gov't. Print. Off., 1973, 1; *99*:42, 62.

⁷⁰⁰ U. S. Bureau of the Census, *1970 Census of Population, Subject Reports, State of Birth*, Washington, D.C., U. S. Gov't. Print. Off., 1973; *98*:1.

⁷⁰¹ U. S. Bureau of the Census, *Statistical Abstract*, Washington, D.C., U. S. Gov't. Print. Off., 1973; *99*:39, 65.

⁷⁰² U. S. National Commission on the Causes and Prevention of Violence, *To Establish Justice, To Insure Domestic Tranquility*. New York: Praeger, 1970; *99*:xxiv–xxv.

⁷⁰³ VALENTINE, TOM, *Psychic Surgery*. New York: Simon & Schuster/Pocket Books, 1975; *171*:all.

⁷⁰⁴ VALINS, STUART, "The Perception and Labeling of Bodily Changes as Determinants of Emotional Behavior," in *Physiological Correlates of Emotion*, ed. Perry Black. New York: Academic Press, 1970, pp. 229–43; *128*:all.

⁷⁰⁵ VALLEE, JACQUES, ARTHUR HASTINGS, and GERALD ASKEVOLD, Remote Viewing Experiments Through Computer Conferencing," *Proceedings of the IEEE*, 64, 1976, pp. 1551–52; *147*:all.

⁷⁰⁶ VASILIEV, LEONID, *Experiments in Distant Influence*. New York: Dutton, 1976; *149*:all.

⁷⁰⁷ VAUGHAN, ALAN, "Investigation of Silva Mind Control Claims," *Research in Parapsychology, 1973*, eds. W. G. Roll, R. L. Morris, and J. D. Morris. Metuchen, N.J.: Scarecrow Press, 1974, p. 51; *169*:all.

⁷⁰⁸ VOGT, EVON, and RAY HYMAN, *Water Witching U. S. A.* Chicago: University of Chicago Press, 1959; *33*:104–5; *180*:128–29, *182*:all, *184*:112–16.

⁷⁰⁹ VON DANIKEN, ERICH, *Chariots of the Gods?* New York: Bantam, 1971; *263*:75–78.

[710] WALKER, JEARL, "The Amateur Scientist: Drops of Water Dance on a Hot Skillet and the Experimenter Walks on Hot Coals," *Scientific American*, 237 (August 1977), pp. 126–31; *177*:all.

[711] WALL, PATRICK, "Acupuncture Revisited," *New Scientist*, 64, 1974, pp. 31–35; *248*:all.

[712] WALLACE, ALFRED RUSSELL, *Miracles and Modern Spiritualism*. London: Nichols, 1895; *293*:all.

[713] WALLACE, ROBERT, "Physiological Effects of Transcendental Meditation," *Science*, 167, 1970, pp. 1751–54; *27*:all.

[714] WALLIS, ROY, *The Road to Total Freedom: A Sociological Analysis of Scientology*. New York: Columbia University Press, 1977; *255*:all.

[715] WALSH, JAMES, *Cures: The Story of the Cures That Fail*. New York: Appleton, 1924; *173*:4.

[716] WALTER, V. J., and W. G. WALTER, "The Central Effects of Rhythmic Sensory Stimulation," *Electroencephalography & Clinical Neurophysiology*, 1, 1949, pp. 57–86; *17*:all.

[717] WAPNICK, KENNETH, "Mysticism and Schizophrenia," *Journal of Transpersonal Psychology*, 1 (Fall 1969), pp. 49–67; *291*:all.

[718] "Was Santa a Spaceman?" in *Some Trust in Chariots*, eds. Barry Thiering and Edgar Castle. New York: Popular Library, 1972, pp. 123–28; *266*:125–26.

[719] WATSON, LAWRENCE, and DIXON GUTHRIE, "A New Approach to Psychopathology: The Influence of Cultural Meanings on Altered States of Consciousness," *Journal for the Study of Consciousness*, 5, 1972, pp. 26–34; *291*:all.

[720] WEIL, ANDREW, "Parapsychology: Andrew Weil's Search for the True Geller—Part II: The Letdown," *Psychology Today*, 8 (July 1974), pp. 74–79; *224*:75–76.

[721] WEINER, JOSEPH, *The Piltdown Forgery*. New York: Oxford University Press, 1955; *142*:all.

[722] WEITZENHOFFER, ANDRE, *Hypnotism: An Objective Study in Suggestibility*. New York: Wiley, 1953; *62*:227–36, *65*:247–48.

[723] WEST, DONALD, "The Investigation of Spontaneous Cases," *Proceedings of the Society for Psychical Research*, 48, 1948, pp. 264–300; *47*:281, *138*:all, *163*:268.

[724] WEST, DONALD, "A Mass Observation Questionnaire on Hallucinations," *Journal of the Society for Psychical Research*, 34, 1948, pp. 187–96; *41*:all.

[725] WEST, DONALD, "The Strength and Weakness of the Available Evidence for Extrasensory Perception," in *Ciba Foundation Symposium on Extrasensory Perception*, eds. G. E. W. Westenholme and Elaine Millar. Boston: Little, Brown, 1956, pp. 14–23; *142*:18, *150*:21.

[726] WEST, DONALD, *Eleven Lourdes Miracles*. New York: Helix, 1957; *172*:13, *172*:12.

[727] WEST, DONALD, "Reasons for Continuing Doubts About the Existence of Psychic Phenomena," *Parapsychology Review*, 2 (March-April 1971), pp. 23–25; *149*:23, *149*:23–24.

[728] WEST, LOUIS, ed., *Hallucinations*. New York: Grune & Stratton, 1962; *40*:all.

[729] WHEELIS, ALLEN, *The Quest For Identity*. New York: Norton, 1958; *97*:all.

[730] WHITE, HARVEY, and PAUL LEVATIN, " 'Floaters' in the Eye," *Scientific American*, 206 (June 1962), pp. 119–27; *12*:all.

[731] WHITE, ROBERT, "Motivation Reconsidered: The Concept of Competence," *Psychological Review*, 66, 1959, pp. 297–333; *50*:all.

[732] WHITEHEAD, HARRIET, "Reasonably Fantastic: Some Perspectives on Scientology, Science Fiction, and Occultism," in *Religious Movements in Contemporary America*, eds. Irving Zaretsky and Mark Leone. Princeton, N.J.: Princeton University Press, 1974, pp. 547–87; *255*:all.

[733] WHITING, JOHN, "The Cross-Cultural Method," in *Handbook of Social Psychology*, ed. Gardner Lindzey. Reading, Mass.: Addison-Wesley, 1954, pp. 523–31; *99*:all.

[734] WHITING, JOHN, and IRVIN CHILD, *Child Training and Personality, A Cross-Cultural Study*. New Haven, Conn.: Yale University Press, 1953; *99*:70–74.

[735] WHITSON, THOMAS, and others, "Preliminary Experiments in Group 'Remote Viewing,' " *Proceedings of the IEEE*, 64, 1976, pp. 1550–51; *147*:all.

[736] WHITTAKER, JAMES, *Introduction to Psychology*. Philadelphia: Saunders, 1976; *86*:back cover.

[737] "Why Hop Ye So?" *Time*, May 1, 1944, p. 56; *205*:56.

[738] WIGGINTON, ELIOT, ed., *The Foxfire Book*. New York: Doubleday/Anchor, 1972; *293*:all.

[739] WILHELM, JOHN, *The Search for Superman*. New York: Simon & Schuster/Pocket Books, 1976; *136*:xiii–xiv, 226:177, 226:100–182.

[740] WILLIAMS, GERTRUDE, *Madame Blavatsky: Priestess of the Occult*. New York: Knopf, 1964; *215*:all.

[741] WILSON, CLIFFORD, *Crash Go the Chariots*. New York: Lancer Books, 1972; *265*:all.

[742] WILSON, CLIFFORD, *The Chariots Still Crash*. New York: New American Library/Signet, 1976; *264*:30.

[743] WILSON, COLIN, *The Occult–A History*. New York: Random House, 1971; *97*:38.

[744] WILSON, M. E., and L. E. MATHER, University of Washington, personal communication; *240*:all.

[745] WINKLER, ROBERT, *An Introduction to Bayesian Inference and Decision*. New York: Holt, 1972; *149*:all.

[746] "Witchery in North Dakota," *Time*, April 24, 1944, p. 75; *205*:75.

⁷⁴⁷ WITKIN, HERMAN, "The Perception of the Upright," *Scientific American*, 200 (February 1959), pp. 50–56; *278*:all.

⁷⁴⁸ WOOD, ROBERT, "The n-Rays," *Nature*, 70, 1904, pp. 530–31; *65*:all.

⁷⁴⁹ WOODWARD, KENNETH, and PAMELA ABRAMSON, "Maharishi Over Matter," *Newsweek*, June 13, 1977, pp. 98, 100; *25*:all.

⁷⁵⁰ WYNDHAM, HORACE, *Mr. Sludge, the Medium*. London: Geoffrey Bles, 1937; *214*:227, *214*:260–61, *214*:all, *215*:146.

⁷⁵¹ YERKES, ROBERT, and J. D. DODSON, "The Relation of Strength of Stimulus to Rapidity of Habit Formation," *Journal of Comparative Neurology and Psychology*, 18, 1908, pp. 459–82; *50*:all.

⁷⁵² ZARETSKY, IRVING, and MARK LEONE, eds., *Religious Movements in Contemporary America*. Princeton, N.J.: Princeton University Press, 1974; *102*:all.

⁷⁵³ ZELEN, MARVIN, "Astrology and Statistics: A Challenge," *The Humanist*, 36 (January-February 1976), p. 32; *237*:all.

⁷⁵⁴ ZELEN, MARVIN, PAUL KURTZ, and GEORGE ABELL, "Is There a Mars Effect?" *The Humanist*, 37 (November-December 1977), pp. 30–35; *237*:all.

⁷⁵⁵ ZÖLLNER, JOHANN, *Transcendental Physics*, trans. Charles Massey. London: Harrison, 1880; *293*:all.

⁷⁵⁶ ZORAB, GEORGE, "The Earthquake Effect: D. D. Home's Unique and Powerful PK Phenomenon," in *Research in Parapsychology, 1976*, eds. J. D. Morris, W. G. Roll, and R. L. Morris. Metuchen, N.J.: Scarecrow Press, 1977, pp. 9–11; *214*:9.

⁷⁵⁷ ZUBEK, JOHN, ed., *Sensory Deprivation*. New York: Appleton, 1969; *22*:all.

Glossary

Glossary

NOTE: Many of these terms, in other contexts, have definitions other than those given here.

Acupuncture. A Chinese medical procedure based on the theory that stimulation with a needle at particular points on the skin has a therapeutic effect on organs and other areas of the body with which these points are functionally linked.

Afterimage. The temporary continuation of a sensory experience after stimulation has ceased.

Alchemy. A forerunner of modern chemistry, which was based on numerous occult notions and which unsuccessfully sought various ends, including transmutation of base elements into gold.

Alienation. Estrangement from something—for example, society—that is of great significance in one's life.

Amphigory. An impressive-sounding nonsense statement.

Anesthetic. Any substance or procedure that produces loss of sensation and feeling.

Animal magnetism. An early name for what is now called hypnosis; based on the notion that therapeutic effects could result from altering "magnetic fluids" of the body.

Apparition. The sight of a ghost or spirit.

Archetype. Symbolic and mythical images that Carl Jung believed were transmitted genetically.

Asceticism. Self-denial of sensory pleasures and indulgences.

Astral. A nonphysical realm of human experience postulated by some occultists.

Astrology. The belief that the position of the heavenly bodies, particularly at the moment of birth, is related to personal destiny.

Atlantis. According to the writings of Plato, an advanced island civilization that sank beneath the waters of the Atlantic Ocean in ancient times; thought by some occultists to have actually existed.

Aura. A region of intensified brightness seen around people and occasionally objects; sometimes thought to be psychic in origin.

Autogenic. A training procedure by which one learns self-control of physiological responses.

Autokinetic. Illusory movement of objects that is perceived under conditions
of darkness.

Automatism. A complex behavior that is performed without conscious
awareness.

Autonomic. The peripheral nervous system that serves the internal organs
of the body.

Bermuda Triangle. A region of the Atlantic Ocean roughly bounded by
Florida, Puerto Rico, and the island of Bermuda.

Biofeedback. The process of measuring and displaying, by means of instruments, subjects' physiological reactions, which they then can learn to
control.

Brain rhythm. The rhythmic, synchronized firing of neurons in the brain.

Catharsis. Relieving pent-up feelings through expressing them.

Cerebral hemisphere. One half—right or left—of the cerebrum.

Cerebrum. The more recently evolved portion of the brain, which, in humans, envelops most of the rest of the brain and which is generally
responsible for higher mental functions.

Chiropractic. A physical therapy based on the belief that diseases arise from
pinched nerves caused by dislocations of the spine and that adjust-
ments of the spine can therefore cure disease.

Clairvoyance. Perception of an event without the use of the ordinary
senses—in other words, through extrasensory means.

Classical conditioning. Learning to make, to a new stimulus, a response that is
similar to one already made to an old stimulus with which the new
stimulus is paired.

Collective behavior. Spontaneous behavior that is mutually reinforced and
enhanced by members of a group acting in a similar fashion.

Collective unconscious. According to Carl Jung, unconscious images and
concepts that are genetically transmitted and are common to all humans.

Complementary colors. Colors that are uniquely related to each other in
certain respects; for example, the predominant afterimage of a color
is its complementary color.

Conditioning. A basic learning process by which new stimulus-response
connections are established.

Conscious. Ordinary waking awareness.

Constellation. A group of stars named after the figure that the stars, by
tradition, are thought to form.

Conversion reaction. An illness or incapacity, with no observable organic
impairment, that arises from psychological needs or suggestion.

Correlation. Related incidence or variation in different events.

Cryptomnesia. Memories that are not ordinarily available to waking consciousness, the origins of which are therefore likely to be viewed as mysterious.

Decline effect. According to parapsychologists, the tendency of subjects who initially perform well on tests of psychic ability to show a decline in performance over a period of time.

Déjà vu. The feeling that the present situation is duplicating an experience from the past.

Delirium. An altered state of consciousness characterized by frenzied irrational thought, brought on by various conditions, including fever.

Delusion. A belief that has no basis in fact.

Dervish. A Moslem group that specializes in ecstatic practices.

Dianetics. A folk psychology originated by L. Ronald Hubbard and distinguished by the notion that most psychological problems stem from traumas experienced before birth in the womb or in prior lives.

Dishabituation. Heightened sensitivity of the nervous system due to the presence of new, varied, or unusual stimulation.

Dissociation. A state in which originally or ordinarily conscious activities are carried on without conscious awareness.

Divining. Foretelling events by means of some magical procedure.

Dowsing. Searching for underground water or other substances by holding a device that supposedly indicates by its movements the presence of the desired substance.

Driving. The artificial activation of a sensory area of the brain by a stimulus with a frequency approximating the brain rhythm in that area, thus producing illusory sensations.

Ecstasy. A state of intense absorption and extreme joy.

Eidetic. A mental image, particularly of a remembered experience, that approaches the reality and vividness of a current sensory experience.

Emotional contagion. The spontaneous mutual reinforcement and enhancement of feeling that can occur in a group that is subject to the same emotional arousal.

Endorphin. A naturally occurring substance, found in emotional centers in the brain, that chemically resembles opiates and that produces euphoria.

Engram. A neural memory trace.

Enkephalin. A naturally occurring substance, found in emotional centers in the brain, that chemically resembles opiates and that produces euphoria.

Existentialism. A school of philosophy dealing with problems of existence, particularly in modern society.

Exorcism. A ritual performed on behalf of people thought to be possessed by evil spirits in an effort to drive the spirits away.

Extrasensory perception (ESP). Perception of an event that is not known through any ordinary sense.

Fakir. A follower of a religious or philosophical discipline who displays, or seems to display, remarkable control over bodily processes.

Floaters. Detached cells in the eye, which are seen as transparent dots that seem to "float" in the visual field.

Flying saucer. Early name for unidentified disclike objects seen in the sky; now generally called unidentified flying objects, or UFOs.

Ganzfeld. A "blank" visual field produced artificially, useful for producing and studying various perceptual effects.

Genetic. Transmitted by heredity, through the genes.

Glossolalia. Dissociated speech, sounding like gibberish, which some people interpret as fragments of a language never learned by the speaker.

"Golden age". An ancient period of wonderful and magical accomplishments that is postulated by various myths and beliefs.

Habituation. The decline in the response of the nervous system to a monotonous stimulus.

Hallucination. The technical term for the perception, in a waking or semiwaking state, of objects or events that have no objective existence.

Haunting. The frequenting of a particular place by ghosts or spirits.

Heredity. The biological transmission of genetic traits from parents to offspring.

Homeostasis. The tendency of the body to seek and maintain a normal state of functioning when this state is upset by deprivation or other threats.

Horoscope. The determination of the pattern of the heavenly bodies at some moment—for example, at the time of birth—together with the meanings ascribed to this pattern by astrology.

Hypersthesia. Heightened sensitivity to stimuli.

Hypermnesia. Exceptional ability to remember past experiences.

Hyperventilation. Excessive respiration or "overbreathing," which can produce abnormally low levels of carbon dioxide in the blood and, as a consequence, various alterations in consciousness.

Hypnagogic. The drowsy state just before falling asleep, often accompanied by dreamlike imagery.

Hypnopompic. The drowsy period between being asleep and waking up, often accompanied by dreamlike imagery.

Hypothalamus. A region of the old brain involved in emotional response.

Hysteria. A general tendency toward dissociation, often characterized by conversion reactions.

I Ching. A set of ancient Chinese proverbs, which, if selected according to a certain random process, are thought by some to provide guidance that is particularly suited to the individual who consults it.

Identity. Feelings dealing with one's own competence, personal worth, life goals, etc.

Ideomotor. An involuntary response triggered by a specific thought or suggestion.

Illusion. A sensory experience that is misleading or is misinterpreted.

Imagery. The mental reproduction of a remembered or imagined sensory experience.

Inhibition. The suppression of neural impulses through the action of inhibitory neurons.

Kirlian photography. Photography done by passing a high voltage electric current through an object in contact with photographic paper; the electrical discharge forms an "aura" around the image of the object on the photograph.

Limbic system. An area of the brain closely related to emotional responses.

Macrobiotics. An approach to nutrition characterized, among other things, by the notion that an ideal diet consists entirely of grains.

Mania. A mental state characterized by extreme excitement and enthusiasm.

Mantra. A sound used as an object of contemplation by some meditators.

Masochism. Deriving pleasure from what is ordinarily a painful stimulus.

Medium. Someone who claims to be able to contact spirits, which then manifest themselves in various ways.

Mental medium. A medium who acts, while in trance, as if possessed by a spirit, so that the medium's utterances are claimed to be communications from the spirit.

Mentalist. A magician who specializes in magic that appears to be psychic.

Metaphysics. The branch of philosophy that concerns itself with the ultimate nature of reality.

Multiple personality. A condition in which the individual displays, at different times, two or more distinct personalities, each of which leads a somewhat independent existence from the others.

Mystery house. A house or cabin built on a slant in order to create illusions having to do with perception of the upright.

Mysticism. Pertaining to experiences of feeling in contact with a universal essence of goodness and truth, characteristically accompanied by intense absorption and ecstasy.

Neuron. A single nerve cell; the basic structural unit of the nervous system.

New brain. A term sometimes used to designate the cerebrum; called "new" because it developed relatively recently in the course of evolution.

Nirvana. In Hindu and Buddhist thought, the attainment of a mystical, egoless state.

N-rays. The name given by R. Blondlot to a new form of radiation he claimed to have discovered.

Numerology. A system of personal forecasting based on the notion that one's address, phone number, and other numbers of a personal nature foretell one's life experiences.

Obsession. Persistent thoughts that one cannot control.

Occult. Pertaining to beliefs or practices that seek to explain or influence observable events, but that are generally considered ill-founded, particularly by experts in relevant fields of knowledge.

Old brain. The lower portion of the brain that developed relatively early in the evolutionary process; responsible for basic bodily functions.

Operant conditioning. Learning a new behavior that will enable one to gain a reward or avoid a punishment.

Orgone. The basic form of energy in the universe, according to Wilhelm Reich; in particular, he believed this energy could be concentrated for therapeutic purposes by an "orgone energy accumulator."

Ouija. A method of expressing unconscious memories and feelings by allowing one's hand to guide involuntarily a pointer to various words, letters, and numbers on the smooth surface of a board; thought by some to reveal information through paranormal means.

Out-of-body experience. The feeling that one's consciousness is detached and free from one's physical body.

Palmistry. A system of physiognomy based on the notion that features of the palms of one's hands—the lines, the mounds, and so on—are indicative of particular life experiences.

Paranoia. A mental disorder characterized by delusions of persecution or of grandeur.

Paranormal. Pertaining to events thought by some to arise from processes outside the range of ordinarily accepted forces.

Parapsychology. The psychological study of experiences thought to be paranormal.

Parasympathetic. The branch of the autonomic nervous system generally responsible for quieting the internal organs of the body.

Past-life. The life one has led during a previous incarnation.

Perception. The more or less immediate appraisal of a stimulus that is based not only on sensory input, but also on one's present needs and prior conditioning.

Peripheral nervous system. The nervous system outside of the brain and spinal cord; serves the external body and interal organs.

Phosphenes. Sensations of patterns and light that arise from stimulation of the eye by pressure or any stimulus other than light.

Phrenology. The study of surface features of the skull, thought by some to reveal psychological capacities of the corresponding areas of the brain underneath the skull.

Physical medium. A medium who claims to contact spirits that express themselves through various physical manifestations.

Physiognomy. Systems of character and personality diagnosis, such as palmistry, which base their interpretations on certain external features of the body.

Physilogy. The science that investigates the ongoing processes and functions of the organs and other components of the body.

Placebo. A medical procedure, such as a sugar pill, the effectiveness of which is based on suggestion.

Polarity therapy. A therapy based on the belief that disease results from imbalances in energy fields of the body that therapists can treat by various manipulations of the body.

Poltergeist. A ghost or spirit—sometimes thought to be the rebellious "psychic spirit" of a living person—that causes physical disturbances.

Possession. The feeling that one's "self" has been "taken over" by an external agent or personality.

Precognition. Foretelling the future through psychic means.

Projection. The ascription of one's own traits to someone or something else.

Proprioceptor. Receptors in the inner ear and in the tissues of the body that provide a sense of body position and movement.

Psi. The technical term for communication and influence between organisms, which, some believe, takes place through nonphysical means.

Psi-missing. Exceptionally poor performance on tests of psi ability, which is interpreted by parapsychologists as a sign of psychic capacity that can sense what is desired in order to do the opposite.

Psychedelic. A substance or stimulus that creates hallucinations or similar alterations in consciousness.

Psychic. The popular term for communication and influence between organisms, which, some believe, takes place through nonphysical means.

Psychokinesis. Psychic influence over an object, without the use of physical contact or energies.

Psychometry. Determining, through psychic means, the characteristics of a person through handling an object belonging to that person.

Psychosomatic. Pertaining to physical illnesses that result from psychological stress or influence.

Psychotic. Serious mental disorders, characterized by loss of contact with reality and often resulting in institutionalization.

Pyramid power. A power that some claim is present in correctly positioned pyramid structures and that is capable of such feats as preserving meat and keeping razor blades sharp.

Pyramidology. The belief that the dimensions of the Great Pyramid embody highly advanced scientific knowledge as well as prophecies of future events.

Radiesthesia. The practice of diagnosing disease, searching for lost objects, and so on, usually by holding a pendulum, which indicates by its movements the information being sought.

Reading. Any method of determining one's personal destiny or personal characteristics from the study of external events; examples are astrology, numerology, and Tarot cards.

Receptor. A nerve cell or group of such cells, specialized for sensory reception.

Reflexology. A branch of zone therapy that assumes that pressure applied to certain points, particularly on the soles of the feet and on the hands, will have a therapeutic effect on diseased parts of the body that are somehow linked to these pressure points.

Reincarnation. The process by which, some believe, souls return to earth, after death, in a new life form.

Reinforcement. Any stimulus that strengthens a learned response; for example, a reward in operant conditioning.

Replication. The duplication of a study by independent investigators to determine the reliability of the initial findings.

Repression. The process of forgetting—or "putting out of" one's conscious mind—disturbing images, thoughts, or feelings.

Retina. The area at the back of the eye that contains the receptors for vision.

Rorschach test. A projective personality test that requires the subject to interpret ink blots.

Samadhi. In Hindu thought, a state of heightened consciousness.

Satori. In Buddhist thought, the attainment of enlightenment.

Scientology. The religion that grew out of dianetics.

Seance. A gathering of persons for the purpose of contacting the spirits.

Self-fulfilling prophecy. The process by which people's expectations are fulfilled through their own behavior, they being unaware of the connection between their behavior and the fulfillment.

Sensation. The raw impression of a stimulus as received by an organism, unaffected by prior conditioning and present needs.

Set. Stereotyped behavior arising from prior conditioning or present needs.

Sidereal astrology. A system of astrology that takes into account the precession of the earth's axis.

Somatic. The peripheral nervous system that serves the external body, as distinct from the internal organs.

Spheroidal state. The state in which a liquid, in contact with a very hot surface, forms tiny droplets and an insulating barrier as it rapidly turns to gas.

Spirit. The essence of a human or other organism that is thought by some to exist independently of the physical body and therefore to survive bodily death.

Spiritualism. The belief and practice that assumes the existence of spirits, which can be contacted in various ways.

State of consciousness. Any of several distinct or altered states of awareness, including, for example, those associated with dreaming, hypnosis, and ecstasy, as well as ordinary waking consciousness.

Stigmata. Marks or wounds resembling the wounds of the crucified Christ, thought by some to be supernatural in origin.

Subconscious. Mental processes such as regulation of basic bodily functions, automatic behaviors, and so on—not usually thought of as part of one's personality—that occur outside of conscious awareness.

Sublimation. The redirection of basic impulses—particularly sexual—into more socially acceptable channels.

Subliminal. Referring to a stimulus that is too weak to be perceived consciously, but that may be perceived subconsciously.

Subluxation. A dislocation of the spinal column, which, according to chiropractic theory, pinches spinal nerves, thus causing illness or disease in the part of the body served by these nerves.

Subvocalization. Subtle activation of the vocal cords in many people that correlates with the words that they are thinking at the moment and that can sometimes be detected by others.

Sufism. A Moslem sect noted for its mystical beliefs and practices.

Sun-sign. In astrology, the constellation closest to the sun at the moment of birth.

Supernatural. In religious belief, a realm of existence and meaning beyond the ordinary physical world.

Surrealism. A movement in art and literature that emphasizes the expression of unconscious images.

Sympathetic. The branch of the autonomic nervous system that is generally responsible for activating the body to deal with emergencies.

Synchronicity. Carl Jung's theory that widely separated events are sometimes linked in a meaningful fashion even if there is no causal relationship—either direct or indirect—between them.

Synesthesia. The capacity to experience sensations of several kinds as a result of stimulation of one sense only.

Tantrism. An Eastern discipline involving sexual practices.

Tarot. A set of cards with symbolic images that are used to forecast one's destiny.

Telepathy. Communication between individuals that, some believe, occurs through nonphysical means.

Totem. An animal with which a group of people identifies and around whose symbol people develop rituals.

Trance. A waking state in which unconscious processes temporarily, but more or less totally, dictate mental and overt activity.

Transcendental. Psychological functioning that goes beyond ordinary levels of experience.

Transducer. A device, such as a sense organ, that converts energy from one form to another.

Tropical astrology. The most popular system of astrology, which fails to take into account the precession of the earth's axis.

Unconscious. That part of one's personality that, for example, because of repression, is not available to ordinary consciousness.

Unidentified flying object (UFO). Something seen in the sky that resembles a flying object, the identification of which is uncertain; thought by some to signify visits of craft from outer space or other mysterious phenomena.

Unitary consciousness. The limited capacity of consciousness, which restricts processing of information ordinarily to a single train of thought.

Vision. The popular term for the perception, in a waking or semiwaking state, of objects or events that seemingly have no objective existence.

Vitreous humor. The jellylike substance that fills the major portion of the eyeball.

Witching. Searching for underground water or other substances by holding a device that supposedly indicates by its movements the presence of the desired substance.

Xenoglossia. Facility in a language that one has never learned.

Yerkes-Dodson Law. A statement of the relationship between motivation and performance.

Zen Buddhism. A Buddhist contemplative sect.

Zone therapy. A system of therapy that assumes that the body is divided into ten vertical zones and that the body areas within each zone are linked so that pressure applied to specific points will have a therapeutic effect on certain other areas within the same zone.

Index

Index